T0313283

OFFICIAL (ISC)²®
GUIDE TO THE
CAP® CBK®
Second Edition

OTHER BOOKS IN THE (ISC)²® PRESS SERIES

OFFICIAL (ISC)²®
GUIDE TO THE
CAP® CBK®
Second Edition

Patrick D. Howard, CISSP, CISM

SECURITY TRANSCENDS TECHNOLOGY®

CRC Press
Taylor & Francis Group
Boca Raton London New York

CRC Press is an imprint of the
Taylor & Francis Group, an **informa** business
AN AUERBACH BOOK

CRC Press
Taylor & Francis Group
6000 Broken Sound Parkway NW, Suite 300
Boca Raton, FL 33487-2742

© 2013 by Taylor & Francis Group, LLC
CRC Press is an imprint of Taylor & Francis Group, an Informa business

No claim to original U.S. Government works

Printed in the United States of America on acid-free paper
Version Date: 20120326

International Standard Book Number: 978-1-4398-2075-9 (Hardback)

Library of Congress Cataloging-in-Publication Data

Howard, Patrick D.
    Official (ISC)2 guide to the CAP CBK / Patrick D. Howard. -- 2nd ed.
        p. cm. -- ((iSC)2 Press series)
    ISBN 978-1-4398-2075-9 (hardback)
    1. Computer networks--Security measures--Examinations--Study guides. 2. Computers--Access control--Examinations--Study guides. 3. Administrative agencies--Information resources management--Security measures--United States--Examinations--Study guides. 4. Telecommunications engineers--United States--Certification. I. Title. II. Title: Official ISC2 guide to the CAP CBK. III. Title: Official (ISC)2 to the Certified authorization professional CBK.

    TK5105.59.H673 2012
    658.4'78076--dc23   2012004044

Visit the Taylor & Francis Web site at
http://www.taylorandfrancis.com

and the CRC Press Web site at
http://www.crcpress.com

Contents

Chapter 3   Establishment of the Security Control Baseline 139

Chapter 7   Security Controls Monitoring

Preface

On the day I turned 16, my sister drove me to the Department of Motor Vehicles Office in Anadarko, Oklahoma, to take my long-anticipated driving test. Unfortunately, I failed in this first attempt at the test as well as the second. I was finally able to pass the test on the third try and obtained a much-cherished license to operate a motor vehicle. This license meant that the state certified that I had met minimum driving standards, and it served as my authorization to drive a car in the state of Oklahoma and wherever else the license was recognized. The subject of this book is similar to the motor vehicle operator licensing process I experienced firsthand in 1965. The system authorization methodology includes testing against an established standard, followed by authorization to operate granted based on this testing. Although system authorization relates to information systems rather than to anxious teenagers awaiting their fate, these processes have much in common.

System authorization has become a major topic of discussion in the information security arena since the early 2000s, at least in U.S. government circles. Many government organizations are currently engaged in employing system authorization processes in response to the requirements of the Federal Information Security Management Act (FISMA). FISMA, with its emphasis on measuring progress in the implementation of information security within the federal government, has elevated system authorization into the preeminent position of being the government's primary risk management approach in the field of information technology security. Although system authorization is not new, its preeminence is, and its newfound acceptance promises to solidify its position for many years to come. System security authorization has been employed in government for over 20 years, and it is becoming recognized outside government for the promise it holds as a practical approach for identifying and documenting business requirements for security, for ensuring that cost-effective controls are functioning appropriately, and for ensuring that weaknesses in protective controls are managed effectively. This book demonstrates the practicality, comprehensiveness, and effectiveness of system authorization as a risk management methodology for information technology systems in both public and private organizations.

This volume describes a usable approach for top-down implementation of information technology security in an organization. It highlights approaches to system
authorization that can be successfully implemented in most organizations, both public and private. The book will help readers make sense of official guidance that has
been published on system authorization and on its related processes. In addition,
this book seeks to simplify the system authorization process and clarify the number
of guidelines related to this topic that have been published over the years. Those
hoping for an introduction to the world of system authorization are struck by the
relative bounty of information, some of which appears to be in conflict. This book
will help readers understand how various, seemingly disparate processes, some old
and some new, are combined into a coherent, unified risk management methodology.
The book provides a consistent view of those processes through the perspective of
an enterprise information technology security manager or chief information security officer (CISO), with a view toward following U.S. government guidance on the
subject. In so doing, it provides nongovernment CISOs guidelines on why and how
system authorization can be implemented in their organizations even though they
are not subject to federal information security legislation. Finally, the book is based
on real-world experience in system authorization, and it describes the most current
thinking on the topic based on my personal involvement in system authorization
activities since 1989.

This book is intended to benefit those who are classified as security practitioners or
those charged with implementation or evaluation of security controls at either the
system or the security program level. This is translated to mean information system
security officers (ISSOs), security managers, certifiers, and developers in public and
private arenas. Those who are charged with developing an information security program for an organization will benefit from this volume most because it provides an
overview of all the various components of system authorization. After reading this
book, those tasked with certifying an information system should be able to document the status of system security controls. Those charged with securing a system
at the system security officer or system administrator level can benefit by gaining
an appreciation for how security for a system can be ensured through standard,
repeatable processes. Those who own a system can benefit from reading this book
and gain an appreciation for approaches to ensure that their system has been properly secured. The processes described in this book apply to security professionals
both inside and outside government organizations. Program managers and system
developers can also gain insights from this material that will help them in effectively
developing secure systems.

On the other hand, this volume is not intended to serve as an introduction to the information technology security field, and individuals who are new to information security may have difficulty understanding this material until they have grasped the concepts, practices, principles, and definitions used in the business.

Since publication of *Building and Implementing a Security Certification and Accreditation Program* in 2006, system authorization remains a major topic of discussion in the information security world. There have been many developments during this time that warrant publication of this updated text, including an update of the title itself.

Today, government agencies are still responding to the system authorization requirements of the Federal Information Security Management Act (FISMA). However, they are now more successful in doing so since upward of 90% of the government's information systems have undergone some form of system authorization, and senior management is much more familiar with FISMA requirements, including system authorization. In addition, reciprocity between government agencies has led to widespread acceptance of system authorization documentation as a basis for establishing trust. And although there has been limited growth in use of system authorization outside the federal government, companies doing business with the government must meet FISMA standards, and consequently their acceptance of system authorization is well established.

While system authorization remains as preeminent today as it was in 2006, it has come under assault for its perceived emphasis on documentation and process at the expense of "real security." In a related development, several proposals have been put forward in Congress to update FISMA and make it less compliance driven and more risk management focused. At least two proposals are currently under review, and there is reasonable expectation they will be merged and become law.

Related to this development, the National Institute of Standards and Technology (NIST) has refined its guidance related to system authorization. NIST has begun to emphasize continuous monitoring and has integrated system authorization squarely into its risk management approach, which is now comprised by the six-step risk management framework. The terms *certification* and *accreditation* are being deemphasized, and system authorization is now the label du jour. The value of the NIST approach to system authorization is demonstrated by stated Department of Defense and director of Central Intelligence plans to follow NIST system authorization guidance as closely as possible, which is reflected in NIST's revision of Special Publication 800-37.

Another important development since I initially wrote this book has been the creation of a certification program for system authorization practitioners sponsored by the (ISC)²® (International Information Systems Security Certification Consortium). Today, there are hundreds of Certified Authorization Professional (CAP®) certification holders who have met certification requirements for experience and knowledge of a system authorization Common Body of Knowledge (CBK®), and the Department of Defense has recognized this certification as part of its initiative to require personnel performing information security tasks to be formally certified. The update of the CAP® CBK® and the recent revision of NIST SP 800-37 are the primary reasons a revised edition is necessary.

This book consists of 10 primary sections. Chapters 1 through 7 describe each of the domains of the (ISC)²® CAP® CBK®. This is followed in Chapter 8 by a case study of the establishment of a successful system authorization program in a major U.S. government department. Chapter 9 speculates about the future of system authorization. Finally, the book provides a collection of helpful samples and additional information in the appendices.

Acknowledgments

I would like to express my gratitude to four people who were instrumental in the creation of this book. First, Tom Peltier, president of Peltier and Associates, friend and mentor, planted the seed that led to this volume and convinced me that I had something to say on the subject. Victoria Lord, director of Enterprise Information Technology Security Division at the U.S. Department of Transportation, allowed me to apply the concepts and processes described in this book and provided her trust in my capabilities as a program manager and security professional. Kelvin Taylor, of Titan Corporation and a fellow traveler in the unending quest for system authorization perfection, served as my sounding board on these principles and practices and is one of the most positive people I have ever met. Finally, Lisa Schlosser, chief information officer at the Department of Housing and Urban Development, provided encouragement to strive for the impossible, had confidence in my system authorization expertise, and gave me the opportunity to apply it under her guidance on numerous occasions over the past 13 years.

About the Author

Patrick D. Howard, CISSP, CISM, is a senior consultant for SecureInfo, a Kratos Company. He has over 40 years experience in security, including 20 years service as a U.S. Army Military Police officer, and has specialized in information security since 1989. Mr. Howard began his service as the Chief Information Security Officer for the National Science Foundation's Antarctic Support Contract in Centennial, Colorado in March 2012. He previously served as CISO for the Nuclear Regulatory Commission in Rockville, Maryland from 2008–2012, and for the Department of Housing and Urban Development from 2005–2008. Mr. Howard was named a Fed 100 winner in 2007, and is the author of three information security books: *The Total CISSP Exam Prep Book,* 2002; *Building and Implementing a Security Certification and Accreditation Program,* 2006; and *Beyond Compliance: FISMA Principles and Best Practices,* 2011. He is a member of the International Information Systems Security Certification Consortium's Government Advisory Board and Executive Writer's Bureau, which he chairs. Mr. Howard is also an adjunct professor of Information Assurance at Walsh College, Troy, Michigan. He graduated with a Bachelor's degree from the University of Oklahoma in 1971 and a Master's degree from Boston University in 1984.

Chapter 1

Security Authorization of Information Systems

Security authorization includes a tiered risk management approach to evaluate both strategic and tactical risk across the enterprise. The authorization process incorporates the application of a Risk Management Framework (RMF), a review of the organizational structure, and the business process/mission as the foundation for the implementation and assessment of specified security controls. This authorization management process identifies vulnerabilities and countermeasures and determines residual risks. The residual risks are evaluated and deemed either acceptable or unacceptable. More controls must be implemented to reduce unacceptable risk. The system may be deployed only when the residual risks are acceptable to the enterprise.

Certified Authorization Professional (CAP®) Candidate Information Bulletin,
November 2010

Introduction

I once made the acquaintance of an information system security officer (ISSO) in a federal department who had what he defined as airtight security for his major application. During my assessment, I found that he had implemented government security authorization guidance for his application as well as could possibly be imagined and had fully documented all the controls protecting the system. Three years later when I returned to recertify the system for reauthorization, the system could not be recertified. When I was told that the ISSO had been transferred, the problem became quite clear to me. The process that the ISSO had used to protect his system was limited only to his single, well-protected application and had not been institutionalized elsewhere in the organization.

To be effective, a system authorization program must be greater than the efforts of isolated, well-intentioned individuals like this ISSO and must be implemented on an enterprise-wide level. A program implemented at this highest organizational level first and foremost permits consistency across the entire organization. Further, the implementation of a successful enterprise system authorization program can greatly promote the implementation of a likewise effective information security program for an organization.

An enterprise security authorization program can be considered successful if it provides an effective means of identifying and meeting requirements, permits efficient oversight of its activities, and provides assurance that necessary controls are implemented at the system level. For the purposes of this discussion, an enterprise program is one that supports the entire organization and that either is independent of any other program or has a significant degree of independence to implement guidance of a higher-level program. This equates to a corporate- or department-level government organization. An enterprise program is distinct from its business unit-level components, which relate to elements of the overall enterprise program. Security authorization for a line of business will normally focus on an interrelated grouping of information technology systems that support a tightly focused business function.

The information contained in this chapter applies to efforts to build an enterprise security authorization program from the ground up, as well as efforts to expand an existing program with additional capabilities or with a revised orientation. This chapter discusses the ingredients necessary to construct a successful enterprise system authorization program. This includes information sections on key elements of such a program; a detailed discussion of system authorization roles and responsibilities; incorporation of system authorization into the system development life cycle (SDLC); causes of the failure of many system security authorization programs; system authorization project planning; elements of an organization-level system inventory process; and the work of dealing with interconnected systems. Also, this chapter provides an overview of the application of the Risk Management Framework (RMF) of the National Institute of Standards and Technology (NIST) to information systems as well as fundamentals of information system risk management according to NIST Special Publication (SP) 800-37, Revision 1.

System authorization is a comprehensive methodology that consists of a number of individual processes, most of which the reader will probably recognize. It is the combining of these related processes into a unified risk management approach that gives a system authorization methodology its real value. Although there are many well-known approaches to implementing a risk management program, there is a need for a coherent methodology to manage risks at the individual system level. To meet this requirement, the risk management approach would need to be sufficiently integrated to provide for consistent inputs and outputs from each process in the methodology; on a microlevel, it would provide assurance that necessary controls are implemented at the lowest level of technology in each organizational element; and on the macrolevel, it would serve the entire organization as a foundation for the enterprise information technology security program. The system authorization approach to risk management ties these necessary security processes together to create a pathway to success. Figure 1.1 shows how the system security authorization processes interrelate.

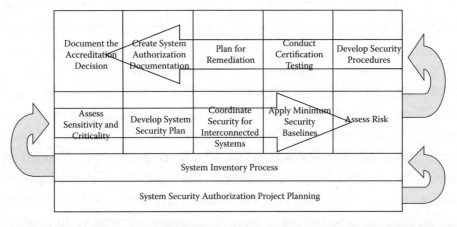

Figure 1.1 **Interrelationships of system authorization processes.**

Legal and Regulatory Framework for System Authorization

In December 2002, Congress passed the Federal Information Security Management Act (FISMA). This new federal law has done more to elevate the importance and visibility of system authorization than any other single event in the history of U.S. government. Certification in the form of accreditation did not begin with FISMA. In fact, it had been established as a formal information technology security methodology with the publication of Federal Information Processing Standard (FIPS) 102 in 1983, and it was elevated in significance with the enactment of the Computer Security Act of 1987 and with the publication of Office of Management and Budget (OMB) Circular A-130, Appendix III, which implemented the Act.

This was followed by the publication of National Computer Security Center (NCSC) Technical Guideline NCSC-TG-029, *Introduction to Certification and Accreditation,* by the National Security Agency (NSA) in January 1994, which provided practical instructions on the application of certification and accreditation for Department of Defense (DOD) information systems. However, system authorization had never truly taken off elsewhere in government outside DOD where the DOD Information Technology Security Certification and Accreditation Process (DITSCAP) had been implemented. Unfortunately, the DITSCAP process, though ideal for the highly sensitive systems operated in support of the national defense mission, was never broadly adopted for use elsewhere in government. This was only partially remedied by the National Information Assurance Certification and Accreditation Process (NIACAP), which was published in 2000. Today, the DOD Information Assurance Certification and Accreditation Process (DIACAP) is the approved system authorization process. DIACAP defines formal department-wide system authorization activities, tasks, and management processes used to maintain the security posture throughout the life cycle of a DOD information system. DIACAP was developed by the NSA and superseded DITSCAP with the publication of DOD Instruction 8510.01 on November 28, 2007. A major change in DIACAP from DITSCAP is the requirement for implementation of information assurance (IA) controls as the primary set of security requirements for all automated information systems (AISs). The IA controls are determined according to the system's mission assurance category (MAC) and confidentiality level (CL). In addition, the Committee on National Security Systems (CNSS) is authorized to establish requirements pertaining to national security systems operated or used by all executive departments, agencies, and U.S. government contractors who own, procure, use, operate, or maintain national security systems.

However, it was only with FISMA (which was followed closely by publication of NIST SP 800-37) that certification, accreditation, and system authorization were given the boost that has effectively raised their visibility throughout government and into the consciousness of most all federal executives and managers.

External Program Drivers

There are certainly internal drivers for system authorization, but there are external requirements pointing to its need as well. In recent years, public laws, such as Sarbanes–Oxley, the Health Insurance Portability and Accountability Act (HIPAA), the Gramm–Leach–Bliley Act (GLBA), Clinger–Cohen, as well as FISMA, have pointed toward the need for more effective implementation of security in government organizations and have increased the need for them to concentrate on regulatory compliance as a primary business driver. The fervent work of NIST staff in the United States as well as the development of International Organization for Standardization (ISO) 17799 and its spread throughout the developed world have accompanied this renewed emphasis on security and accountability. In the private sector, successful prosecution of executives in large American corporations like Enron, WorldCom, and Global Crossing have pointed to the need for management accountability and due diligence. In addition, since September 11, 2001, the war on terrorism and the establishment of the Department of Homeland Security have heightened awareness of security in general and management's role in the protection of its resources, especially its critical infrastructure and personnel.

System-Level Security

It should be noted that the objective of system authorization as used in this volume is to ensure the security of an information technology system. It is not meant to ensure the security of an organization, a security program, a person or persons, or a manual process. There are other processes available to measure and ensure the effectiveness of these, but the focus of our attention will be on computer systems, which are viewed as distinct units in the construction of a successful information technology security program. With this model, a security perimeter is established for individual critical resources according to system boundaries, rather than constructing a single, extended security perimeter to protect all critical resources the organization chooses to protect. The approach works because systems are distinct, their limits can be defined in practical terms, and security is comparatively easy to implement at the system level. On the other hand, the enterprise security is more difficult to define, and implementation of security controls enterprise-wide is far less practical. This approach envisions the implementation of an organization-wide security architecture through the identification and implementation of its aspects at the system level.

Perhaps the key aspect of the system authorization methodology described in this volume is its concentration on systems as building blocks for an organization's information security program. This is based on the notion that it is more practical to define security requirements for an individual system than for an entire enterprise.

Defining System Authorization

Before proceeding, it is necessary to define our terms. System authorization comprises what was formerly known as certification and accreditation as the methodology used to ensure that security controls are established for an information system, that these controls are functioning appropriately, and that management has authorized the operation of the system in its current security posture. Implied in this definition is that system authorization relates to the security of an information system. Consequently, both "system authorization" and "security authorization" are commonly used to identify this process. Although the terms *certification* and *accreditation* are in most cases used together to define a comprehensive process, certification and accreditation are distinct from each other and are performed separately by different entities at different times for different but related purposes. *Certification* is the process by which the effectiveness of security controls is assessed, and *accreditation* is the management decision (based on that assessment) to permit an information system to operate at its current security posture. It is possible to perform each of these two processes by itself, but it would be either incomplete or risky. Performing certification on a system without continuing on to an accreditation decision misses an opportunity for fixing accountability for remediating weaknesses uncovered in the certification process. On the other hand, an authorizing official who chooses to accredit a system without first having the adequacy of security controls certified is taking a very large risk. For the purpose of this text, system authorization is an overarching process that includes certification and accreditation and serves as the basis for an official management decision by a senior organizational official to authorize operation of an information system with an explicit acceptance of the risk of its operation to the organization and based on the degree to which agreed-on security controls have been implemented.

Resistance to System Authorization

To many, the system authorization process and certification and accreditation specifically are dirty words because they equate them with expensive and time-consuming paperwork foisted on them by unknowing and uncaring bureaucrats. The process has been viewed as an unnecessary requirement that provides no return on investment, challenges managers with a need to dip into already-limited resources, preventing them from meeting other more pressing priorities with which they must contend. When confronted with requirements to implement system authorization for the first time, the natural reaction is to wonder why it is needed because the system has survived without it. Most consider it "a government thing" that is not really relevant to the private sector. Those more familiar with system authorization complain that it is too heavy on assessment and not heavy enough on remediation or that concentrating security on systems is too granular to be effective. Others who have no familiarity with system authorization think that it relates to individuals and miss the point entirely.

Benefits of System Authorization

Despite negative opinions and experiences of some with system authorization as applied in government over the years, system authorization can provide significant benefits to an organization. Some of the most obvious benefits include

- Helping to maintain the visibility of the information technology security program by drawing attention to it at multiple organizational levels.
- Effectively using it in the exercise of due diligence, allowing management to prove that it is doing the right thing in protecting its assets, and providing a process for meeting requirements and managing risk.
- Providing a means for integrating security across all of its computer systems, allowing consistency in the implementation of security controls.
- Permitting fulfillment of requirements of the information technology security program by helping focus on a unified objective. All the elements of the program—security planning, vulnerability assessment, risk assessment, controls testing, and so on—aim toward achievement of a common goal: the protection of the organization's information technology systems.
- Ensuring that minimum security control requirements are met.
- Ensuring that appropriate, risk-based security controls have been identified and are implemented and functioning as designed.
- Promoting management involvement through the designation of program-related roles and responsibilities, by fixing accountability for the secure operation of the system, and by measuring the effectiveness of managers in mitigating risks to the system.
- Saving effort and resources by consolidating individual processes into an integrated program.

Key Elements of an Enterprise System Authorization Program

A system authorization program is comprised of a wide variety of people, processes, and technologies. Each of these various elements is important, but there is a small subset of program components that can truly be classified as essential to the success of the program. These are the deal breakers. If they are not in place or do not function effectively or completely, implementation of the program will be hampered, and the success of the entire program may be jeopardized. Of course, it is possible for a program to crash and burn even if all of the essential elements described are present. However, chances of success are greatly improved when a program has effectively addressed these elements. The following paragraphs identify and explain program elements that are critical to the success of any system authorization program. Because of their importance to the success of the program, the following components should be designed into the program from its inception.

The Business Case

The establishment of an enterprise system authorization program has to be based on a strong business case that documents its key benefits to the organization. This business case highlights for management the reasons why the program is necessary for the organization, and it establishes early on that there is a business need for the program. These benefits of an enterprise system authorization program include

- *Due Diligence*: The system authorization program provides a means for exercising due diligence. It assures management that security has been appropriately addressed through the implementation of a comprehensive, documented process that produces evidence of this assurance.

- *Accountability*: The program provides mechanisms for making executives, managers, and employees at multiple levels of the organization accountable for the security of the systems that they either use or are responsible for.

- *Implementation*: System authorization facilitates the management of risks. It provides a mechanism for ensuring that security issues are addressed by means of its requirements for remediation plans and oversight of corrective action. The program provides a road map for fixing as well as identifying weaknesses and formalizes security control identification, implementation, and evaluation.

■ *Visibility*: The system authorization program provides visibility to information technology security across the organization by addressing issues at several levels.

■ *Cost-Effectiveness*: Finally, the system authorization program provides a cost-effective approach for securing systems through the establishment of repeatable processes that regularize security tasks and lend themselves to management oversight.

When developing the business case for the system authorization program, it is important for the chief information security officer (CISO) or security program manager to enlist the support of allies. By building partnerships with other organizational executives, the CISO can create a more convincing case for the program. Although the CISO must play the role of program champion, he or she needs to seek the support of other influential individuals as cochampions. This can be done by meeting with and working closely with managers of other organization programs and operations to convince them of how the system authorization program can help them meet their business needs. Building these relationships is discussed further in this chapter.

Goal Setting

In designing a system authorization program for the enterprise, goals and objectives for the program must be established and effectively communicated across the enterprise. When considering program goals, it is important to understand that the program must be

■ *Realistic*: The program must solve a realistic business problem. Small organizations or those without significant investments in information technology resources realistically do not need a formalized system authorization program like those described in this volume. In these cases, less-elaborate programs that include risk assessment and acceptance will probably meet the needs of such organizations.

■ *Comprehensive*: The system authorization program needs to leave no stone (or system) unturned. One of the program's greatest benefits is standardization of processes, requirements, and outcomes. Failure to require all organizational elements to comply with program requirements risks the loss of this standardization.

■ *Integrated*: The program must integrate requirements from multiple sources under a centralized authority. Requirements that have an impact on security must all be brought into the system authorization house so that they can be addressed as part of an integrated program.

- *Achievable*: The program must be achievable with resources that are or will be reasonably available. There is no need to design an elaborate program that is impressive to behold but can never be implemented due to its complexity or cost. The program must be able to harness the skills of those readily available in the organization.

- *Effective*: An ineffective system authorization program may very well be worse than no program at all because of the basic planning and implementation required to establish the program initially. If the system authorization initiative does not achieve its goals, then the effort that has been expended on it has been wasted with no obvious benefit, further deteriorating any element of goodwill that may have existed previously.

- *Supported*: The system authorization program must have genuine support to work effectively. If no one supports it, or if it is only supported by a limited number of individuals in a minimal number of organizational elements, it will fail. Executives must provide their active support, especially in its early stages, by providing resources to the initiative; business managers must exercise continuing support; technicians must understand the benefit of the program and support it through their day-to-day control of system controls; and users must see evidence of enhanced security provided by the program to perform the security functions inherent to their jobs.

- *Enduring*: A system authorization program must be designed for the long term. It is not a temporary solution for a short-term problem. The program must be designed to permit continuous improvement in the security posture of the organization. And, because of the threats inherent in the nature of the modern workplace, an optimum security posture can probably never be achieved; even if it is, this posture cannot be maintained without a system authorization program.

The most effective approach to setting program goals and objectives is for the organization information technology security director or CISO to be the individual charged with this responsibility because he or she is the rightful owner of the program. Goal setting must be closely tied to the development of the business case for the program and must be underwritten by senior organization management. Knowledge of the organization, its culture, its personalities, and its security posture is essential in this process. Other areas that the CISO should consider as part of the program goal-setting process are the effect that other programs and initiatives may have on system authorization (e.g., strategic enterprise information technology planning, mergers and acquisitions, etc.) and the resources available. There is no need to plan a 2-week vacation in Maui when you cannot afford the trip to the airport.

Tasks and Milestones

For the system authorization program to be effective, the CISO or dedicated program manager must establish tasks that need to be performed and a schedule for their completion. These tasks must be established from the perspective of identifying how approved program goals and objectives will be achieved. Both short-term (immediate certification of systems) and long-term goals (achieving an established performance objective as an organization) need to be addressed. Tasks and milestones need to be consolidated into a coherent high-level program management plan that is disseminated to program participants and other organization managers under the authority of executive management. This program-level plan cannot simply be developed and then reviewed annually. It must be a driver itself that is used frequently in monthly and quarterly updates, and it should provide the basis for development of objectives for individual performance plans of key program players.

Program Oversight

The execution of the system authorization program must be constantly measured to ensure that it is being implemented effectively and to ensure that established program requirements are being met. The program oversight function must be responsive to the needs of the organization, and this is best served through a dedicated tracking process established by the CISO or system authorization program manager. Metrics that can be used to measure the successful implementation of the program are outlined further in this chapter. The CISO should seek frequent feedback from program participants on their view of the program and ways in which it can be improved, and the CISO must be responsive to their concerns either by making suggested changes or by explaining why their recommendations cannot be employed. Program requirements must be subject to a well-defined enforcement mechanism and schedule. The enforcement effort should not be half-hearted, capricious, or irregular. System owners and business managers should know how compliance inspections will be performed and when they will be conducted.

Oversight of the program also needs to include provision of assistance and advice to program participants. This assistance should extend to the area of problem escalation on either an immediate or a periodic level. The CISO or system authorization program manager should either create or be part of an escalation plan by which issues related to the program can be identified, reported, and resolved on an immediate basis. In addition, the CISO should schedule regular meetings to explain program initiatives and their impact. Such meetings should be conducted for systems owners, ISSOs, and authorizing officials when necessary.

Should one exist (and one should), a security oversight committee can assist in performance of the system authorization program oversight function. This group will probably meet on a periodic basis with representation of broad organizational elements well suited for oversight of program compliance and for establishing program goals. To be effective, the security oversight committee must have access to performance metrics to perform its program evaluation function and must have the authority to establish or recommend changes to program objectives and strategies. The CISO should closely coordinate with this group as it reviews objectives and goals and assesses progress toward those goals and as best possible use its findings as justification for resources for the program.

Visibility

Without consistent management support, the system authorization program will lose effectiveness and will eventually die. To preserve the attention it needs, the CISO will have to work hard to maintain management support by providing frequent updates on program status, needs, and benefits. As part of his or her participation in regular organization staff meetings, the CISO should make reporting on system authorization one of the hot buttons. The CISO should brief executive management on project plans for significant program initiatives (e.g., recertification of a large number of systems due to a facility upgrade) and should consider couching problem resolution in terms of system authorization program implementation. For instance, implementation of a biometric solution can be presented not only as another control that provides security to information systems but also as a means of mitigating residual risks in the operation of the system that were previously identified during certification testing.

The CISO should take every opportunity to maintain the interest of upper management because it has control over the lifeblood of the program: resources. The CISO must offer those in upper management frequent written updates, involve them in program issues during routine staff meetings, and get on their schedule to brief them when their direct input is required on program issues. In addition to offering formal briefings to keep C-level executives in the loop, brief, well-written e-mail messages can also be an effective means of communicating program status to upper management, and these messages keep the program visible. Focusing such messages on the program's support to other ongoing initiatives helps elevate the program's usefulness in their eyes. This is most effective when concrete metrics can be pointed out, such as delays in schedules or the number of security weaknesses that can be resolved through the selection of a particular course of action. In addition to topical e-mail, system authorization program status should be integrated into other reports as much as possible. For instance, weekly reports from the CISO should most assuredly include a paragraph on program status, and information technology security input regarding the status of an organizational initiative like implementation of a new accounting system should use system authorization terms and program objectives as fully as possible.

CISOs should remember that in their drive to gain the ear of senior executives, they should avoid using any increased visibility or influence to draw unnecessary attention to the failures of individual program participants. Although this may very well be required on occasion, this tactic should be rarely employed and only after making every effort first to resolve the difficulty personally. Seeking the cooperation of system owners and business unit managers involved in the program must be maintained at a high priority, and using upper management to hammer them into cooperation may be effective in the short term but is detrimental to the program in the long run.

Resources

Funding for system authorization initiatives is the lifeblood of the program. The decision to establish an enterprise program must be followed with a commitment to invest in the resources of people, processes, and technology required to implement and maintain the program. This begins with a realistic definition of program requirements, not a wish list. A realistic budget for the program can be developed by first estimating the man-hours needed to perform project tasks because labor and personnel costs will make up the lion's share of program expenditures. Costs to certify individual systems vary greatly, but reasonably realistic man-hour estimates based on system type and level of effort are provided in Table 1.1. Other costs include program management costs (addressed further in this chapter), costs for developing program guidance, training costs, and costs for the purchase of development-automated

Table 1.1 Man-Hour Planning Estimates			
Certification Level	**Duration of Testing**	**Number of Personnel**	**Man-Hours**
Low	1 day	1	8
Moderate	2–3 days	2	32–48
High	5–10 days	4	160–320

tools. Once the program is established and operating, the program manager must continue to develop, submit, and justify program budget requirements. When the program manager anticipates resistance in initial funding for the program, the program manager should consider a salami-attack-like approach, with program objectives quantified individually, allowing them to be funded incrementally depending on funding available. Using the repeatable processes and quantifiable metrics described in this volume, program operating costs can be readily estimated, making the job of defending the program budget much easier.

Program Guidance

Once program goals, objectives, tasks, and milestones have been developed and resource requirements have been identified, then it is time to begin documenting what the program is and how it will be implemented. This is achieved through the development and publication of system authorization guidance. By guidance, I mean documented policies, standards, guidelines, and procedures. This documentation set establishes mandatory program requirements (policy, standards, and procedures) and offers useful but optional advice (guidelines). As a reminder, guidance documentation should always stress that the purpose of the system authorization program is to meet an organizational business requirement and is based on a combination of legal, contractual, operational, and other business drivers; it is not simply a security program for its own sake.

System authorization guidance documentation is developed at the CISO level using the existing organization guidance structure (i.e., policy library) to give program documentation added authority and credibility. As part of this guidance development process, the CISO needs to assess any existing security guidance documentation to determine if it can be used to establish the program by updating it or if it needs to be replaced entirely. The CISO should also look to follow a guidance policy life-cycle approach, shown in Table 1.2. Program guidance begins with developing a policy statement. This is a brief (no more than one page) document that establishes the program and is signed at the highest level of the organization. A sample enterprise-level system authorization policy is provided in Table 1.3. Program-related terms and definitions must be described in a system authorization glossary, preferably at this highest level where it will be most visible.

Based on the policy establishing the program, enterprise-level system authorization standards are developed to establish particular program requirements. These standards facilitate implementation of the high-level policy by elaborating on program

Table 1.2   System Authorization Guidance Development Life Cycle

Phase	Task	Activity
Development	Creation	Plan for, research, and write the policy
	Review	Complete an independent policy review prior to approval
	Approval	Obtain management approval of the policy
Implementation	Communication	Disseminate the policy
	Compliance	Implement the policy
	Exceptions	Manage cases if full implementation is not possible
Maintenance	Awareness	Ensure continued awareness of the policy
	Monitoring	Report and track compliance with the policy
	Enforcement	Handle violations of the policy
	Maintenance	Keep the policy current
Disposal	Retirement	Retire the policy when it is no longer required

Table 1.3   Sample Enterprise System Authorization Policy

Based on a certification package that contains an up-to-date security plan, risk assessment, security test and evaluation (ST&E), and plan of action and milestones (POA&M), each XYZ Agency general support system and major application will be evaluated for authorization to operate. The XYZ Agency senior management official, who is responsible for the business process supported by the system and who exercises budgetary control over the system, must authorize the system prior to its being allowed to go into production for newly developed systems or those undergoing major updates or must authorize systems in production to continue to operate. This authorization must be made in writing based on implementation of its security plan before beginning or significantly changing processing in the system. Operation of the system shall be reauthorized at least every 3 years.

requirements in more detail. Standards should be set for the entire spectrum of the program to establish minimum security baseline requirements that must be met. Minimum security baseline standards are addressed in detail in Chapter 3.

The next type of program guidance to be developed is enterprise-level system authorization guidelines. These are written as work aids, templates, samples, checklists, and instructions that are designed to assist in the development of program documentation and in meeting program requirements. This type of documentation is highly valuable because it facilitates consistency in program documentation. Although the use of guidelines is optional, they should be so well written and so easy to use that their use will be practically universal. They should represent the simplest, most effective, and best ways to perform a task. Ensure that when templates and samples are provided users understand these need to be tailored to their own specific needs. Otherwise, the use of out-of-the-box system authorization products without thought can lead to the organization being held liable for noncompliance with rules that are actually nonapplicable.

The final component of an integrated set of system authorization policies is security procedures. Development of security procedures is accomplished on several levels. At the enterprise level, responsible organizations develop procedures that apply to all systems throughout the organization. At the business unit level, managers prepare procedures that apply only to those systems in their area of responsibility, but with which all systems must adhere. Finally, at the system level, the system owner is responsible for creating procedures that implement program policies, standards, and procedures of higher-level organizations. These system-specific procedures apply only to a particular information technology system and present the most detailed requirements of all policy documents. The development of security procedures is addressed in more detail in Chapter 4.

The system authorization guidance must describe a methodology for performing program tasks. This means that it must present a flow of how certifications and accreditations will be performed and how program processes, tasks, and activities interrelate. An example of system authorization process flow is presented in Figure 1.2. Program guidance documentation must describe each process, what each is designed to achieve, the output from each, responsibilities for the process, and timelines for completion.

System authorization policy and guidance should be precise, clear, and as brief as possible to enhance understanding and to limit confusion. It should be located in the same repository and should be tightly controlled by the CISO. For every new policy document created, an old one should be removed to avoid its continued use. Stability of documentation is a useful goal, particularly in light of the fact that system authorization documents are being used at very low levels of the organization. System administrators rely on clear and stable documentation in developing security plans, minimum security baseline self-assessments, and other documentation, and they expect that once they learn how to comply with the rules, the rules will not be changing frequently. Other desirable characteristics of system authorization policy documentation include ease of access (preferably it will be accessible from the corporate intranet); seamless integration into the organization's policy structure; consistency with other policy documentation, particularly other system authorization

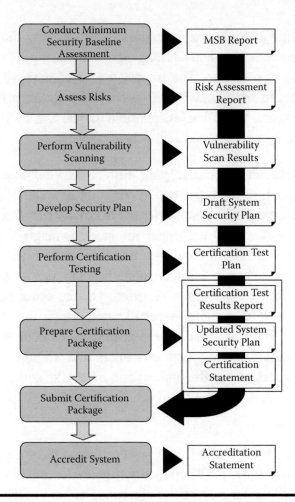

Figure 1.2 **System authorization process flow.**

policies and standards; readability by an average reader; that it is up to date; and applicability to the needs of the organization.

Limiting the amount of system authorization policy documentation in circulation will facilitate ease of maintenance as well as make it more readily accessible and useful. The golden rule of policy documentation—"less is more"—should be adhered to because an overly abundant set of rules and regulations stifles application of discretion in the security of systems as well as innovation in identifying solutions to control implementation.

Special Issues

In terms of guidance and establishing program parameters, there are three special issues that must be addressed as part of the enterprise security system authorization program: establishing accreditation boundaries, determining the level of effort of system authorization activities, and defining significant changes and events that warrant reaccreditation of a system. The importance of addressing these three areas normally arises early in any discussion of system authorization policies, procedures, and practices. Therefore, the official responsible for the agency's system authorization program would be well served to give them priority.

One of the most difficult and challenging problems for authorizing officials and CISOs is identification of appropriate accreditation boundaries for agency information systems. Accreditation boundaries are normally based on the components of an information system that are under the same management authority. Care must be taken to ensure that boundaries are not overly expansive (i.e., include unrelated hardware, software components), making the system authorization process more difficult to apply than required. On the other hand, definition of narrow boundaries results in multiple certification efforts that will increase their cost to the agency. To ensure that system accreditation boundary definitions do not impede certification efforts, system owners and authorizing officials must understand their importance to the process and must take action to establish them prior to the initial risk assessment and the development of the security plan for the system.

Determination of the level of effort and resources required for performing system authorization should be made in accordance with procedures established by the CISO or other security official as part of the enterprise system authorization program. An enterprise-level determination will inform decisions of the authorizing official, system owner, and certifying agent with respect to defining work requirements for authorization of individual systems. Questions on level of effort normally arise in the context of certification testing performance. The scope, rigor, and complexity of testing and test procedures should vary according to the security categorization of the system. This ensures that the effort is commensurate to the risk associated with the system and is cost-effective.

Finally, for systems that have successfully undergone system authorization and are in operation, circumstances that necessitate reaccreditation need to be defined clearly in agency security policy and procedures. Significant changes in a system or its operating environment must trigger a new system authorization for the system. Definitions of such events will be unique to the organization, although there is a need to define and document them uniformly to prevent confusion over what constitutes a significant change or event.

Program Integration

CISOs will have to integrate the system authorization program with other organization programs and activities, both those they control and those they do not. High on the list of priorities will be initiating discussions with individuals responsible for incident response, disaster recovery, system development, auditing, resource management, capital investment planning, personnel security, project management, information technology operations, human resources, physical security, general counsel, performance measurement, the security oversight committee, education and training, the configuration control board, enterprise architecture, and contracting. The relationships of these contacts to the system authorization program are detailed elsewhere in this chapter.

System Authorization Points of Contact

Although the CISO has direct responsibility for the success of the organization's system authorization program, he or she has to rely on many others to be successful. One of the first objectives for achieving success in building a program is the development of a system authorization work group. Such an informal organization would consist of key players across the organization who can contribute to the effectiveness of the program. The CISO should strive for the involvement of system owners, points of contact from key lines of business, adjunct members from external sister organizations, and points of contact from interconnected systems.

Individuals who function most effectively as members of a system authorization work group are those who have knowledge of the organization's operations, management structure, leadership hierarchy, business strategies, and initiatives and plans, as well as its systems and information technology architecture. Security qualities that point to success as a work group member are a basic understanding of security principles and practices, sound knowledge of system authorization policies and processes, and a general knowledge of risk management principles, as well as knowledge of specific risks to organization information technology assets. Therefore, the team should have a good mix of members with business, information technology, and security backgrounds.

Measuring Progress

An effective system authorization program requires defined metrics to allow the CISO to know how well it is functioning. The CISO should establish a process for measuring the effectiveness of the program so that he or she can rapidly determine shortfalls and redirect efforts to trouble spots. The system authorization processes described in this volume are designed to produce information that the CISO can use to monitor the progress of the program at several levels throughout all the stages. Common measures of success that can be used in monitoring program effectiveness include

- *Time*: Measuring the completion of program requirements according to a predetermined schedule to determine if they are being completed in a timely and efficient basis.

- *Task*: Measuring discrete program elements such as preparation of security plans, risk assessments, certification tests, and so on. Tasks of this nature have established start and end dates and follow a measurable development process, allowing the security manager to determine if they are being performed on time and according to standards.

- *Cost*: Measuring the amount of financial resources expended in performance of program requirements. This is primarily related to man-hours utilized in performing program tasks but also includes expense elements such as contracting, training, travel, and supplies. Costs are measured against an established program budget, and deviations are readily discernible.

- *Number of Systems*: Measuring the scope of the program is achieved by measuring the number of general support systems and major applications within its scope. The system inventory process will produce this metric and is addressed in detail elsewhere in Chapter 1.

- *Sensitivity and Criticality*: Measuring a system's relative need for protection and its relative importance to the organization permits the manager to determine if the system's security protection requires additional emphasis, more resources, increased priority, or elevated scrutiny. Chapter 2 defines the process for assessing system sensitivity and criticality.

- *Risk*: Measuring the number and severity of weaknesses in information systems that are certified and accredited. The identification of risks and determination of their severity follow a well-defined process that produces consistency in findings. The risk assessment process is described in Chapter 3.

- *Level of Effort*: Measuring to establish the amount of time and expertise required to perform certification testing. The level of effort is defined in predetermined standards and is applied according to the sensitivity and criticality of the system. This ensures that the rigor of certification testing is commensurate with the needs of the system. Certification levels of effort are discussed in Chapter 5.

- *Improvements*: Measuring the status, rate of completion, and adequacy of corrective actions taken in response to correct deficiencies in security controls. The plan of action and milestones or remediation plan is normally used by the security manager to measure the success or failure of remediation efforts, and the process is further discussed in Chapter 4.

■ *Number of Systems Accredited*: This measurement gives a direct indication of the bottom line. The goal of the system authorization program is to accredit 100% of the organization's systems. Counting the number of signed, approved system authorization packages readily allows the security manager to establish the level of progress toward this goal. Documentation and approval aspects of the accreditation process are defined in Chapter 6.

Use of these metrics allows CISOs to measure progress toward accomplishment of program requirements and gives important feedback that can be used to inform management of the security posture of the organization's information systems. These metrics permit a comparison of different organizational elements to establish where increased emphasis and priority are needed. They allow identification of trends that require resolution at the enterprise level, such as implementation of a strong authentication solution. And, because easily quantified, common metrics are used, they allow CISOs to benchmark the status of their organization's program with that of other organizations. FISMA has been effective in its establishment of useful metrics that allow Congress to compare the level of security in major government departments and agencies.

Managing Program Activities

At any given time, CISOs will have a wide variety of system authorization initiatives and activities taking place, and they have overall responsibility for the adequacy of their results and the timeliness and cost-effectiveness of their completion. A tracking process allows CISOs to use the metrics described to monitor the progress and status of these activities to identify problems before they become bigger problems. Key elements of project tracking include

■ *Problem Forecasting*: Program managers as much as possible should aim to forecast difficulties for management, allowing them to be not only the bearer of bad news but also the providers of an accompanying solution. Knowing the dependencies related to a project's progress allows CISOs to project potential difficulties before they occur, and focusing on the critical path allows them to concentrate on the tasks that matter most to the successful completion of the project and ensures that they are not distracted by minutiae.

■ *Tracking External Projects*: CISOs must also be aware of and track the progress of ongoing projects for which they do not have responsibility but that have an impact on the system authorization program. This could include development of new systems, consolidation of existing systems, or interconnection with external systems. Processes that address events such as these are discussed in more detail further in this chapter.

■ *Reporting*: The information that the CISO gathers to maintain visibility of program activities should be translated into reports to apprise management, supporting elements (e.g., certifying agents), and supported elements (e.g., system owners) of project status. Regular status reporting to management helps to maintain management support and aids in team building when dependably communicated to other program participants.

■ *Resource Tracking*: Close tracking of resources expended in the performance of program activities allows the CISO to monitor and respond to deviations in the budget estimate. This helps him or her identify requirements for additional resources to ensure that critical projects can be completed even when over budget.

Management of system authorization projects is further described elsewhere in Chapter 1.

Monitoring Compliance

If the system authorization program manager only needed to meet certification requirements by identifying weaknesses and risks, his or her job would be simpler but incomplete. After a system has been certified, the CISO needs a process to monitor the system's continued compliance with requirements, measure progress in implementing corrective actions to address weaknesses, and track risks that authorizing officials have accepted. The process needs to include the following capabilities:

■ *Vulnerability Scanning and Checking*: The compliance-tracking process needs to include the use of automated vulnerability scanning tools to periodically verify the ability of a system's technical controls to protect against known exploits. These should be performed as often as weekly for the most sensitive systems, but no less frequently than quarterly for any system.
In addition to automated scanning, physical spot checks of security practices should be performed to ensure compliance. This includes reviews of documentation (such as audit trails, facility access logs, system change request forms), as well as observations of how system personnel comply with documented procedures.

■ *Recertification Tracking*: The process must provide for tracking the need for periodic recertification of systems to ensure that full and interim accreditations are not allowed to expire. Associated with this is the CISO's need to monitor systems for which accreditation has been denied to ensure that the systems do in fact terminate processing or do not begin processing.

■ *Monitoring Accepted Risks*: The CISO should maintain an inventory of all risks that accrediting authorities have accepted and do not plan to mitigate due to cost or other operational considerations. The purpose of this is to ensure that these risks do not present exposures to other systems in the enterprise and to allow them to be reassessed when changes in the environment occur.

■ *Tracking Changes in the Environment*: The tracking process must provide for monitoring changes to systems environments to identify additional requirements for protection. This process must be closely tied to the incident response capability to allow knowledge of incidents that may have an impact on the enterprise.

■ *Tracking Audit Findings*: The CISO must be able to maintain visibility of security-related findings from internal and external audits and must ensure their integration into remediation plans developed through system certification.

■ *Reviewing Security Documentation*: The process should track the currency of security documentation (i.e., security plans) by reviewing it to ensure it has been reviewed and updated by system owners annually to account for changes to the system and its security posture.

■ *Validating Corrective Action*: Once system owners report through the plan of action and milestones process that corrective action has been completed, the process must provide the capability to spot check reported corrective actions to provide assurance that they fully mitigate the weakness and that they will prevent the weakness from reoccurring.

Providing Advice and Assistance

From the perspective of the senior manager, one of the primary services rendered by the system authorization program manager is offering advice and assistance. Advice and assistance are important to others in the organization, so this is essential both vertically and horizontally. The CISO needs to establish a process that maximizes consistency while minimizing ad hoc readings and opinions that may not withstand scrutiny when applied enterprise-wide or over time. Other considerations for the system authorization program manager when providing advice and assistance include

■ *Having Knowledge of the Program*: The program manager is expected to be the absolute subject matter expert and resident "guru" who offers the most reliable information on the system authorization program and how it works. Advice provided regarding processes, policies, and products must be based on a thorough knowledge of all aspects of the program as a result of personal experience.

■ *Understanding of Compliance*: When offering advice or providing assistance, the program manager must avoid the urge to rule from "on high." Though he or she may be charged with establishing program requirements and enforcing compliance, the manager must understand the perspective of the individual seeking advice and should offer solutions rather than simply responding that there will be no alternative but compliance. It is always better to offer advice and assistance with an aim toward relationship building based on an understanding that compliance starts from the bottom up, not from the top down.

■ *Limiting Assistance*: The program manager must understand that many requests for assistance are based on a desire by the requestor to avoid responsibility. Be on the lookout for this tactic and avoid the trap of doing the work for system owners, ISSOs, and authorizing officials.

■ *Accepting Suggestions*: Program managers should also understand that just because an idea does not originate with them that it is not a good one. Program managers must be open to suggestions, recommendations, and new ideas received from program participants and give them credence because they may very well be based on hard-earned experience.

■ *Making Promises*: System authorization program managers must be careful in making promises in response to requests for advice and assistance. Promises may be difficult to keep once they are made, particularly when they have not been well thought out. Program managers must not promise an authorizing official that they will recommend that a system be certified until certification testing has actually been performed and results have been reviewed. Breaking promises is a quick way to lose credibility with those for whom it is most important. Program managers should work to manage expectations with honest answers rather than with easy promises.

■ *Seeking Advice*: Program managers, although they may be the resident experts, will not always have all the answers. When this happens, they should seek external advice and assistance by approaching an expert outside the organization. This might range from a phone conversation with a counterpart in a sister organization to discuss how a similar problem there may have been solved or presentation of a proposal to a higher-level organization (for government agencies, perhaps this will be approaching NIST for more detailed guidance).

■ *Recording Agreements*: Agreements made as a result of offering advice and assistance, which commit the program manager to provide assistance in the future, need to be recorded to ensure that they are met when the time comes. If the CISO offers to expedite his or her annual review of security compliance as requested by a system owner, then the work must be scheduled to ensure that it happens. Again, credibility is an asset that is difficult to reestablish once it is lost.

Responding to Changes

Another essential ingredient to the success of the system authorization program is ensuring compliance with external requirements. To do this, program managers must establish a process for ensuring they are aware of changes that affect the program and that permit them to develop an understanding of the impacts of the changes. Examples of changes that could change the ground rules for the program might include the passage of new laws and dissemination of new regulations; requirements associated with new business agreements and contracts; new business models and initiatives; mergers and acquisitions; and new operating locations. If not careful, external changes can lead to requirements for major changes in the system authorization program, even a potential program reinvention if these changes are not fully researched and understood. In implementation of a process that allows them to be proactive in addressing potential impacts, program managers must know when and how to contest proposed changing conditions when warranted. Frequently, threatened changes are based on changes of personnel in the hierarchy and are made without knowledge of their impacts. CISOs must revisit the program business case and use it to present a convincing case for maintaining the status quo.

Program Awareness, Training, and Education

Developing and managing system authorization-related awareness, training, and education are also essential elements to sustain the program over the long term. A system authorization program can be implemented in the short term with the use of external resources (i.e., contractors and consultants). However, to maintain the program, its requirements have to be internalized to be performed by assigned personnel. Program awareness ensures that every individual in the organization is familiarized with program objectives, processes, and benefits so that they understand the value of the program to their own work. Next, training provides more specialized schooling to program participants in system authorization requirements specific to their program roles. System owners, ISSOs, system administrators, managers, and executives form the target audience for this training. Finally, education should be provided to those involved in the program who, because of the nature of their program roles, require professional-level expertise in system authorization concepts, principles, and best practices. The CISO, others performing program manager functions, certifying agents, and certain ISSOs who are responsible for highly sensitive systems should receive professional system authorization education.

In developing and delivering awareness, training, and education opportunities, the program manager should work with the organization's training function to ensure it

Table 1.4 Example of a System Authorization Training Plan			
Priority	Target Audience	Description of Training	Duration
1	System owners/project managers	Overview of system authorization and the role of the system owner/project manager	2 hours
2	Approving authorities	Overview of system authorization and the role of the approving authority	1 hour
3	System security officers (ISSOs)	Implementing system authorization at the system level and the role of the ISSO	4 hours
4	IT security oversight board	Overview of system authorization	1 hour
5	Business unit security points of contact	Oversight of system authorization activities	4 hours
6	System administrators	Compliance with minimum security baseline controls	4 hours
7	System developers	Integration of system authorization into the system development life cycle	4 hours
8	General users	Awareness of system authorization	1 hour

is fully integrated to allow the use of existing mechanisms for documenting attendance, posting to personnel records, requesting funding, and so on. As they always say, there is no need to reinvent the wheel. Once system authorization requirements have been integrated into the organization's training program, there will be less difficulty in scheduling time to train employees and to obtain resources required to present the training. Table 1.4 provides planning estimates for establishing system authorization awareness, training, and education requirements.

Using Expert Systems

Another essential element of the enterprise system authorization program is the evaluation, development, and utilization of automated tools to assist in the implementation of the program. Expert systems can be useful in developing program documentation and ensuring consistency. The program manager must decide which processes are ripe for automation and whether useful tools can be acquired or developed within the limits of available resources. Processes that lend themselves most readily to automation are those related to identification of controls, assessment of risks to those controls, documentation of vulnerabilities in the controls, and correction of weaknesses in these specific controls—in other words, the security plan, risk assessment, certification testing, and remediation planning processes. There is an array of products available that automate system authorization processes, including the minimum security baseline assessment, security plan development, risk assessment, aspects of certification testing (i.e., vulnerability scanning and baseline configuration checking), and remediation planning. However, care must be taken to ensure that the output of these various tools can be integrated to allow compliance with program requirements in a coherent way.

The tools that most effectively support system authorization are those that centralize data collection, permit assessment of security posture against established standards, ease calculation of risks, consolidate development of security documentation (e.g., generation of security plans and certification test results reports), generate action plans, permit tracking of individual project work, and facilitate periodic reporting on program status (e.g., quarterly and annual FISMA reporting). The cost to purchase or develop tools is a key consideration, and costs to provide continuing training to users must be factored in because there is normally a significant need to train new program participants. When establishing a program and assessing the viability of using automated tools, it is important to determine first who the prospective users are going to be. Will they be employed for external certifying agents or system owners and ISSOs? The answer to that question has an impact on requirements for ease of use and consistency. When selecting a tool, the CISO needs to make sure that program requirements are used to drive the selection and that tool capabilities are not used to drive the program.

Waivers and Exceptions

Although not as essential as the other elements listed previously, a process for considering waivers and exceptions to program requirements is normally a part of a successful system authorization program. As a component part of program enforcement, the CISO must know how to identify when waivers of program policies and standards are warranted in the interest of the overall mission of the organization. Considerations relating to schedules and costs have to be weighed to see if they can be accommodated without unduly jeopardizing the security of the system and the enterprise. There may be short-term circumstances that give rise to waivers of program requirements. For instance, it may make sense to honor a request to delay development of a system contingency plan for the system until the organization has decided on an organization-wide recovery strategy. Another example would be to grant a waiver to requirements until the organization has completed its plans for relocation to a new data center. Both of these examples relate to circumstances beyond the control of the affected system owner, are relatively short term in nature, and have established dates by when the security deviation will no longer apply.

On the other hand, there may be cases when an exception is appropriate for a security deviation because of other long-term conditions. This could relate perhaps to minimal cost benefit in meeting program requirements (i.e., implementation of strong authentication on a company parking space registration system). A formal process for reviewing and approving waivers for short-term deviations and exceptions to policy for long-term deviations can be established and managed, but it may prove to be time-consuming and eventually unwieldy because tracking of waivers and exceptions is a labor-intensive process and by definition requires management by exception. The CISO will be better served in addressing these deviations using an existing certification process: one that is used to identify risks to systems assets that are acceptable and that leads to executive management acceptance of those risks.

Although the system owner and the authorizing official are the primary players in the risk acceptance process, the CISO can still exercise authority in this process through oversight of risks that have been accepted across the organization's information systems. The CISO should establish a basis for evaluating accepted risks to ensure that decisions are consistent and coherent in a broad context and are realistic and achievable at the system level. A decision-making framework for the CISO should be based on knowledge of the organization, its business processes, and business drivers. The CISO must also apply his or her evaluation based on expertise of the organization's security architecture. Finally, it must be based on a firm commitment from management to provide backing to the decisions the CISO makes regarding risks that should not be accepted. This will allow the CISO to stick to his or her guns when pressure mounts.

NIST Special Publication 800-37, Revision 1, and the Application of the Risk Management Framework to Systems

In February 2010, the NIST updated its guidance relating to authorization of information systems with its publication of NIST SP 800-37, Revision 1, Guide for Applying the Risk Management Framework to Federal Information Systems: A Security Lifecycle Approach. It replaced the earlier version of SP 800-37 originally published in May 2004 under the title, Guide for the Security Certification and Accreditation of Federal Information Systems. The purpose of this section is to review this latest guidance.

By omitting it from the title, NIST signaled its move away from use of the system authorization terminology in favor of system authorization. However, the principle tenants of system authorization were carried forward in the new special publication, but as one can surmise by the title, are addressed in the context of risk management. The system authorization process described in NIST SP 800-37, Revision 1, is designed to be used by all federal organizations, including the DOD organizations and intelligence community elements, as well as agencies of civilian government. NIST's new authorization process abandons the four phased certification and accreditation process in favor of a six-step authorization process. The new process emphasizes risk management, near-real-time awareness, automation, program management, and continuous monitoring as the basis for protecting government information systems. In addition, new roles and responsibilities at various levels within government organizations and supporting contractor organizations are identified in the new NIST system authorization guidance.

According to its authors, NIST SP 800-37, Revision 1, was developed as part of the Joint Task Force Transformation Initiative to provide a unified information security framework for the entire federal government. For this purpose, an Interagency Working Group was established with representatives from the civil government, defense, and intelligence communities, under the direction of project leader Dr. Ron Ross of NIST.

Two of the primary drivers for NIST's development of NIST SP 800-37, Revision 1, were to avoid duplication of effort and ensure that NIST publications compliment security standards and guidelines for national security systems. Its goal in collaborating with the Office of the Director of National Intelligence (ODNI), the DOD, and the CNSS in the project was to establish a common foundation for information security across the entire federal government, leading to more uniform and consistent management of risk resulting from operation and use of information systems. An additional objective of the project was to provide a basis for reciprocity in the acceptance of security authorizations across government organizations and to facilitate system authorization-related information sharing.

Overview

The common framework described in NIST SP 800-37, Revision 1, transforms the traditional certification and accreditation process into the RMF. The emphasis of the revised process is on

- Building information security controls into government information systems by applying up-to-date management, operational and technical security controls.

- Maintaining awareness of the security posture of information systems through the application of "enhanced monitoring processes."

- Providing senior leaders essential information to facilitate decision making with regard to risk acceptance.

NIST describes the RMF as having the following characteristics:

- Implementation of continuous monitoring to promote near-real-time management of risk in information systems and ongoing information system authorization.

- Use of automation to drive decision making by providing senior leaders information necessary to make cost-effective, risk-based decisions on the operation of information systems supporting their core missions and business functions.

- Integration of information security into the SDLC and the enterprise architecture.

- Emphasis on the selection, implementation, assessment, and monitoring of security controls and authorization of information systems.

- Linkage of system-level risk management processes to risk management processes at the organization level by means of a risk executive (function).

- Establishment of distinct responsibility and accountability for security controls for information systems inherited by those systems.

Authority and Scope

NIST SP 800-37, Revision 1, was developed by NIST under the authority of the FISMA, Public Law (P.L.) 107-347. FISMA assigns NIST statutory responsibility for developing information security standards and guidelines, including minimum requirements for federal information systems, with the exception of national security systems. In addition to FISMA, NIST's new system authorization guidance comports with OMB Circular A-130 and therefore does not supersede the existing authority of the director of the OMB.

NIST has encouraged the use of its revised system authorization guidance by nongovernmental organizations on a voluntary basis. Generally, special publications are developed and published by NIST for guidance purposes. However, NIST special publications mandated in an FIPS must be adhered to by federal agencies other than for national security programs and systems. For instance, FIPS 200 mandates the use of SP 800-53. In addition, OMB policies state that for other than national security programs and systems, federal agencies must follow certain specific NIST special publications but are permitted flexibility in how they apply the guidance. This allows federal agencies to apply the concepts and principles of the NIST special publications according to and in the context of the agency's missions, business functions, and environment of operation.

While not required for national security systems, the guidelines were broadly developed from a technical perspective to complement similar guidelines for national security systems, and NIST asserts that they may be used for such systems. In addition to private sector organizations, NIST encourages state, local, and tribal governments to consider using its system authorization guidance.

Purpose and Applicability

The purpose of this publication is to provide guidelines for applying the RMF to federal information systems to include conducting the activities of security categorization, security control selection and implementation, security control assessment, information system authorization, and security control monitoring. NIST developed the system authorization guidelines to

- Link management of system-related security risks to organization mission/business objectives and its overall risk strategy.
- Improve security authorization decisions through continuous monitoring, transparency of security and risk management information, and reciprocity.
- Ensure security requirements are integrated into the enterprise architecture and system development life-cycle processes of the organization.
- Improve security of government information and information systems through implementation of appropriate risk mitigation strategies.

Target Audience

NIST SP 800-37, Revision 1, provides guidance to individuals involved in the design, development, implementation, operation, maintenance, and disposition of government information systems. That is, it serves personnel engaged in every phase of a system's life cycle. This includes those assigned security responsibilities in the following areas:

- Mission/business ownership responsibilities or fiduciary responsibilities, including heads of federal agencies, chief executive officers, and chief financial officers.

- Information system development and integration responsibilities to include program managers, information technology product developers, system developers, systems integrators, enterprise architects, and security architects.

- System or security management and oversight responsibilities, including senior leadership, risk executives, authorizing officials, chief information officers (CIOs), CISOs, and the like.

- System and security control assessment and monitoring responsibilities to include system evaluators, assessors and assessment teams, independent verification and validation assessors, auditors, and information system owners.

- Information security implementation and operations responsibilities, including system owners, common control providers, information owners, information stewards, mission/business owners, security architects, and ISSOs.

Fundamentals of Information System Risk Management According to NIST SP 800-37, Revision 1

NIST SP 800-37, Revision 1, states that the fundamental concepts of information system-related security risk management include establishment of an organization-wide view of risk management and the application of NIST's RMF; integration of information security requirements into the organization's SDLC and other management processes; establishment of information system boundaries; and allocation of system-specific, hybrid, or common controls to information systems.

NIST SP 800-37, Revision 1, like its predecessor, provides guidance on the protection against risks to information systems. This concentration on information system-level protection and the exclusion of organization-level risks reinforces one of the primary weaknesses in NIST's early FISMA-related implementation guidance. Only recently with the publication of SP 800-39 has NIST addressed risk management from an enterprise perspective. NIST SP 800-37, Revision 1, describes four concepts inherent in the management of system-level risks:

■ Application of risk management principles to organization strategic planning and processes.

■ Addressing information security requirements as part of organization system development life-cycle processes.

■ Establishment of useful boundaries for information systems.

■ Classification of information system security controls as system-specific, hybrid, or common controls.

In the following paragraphs, more specific information on NIST's recent guidance in each of these areas is provided.

Guidance on Organization-Wide Risk Management

Although NIST SP 800-37, Revision 1, is designed to provide guidance on managing risk at the information system level, NIST takes care to anchor its system-level guidance to a framework that addresses risks at various levels of an organization. To properly address information security risks holistically, the involvement of the entire organization is necessary. Effective risk management must be supported by individual employees who develop, implement, and operate the information systems used to support the agency mission. In addition, risk management requires effective oversight by project managers and midlevel managers. Finally, an organization-wide risk management program requires the support of senior leaders to provide strategic vision, goals, and objectives for the organization. Full integration of risk management principles and best practices must be applied at every level of the organization and must be embedded in all information-related activities holistically. NIST provides a graphic illustration (provided in Figure 1.3) of the three-tiered approach to risk management described in NIST SP 800-37, Revision 1. It shows that risk-related concerns are addressed at the enterprise or organization level, the mission and business process level, as well as the information system level.

Organization Level (Tier 1)

The organization level (Tier 1) addresses risk from an enterprise-wide perspective through the development of an organization-wide governance structure and of a comprehensive enterprise risk management strategy. This strategy requires the following:

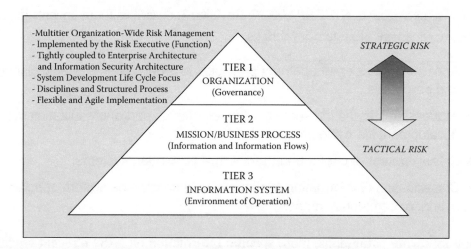

Figure 1.3 **Risk management approach.**

- *Assessment of Risks*: Processes for assessing information system-related security risks and other types of risk that may be of concern. Normally, risk assessment processes will adhere to NIST SP 800-30, which provides an approach for performing system-level risk assessments.

- *Evaluation of Risks*: Procedures for evaluating the significance of the risks identified through risk assessment. Prioritization of risk should normally follow NIST SP 800-30 as well.

- *Mitigation of Risks*: The strategy must identify the types and extent of corrective actions and mitigation measures that will be employed to address identified risks following the established mitigation priorities. NIST SP 800-53 provides a wide range of security controls as a basis for this activity.

- *Acceptance of Risk*: The organization must define the level of risk it is willing to accept. That is, the organization's risk tolerance must be identified. With the publication of NIST SP 800-39, standard guidance for determining an organization's risk appetite is now available.

- *Monitoring Risk*: The organization must include in its risk management strategy a description of how it will monitor risk on a constant basis. Changes to information systems and their operational environments necessitate continuous monitoring of risks to information.

- *Risk Management Strategy Oversight*: The strategy must also describe the nature and extent of oversight to be exercised to ensure that the strategy itself is properly implemented.

This risk management strategy is disseminated throughout the organization by means of the organization's governance structure. All agency officials as well as contractors who exercise programmatic, planning, development, acquisition, operational, or oversight responsibilities should be made aware of the risk management strategy. NIST's guidance stresses that the risk management strategy is appropriate for every level of the organization by identifying specific information security-related roles as recipients. These include authorizing officials, CIOs, senior information security officers, enterprise information security architects, information system owners and program managers, information owners and stewards, ISSOs, information system security engineers, information system developers and integrators, system administrators, contracting officials, and system users.

Mission/Business Process Level (Tier 2)

The risk decisions made at Tier 1 inform the mission and business process risks identified in Tier 2, the mission/business process level. The activities associated with Tier 2 are closely related to the enterprise architecture. These activities include

- Identifying the core missions and business processes for the organization, as well as those assigned to subordinate elements of the organization.

- Prioritizing missions and business processes according to their relationship to the organization's goals and objectives.

- Defining the types of information needed by the organization to successfully carry out identified missions and business processes as well as defining the organization's internal and external information flows. NIST SP 800-60 is designed to assist in making such information type decisions.

- Developing an information protection strategy for the entire agency and incorporating general information security requirements into all core missions and business processes.

- Specifying the authority granted to subordinate organizations (bureaus, offices, divisions, etc.) for assessment, evaluation, mitigation, acceptance, and monitoring of risks.

NIST is careful to clarify the need to consider granting autonomy to subordinate organizations responsible for carrying out supporting missions and business processes that have already developed processes for assessing, evaluating, mitigating, accepting, and monitoring risk to ensure a cost-effective approach. However, such flexibility could lead to a variety of acceptable risk assessment methodologies and practices, necessitating identification of a process for synthesizing the resulting risk-related information to ensure that the output can be properly correlated to be meaningful.

Information System Level (Tier 3)

Tier 3 of the risk management pyramid concerns risks at the information system level. As with Tier 2, risk decisions at this level are informed by those made at higher-level tiers in the model and ultimately have an impact on security controls selected and implemented to protect individual information systems. Tier 3 is the primary focus of NIST SP 800-37, Revision 1, and is familiar turf to those versed in NIST's FISMA-related guidance. Tier 3 also touches on those security requirements defined in NIST SP 800-53 and the management, operational, and technical security controls it defines. Tier 3 activities include allocation of security control components of the information system in the form of system-specific, hybrid, or common controls according to the information security architecture developed by the organization as part of Tier 2 activities. NIST's guidance for Tier 2 reminds the reader that security controls should be traceable to organizationally established security requirements to ensure they are satisfactorily addressed in the design, development, and implementation of the system. The NIST guidance also points out that security controls can be provided either by an organizational entity or by an external provider. In the case of external providers of security controls, provisions for ensuring the adequacy of provided controls must be arranged as part of the agreement between the organization and the external provider.

Guidance on Risk Management in the System Development Life Cycle

Just as noted previously, NIST's guidance in SP 800-37, Revision 1, emphasizes the need for risk management tasks to be initiated early in the SDLC to properly shape the security capabilities of the information system. Failure to perform risk management tasks during the initiation, development, and acquisition phases of the SDLC will require them to be addressed later in the life cycle, increasing implementation costs. Definition of system functional and nonfunctional requirements is performed early in the SDLC, usually as part of the initiation phase. Identification of business requirements for security should be considered as part of the overall requirements definition effort in the initiation phase to ensure they are addressed early in the life cycle of the system. Ensuring that security controls are incorporated into system requirements can best be accomplished through the use of an integrated project team established for the system. Capable security personnel should be included in the staffing of the integrated project team, allowing them to be involved in all system development activities beginning with the initial definition of security requirements in Tier 1 and Tier 2 to the selection of security controls in Tier 3.

Every effort must be made to ensure that risk management tasks are completed prior to the information system going into operation, particularly authorizing official acknowledgment of the risks operation of the system poses to organizational assets and operations. In addition, the system's continued operation should be contingent on adequately addressing system-related security risks on an ongoing basis.

Security-relevant information (i.e., certification test results, system security plan, etc.) developed during SDLC activities should be leveraged to help eliminate duplication of effort, minimize and standardize documentation, define common controls, promote reciprocity, and eliminate unnecessary costs resulting from uncoordinated activities. Also, the reuse of security information ensures increased consistency of information used throughout the life cycle of the information system.

Besides the inclusion of information security requirements in SDLC processes, security requirements must be integrated into the organization's program, planning, and budgeting processes. This will ensure resources are identified in a timely fashion and are available when required to meet program and project milestones.

NIST's Risk Management Framework

The RMF, which is updated in NIST SP 800-37, Revision 1, provides a structured process to fully integrate information security and risk management activities into the SDLC in a disciplined fashion. The RMF primarily targets activities in Tier 3 of the risk management pyramid, but also interconnects with activities in Tiers 1 and 2, for example, informing authorizing officials of systems-level risks that may have an impact on the overall organization risk profile. The six steps of the RMF are as follows:

- *Categorize*: Categorization of the information system and the information it processes, stores, and transmits is conducted by means of an impact analysis.

- *Select*: This step identifies an initial set of baseline security controls for the information system according to its security categorization. This is then followed by tailoring or adjusting and supplementing the security control baseline as necessary to address organizational assessment of risk as well as local conditions.

- *Implement*: The next step is to implement the security controls identified in Step 2 and describe how they have been implemented in security documentation.

- *Assess*: Following their implementation, security controls are formally assessed to determine "the extent to which the controls are implemented correctly, operating as intended, and producing the desired outcome with respect to meeting the security requirements for the system."

- *Authorize*: This step leads to authorization of the information system to operate by a senior agency management official based on its risks to organizational operations and assets and a decision that the risk is acceptable.

- *Monitor*: The final step in the RMF focuses on ongoing monitoring of information system security controls for effectiveness, documentation of changes to the system, performance of security impact analyses of system changes, and provision of status information to designated officials on the security posture of the system.

NIST's RMF is graphically portrayed in Figure 1.4.

NIST's risk management guidance provides organizations a significant degree of flexibility in implementing the RMF. The success of an agency's risk management efforts rests on a consistent approach such as the RMF, which is consistently and effectively applied to all its risk management processes and procedures.

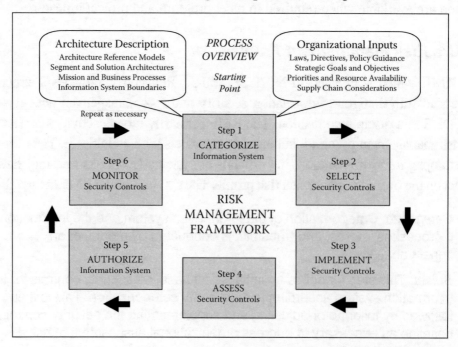

Figure 1.4 **NIST's Risk Management Framework.**

Guidance on System Boundary Definition

Identifying appropriate boundaries for organizational information systems is a major challenge for system owners, authorizing officials, CIOs, and CISOs. The updated guidance provided in NIST SP 800-37, Revision 1, stresses the importance of clearly defined boundaries. System boundaries establish the scope of protection for an information system and encompass the people, processes, and information technology components that are part of the system. System boundaries are established as part of the initial (categorization) step of the RMF and prior to the development of the system security plan. The expansiveness of system boundaries is a primary consideration of their definition; if the boundary is drawn too large, there will be an excessive number of system components and perhaps unnecessary complexity, making the risk management unwieldy and complex. On the other hand, boundaries that are too restrictive increase the number of systems and inflate security-related costs of protecting them.

NIST's revised system authorization guidance does not strictly define what constitutes a system and provides organizations significant flexibility in making determinations for system boundaries. However, the guidance suggests three primary considerations for defining system boundaries, noting that information resources identified as a system for risk management purposes will

- Normally be under the same direct management control. (However, the guidance clarifies that multiple information systems under the control of several managers may be considered as independent subsystems of a more complex information system.)
- Usually support the same mission/business objectives or functions and have the same basic operating characteristics and information security requirements.
- Reside in the same general operating environment or in various locations with like operating environments in the case of a distributed information system.

Since systems change over time, these considerations should be revisited periodically as part of the monitor step of the RMF to ensure the commonality of system components and subsystems. The NIST guidance points out that these considerations are not meant to restrict an organization's ability to establish boundaries that make sense in the context of the organization's mission and business operations to promote effective information security while making use of its available resources.

While the decision on an information system's boundary definition resides with the information system owner, the owner must be careful to consult with authorizing officials, the CIO, CISO, and the risk executive (function) in this process, including when system boundaries require modification. The NIST guidance suggests that the risk management implications of the system boundary definition process demand an organization-wide approach that is informed by mission and business requirements, technical considerations, and programmatic costs to the organization.

Guidance on Software Application Boundaries

NIST guidance pays particular attention to how software applications (e.g., database applications, Web applications) should be addressed in the system boundary definition. Software applications depend on resources provided by a hosting system and therefore leverage the security controls provided by the hosting system. However, additional application-specific security controls must be provided by the respective software application. The owners of applications and hosting systems must coordinate with each other to ensure that protection of the system and risk management activities are performed as seamlessly as possible. This coordination should include

- Selection, implementation, assessment, and monitoring of security controls for hosted applications.
- Evaluation of the effects of changes to hosted applications on the overall security state of the hosting information system and the missions and business processes it supports.
- Evaluation of the effects of changes to the information system on hosted applications.

Software application security relies on effective configuration management for both hosted software applications and hosting information systems and on sharing of security control assessment results. Application-specific security controls are to be assessed for effectiveness when applications are added to the boundary of the hosting information system after it has been authorized to operate. Hosting system owners must ensure that hosted applications do not affect the security health of the hosting system. This is accomplished by obtaining necessary information from application owners to conduct security impact analyses of changes as needed.

Guidance on Complex Systems

The protection of a complex information system can present significant challenges to an organization with respect to applying security controls. To lessen this challenge,

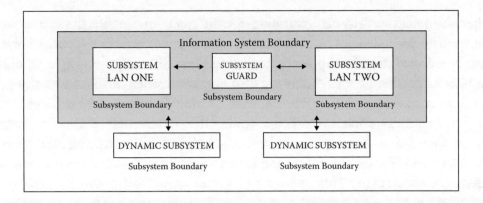

Figure 1.5 **Complex system decomposition. LAN, local-area network.**

NIST guidance suggests that system owners should consider the feasibility of deconstructing complex systems into more manageable subsystems. Decomposing an information system into manageable subsystems, each having its own boundary, permits targeted application of security controls to achieve security requirements and facilitates cost-effective risk management. This should be performed in collaboration with the authorizing official, CISO, information security architect, and information system security engineer, who together examine the purpose of the information system. When considering decomposition of complex information systems, the organization must ensure that separate subsystems are able to work together in both a secure and a functional manner. The FISMA guidance provides an illustration of the concept of decomposition for a complex information system as shown in Figure 1.5.

Security control selection and allocation for a complex information system are driven in large part by the information security architecture. The security architecture addresses requirements for monitoring and controlling communications across subsystem boundaries and provision of systemwide common controls to meet subsystems security requirements through inheritance of these common controls. The NIST guidance suggests categorizing each identified subsystem as a possible approach to selection and allocation of security controls. This approach does not change the overall categorization of the complex system but allows definition of more targeted security controls for each subsystem rather than implementation of higher-impact controls for every subsystem. NIST also offers an alternative approach with the bundling of smaller subsystems with larger subsystems within the overall complex information system, categorizing each of the combined subsystems, and allocating security controls to the aggregated subsystems as needed. In the case of complex systems, subsystems may exist as complete systems but are generally not treated as independent entities due to their interdependence and interconnectivity.

When subsystem security categorizations are different, information flows, interfaces, and security dependencies must be examined, and interconnection security controls must be selected to address potential vulnerabilities. Similarly, security controls for the interconnection of subsystems are also employed when different security policies (e.g., access controls) are implemented or are administered by different organizational entities (officials or offices). Testing the effectiveness of security controls in a complex information system is best accomplished by combining security control assessments for the subsystem and then addressing system-level interface issues among the subsystems. This approach promotes cost-effectiveness by scaling the level of effort of the assessment according to the subsystem security categorization and allowing for reuse of assessment results at the overall system level. After all subsystems have completed an initial security control assessment, action must be taken to ensure that

- All security controls not addressed in subsystem assessments are assessed for effectiveness.

- Subsystems interface to meet the security requirements of the complex information system.

Guidance on the Impact of Technological Changes on System Boundaries

The task of establishing information system boundaries is complicated by changes to information technologies and computing paradigms of the system, which compound the difficulty of protecting the missions and business processes the system supports. NIST guidance provides discussion of the concept of dynamic subsystems and external subsystems and how they are to be addressed when defining boundaries for information systems. In particular, service-oriented architectures, cloud computing, and other net-centric architectures present organizations with significant challenges due to their pervasiveness and expanding use.

Guidance on Dynamic Subsystems

Ideally, subsystems will be defined during the initiation phase of a system's life cycle and in system categorization. However, often subsystems are incorporated into the boundary of an information system following system initiation. If such dynamic subsystems are identified in the system design and appropriate security controls are reflected in the security plan, the initiation of the subsystem will not generally have an impact on the external boundary of the information system. However, this action does have an impact on the other subsystems within the boundary.

Dynamic subsystems may be owned by external providers through contracts, licensing agreements, lines of business arrangements, interagency agreements, or other arrangements. In this situation, the organization must consider the capabilities of the subsystem and must be prepared to reassess the information system as a whole to determine the impact of adding the system on existing security controls. A security impact analysis will provide a mechanism for evaluating the functions the subsystems perform, interfaces with other subsystems and connections with other information systems, and how they have an impact on other subsystems and permit update of the system design and incorporation in the security plan. Once they have been determined to conform to identified constraints and assumptions, subsystems can be dynamically added (or removed) from the information system without having to reassess the entire system.

Guidance on External Subsystems

NIST defines *external subsystems* as those subsystems or components of subsystems that lie outside the direct control of the organization that owns the information system and authorizes its operation. External subsystems may take the form of computing services employed by a government organization to process, store, and transmit its information and services developed or operated by an external provider, either public or private.

According to FISMA and OMB policy, external subsystems are required to meet the same security requirements as systems operated internally by government organizations. Government agencies require assurance that security requirements can be and are being met by external systems and rely on the amount of trust that is established with the relationship. This level of trust is often based on the control the organization is able to apply to the external service provider with respect to how it employs and operates required security controls and the evidence that can be produced to permit an assessment of the effectiveness of those controls. Trust may also be based on the positive experience the organization may have through a long-term relationship with the external service provider or perhaps the demonstrated ability of the service provider to take appropriate corrective action when issues surface. On the other hand, NIST guidance points out several factors that can complicate the level of trust issue, including

■ Lack of clarity in the delineation between what is owned by the external entity and the organization. For example, an agency-owned platform is used to execute application software developed by an external provider.

Chapter 1

- Limits on the control the organization has over the external provider (e.g., inability to specify a geographical location for the storage of its information).

- Possible rapid change of external subsystems, making it difficult or impossible for the organization to gain assurance that security requirements are being met by the external provider.

- Need for incorporation of critical externally provided subsystems or services into existing organizational systems rapidly, thereby restricting the ability to properly assess the effectiveness of necessary controls.

These factors point to the fact that it may not be feasible to rely on traditional means of verifying the security of a subsystem through clearly defined requirements, design analysis, testing, and evaluation prior to deployment. Consequently, government organizations may have no alternative other than to depend on the trust relationships they can establish with the external provider. However, organizations need to apply a risk-based approach in assessing the use of external subsystems and services and consider their use only after determining information and process flows and that they can accept the risk of any potential adverse impact. However, risk acceptance when the external subsystem owner or service provider cannot fully meet security expectations should be based on the implementation of compensating controls. Otherwise, the organization may have to accept a greater degree of risk or determine that the risk is too great to accept and decline use of the external service or subsystem.

Guidance on Security Control Allocation

NIST's new system authorization guidance identifies three classifications for security controls for information systems based on responsibility for their provision:

- *System-Specific Controls.* This category includes controls that are intended for the protection of a specific information system only, and their implementation and maintenance are the responsibility of the system owner.

- *Common Controls.* These include controls that are common to multiple information systems and fall under the responsibility of the common control provider for implementation.

- *Hybrid Controls.* This category of controls includes those that have characteristics of both system-specific and common controls, with shared responsibility for their implementation.

Organizations must develop a process for allocating security controls to information systems consistently in accordance with their enterprise architecture and information security architecture. NIST stipulates that this activity is to be performed on an organization-wide basis and is to involve a wide variety of personnel exercising information security responsibilities, including authorizing officials, system owners, the CISO, enterprise architect, information security architect, ISSOs, common control providers, and the risk executive (function).

NIST guidance on security controls allocation encourages organizations to identify and implement common capabilities that can support multiple information systems as fully as possible to promote efficiency and effectiveness and adds that this is best accomplished as part of the information security architecture. This approach calls for owners of information systems that rely on common controls delivered from another system or systems or otherwise from a common control provider to identify them in their security planning and documentation as inherited controls. Hence, the value of common controls identification is to promote cost-effectiveness and consistency in the application of information security controls throughout an organization and to simplify risk management activities. The benefit of security controls allocation as system-specific, hybrid, or common controls permits discrete assignment of responsibility and accountability for their development, implementation, assessment, authorization, and monitoring to specific organizational officials.

NIST guidance indicates that organizations have a significant degree of latitude in deciding how specific SP 800-53 controls or families of security controls will be allocated. NIST's guidance does stress the need to establish effective communications among all parties involved in common and hybrid controls arrangements. For example, effective communication between common controls providers and system owners inheriting those common controls includes sharing authorization information and continuous monitoring results as well as making system owners aware of changes to common controls that may affect the security of their information system. NIST SP 800-37, Revision 1, provides an illustration (shown in Figure 1.6) of the organization-level security control allocation to show the relationship between system-specific, common, and hybrid controls in the context of the RMF and how it informs authorization decisions regarding the ongoing security state of information systems and their supported missions and business processes.

Guidance on Applying the Risk Management Framework

The purpose of this section is to describe how NIST's RMF is applied to information systems as it is presented in NIST SP 800-37, Revision 1. NIST's revised guidance for system authorization provides a set of well-defined risk-related tasks to be

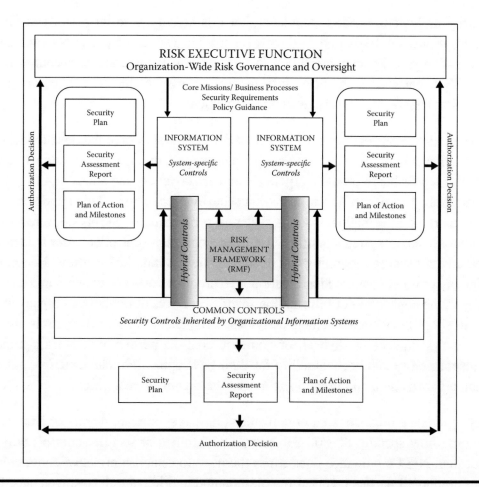

Figure 1.6 **Concept for security control allocation.**

performed by specified individuals assigned defined organizational roles. Specific tasks are accomplished either concurrent with or as part of other SDLC processes. This arrangement takes into account appropriate dependencies to ensure organizations effectively integrate system-level security risks into their SDLC processes.

NIST guidance for each RMF task includes identification of the individual or group with primary responsibility for its performance, the roles associated with supporting task completion, the SDLC phase the task is associated with, and references related to the task. In addition, NIST elaborates on supplemental guidance on how the task is accomplished.

The NIST guidance explains that there may be variance in how organizations implement RMF tasks to include the order and manner tasks take place and the identification of primary and supporting roles. The order of RMF tasks is intended to be sequential. However, organizations may identify situations for which divergence with the prescribed order may be necessary, to include the need for iterative cycles between tasks and the need to revisit tasks, and occasions when efficiency or cost-effectiveness can be gained. Regardless of the task ordering followed, the final step before placing an information system into operation must always be explicit acceptance of risk by an authorizing official.

The level of effort expended when implementing RMF tasks should correspond to the security categorization of the system according to the new NIST system authorization guidance. Security categorization highlights the systems that support the organization's most critical or sensitive operations and assets, and these are the systems that require the greatest attention and effort to ensure their protection. NIST further clarifies that most RMF tasks may be performed by either internal resources or external providers based on appropriate contractual agreements.

Based on the maturity of its processes and activities, organizations may find it advantageous to expend more effort on certain RMF tasks and fewer resources on other tasks. The NIST guidance notes that the RMF is life-cycle based, and consequently the need to revisit various tasks over time will be necessary depending on the manner in which changes to the information systems are managed. The RMF provides a path for the management of system-level information security-related risks. However, it must be viewed in the context of the larger enterprise-wide risk management performed by senior agency leaders. Consequently, the RMF must provide a systematic means for mitigating system-level risks while simultaneously supporting the organization's core mission and business operations in a highly dynamic environment.

The NIST guidance indicates that RMF steps and tasks are applicable to both systems under development and to legacy information systems. With respect to legacy systems, RMF Steps 1 through 3 can be applied to validate the security categorization to ensure appropriate security controls have been selected and implemented. These activities may be considered to be a gap analysis to determine if necessary and adequate security has been properly chosen and employed. Any security control weaknesses identified can then be addressed by performing RMF Steps 3 through 6 as one would do with a system in development. If the gap analysis reveals no weaknesses in security controls and a current security authorization in effect, then the system owner can proceed to continuous monitoring. However, if a current security authorization is not in place, the system owner must perform RMF Steps 4 through 6.

Chapter 1

Finally, the NIST guidance tells us that RMF tasks are applicable to both information system owners and common control providers. In addition to supporting the authorization of information systems, RMF tasks apply to selection, development, implementation, assessment, authorization, and ongoing monitoring of common controls inherited by information systems. Common control providers execute RMF tasks to ensure information system owners have assurance that the security capabilities provided by the common controls meet their system security requirements.

Summary of NIST Guidance

Revision 1 to NIST SP 800-37 includes a number of key changes that are important for understanding the current manner in which government organizations and private contractors perform services for the government-authorized information systems. The new organization-wide RMF described in the publication provides guidance that establishes the organizational context for system authorization in that enterprise-level mission, and business aspects of risk management are addressed for the first time. This permits an organization to determine the boundaries for risk acceptance. The new system authorization guidance also highlights critical aspects of integration of risk management into an organization SDLC process to ensure identification of security-related requirements at an early stage and to permit standardization of security artifacts and processes to reduce costs and ensure consistency of quality.

The revised guidance updates the RMF, which identifies the six steps necessary in providing security and managing risk throughout the life cycle of an information system. Using the structured approach provided by the RMF, an organization can have assurance that an information system has been thoroughly categorized, that appropriate security controls have been selected, that these controls have been properly implemented, that they have been assessed in a formal manner, that the system has been approved by a management official, and that the security posture of the system is continuously monitored for deviations from the authorized baseline.

NIST in its revised guidance provides an update on definition of information system boundaries to address in particular the relationship of systems and subsystems and the impact of changing technology. It provides instructions on decomposition of complex systems, consolidation of small systems into larger systems to facilitate risk management and how dynamic subsystems and external subsystems and services have an impact on the boundaries of organizational information systems.

Finally, the new guidance elaborates on the relationship between system-specific, hybrid, and common controls and how they can be employed to enhance accountability and responsibility for their implementation and maintenance.

System Authorization Roles and Responsibilities

One's view of the system authorization program will be driven by perspective and needs. The program from the perspective of the approving authority may appear to be a means of ensuring that the operation of the system poses no significant risk to the organization. To the system owner, the program may be viewed as a management process that provides assurance that the owner's system is safe from intruders, viruses, and other adverse events. To the security officer, the program may be considered as an approach for facilitating the implementation of essential security controls. And to the system administrator, the system authorization program will appear to be a vehicle for defining security requirements and measuring the security posture of the system. The utility of the system authorization program can then be said to be in the eye of the beholder. However, for the program to be effective, the roles and responsibilities for these individuals and others need to be set down in writing to prevent overlap while ensuring that all are addressed comprehensively.

Primary Roles and Responsibilities

There are five primary roles associated with the system authorization program: the CISO, the system owner, the ISSO, the certifying agent, and the approving authority. These are considered the primary roles because they are the players who have the greatest impact on the success or failure of the program.

- *Chief Information Security Officer*: The CISO normally serves as the organization's senior agency information security officer (SAISO) as required by FISMA. The CISO's primary responsibility is information security, and he or she carries out the FISMA-related functions assigned to the CIO. The CISO exercises overall responsibility for the organization's information technology security-related programs, such as risk management, policy development and compliance monitoring, security awareness, incident investigation and reporting, and often contingency planning. The CISO is normally charged with responsibility for the enterprise-wide system authorization program as well. The CISO's system authorization responsibilities include establishing the program and ensuring enforcement of program-related policies. FISMA requires the CISO to possess necessary professional qualifications and to be in charge of the agency information security office. This position is referred to as the *senior information security officer* in NIST guidance.

■ *System Owner*: The system owner is the official who bears the primary responsibility for the security of an information system. The system owner establishes the sensitivity level of the system based on the data it processes and thus establishes the basis for the kinds of controls needed to protect the system. The system owner exercises this responsibility over the full life cycle of the system from its initial development to its final disposition. The system owner ensures that controls are implemented, requests resources to ensure implementation is accomplished, oversees the continued effectiveness of controls day to day, and oversees remediation of weaknesses in controls. The system owner initiates system authorization activities, ensures that resources are available, prepares the system security plans, and monitors preparation of the accreditation package from initiation to final system accreditation. The relationship between the owners of the major application and general support system owners must be close and well defined. Because major applications are normally connected to or hosted on a general support system, the owner of the major application must to a large degree rely on the owner of that supporting system to provide a substantial amount of the security for his or her application.

■ *Information System Security Officer*: The ISSO serves as the principal staff advisor to the system owner, who appoints the ISSO. Under the system owner's authority, the ISSO is responsible for securing the system and managing all security aspects of the system. The ISSO closely monitors the day-to-day security of the system as well as routinely monitors the effectiveness of controls. He or she controls security mechanisms, performs security activities and tasks, develops and enforces security procedures for the system, follows up on incidents, and advises the system owner on security-related matters. The ISSO plays the most significant role in the certification of the system by serving as the point of contact for the certifying agent and assembling the security accreditation package.

■ *Certifying Agent*: The certifying agent is the independent authority charged with assessing the security controls protecting a specific information system to determine if they are implemented correctly, are operating as intended, and produce the desired outcome. The certifying agent also recommends corrective action to reduce or eliminate vulnerabilities in assessed controls. To ensure independence, this role is normally performed by an individual assigned to another part of the organization or who is a contractor or consultant tasked with performing this function on a short-term basis. This position is referred to as the *security control assessor* in NIST guidance.

■ *Approving Authority*: The approving authority, accrediting official, authorizing official, or designated approving authority (DAA) is the senior management official responsible for deciding if a system should be allowed to operate. Inherent in this role is the responsibility for accepting any residual risks to the system. The approving authority is the executive who has the authority and ability to evaluate a system's security risks. This normally requires budget authority over the system, oversight of business processes supported by the systems, and knowledge required to determine the acceptable level of risk to the agency that operation of the system may present. In government agencies, only a government employee may serve as an approving authority. This position is referred to as the *authorizing official* in NIST guidance.

It is important that different individuals are chosen to perform these primary roles to ensure separation of duties. Emphasis on this important security principle means that independence is maintained and that a structure that promotes checks and balances is established. The relationships between these positions must be clearly spelled out in organizational policy so that there is no duplication of effort while ensuring that responsibilities and accountability for all critical tasks are assigned.

Other Roles and Responsibilities

Secondary system authorization roles include the CIO, the information technology security program steering committee, the auditing staff, data owners and custodians, system administrators, business unit managers, project managers, facility managers, and executive managers. Individuals serving in these positions are indirectly involved in the program and support those in primary positions by performing the duties specified in the following paragraphs.

■ *Chief Information Officer*: The CIO has overall responsibility for the execution of an organization's information technology security program and delegates authority to the CISO for the management of the enterprise system authorization program. The CIO supports the program through oversight, maintaining visibility of the program across the organization and with senior management, and through the provision of resources for its execution. The CIO assists senior agency officials with their security responsibilities and reports annually to the agency head on the effectiveness of the agency information security program.

■ *Approving Authority Designated Representative*: This is an individual who is appointed at the discretion of the approving authority to coordinate and carry out the necessary activities required during authorization of an information system. This individual is empowered to make decisions regarding the planning and resourcing of the effort, acceptance of the system security plan, and determination of risk to agency assets, among other tasks. Often, the *approving authority designated representative* is given responsibility for preparing the accreditation decision memo and obtaining the signature of the approving authority. However, the representative is not authorized to make the security accreditation decision or sign the decision memo. This position is referred to as the *authorizing official designated representative* in NIST guidance.

■ *Information Technology Security Program Steering Committee*: The committee provides high-level oversight of the organization's information security program and provides direction on program goals, resources, and initiatives. In this context, the committee provides indirect supervision and oversight of the enterprise system authorization program.

■ *Auditor*: This function provides for an independent assessment of the viability of the overall program by looking at the effectiveness of individual program components. Auditors ensure that the system authorization program provides an adequate level of security assurance by reviewing program practices and procedures to ensure that controls are documented, that risks are identified and prioritized, that controls are tested, that weaknesses are identified and corrective actions are specified and are tracked, and that systems have been authorized to process by a senior management official.

■ *Information Owner/Custodian*: The owner of the information processed by an information system and the custodian who serves as the owner's agent are responsible for ensuring that the system owner is aware of requirements for protecting his or her information based on its sensitivity. Most often, the information owner and the system owner are one and the same, but the information owner is distinguished as the official who has statutory or operational authority for specified information and who should therefore be well positioned to know the impact of the information's unauthorized disclosure, its corruption and loss of integrity, and its unavailability. The information owner should establish rules for appropriate use of the information as well as its impact levels, which are then used to establish security control requirements. This position is also referred to as the *information owner/steward* in NIST guidance.

■ *System Administrator/Manager*: The system administrator or manager is charged with the day-to-day administration and operation of the system and is responsible for the implementation of many of the technical and operational controls employed to protect the system. Primary security-related functions performed by the system administrator include ensuring that configuration and change-control processes are followed; activating, deactivating, and monitoring user accounts; performing backups; implementing hardware and software changes; monitoring system performance; and notifying the ISSO of all system decisions he or she makes. The system administrator works for the system owner; works closely with, but separately from, the ISSO; and demonstrates controls to the certifying agent during certification testing.

■ *Business Unit Manager*: Although business unit managers often function as system owners, their system authorization responsibilities generally include disseminating security information to subordinate personnel, reporting and responding to security incidents, determining priorities and resources for implementing corrective actions to mitigate identified risks in relation to their areas of responsibility, and enforcing security controls and associated personnel actions. Generally, the business unit manager's role relates to the implementation and maintenance of security controls.

■ *Project Manager*: For the purpose of this discussion, the project manager is the official who is tasked with performing system owner-related functions for a system in development. In this respect, the project manager is responsible for the overall procurement, development, or integration of an information system. The project manager fulfills all the system authorization responsibilities of the system owner described relative to a system in the development phases of its life cycle but is not responsible for system operation or maintenance.

■ *Risk Analyst*: The specialist trained to conduct a risk assessment for an information system is the risk analyst. The risk analyst supports the risk-related activities of all members of the system authorization team.

■ *Facility Manager*: The individual performing this role is responsible for the implementation and maintenance of physical and environmental controls protecting information technology systems located in facilities he or she manages.

■ *Executive Management*: Executive managers play a crucial role in overseeing the system authorization program, establishing policy, apportioning resources, and enforcing requirements. Most important, senior executive management can increase visibility of the program and ensure its success through support and emphasis.

■ *Authorization Advocate*: This role has been established in many organizations to manage, coordinate, and oversee all security authorization activities of the organization. The advocate works with the CISO, authorizing officials, and system owners agency-wide to ensure that authorization activities are given priority and are carried out effectively.

■ *User Representative*: The individual performing this role represents the operational interests and mission needs of the user community throughout the authorization of an information system. The user representative identifies unique mission requirements and risks, serves as a liaison to the user community throughout the system's life cycle, and assists in the system authorization process as needed.

Additional Roles and Responsibilities from NIST SP 800-37, Revision 1

NIST's recent system authorization guidance identifies several additional roles that are integral to the risk management process at the organization level.

- *Head of Agency or Chief Executive Officer*: This individual is an organization's highest-level senior official responsible for exercising overall responsibility for providing risk-based security for information assets of the organization. This includes ensuring integration of information security management processes with strategic and operational planning processes and that senior agency officials provide information security for the information and systems under their control. The agency head also ensures there are sufficient trained personnel available to ensure compliance with internal and external information security requirements.

- *Risk Executive (Function)*: The risk executive or function is an individual or group who ensure risk for individual systems are considered from an organization-wide perspective with regard to the overall strategic goals and objectives of the organization. This role is also responsible for ensuring that management of system-related security risks is consistent across the organization, reflects the organization's risk tolerance level, and is considered along with other types of risks to ensure mission or business success.

- *Common Control Provider*: This role is performed by an individual, group, or organizational element given responsibility for the development, implementation, assessment, and monitoring of common controls. Common control providers document common controls (normally in a security plan), ensure that common control assessments are performed by qualified/independent assessors, document findings of assessments, and maintain a plan of action and milestones for all controls with weaknesses. They must also make security documentation available to system owners whose systems inherit common controls.

- *Information Security Architect*: This is an individual, group, or organizational element that ensures information security requirements are properly addressed in the organization's enterprise architecture. This role serves as the liaison between the enterprise architect and the information system security engineer and coordinates with system owners, common control providers, and ISSOs regarding allocation of security controls as either system-specific, hybrid, or common controls. Also, the information security architect role coordinates with other roles about the system boundary definition, determination of the severity of weaknesses, corrective actions related to POA&M (plan of action and milestone) weaknesses, security alerts, potential adverse effects of identified vulnerabilities, and so on.

■ *Information System Security Engineer:* This is an individual, group, or organization assigned responsibility for system security engineering activities. Information system security engineering captures and refines information security requirements and ensures they are integrated into information technology products and systems by means of security architecture, design, development, and configuration. This role supports development team activities such as design and development of information systems or modernization of legacy systems.

Documenting Roles and Responsibilities

As we discussed further in this chapter, roles and responsibilities must be documented in the security plan for each system. The specific tasks that must be performed by these system authorization players are also identified in system-level and program-level procedures. In such documents, it is normally better to make reference to the position rather than to the individual holding the position to avoid the need for revisions of the procedures when individuals change jobs or otherwise depart. Organizations also need to document and continually update system authorization roles and responsibilities in program policy documentation to ensure they are mutually supporting. Other roles and responsibilities are typically fluid and short term in nature. As such, they need only be documented in general terms as conditions warrant.

The CISO should document as many system authorization positions as possible. This may be achieved using assignment orders or letters of appointment for each individual involved with the program. This cannot be achieved without management support, and a policy or directive signed by senior management will normally be required for this. At the very least, those functioning in the five primary program roles should be formally designated in writing. Others involved on the periphery of the program should also be identified, perhaps in a less-formal way by being listed on the CISO's intranet site. The system authorization program manager will find it beneficial to maintain up-to-date lists and matrices of personnel performing program functions, and this is best supported through creation of a contacts database. An example is shown in Table 1.5.

Job Descriptions

Generally, it is a good idea to stipulate system authorization responsibilities in the position descriptions of those involved in the program. The value of including security requirements in an individual's job description is that it sets expectations for performance of security functions and provides a basis for holding the individual

	Table 1.5	Example Contacts Database		
Name	**Position**	**Organization**	**Phone**	**E-mail**
Hector Blanco	Nutria system owner	Research division	x8650	hblan@acme.com
Roberta Jones	Security manager	Finance division	x8740	rjones@acme.com
Thomas Wild	Payroll ISSO	Administration	x8634	twild@acme.com
Frank Hostler	Security manager	Administration	x8552	fhost@acme.com
Murray Booker	LAN ISSO	IT operations	x8907	mbook@acme.com
Felix Gottlieb	Security manager	Southern region	345-678-9012	fgott@acme.com

accountable for the performance of those duties. However, unless an individual performs system authorization functions at least 50% of the time, there is little need to specifically cite these responsibilities in a job description. However, security responsibilities should be prominently included for those holding any of the five primary system authorization roles described. Examples of job description wording for each of these key positions are provided in Table 1.6.

Position Sensitivity Designations

The positions of individuals holding key system authorization-related positions should be designated as highly sensitive due to the need for them to have access to all vulnerability information for information technology systems, knowledge of security controls functionality, knowledge of the system's security posture, and their involvement in the mitigation of system security weaknesses. This access and involvement require reliable and trustworthy personnel; consequently, their background information should be screened more thoroughly and more frequently than for other employees. Because of the costs associated with screening of this nature and the high level of trust involved, organizations should consider performance stipends for personnel holding such positions to encourage stability and to avoid frequent turnover.

Personnel Transition

When individuals holding these positions do depart, the primary concern is ensuring that a capable individual is available to assume the responsibilities. When possible, a replacement should be identified before the incumbent departs to provide overlap and smooth the transition. The incumbent should give the incoming

Position	Job Description Entry
	Table 1.6 Sample Job Description Wording
CISO	Establish the organization system authorization program and develop program policy; assist in the implementation of the program; oversee program activities and provide management regular reports of program effectiveness.
System owner	Implement organization system authorization policy through identification and implementation of risk-based security controls for assigned systems; manage the security of information technology systems by monitoring system activities and controls effectiveness.
ISSO	Assist the system owner in complying with the organization system authorization program by identifying and implementing risk-based controls, monitoring controls status, and managing corrective actions.
Certifying agent	Perform independent testing of information technology system security controls and make recommendations regarding the potential accreditation or reaccreditation of the system.
Approving authority	Based on certification testing of security controls, approve assigned information technology systems for operation with regard to residual risks to the operation of the system and specify risks for which acceptance has been granted.

individual an overview of the organization's system authorization policies, procedures, and activities to include pending remedial actions, the certification/recertification schedule, the compliance review schedule, and any other pending issues and activities. In the case of very sensitive systems, the ISSOs and system owners should review all system authorization-related documentation (i.e., the system security plan and risk assessment) to ensure that they are familiar with the contents of documents that describe risks to their system and the controls implemented to protect it. Although a transition of this nature does not require that the documents be updated, a formal indication that the incoming individual has reviewed the documents is a clear need. A signature on a document review sheet as described in Chapter 3 will serve this purpose. The CISO should closely monitor personal transitions affecting assigned approving authorities and be prepared to brief replacements to ensure they understand their new roles as accrediting officials.

Time Requirements

At the system level, system authorization-related duties do not normally require full-time concentration. These duties are generally performed as collateral duties by an individual assigned to complementary functions (i.e., system administration, system management, database administration, etc.). In such cases, the individual has to make his or her system certification tasks priorities at key stages of the system authorization process. At times, depending on the size of the organization, system authorization will be full time. However, there may be months when no significant system authorization activity occurs at all. As an alternative, organizations may find it advantageous to make computer security activities for a group of several systems the full-time responsibility of a single, dedicated employee. This permits the individual to concentrate on performing security-related tasks (including system authorization) specifically, and it provides the organization consistency of performance and greater assurance that security functions are being properly administered. The decision to employ a full-time security manager in this fashion must be based on resource considerations. However, the sensitivity and criticality of the systems for which the individual may be responsible should also be factored into determination of resource priority setting. A job analysis should be conducted to determine if a full-time security position is necessary, and it should consider elements such as separation of duties, need for independence, level of compliance required and consequent scrutiny necessary, and the security posture of the systems; those with extensive remediation plans will most benefit by the assignment of a full-time security officer on at least a temporary basis.

Expertise Requirements

Specialized knowledge, skills, and abilities are required to perform system authorization tasks. Project management expertise is essential for the security manager or any other individual who provides dedicated system authorization program leadership. Individuals at this level of program management must know system development principles and practices to promote integration of system authorization efforts into the organization's system development life-cycle methodology and into individual system development projects. All personnel involved in primary system authorization positions must be familiar with platform-specific technical controls and operations, and they must understand particular hardware and software products used in the organization's processing environment. Further, each system authorization specialist needs familiarity with the organization, its structure, its leadership, its mission and goals, and its culture and language and with key business or mission initiatives that it is pursuing. General expertise in the areas of administrative staffing and coordination, information technology security terminology, practices, methodologies and procedures, interpersonal communications, and technical writing skills are also key attributes for individuals assigned to these positions. In addition, personnel must meet organizational background screening requirements and must be able to receive and maintain appropriate security clearances and access credentials required to perform their functions. In all positions involved in the system authorization program, individuals must have educational credentials commensurate with the level of responsibility required. Perhaps most important of all is the individual's level of credibility.

Credibility of system authorization personnel can be further established through reliance on professional certification. Although there are many to choose from, the professional certifications that are most useful to system authorization practitioners are those related to security management, such as the Information Systems Audit and Control Association's (ISACA) Certified Information Security Manager (CISM) credential and the Certified Information Systems Security Professional (CISSP)® certification of (ISC)²® (International Information Systems Security Certification Consortium). However, when engaged in certification testing, certification in specific technologies is often beneficial.

Using Contractors

In most cases, system authorization functions will be performed by organization employees. This is almost always the case with the CISO, system owner, and the authorizing authority positions and is only somewhat less so for the ISSO. Use of employees in these positions provides an element of stability, thereby minimizing training time required, fostering competence in duty performance, and reducing the amount of personnel background screening required. However, because of the need for independence inherent in the position, the role of the certifying agent is often performed by consultants or other individuals under contract. The use of contractors for this function is sound not only because of the independence they offer but also because of the breadth of experience and knowledge of system authorization activities, practices, and methodologies their specialization may permit. Requirements for contractors need to be well defined in statements of work and contract terms to ensure the scope of their work is clearly defined, the methodology to be used is specified, timetables for performance are detailed, and deliverables to be produced are clearly documented. Although contractors are not suited to perform all system authorization functions, they can be effective partners in system authorization efforts and can offer checks and balances in program execution. Building a good partnership with supporting contractors can lead to an effective working relationship that is as stable, reliable, and consistent as one experienced with assigned employees. The use of contractors is the most cost-effective approach for the role of certifying agent and should also be considered for other less-significant system authorization roles, such as data custodian, system administrator, and project manager.

Routine Duties

A day in the life of an individual assigned to a system authorization role involves a wide variety of activities that must be performed routinely and performed well to provide the level of consistency necessary for an effective program. A typical manager involved in system authorization will be regularly involved in the following types of tasks:

- Scheduling tasks to be performed and coordinating work that is under way.

- Reporting on the status of system authorization activities on a recurring basis to include both report submission and face-to-face updates with the management staff.

- Providing routine system authorization-related advice and assistance to members of the organization.

- Attending periodic and ad hoc meetings with system owners whose systems are being certified, with certifiers who are engaged in performing system certifications, and with organizational management to provide updates on program status.

- Reviewing documentation for quality control purposes, presenting these deliverables to supported organizations, and responding to customer comments and questions about the deliverables.

- Overseeing ongoing system authorization efforts and spot-checking compliance.

- Acting as an intermediary for the system owner and supporting certifying agent to ensure that requirements are being accurately understood and organizational requirements for certification and activities are being met. The definition of boundaries between systems is a common issue that calls for the intercession of the program manager.

- Offering solutions for implementing the organization's system authorization methodology or ruling on whether a particular planned approach will comply with policies and standards.

- Educating personnel on system authorization practices and procedures. This may take the form of telephone discussions, one-on-one briefings to executive managers, presentations to small groups of managers, and formal training sessions presented to large groups of employees. These education sessions seek to educate recipients on what system authorization is, to describe the program, to detail how the program is being implemented in the organization, and to define what roles and responsibilities for system authorization are. Education responsibilities also usually include mentoring of personnel assigned to the system authorization program staff.

■ Justifying findings and recommendations detailed in certification documentation. The program manager must be able to work with system owners, business unit managers, authorizing authorities, and senior management to explain the documentation, the methodology used, the weaknesses identified, and the corrective action recommended. The program manager must have total familiarity with these issues to provide assurance in the quality of work performed and their soundness as a basis for planning and decision making.

■ Participating in system development activities. In this capacity, the program manager serves as a subject matter expert to describe system authorization objectives, methodologies, products, and, most important, how the security interfaces with the system development process. The program manager must be careful not to become overly involved in requirements' definition and analysis and system design tasks. Failure to heed this advice can quickly outstrip the time the project manager has available. It is also better to maintain a certain degree of distance from the nuts and bolts of the system development project to be able to remain independent when it is time to certify the system.

Organizational Skills

Dealing with a large number of people on a multitude of systems issues requires that the system authorization program manager be well organized and fully on his or her game regarding requirements, obligations, promises made, and discussions conducted. Therefore, the program manager must either have a photographic memory or be able to rely on meeting notes, records of conversations, and lists of things to do to stay organized. The volume of information that the program manager must be able to access readily mandates that well-thought-out filing systems for both electronic and hard-copy information be established and maintained. These systems need to allow recovery of information related to system-level and program-level activities for a period of at least 3 years. It is also particularly important to have e-mail files available to document decisions made, agreements reached, and work performed.

Organizational Placement of the System Authorization Function

There is one final issue to discuss relative to system authorization roles and responsibilities, and that is to establish the most effective organizational placement of the system authorization function. To be most effective, responsibility for system authorization should reside with the CISO. This places the responsibility for the program where it belongs, firmly in the hands of the senior security professional. To ensure the program receives the management support, emphasis, and visibility it requires, the CISO should report directly to the chief operating officer or chief executive officer of the organization. This also permits the degree of independence the CISO needs to monitor and report on system authorization activities enterprise-wide.

Program relationships with other organizational elements are shown in Table 1.7, which lists and describes the relationships between various organizational functions and the system authorization program.

As in most processes, employees are the most important components, and matching the right personality to the right role can mean the difference between success and failure of a system authorization program. The program relies on five primary roles and their attendant responsibilities: the system owner, the authorizing official, the CISO, the ISSO, and the certifying agent. Each of these roles must be competently performed, and each role and responsibility must be documented to complement the other primary roles. Managers must make wise choices regarding the selection of personnel to fill these key positions, must motivate individuals in supporting secondary roles, and must mobilize the support of other organizational functions to ensure the program's success. Through the effective interplay between these various roles, both the efficiency of the system authorization program and the separation of critical functions can be assured.

The System Authorization Life Cycle

In a perfect world, security would be a primary factor in considering the feasibility of developing a new system. Early in the planning stages, the sensitivity of data would be defined, risks to processing would be identified, and security controls necessary to protect the system would be determined. When this happens, security becomes an integrated part of the project, and controls are incorporated into the system design. Implementing security in this fashion saves money, time, and aggravation. Unfortunately, for a variety of reasons, this does not always happen, and security considerations do not surface until well into the project when it is too late for them to be efficiently addressed, making them more difficult, more costly, and less practical to implement. In fact, systems often go fully into production without any formal identification of security requirements. Consequently, security employed in this manner almost always results in the security function being put in

Table 1.7 *Functional Relationships to the System Security Authorization Program*	
Function	***Relationship***
Incident response	Provide input for remediation plans
	Access for certification test plans and system security plans
	Review security documentation for impact of risks/vulnerabilities
	Trigger review of need for recertification
Security awareness and training	Provide input for the system security plan and certification test
	Draw on rules of behavior
	Review/track findings
Data classification	Define data sensitivity for system authorization inventory
	Provide input to system security plan
Risk management	Support plan of action and milestones (POA&M) process
Compliance/enforcement	Support system authorization assessment processes
	Provide input into POA&M process
	Monitor compliance of system authorization processes with established policy and guidance
Contingency planning	Provide input for system security plan and certification test
	Review/track findings
Auditing	Review findings during regular audits
	Oversee system inventory
	Validate security documentation
Resource management	Obtain funding for system authorization program management
	Obtain funding for system-level risk remediation
Information technology security oversight	Monitor system authorization program goals and strategies
	Monitor POA&M process
Record retention	Establish retention periods for system authorization documentation
Physical security	Implement/maintain physical security controls
	Review/track findings
Facilities management	Provide input for security plan and certification testing
	Review/track findings

continued

Table 1.7 (continued) Functional Relationships to the System Security Authorization Program	
Function	*Relationship*
Supervision and management functions	Provide input for security plan and certification testing
	Enforce policies and procedures
	Report incidents
	Recommend disciplinary action
	Obtain security awareness
	Implement/maintain security controls and corrective actions
	Review/track findings
Departmental management	Provide input for security plan and certification testing
	Enforce policies and procedures
	Review/track findings
Chief privacy officer	Provide privacy input into system authorization inventory, system security plan, and certification testing
	Review/track privacy-related findings
	Perform privacy impact assessments
Information technology services	Review/track findings
	Respond to incidents
	Implement system authorization-driven security architecture
	Implement controls
Human resources	Review/track findings
	Implement/maintain personnel security controls (e.g., background screening)
	Oversee disciplinary action
	Hire, transfer, and terminate process ownership
Legal	Review memorandums of understanding/agreement (MOUs/MOAs)
	Review contracts
	Coordinate disciplinary actions
	Advise designated approving authorities (DAAs)
Contracting/purchasing	Review MOUs/MOAs
	Contract certification and accreditation (C&A) support
	Review statement of work (SOW)
	Implement contract security clauses

an adversarial role, giving it a reputation as enforcement "heavy" as a result of this often-seen scenario.

System authorization aims to rectify this state of affairs by providing an accepted, proven methodology for determining business needs for security and presenting a prescription for addressing them at the appropriate stage in the system's life cycle. The system authorization framework can be effectively employed for new systems in development and implementation, for operational systems, for systems undergoing change, and for systems being retired. Most people are familiar with authorization of operational systems in which an owner of a legacy system that has been in production for years "gets religion" and decides the system needs to be certified and accredited. (This normally happens because he or she is directed to do this by someone higher in the food chain.) So, kicking-and-screaming system authorization is initiated with little likelihood of a change in the system's authorization to process, except to document that it has been formally approved to process. The problem with this scenario is that management knows that the system is not going to be shut down if significant weaknesses are found because the system has already been operating without negative consequences for a long time. This antisecurity bias points to a major obstacle in accrediting systems already in production.

A better alternative is to begin the system authorization process parallel with system development to ensure system authorization activities are performed at the appropriate time in the appropriate manner to the appropriate degree so that security and system authorization can become a solution rather than a hindrance. NIST's recent update of SP 800-37 details how its new RMF can be effectively integrated into the SDLC to ensure risk is properly managed at the information system level.

The first step in making sure this happens must take place long before a development project is kicked off. It begins with education of project managers, system developers, and employees at large on the role of security, the importance of integrating security into information technology systems, and how system authorization plays a role in system development. Unless program managers are aware of these things, the phone call inviting the information technology security staff to a meeting at which managers will be informed about a new project will never be made. The information technology security team must make system authorization a prominent part of its ongoing security awareness efforts to ensure that the security function is brought into the picture early in the initiation phase. System developers should be aware of system authorization procedures and requirements to allow them to understand the process and to permit them to address security requirements as they construct the system. Finally, employees must be aware of the program and what it is designed to achieve to prepare them for roles they may potentially play in system authorization.

The services delivered through the system authorization process are ideally suited to ensure that security is fully integrated into the system design, permitting the system to begin processing securely with full authority to process from management without having expended additional funds and resources to make that happen. Table 1.8 is taken from NIST SP 800-64, and it identifies various security activities according to order of performance in the SDLC.

Initiation Phase

The risk assessment, when performed as part of the initiation phase, provides a mechanism for documenting the sensitivity of the system, for identifying threats to the system and potential vulnerabilities, for calculating and ranking risks inherent to the system's operation, and for selecting controls necessary for protecting the system. Control selection also addresses identification of controls necessary to implement established minimum security baselines and controls necessary to ensure compliance with statutory, legal, operational, and contractual obligations. It also allows the system owner to determine how the system will meet the organization's minimum security control standards and if those standards are stringent enough to protect system data. When done properly and at the right time, the results of the risk assessment can feed directly into the requirements analysis process and can allow them to go from "security requirements" simply to consideration as requirements. Ideally, there will be no distinction of this type.

A plan of action and milestones are generated as a result of the risk assessment to document controls that must be implemented to address potential risks and any identified weaknesses. The remediation plan serves as an effective tool for managers to know what needs to be done relative to each risk-based control, what resources are necessary to accomplish the corrective action, the individual who is responsible for the task, and the schedule for implementing the control. In addition, the risk assessment provides a risk ranking for each control recommended, allowing the project manager to prioritize how potentially limited resources can best be utilized.

As part of definition of requirements, controls are defined in increasing detail and are further refined as the system progresses through development, implementation, and into production.

Table 1.8 Information Technology Security Activities in the SDLC		
Phase	**SDLC Activities**	**Security Activities**
Initiation	Needs determination	Security categorization
	Perception of a need	Preliminary risk assessment
	Linkage of need to mission and performance objectives	
	Assessment of alternatives to capital assets	
	Preparing for investment review and budgeting	
Acquisition/ development	Functional statement of need	Risk assessment
	Market research	Security functional requirements analysis
	Feasibility study	Security assurance requirements analysis
	Requirements analysis	Cost considerations and reporting
	Alternatives analysis	Security planning
	Cost-benefit analysis	Security control development
	Software conversion study	Developmental security test and evaluation
	Cost analysis	Other planning components
	Risk management plan	
	Acquisition planning	
Implementation	Installation	Inspection and acceptance
	Inspection	System integration
	Acceptance testing	Security certification
	Initial user training	Security accreditation
	Documentation	
Operations/ maintenance	Performance measurement	Configuration management and control
	Contract modifications	Continuous monitoring
	Operations	
	Maintenance	
Disposition	Appropriateness of disposal	Information preservation
	Exchange and sale	Media sanitization
	Internal organization screening	Hardware and software disposal
	Transfer and donation	
	Contract closeout	

Acquisition/Development Phase

The primary activities performed during the acquisition/development phase include analysis of security functional requirements, analysis of security assurance requirements, cost-benefit analysis of security controls, selection of security controls, and development of the system security plan. During this phase, the system security plan is initiated to begin to document the system description, ownership, environment, technical architecture, interconnectivity, applicable directives and drivers, system sensitivity, and controls mapped to the minimum security baseline for the organization. Although begun during the acquisition/development phase, the security plan is revised and updated throughout the implementation and operation phases as well.

Certification test plan development begins with the acquisition/development phase when tests necessary for measuring the effectiveness of controls are documented in a certification test plan. All weaknesses identified during the risk assessment are included in the certification test plan as well as all other controls that may be categorized as implemented (although there are normally very few of these at this stage of the system's development). For each control, a specific test is designed along with expected results and evidence required to substantiate that it meets requirements. This test development process is covered in Chapter 5.

Implementation Phase

Once the certification test plan has been developed, it is then executed during the system implementation phase to ensure required controls are in place and are functioning properly. Because the information technology security function has been involved in the project from its inception, the certification test plan can be developed in time to be performed as part of acceptance testing, thereby reducing coordination time and execution costs. The results stemming from use of the certification test plan are recorded in the certification test plan results report, which becomes part of the system authorization package for the system. Any controls that do not meet predefined standards are documented in an updated remediation plan for submission to the approving authority as part of the certifier's recommendations. The security plan is also updated to record the results of testing and to document whether controls either are in place or are planned.

Following this integrated approach, the approving authority will have all necessary documentation to make a decision authorizing the system to process prior to the system being approved to go into production and as an element of the larger process for approving the system to operate based on both performance and security conditions being met. This is the ideal solution and is pure heaven for the CISO.

Operations/Maintenance Phase

Once operational, system owners must then maintain the security of the system so it stays secure. Owners must exercise controls that permit continuous monitoring of the security environment and review the system's security for the potential need for recertification and reaccreditation following certain types of incidents or situations, commonly known as significant events. Significant events include serious security incidents (an intrusion or severe virus/worm attack, for example); recognition of the potential for the introduction of new threats (terrorism) or low-frequency risks not previously considered (perhaps a tsunami); changes in the user community (additions due to an acquisition); changes in data sensitivity or system criticality; changes in system hardware and software components (a rehosting); a new interconnection with another system; occupation of new or upgraded facilities; or an expansion in system functionality. Prior to diving headlong into a full-blown recertification based on one or more of these conditions being met, a more reasonable approach is first to evaluate the need for recertification by reviewing the impact of the change. This is best accomplished by means of a risk assessment.

During the operations phase, the organization's configuration management process can be used to trigger recertification of systems. As the configuration control board addresses changes in the environment, connectivity, or other conditions of operation, the security representative (assuming there is one) then should evaluate the change to determine if recertification is warranted. A policy needs to be developed to provide guidance on what sorts of changes constitute grounds for recertification of a system and how this will be accomplished. The same principle applies to the incident response function. When an incident has an adverse impact on the data processed by a system or impairs or circumvents its controls, these new conditions should be evaluated in light of the existing system authorization package to determine if recertification is necessary. Because a known set of controls has already been identified and a complete system authorization package already exists, the recertification effort can normally be completed relatively quickly when compared to the initial effort.

Reaccreditation must also be performed at normal cycles, and for most systems a 3-year cycle is adequate. However, highly sensitive systems may need to be reaccredited every 2 years or perhaps even more often.

The scope of the periodic reaccreditation should include a full review of all documentation in the system authorization package. Reaccreditation based on other events or situations need only focus on those elements of the initial package that are affected by the change.

Disposition Phase

Finally, the system authorization package is the best starting point for addressing security requirements for systems in the disposal phase of their life cycle. It permits sound decisions to be made on disposal of sensitive data and documents controls to be employed to ensure data is purged from storage devices so as not disclosed to unauthorized individuals. Once it has been decided that a system is no longer useful and decommissioning is warranted, system authorization activities should be addressed to provide assurance that system assets are properly disposed of, accounted for, and approved. Confidential data processed by the system in all its forms must be purged from hardware, destroyed if no longer needed, or shredded in the case of hard-copy reports and forms to ensure sensitive information is not disclosed. For historical purposes and potential future use, the integrity of the data must be ensured through proper archiving and storage techniques. Availability concerns must be addressed to ensure the future needs for system data can be met to include availability of storage media and hardware/software platforms to allow access to the media.

To address system disposal issues, a risk assessment of system confidentiality, integrity, and availability needs during this phase should be conducted, and a remediation plan documenting required actions and milestones for ensuring protection of system resources needs to be developed. Once requirements have been identified in the remediation plan and required actions have been taken, verification using the certification test plan can be performed to provide assurance that all assets have been accounted for and protected. A certifier who conducts this minicertification testing uses a certification statement to document these activities and to make recommendations to the approving authority regarding disposal-related security issues. The final step in the disposal is the approving authority declaring his or her decision to retire the system and addressing all reasonable risks to system resources. This decision should be documented in an approving authority statement.

It stands to reason that system authorization activities performed during the disposal phase are scaled-down versions of the processes employed earlier in the system's life cycle. The risk assessment, remediation plan, and certification test plan follow the same process for the same purpose, but the scale of the activity is normally much reduced. However, organization-wide systems that are interconnected to many other systems are a notable exception because tracing these data links can be an imposing task.

Most often, the retirement of one system is accompanied by the implementation of a replacement system. It makes sense to link the life-cycle activities of incoming and outgoing systems to ensure that security requirements for each are addressed simultaneously and comprehensively.

Another task that must be addressed as part of the disposal phase is the disposition of system hardware and software that can be reused with other systems. In addition, disposition of documentation for hardware and software must be decided. Employees who are to be terminated or reassigned due to the system's retirement should be required to sign nondisclosure agreements to protect against the release of confidential information. Finally, the system needs to be formally removed from the organization's system inventory using the existing formal process, ensuring that the justification for the retirement is fully explained.

Challenges to Implementation

Many organizations either fail to develop mature SDLC methodologies or allow them to lapse into a coma because of the demands placed on rapid development and implementation of systems. The need to speed the development cycle to meet pressing business needs (such as accelerating the development of an enhanced feature to match the release of one of your major competitors) overwhelms the ability of the SDLC model to keep pace. Too often in such situations, security becomes an afterthought, if a thought at all, because of preconceived ideas that security impedes progress and is costly besides. It is difficult to implement a system authorization process in a setting like this, but it can be done. A good strategy for addressing this assault on the viability of its system authorization program is to establish a two-track certification methodology: One track is a full-system authorization track for systems being developed on a normal schedule in which the full SDLC methodology can be implemented, and the second track is an abbreviated system authorization methodology in which time is an overriding concern with adherence to tight schedules. This latter track will lead to an interim certification that is more responsive to organizational needs while providing some degree of assurance that security controls have been addressed in the design and have been implemented prior to going live. This abbreviated methodology should only apply in about 25% or less of an organization's development efforts. However, it is not a precise fit in that even systems with highly sensitive data may need to be certified using this abbreviated approach when the business situation demands expedited development.

As an alternative to a specialized "quick fix" methodology, an organization can fine-tune its standard system authorization methodology to be fully responsive to any and all demands system development requirements place on it. When the methodology invariably takes 6 months to run its course, its utilization will be minimized. If, however, the methodology can lead to accreditation in 2 months or less, then it will be flexible enough to support even the most demanding time-to-market scenarios. A responsive system authorization program such as this will prove to be far less onerous than developers have come to expect and has a greater-than-average chance of being accepted and employed.

Not only can the system authorization process support the system development methodology, but also SDLC products can support the implementation of an effective system authorization program. The system concept, feasibility study, requirements document, system design, implementation plan, and test plan provide highly valuable information for determining data sensitivity, assessing risks, evaluating applicability of minimum security controls, and constructing a certification test plan for testing controls.

According to the most widely used system authorization methodologies, the system authorization process has a life cycle of its own. It generally consists of four phases: the precertification phase, followed by validation, then accreditation, and finally postaccreditation. Table 1.9 shows the labels used in NIST SP 800-37, NIACAP,

Table 1.9   Comparison of C&A Methodology Life-Cycle Phases

Methodology	Phase 1	Phase 2	Phase 3	Phase 4
NIST[a]	Initiation	Security certification	Security accreditation	Continuous monitoring
NIACAP	Definition	Verification	Validation	Postaccreditation
DITSCAP	Definition	Verification	Validation	Postaccreditation
DIACAP[b]	Initiate and plan	Implement and validate	Make C&A decisions	Maintain ATO/reviews

[a] Prior to the publication of NIST SP 800-37, Revision 1, which establishes the six-step Risk Management Framework.

[b] DIACAP includes a fifth phase: decommission.

and DITSCAP methodologies, along with the primary activities associated with each of these four phases. As an exception, DIACAP has five phases: initiate and plan, implement and validate, make certification and accreditation decisions, maintain authorization to operate (ATO)/review, and decommission. To summarize this approach, the precertification phase comprises tasks performed in preparation for certifying a system; actions related to actual certification are performed in the validation phase; the accreditation phase addresses accreditation of the system; and finally actions performed after the system is accredited are covered during the postaccreditation phase. Although this taxonomy helps organize the system authorization process, it is much more useful to connect specific system authorization activities with the more broadly accepted system development methodology as shown in Table 1.8.

Integration of system authorization into the SDLC is promoted by the consistency of the role of the project manager/system owner in each of the two processes. The project manager plays the lead role in the development project, and this is certainly not at odds with his or her responsibility that he or she is expected to exercise over implementing security for the system. In system authorization terms, the system development project manager performs the complementary role of system owner. In this case, the mapping between the two roles is direct.

Inclusion of system authorization processes and products in an organization's system development methodology can substantially raise the visibility of a security program, particularly with management. Integration of security requirements at an early stage along with other system requirements makes them far less onerous. In fact, it helps define them more clearly and permits one to consider them in practical ways. It is far easier to convince a project manager during the design stage that encryption for the system is important than it is to convince him or her after the system has been operational for a year.

Why System Authorization Programs Fail

Unfortunately, the history of system authorization is marked by the frequent failure of well-intentioned programs. The following paragraphs identify a number of reasons that programs fail. By studying the causes of these failures, we can perhaps discover the pitfalls to be avoided when designing and implementing an enterprise information technology system authorization program.

Program Scope

Often, programs are unsuccessful because they fail to identify and inventory systems effectively. When the program is not applied evenly across all organization information technology systems, controls are not comprehensively applied. Therefore, vulnerabilities in the enterprise processing environment open up and increase the potential for threats to exploit vulnerabilities in security controls that have been implemented.

Management must actively concentrate on the identification and inventory of all systems without exception. As stated previously, failure to effectively make all of the organization's systems subject to the program will risk security gaps and uneven application of controls and resources. It is therefore important to ensure that all systems are identified, that a 100% inventory is conducted, and that the inventory is updated regularly (at least annually).

Assessment Focus

A program can also fail to mature and never advance beyond mere assessment of controls. This constitutes only half a program. Identification of security weaknesses, although essential, is only part of a comprehensive program. Assessment must be followed by remediation. Action to correct deficiencies is needed to complete the program. A mature program also provides mechanisms for an iterative process of assessment and remediation to ensure that, as systems change, controls change appropriately in response to vulnerabilities that accompany changes. An extension of the lack of program maturity failure is management's inability to connect system authorization to budgeting for resources. As weaknesses are identified and corrective actions are prescribed, there has to be a process for providing the necessary resources to ensure these actions can be completed. Without the resources to take corrective action, the program is reduced to merely an emasculated assessment process.

Short-Term Thinking

In many cases, system authorization programs fall prey to an organizational attitude that prevents a focus on long-term, strategic requirements, which prevents a system authorization program from getting off the ground. Organizations in this category never get a glimpse of the future due to a concentration on present-day requirements. Such thinking leads to implementation of point solutions that cannot be integrated into an overall security architecture because one does not exist. An organization that is buried in fixing short-term problems will never be able to get beyond that level of immaturity until strategic programs like system authorization can be launched.

Long-Term Thinking

Conversely, an organization that focuses its energy at the strategic level alone usually fails in its efforts to implement an effective system authorization program. A comprehensive, integrated security architecture is a thing of beauty once it has been developed. However, if the requirements identified in the security architecture cannot be translated down to the implementation level, it is similar to a bird without wings. A system authorization program that emphasizes strategic solutions will eventually fail without resting on a foundation of system-level building blocks that serve as entities through which security solutions are implemented.

Poor Planning

System authorization programs do not develop and implement themselves. It takes effort and resources to establish them, and they do not happen overnight. Failure to recognize the costs of establishing such programs can lead to a lack of follow-through on program requirements and can lead to the need to start over continually. The frustration of fits and starts of this nature will fray management confidence in the program, leading to its eventual scrapping before it ever gets off the ground. To avoid unpleasant surprises, the security manager cannot afford to be unrealistic about program costs. Other ways that inadequate planning diminishes a program's likelihood of success include

- Failure to ensure that program requirements are realistic, leading to waste of critical resources and loss of program credibility. Similarly, the failure to tailor system authorization requirements to real organizational needs can cause weaknesses in program implementation.

- Failure to assign responsibility to the most appropriate staff element or individual can greatly reduce chances for success. For example, the audit function is not in a good position to manage the system authorization program because of its need to remain independent. Assignment of program responsibilities to the CISO is a better approach and a wiser decision.

- Failure to integrate the system authorization program with other processes can doom a program from the start because of the effect of competition for time and resources.

- Failure to train personnel in their system authorization roles and responsibilities can put a drag on your program and keep it from achieving the level of professionalism it requires.

■ Failure to correctly identify assumptions can lead to misconceptions about the nature of the program. Organizations that fail to make sound assumptions about system authorization programs may find themselves doomed by the effects of not preparing for the amount of time required and the costs associated in establishing and operating the program or may assume unrealistic expectations about what the program can actually achieve. On the other hand, organizations should not assume that the program is for government entities only or that it is not necessary in the organization's current circumstances.

■ Finally, failure to recognize the limitations of system authorization can contribute to poor planning for implementation of the program. Planning must accurately set expectations for the program and its goals.

Lack of Responsibility

Programs also fail because they do not fix responsibility at the system level and at the program level. There has to be balance and separation between these two levels. The program must distinguish program-level responsibilities that are applied enterprise-wide from system-level responsibilities that apply to individual systems. In practical terms, a single entity cannot perform both and you would not want them to do so. On the other hand, if the program does not fix responsibility at either level, it risks failure.

Excessive Paperwork

In other cases, history has shown that system authorization programs have failed when they lost sight of their goals and became bogged down in bureaucracy. A slow choking death by paperwork in such cases is usually well deserved because such programs have clearly failed to deliver. One cannot expect program participants to embrace a program that buries them in paperwork that they perceive to be unwarranted, unnecessary, and onerous.

Lack of Enforcement

Failure to enforce system authorization policy properly can kill an otherwise-sound system authorization program. Program requirements are necessary but plentiful, particularly at the system owner and ISSO levels. If there are not processes in place to enforce program requirements, the program will become inconsistent and ineffectual and will fall into disuse once those with program responsibilities perceive or observe that accountability for system security improvements is lacking. A program that is inconsistent in its treatment of program participants, individuals, organizations, solutions, or processes leads to ineffectiveness eventually. The system authorization program's failure to be evenhanded and consistent causes confusion in meeting requirements. Inconsistency in program management can also cause difficulties in performing review and audit tasks and uneven results due to a failure to provide consistent guidance. Programs in this category permit participants to shop for the answer they desire. Everyone must be onboard for the program to work on a consistent basis without favoritism. This is often caused by a failure to document program policies and procedures or by a failure to adhere to the established requirements. The level of enforcement can sometimes be driven by the program's failure to overcome strong personalities and forceful (negative) opinions. Such influences may be expressed in terms of support of favored point solutions and support of inadequate alternatives to the program (e.g., security around the perimeter only). These negative influences have to be confronted directly in an early test of management support for the program.

Lack of Foresight

Organizations that fail to adequately understand the benefit of a system authorization program will never consider its implementation. Consequently, a program will never be initiated. Although this is not an outright failure, it is a failed opportunity. Organizations that do not have the foresight to study the benefits of a system authorization program should seriously consider the need to conduct a cost-benefit analysis to assess the potential of the program in enhancing its information technology security program. Such a study could find that implementation of a program could result in increased visibility of the information technology security program, in enhanced tracking of security weakness and corrective actions, in quantifying resource requirements for security, in providing a vehicle for security oversight, and finally in measurement of security program success (or failure).

Poor Timing

A system authorization program can also fail when the organization is simply not ready for it. Perhaps the company is not far enough along in its maturity, or perhaps a real need for the program has not yet evolved. Poor timing is also responsible for the failure of a program when it is established without the personnel, and resources are simply not available due to other, more pressing business needs (i.e., product development).

Lack of Support

Perhaps the most significant obstacle to the implementation of a system authorization program is the lack of support. This is observed in management's emphasis on the program and failure on the part of lower-level program participants to support the program. Program neglect can lead to its starvation in a short time. Management buy-in is necessary to ensure program success because the program can only survive if management stands fully behind efforts necessary to enforce program requirements. Committed management support is needed to ensure that program participants follow through on their obligations. System authorization programs that cannot force active participation and carry through on its requirements often end up in the dustbin of forgotten programs and initiatives. This is also the end result of programs for which management fails to ensure that risks are mitigated, leaving systems excessively exposed to vulnerabilities. Finally, lack of management support can result in a failure to accredit or reaccredit the organization's information systems in a timely or efficient basis. System security authorization program managers should keep management involved in the program through the use of scorecards and metrics coupled with regular and frequent program updates to force management to pay attention.

Those who are governed by the system authorization program must be convinced that it has value for it to be effective. Of all the roles and responsibilities associated with a certification program, the role played by the system owner is unquestionably critical to its success. A program that cannot get system owners to recognize its value cannot succeed because of the reliance any program must place on owners' active involvement. A program that does not apply sufficient energy to obtaining system owner buy-in through training and education efforts and to maintain their involvement through close and continual communications is like expecting a body to function without a heart. Sometimes, an effective tactic for gaining program support is fear. Fear of embarrassment by system owners can enhance their willingness to comply; fear of lawsuits can accomplish the same thing. Willing support can often be obtained when compliance is linked to project funding. Failing the acceptability and effectiveness of these approaches, using the management "stick" may be the only alternative for system owners who fail to comply.

As we have seen, there are several obstacles in implementing system authorization programs. Consequently, many brilliant initiatives never quite deliver what they promise. Programs can falter due to poor planning, lack of support, and failure to understand what a system authorization program can and should be able to deliver. Security managers need to be aware of these pitfalls and need to design and manage their programs to avoid them. Also, they must continually track progress and performance to ensure that the ill effects of these problems do not derail their programs.

System Authorization Project Planning

Authorization of a system is normally an effort that requires the accomplishment of many tasks, and it affects many resources over a period of several weeks or months. Unless the system authorization effort is properly coordinated, effectively organized, and closely managed, achieving a predetermined objective at a projected time will be a virtual accident. As related previously in this chapter, there are myriad things that can go wrong and cause the effort to fail, and the only solution is effective (rather than lucky) project management. This section outlines the role and responsibilities of the individual charged with managing a system authorization project for a single system or for a group of systems, with an emphasis on how managing a system authorization project differs from the management of other types of projects.

Planning Factors

The project management is only completed when the project is finished, and it must be performed for the duration of the effort, it is hoped by the same individual throughout. The system authorization project management function normally requires an additional 10% of the overall project labor effort. This project management surcharge provides a realistic guide for planning the number of man-hours that will be required to organize the effort, coordinate accomplishment of tasks, and oversee the performance of the project team. Using this planning factor, a 6-week system authorization project will require around 3 man-days of dedicated project management support. This factor increases as the number of systems in the scope of the project increases. Speaking in rough terms, a project comprising certification of 10 systems will require a full-time project manager. For a single system, the system owner or ISSO may serve as his or her own project manager. The system owner's availability may limit his or her ability to perform this task, however, and he or she may choose to assign another staff member to perform the project management function as a collateral duty. For a highly sensitive system, a consultant may be called in to perform dedicated project management functions. Normally, an individual is sufficient for the project management role; however, an alternate who has knowledge of most aspects of the project should be available to step in and cover for the project manager when there is a scheduling conflict or during other times of nonavailability.

To be effective, project managers must be knowledgeable, personable, persistent, and involved. They must understand system authorization objectives and methodologies, must have detailed knowledge of system authorization tasks and tools, and must know how to successfully manage a project and the people performing it. The system authorization project is people-centric and requires continual coordination and work toward achieving needed cooperation. It takes someone who can communicate well with others verbally and visually. The interpersonal skills of project managers cannot be stressed too much. Project managers must also be doggedly determined to ensure schedules are met and promises are kept. When someone agrees to do something, project managers should prod people into keeping their agreements and schedules. Finally, project managers must be immersed in the project. They must be continually aware of project schedules, status, risks, problems, and issues to foresee difficulties before they arise. This cannot be done from a distance and can present problems for those performing project management functions only on a part-time basis. Being a project manager is a hands-on exercise.

Dealing with People

Being a "people person" helps project managers understand the roles and responsibilities of individuals involved in the project, those they have control over (and those who control them), those they support, and those who support them. Project managers not only must identify but also must estimate and then solidify the expectations of those affected by the project: the approving authority, the organization staff, the system owner, the CIO, the CISO, the certifying official, the ISSO, the certification team members, the auditors, and the quality control members. Each views the project in a different way with different objectives and expectations. Project managers must understand these points of view and use them to improve the likelihood of success.

The first tasks that project managers must perform is identifying individuals involved in the project at several levels and defining project-related roles and responsibilities. This includes those both internal and external to the supported organization. A contact list should be constructed to identify at a minimum the approving authority, certifying official, team members, ISSO, system administrator, quality assurance personnel, and key management personnel.

Team Member Selection

Another people-related task required of project managers is selection of certification team members. Who makes up the team is a decision of the project manager and should be based on the knowledge, skills, abilities, experience, and integrity of the individual rather than simply determining who is not doing something else more important. Project managers should seek team members who can be critical, impartial, and fair; who have good people skills themselves; who are analytical; and who have sound writing capabilities. Team members should each have a good balance of technical and nontechnical skills. Of course, experience with system authorization in general, and with significant system authorization processes in particular, should be the overriding selection factor. Also, as much as possible, the project manager should evaluate each potential team member based on his or her integrity, character, credibility, and trustworthiness. If project managers have an opportunity to review résumés to select potential members, they should list brief selection criteria and prioritize qualities desired in a candidate. Criteria should also include security clearance and background screening requirements demanded by the project.

Team members may be part of the organization and may be well known to the project manager. Or, they may come from another organizational element, and familiarity will not be ensured. When team members are provided by external entities under contract, it is important to consider and arrange for logistical matters such as time accounting, travel authorization, expense claims, disciplinary actions, and so on. When contractors provide support by assuming responsibility for an aspect of the project in its entirety (i.e., certification testing), the project manager should ensure that there are no secrets regarding man-hours set aside for their slice of the project. Also, the project manager must review the methodology he or she intends to use to be sure it is in balance with other project objectives, work, and schedules. Appendix C contains a sample statement of work.

Scope Definition

The primary questions the project manager must ask when preparing for project initiation is how many systems are within the project scope, what types of systems they are, and how complex the systems are. The scope is also affected by the number of organizations involved and the level of cooperation (with interviews and documentation), the location of systems, the number of people who will be involved, the number of people available to assist with the project, the time available to perform the work, the certification level or levels of systems within the project scope, and finally, what systems do not have to be certified.

Naturally, if more systems are involved in the project, that provides opportunities for economies of scale and a reduction in per system costs based on volume of work performed. But, this is only really true because of similarities in the approach to the work. If the project comprises three systems but there is little similarity between them, then little if any time can be saved. Similarly, time and savings can be achieved if the systems are somewhat alike in design, functionality, and location. In fact, such similarity may provide the potential for grouping tasks even on deliverables.

The biggest drivers in scoping a project besides the number, types, and complexity of systems involved are time and available resources. Time required for a project ranges from as little as 1 month for a single system to a year or more for multiple, complex systems at several certification levels. An average project will run from 3 to 6 months and will involve between 5 and 50 systems. Of course, when a project requires 6 months but deadlines dictate that the project be accomplished in 3, then staffing of the project must be increased to meet the deadline. To scope a project properly, the project manager must know how long it takes to perform tasks for an average system. This normally is based on a high-level project work plan like the one shown in Appendix D, which documents the number of days normally required for standard system authorization tasks. From this baseline project, work plan adjustments for system complexity factors are made to refine it appropriately to address the specifics of the project. From the updated project work plan, a schedule of project activities, milestones, and deliverable targets can be established. For large projects involving multiple systems, a project management tool will help in tracking project performance, making scheduling changes, and supporting reporting require-ments. The project work plan is the project manager's road map to success and his or her greatest aid.

The work plan should include a few key ingredients. The plan should clearly describe work in terms of activities, tasks, and subtasks, each of which is identified through a coherent numbering scheme. The plan must record realistic start dates and end dates for each level of work. Included in the plan should be resources required to complete work at all levels, as well as dependencies between tasks. This helps identify critical work and potential bottlenecks.

One final and highly important issue is the phenomenon known as scope creep, or incremental changes in the scope of work. Although management requests that additional or different work be included in the project can be easily accommodated without difficulty, usually the additional work is insidious and can quite easily result in eventual delays in the project's completion. At the very least, the project manager is obligated to inform management clearly of estimates of the costs of changing the scope and the impact they will have on the project's completion.

Assumptions

Project managers seldom have all the information required to plan for the project. They have to speculate on certain aspects of the project that are not well defined, at least early on in the project. To deal with these uncertainties, they must build assumptions into the project plan. These assumptions are about things like sufficient manpower to staff the project, sufficient time to complete necessary tasks, sufficient funds to permit travel and production of work products, and availability of key personnel for interviews and documentation for review. It is important to document these assumptions and work to validate them as much as possible. When they are considered assumptions, then they can be addressed with management to transform them from assumptions into known planning factors.

Risks

The project manager must also identify in the project plan risks that could potentially prevent the project from meeting its objectives. Lack of manpower risks the ability of the project team to be able to complete project tasks according to schedule or standard. Failure to complete data collection due to lack of cooperation also risks delays in meeting schedules. And, failure to review and provide comments on draft deliverables risks achievement of work product finalization and submission. During the execution phase of the project, the project manager should continue to highlight these risks when reporting project status to management. Whenever possible, risks should be clearly quantified to facilitate their understanding by executive management.

Project Agreements

In the role of project manager, there is the inherent condition of being in a supporting role. The project is being performed in support of some individual or organization. To facilitate understanding between the supporting project team and the supported organization, there should be an agreement on who does what, when, how, and so on. This project agreement sets the ground rules for the project and serves as the basis for setting expectations. It should accompany the project work plan and is normally drafted by the project manager. An example of a project agreement is provided in Table 1.10.

Project Team Guidelines

The project manager may find it necessary to develop guidelines for team members to ensure consistency of work performed. Policies and procedures internal to the

Table 1.10   Project Agreement Outline

1 Document Information and Revision History

2 Project Agreement Approvals

3 Project Mission Statement

4 Project Background

5 Project Overview and Scope

6 Critical Success Factors

7 Project Team

8 Project Timing

9 Project Deliverables

10 Project Approach

    10.1 Phase 1: Project Initiation

        10.1.1 *Time Frame and Deliverables for Phase 1*

    10.2 Phase 2: Data Collection and Analysis

        10.2.1 *Activity 1: Preparation*

        10.2.2 *Activity 2: Data Collection*

        10.2.3 *Activity 3: Data Analysis*

        10.2.4 *Time Frame and Deliverables for Phase 2*

    10.3 Phase 3: Certification Testing

        10.3.1 *Activity 1: Test Plan Development*

        10.3.2 *Activity 2: Test Execution*

        10.3.3 *Activity 3: Documentation of Test Results*

        10.3.4 *Time Frame and Deliverables for Phase 3*

    10.4 Phase 4: Develop Certification Package

        10.4.1 *Activity 1: Prepare Security Plan*

        10.4.2 *Activity 2: Prepare Risk Assessment*

project team should be published based on project agreements to give team members guidance on administrative matters like time reporting, work hours, appropriate attire, travel requests and authorizations, supplies, methodology-related guidance such as use of templates and checklists, lines of coordination and communication, conducting interviews, collecting and accounting for documentation, recording test results, using tools, performing vulnerability scans, and progress reporting require-ments (weekly status reports and problem reporting). This guidance should be dis-seminated prior to the beginning of the project so that all project team members can be trained on them to achieve a common level set. However, as the project pro-gresses, adjustments usually need to be made, and the guidelines have to be updated.

Guidance should be firm and authorized and must be available to and followed by all team members. Posting guidelines in a shared directory is an ideal solution. Having comprehensive, clear, up-to-date guidance on how to do the work is instrumental when bringing on new team members after the project has begun, and it serves as a solid foundation for future projects as well, even though specifics of individual system authorization projects will change.

Administrative Requirements

Project managers must anticipate and identify administrative requirements necessary for their team as well. This allows them to estimate requirements for funding as necessary and supplies as needed. Requirements for and costs of production materials like copy paper, binders, dividers, print cartridges, software tools, references, hardware, electronic media, and the like will surely need to be determined, budgeted for, ordered, and stockpiled. Workspace requirements, including workstations, connectivity, communications, and physical access to facilities, ideally should be settled before the first team member is selected. Travel requirements need to be identified in detail, using realistic planning estimates for airfare, ground transportation, parking, meals, lodging, and so on. This cannot be prepared until the scope is defined and the work plan is developed. It is the project manager's responsibility to manage travel efficiently by making adjustments to the project plan to pool travel requirements and consolidate trips as much as possible. Often, it is advantageous to revise team assignments based on team members' availability to travel. Project managers should also anticipate modifications to the travel schedule because in the course of data collection the scope of the system may include components and operations at other locations, necessitating travel there for testing. Scope changes such as these may cause other changes to the project scope and project plan, particularly as related to milestones and delivery dates. Project managers should also establish and implement a process that accounts for all documentation received throughout the project. This ensures that it can be returned in full to the rightful owner once it is no longer needed.

Reporting

One key responsibility of the project manager is status reporting, which allows the project manager to monitor the progress of the project and to inform management. Reporting requirements need to be defined prior to the project to ensure consistency and to forecast and plan for the level of effort required to gather information for and to develop and provide status reports. Following a standard reporting format and procedures throughout the project is more efficient than frequently changing requirements after the project begins. The project manager should estimate reporting requirements, then stick with them within the constraints of meeting project needs. Also, member input should be kept to a minimum because reporting should be secondary to members' primary responsibility of performing project tasks and documenting results. No more than 5–10% of an analyst's time should be dedicated to progress reporting, as compared to the 25–30% of the project manager's time. Reporting consists of submission of routine ad hoc reports supplemented by face-to-face meetings to elaborate on submitted reports. This can be viewed as beneficial to both the project manager and management, but often project managers disdain reporting as a necessary evil. To avoid this less-than-positive view of status reporting, the project manager must use it to his or her advantage. Reporting can improve support and cooperation rather than intrude on the manager's time. However, the project manager should avoid submitting overly detailed reports. They should be succinct, clear, and to the point, ideally consisting of one or two pages of bulleted items. The report should highlight what has been accomplished during the reporting period (weekly or monthly), what will be accomplished in the next reporting period, and identify problems and impacts (risk). Table 1.11 is an example of a project report.

Problem-related reporting and coordination make up a special class that must be handled carefully. Problems at the lowest level possible should be worked up the management chain only when absolutely necessary. This approach allows the project manager to function as problem solver rather than problem maker. When low-priority issues surface at the top management level first, this runs the risk of alienating those at lower levels, and it may jeopardize long-term cooperation at the expense of short-term gain. Give the system owner a chance to set up interviews and provide documentation first, then give him or her a second chance before reporting to his or her boss that the owner has been uncooperative. Good coordination also includes sharing and discussion of schedule changes with others involved in the project. The schedule that is presented to management at the weekly meeting must be synchronized with dates being used or reported by others involved in the project. Schedule discrepancies can be embarrassing and can quickly erode good relations that have been carefully built up over a long period of time. Finally, reporting by the project manager can be used to manage expectations of management and of supported organizations. By giving them frequent, candid, realistic, and up-to-date information on project status, they will become active participants in the project and build management support when it comes time to getting the accreditation signed. This also allows project managers to inoculate themselves somewhat from

Table 1.11   Project Report

System Authorization Project
Weekly Status Report
Week of February 19–February 25, 2012

Issues to be Resolved/Risks:

Technical: None

Cost: None

Performance: Tom Turner, who has been performing certifications for OST
                        systems has resigned and will depart on Mar. 12th. Interviews
                        for his replacement are now being coordinated.

Summary:

	Technical	*Cost*	*Performance*
System Authorization	GREEN	GREEN	GREEN

Work Status by Business Unit:

- **Administration:**

  - Concluded security tests and evaluations (ST&Es) of seven systems in San Diego; now anticipate delivery of draft C&A packages on Mar. 12th. ST&E of two remaining Admin systems rescheduled for week of Mar. 15th due to lack of scope definition (Diana System) and inadequate current security posture (Zeus).
  - Data collection for three Admin systems (Acme, Ajax, Mercury) behind schedule due to lack of receipt of input from system owner.
  - ST&E for Admin's Mars Web site delayed one week due to nonavailability of system owner. Will be completed on Feb. 27th. Authorization package submission now anticipated for Mar. 12th.
  - Development of certification schedule for Admin regional LANs, Jupiter, and Pluto systems pending receipt of feedback from system owner.
  - Development of Neptune and Venus LAN authorization packages delayed two weeks due to concentration of team on Admin ST&Es. Anticipate submission of both by Mar. 5th.

- **Manufacturing:** ST&E on three systems scheduled for Mar. 2nd. Expect delivery of draft authorization packages on Mar. 12th.

- **Sales:**

  - Saturn System Authorization package on schedule for submission on Mar. 5th.
  - Schedule delayed for four systems due to lack of receipt of 800-53 input.
  - Sales resolved contractor cooperation issue with Apollo System.

- **Research:**

  - A C&A package for the Research LAN is on schedule for delivery on Mar. 5th.
  - Data collection for Research's private Web server on schedule.

continued

Table 1.11 (continued)   Project Report

- **Corporate Headquarters:**
  - Data collection for the Uranus System delayed pending receipt of input from system owner.
  - Certification of the Luna System delayed pending identification of point of contact.
  - ST&E of Achilles Server on schedule for Feb. 26th.
  - Titan System Authorization Package completed and submitted on Feb. 24th.
  - Ares System deleted from OST inventory.
  - Notified that Athena will soon be ready to finish certification. Will coordinate ST&E.
  - Certification responsibility for Hermes System still to be resolved.

System C&A Status by Business Unit

The number of systems reflected in the following table is based on information received directly from business units and may not as yet be reflected in the official systems inventory.

Business Unit	Total Number of Systems	Number of Systems Certified and Accredited Last Year		Number of Systems that Will Be Certified and Accredited This Year		Number of Systems Accredited to Date	
		No.	%	No.	%	No.	%
Headquarters	7	5	71.4%	2	100.00%	0	71.4%
Research	12	7	58.3%	5	100.00%	2	75.0%
Sales	8	6	75.0%	2	100.00%	0	75.0%
Manufacturing	5	3	60.0%	2	100.00%	0	60.0%
Administration	18	5	27.8%	13	100.00%	6	61.1%
Agency Total	**50**	**26**	**52.0%**	**24**	**100.00%**	**8**	**68.0%**

the effects of surprises. It is not reasonable to expect a manager to react positively when told 2 weeks before the projected completion date that the project is 30 days behind schedule. The project manager must take the initiative and initiate the reporting process, avoiding reliance on management to request updates. Because they are likely to assume that no news is good news because of the nature of their positions (with management by exception is the normal mode of operation), they may never request an update until someone other than the project manager reports to them that there are problems. This is never a good situation for the project manager. If there is bad news about the project, it needs to come from the project manager, not someone else. So, the project manager must be proactive.

How does the project manager avoid other pitfalls? Things like delays in meeting project timetables need to be addressed by anticipating them first. Extra time should be built into the project plan, and larger tasks should be broken into smaller pieces, with assigned due dates. This may only be necessary for team members or system owners who have demonstrated an inability to stay on track. Recalcitrance or a lack of participation and cooperation is a matter to be reported to management. The thinking is that if system owners are not responsive to the project manager who is their equal or superior, then perhaps owners will respond to someone who is in their supervisory chain.

Failure to provide support—time and resources—can be attributed to a lack of visibility or urgency on the part of management. The project manager must ensure that management has the facts through timely, regular reporting and by not pulling punches. Management must know the risks involved if the project fails.

Other Tasks

When documenting the project plan, the project manager must ensure that he or she builds in sufficient time for training of the project team. This should include training in the methodology that will be used, particular standards and regulations that apply to systems within the scope of the project, guidelines applicable to project team members, and reporting requirements. In the plan, the project manager must also include tasks for guidance development as well. Rules for conducting interviews, collecting documentation, recording findings and analysis, preparing deliverables, and providing status reports should be given. The plan also must address reporting requirements to ensure that the amount of time they will require is properly estimated and anticipated. Finally, the plan should allow sufficient time for preparing and presenting kickoff and closeout briefings for each system within the scope of the project.

Project Kickoff

The project manager is usually well served when he or she takes the time to prepare and schedule a kickoff meeting for those involved in the project. It is essential to provide a project briefing with management to give feedback on the conception of the project's objective, definition, approach, scope, timetables, and resources, providing management an opportunity to get onboard with the project plan and to give them a chance to query the project manager about particulars. This solidifies management support for the project. It is also important for supported organizations to be given a project briefing for the same reasons. And, if possible, depending on the number of systems in the scope of the project, the project manager may want to provide a kickoff presentation to each system owner to demonstrate commitment to quality, cooperation, and support and to offer the system owner a line of communication for problem resolution should the need arise. A sample kickoff presentation is provided in Appendix E.

Wrap-Up

Likewise, the project manager should be prepared to present a wrap-up or closeout briefing when the project is concluded. This gives management a view of objectives achieved and the success (or failure) to achieve them, as well as summary findings, recommendations, and next steps. In addition, the project manager may want to brief individual system owners as each system is certified to highlight findings and recommendations and to speed up the deliverable review process.

The information that is briefed to managers at the end of the project should be documented separately in a lessons learned report. This historical document summarizes the project with an aim to serve as a starting point for improving the probability of success in future projects. By documenting successes and failures experienced in the project, project managers of future projects will obviously benefit. The time required preparing such a report (which does not have to be more than a few pages) and to collect project work papers will be more than made up for by the increased quality and efficiency of future system authorization efforts. A sample wrap-up briefing is provided in Appendix F.

Observations

The prime responsibility of the system authorization project manager is to ensure that the project is executed smoothly, on time, and within budget and is compliant with project guidance, objectives, and requirements. Success in a project generally means that the systems in the scope of the project will be professionally certified, allowing the accrediting authority to authorize processing. To achieve this goal, the project manager must chart a course to avoid a wide range of system authorization pitfalls that include delays in project performance, lack of support from personnel, lack of adequate documentation, lack of participation by key personnel, and loss of project visibility. Using sound planning techniques, interpersonal skills, and deep reserves of energy, the project manager can usually overcome problems and navigate the project to a successful conclusion.

The System Inventory Process

An effective and workable system authorization program relies on a sound process for identifying and inventorying all the information systems under the control of an organization. Anyone who participated in inventorying systems as part of the Y2K (year 2000) effort knows how imposing a task this can be. The difficulty in inventorying information technology assets is caused by the lack of understanding of what constitutes a system, the failure to distinguish between systems, the rapid rate of creation of new systems, and then the failure to monitor the information technology operating environment. Yet, it is important that a reliable and complete system inventory be created and maintained because it is one of the most important steps in system authorization. The goal of the system inventory process is to provide assurance that systems requiring protection have been identified and are included in security planning and oversight.

Unless systems are known and identified in a centralized, enterprise inventory process, they cannot be protected with any degree of assurance. Managing systems accountability in a rapidly changing environment was previously addressed in this chapter. This section concentrates on the definition of systems and on identifying where one system stops and another begins. Here, we also address the need for monitoring the systems inventory through the use of automated tools to identify previously unknown applications and network servers not only for identification purposes but also to administer updates to the inventory.

Establishing and maintaining a centralized systems inventory program is not an easy task. Fortunately, the task gets easier once it has been established. To build an effective program, there are three critical success factors: continuing management support, clearly documented guidance, and a well-constructed implementation plan.

- Management support for the effort is critical because lines of business at some point will question the need for the inventory process and will escalate their concerns as far up the chain as they are able. Committed management support will ensure that everyone plays the game according to the rules, will disallow invalid exceptions and waivers, and will provide the staying power necessary to see the project through to its conclusion. Management has to be sold on the benefit of establishing a system inventory process, and this is the first crucial step. Security managers will not be able to proceed without management backing no matter how hard they try because they will never be able to use their own pleasing personalities to the extent necessary to earn the willing participation of systems owners. It takes muscle as well as personality. The proposal for presentation to the boss should be built around the fact that an information technology security program cannot function without knowing what needs to be protected, and that this must start with knowing what information technology systems the organization possesses.

- Once approval for the program has been gained, the CISO must document a basic policy on systems inventory. This will be prepared for an executive's signature and needs to be approved at the highest organizational level possible,

Table 1.12 High-Level System Inventory Project Work Plan	
Task One	• Identify general support systems (GSSs) and applications
	• Identify business functions
	• Identify automated information resources
	• Categorize automated information resources as GSS or application
Task Two	• Classify GSS and applications
	• Determine information sensitivity
	• Determine mission criticality
Task Three	• Identify major applications
	• Determine applications that qualify as major applications
	• Determine major application–GSS linkages
	• Map nonmajor applications to GSSs
Task Four	• Submit to CIO
	• Business unit executive review
	• CIO review
	• Publish inventory

preferably by the chief executive officer. This is the document, written in "thou shalt" language, that requires systems owners to identify their systems using an established process. A sample system inventory policy is provided in Appendix G. Naturally, it must be supported by a description of the process to include roles and responsibilities, steps, schedules, formats, and rules for defining systems. Both the policy and the procedures must pass through the organizational staffing chain to gain concurrence and support.

■ Finally, once the policy and procedures have been completed, staffed, and approved, the CISO must develop and oversee the execution of an implementation plan for the initiative. The CISO must develop instructions for complying with policy and procedures, including timetables, tasks, and activities and reporting requirements. Although it is difficult to account for exceptions, execution of the plan for a large organization should take 60 to 90 days, and for smaller organizations (less than 100 systems), it can be accomplished in about a month of diligent effort. A sample work plan for a system inventory project is provided in Table 1.12.

Responsibility

System owners will play the primary role in the inventory process. Their role along with all those involved in the inventory process needs to be defined in writing. System owners in the organization must be identified and must know and accept that they are the owners of the information systems in their area of responsibility. Further, system owners must be trained in the responsibilities inherent in that role. An ISSO needs to be appointed for each system to provide the system owner his or her primary point of contact for system security. The ISSO must also be trained in system security responsibilities. The third person in the inventory process is the line of business information technology security manager. This individual will play a key role in collecting system inventory information from system owners in his or her business unit. And, finally, the CISO as owner of the inventory process will play the largest role in collecting and consolidating inventory submission data and keeping it up to date. All of the roles identified here require a degree of security expertise because this is a security process at its heart, even though it can support other business requirements as well. The data is collected primarily to meet security needs, using security terminology. Hence, the individuals selected for these roles must understand information technology security and preferably must have demonstrated experience in applying it. There are, however, others involved in the process that will have little if any security experience or interest. Business managers own the processes and help define business needs for security based on their knowledge of the importance of the system and the impact of its loss or degradation on the organization or mission. Although it is not necessary for each individual mentioned here to sign off on the inventory form, each should fully concur with the information contained in the submission.

System Identification

The system owner plays the primary role in the initial identification of information systems. He or she can obtain assistance in performing this task from information owners, the CIO, CISO, and others but has the primary responsibility for determining what collections of information resources should be identified as a system, either an application system that supports a tightly defined business process or a general support system that serves as the computing platform for multiple computer applications. When the system owner considers what constitutes a system, he or she may need to consider a wide variety of information technology hardware, software, and processes. The system owner may be responsible for stand-alone computers, applications, office automation systems, word processors, vendor-hosted systems, subscription services, manual processes, mainframe computers, midrange computers, local-area networks, and wide-area networks. A useful and broadly accepted definition of a system comes from OMB Circular A-130:

> The term "information system" means a discrete set of information resources organized for the collection, processing, maintenance, transmission, and dissemination of information, in accordance with defined procedures, whether automated or manual.

Circular A-130 also gives us useful definitions for a general support system, which it says is "an interconnected set of information resources under the same direct management control that shares common functionality. It normally includes hardware, software, information, data, applications, communications, and people." It further defines a major application as "an application that requires special attention to security due to the risk and magnitude of harm resulting from the loss, misuse, or unauthorized access to or modification of the information in the application." These definitions help us to focus on the discrete elements of an organization's information resources that are most useful in determining what needs to be protected.

NIST SP 800-37, Revision 1, provides additional information on tasks with definition of information systems. Specifically, Task 1-3 provides guidance for registering information systems in the organization system inventory.

Small Systems

It is important to separate the assets that constitute general support systems or major applications to avoid placing emphasis where it is not needed. This can happen when other less-significant applications are also included in the system authorization inventory. Limited-purpose applications developed to help a user or small number of users to do work more efficiently, such as databases and spreadsheets, fall into this category. These systems are also distinguished by their near-total reliance on the general support system for their security, as opposed to a major application that has substantial technical controls built into its design. Although such applications also require attention to security because of the harm that can result from loss of confidentiality, integrity, or availability, for system authorization purposes, they are normally addressed as part of the general support system through which they are accessed. This approach helps the organization limit the number of systems for which formal system authorization is exercised, ensuring that visibility for security is apportioned appropriately without losing sight of minor applications.

Complex Systems

Large, complex systems pose another difficulty to development of the system inventory. They are more difficult to certify and accredit not because they are difficult to define but because of their size and complexity. Large, complicated systems, such as corporate finance and accounting or personnel systems, contain multiple processes and subsystems that are combined into a single integrated major application. However, each of these components may in itself be larger than another major application the organization operates. This creates a disparity when it is time to certify the system because the level of effort is so much greater than an ordinary major application. Such systems may also have several different managers responsible for each of its component parts, which clouds the single-ownership principle. For these large, complex systems, system authorization is best approached through their sub-systems. Breaking them into manageable chunks that support a larger whole is for practical purposes the only way to ensure the system is certified and accredited in a timely and cost-effective way.

Combining Systems

Another approach that can be used to streamline the system authorization inventory is the grouping of similar systems. This reduces the amount of documentation that must be developed and maintained, and it is acceptable as long as certain conditions are met. First, systems can be grouped when all of the systems in the group fall under the responsibility of the same system owner. Second, each must process in the same operating environment (e.g., reside on the same server). And, third, each must be protected within a common security perimeter (e.g., are protected by the same set of management and operational controls). This loose set of criteria can be helpful in ensuring that security is applied properly to all systems within the group while doing away with the need for creating superfluous security documentation.

Type accreditation and site accreditation are other system authorization approaches that can be utilized to minimize the demands of creating security documentation without jeopardizing the loss of security visibility. Type accreditation relates to the common system authorization of all systems of a given type that are secured in a like manner. This may apply to an application that is installed and used by multiple users throughout an organization. Although the security perimeter and processing environment of each are similar though not identical, ownership of the system varies greatly in that there are usually multiple system owners involved. On the other hand, with site accreditation, all the systems at a given location (i.e., computer room, data center, facility) are protected within the same security perimeter, have common but often different processing environments, and are certified and accredited under the ownership of the site manager, rather than by individual system owners. Both of these approaches are acceptable solutions for minimizing the number of systems requiring individual system authorization.

Accreditation Boundaries

For the purpose of system authorization, it is important to remember that every-thing must be certified. Consequently, there should be no dispute over the fact that every component of the organization's information system inventory has to undergo the same process. Hence, establishment of accreditation boundaries is more concerned with establishing responsibility for the accreditation of a given information resource, not whether a system has to be certified. Accreditation boundaries are drawn between one or more general support systems or one or more major applications. It is best to proceed based on business processes first, security perimeter second, and ownership last. All information resources related to the same business process (i.e., asset management) should naturally be grouped into the same major application. However, if one component supports two different processes (e.g., two applications reside on the same server), then either server controls can be addressed in each certification (effectively doubling the system authorization burden on the server owner) or the server can preferably be certified as part of a general support system because it is within the same security perimeter. If the same manager functions as the system owner of these two applications, it is possible that they can be grouped into a single accreditation even though they do not support an identical business process because they have consistent ownership and both are within the same security perimeter. The owner of these two major applications can also argue that he or she should own the computing platform, making the case that it should be included in the same accreditation as well.

One principle also to be considered in assessing the security perimeter is to make boundaries as small as possible for systems with elevated levels of sensitivity to ensure that the cost-effectiveness of controls is maximized. For instance, it will be more effective to accredit the most sensitive components of a general support system (e.g., a remote access server) in a separate enclave rather than to attempt to accredit the entire general support system at the high level of sensitivity. It is also not appropriate to accredit the high-sensitivity component at the moderate level of sensitivity of the general support system.

The organization must clearly define the outer boundary of its security perimeter to ensure that security of all its assets is in place at this outermost extent. First, this is done by ensuring that devices that guard the perimeter (i.e., firewalls, routers) are defined as part of a specific system that is to be certified and accredited itself. Systems of this nature are more sensitive, and controls protecting them should be subjected to more rigorous scrutiny. Second, the perimeter must be defined through identification of interfaces and interconnections with systems lying outside the secure perimeter. This is done through coordination and negotiation with system owners of these external systems, which transmit data to and receive data from our organization. There is a great variety of ways to package information resources for accreditation purposes. This flexibility is permitted by the fact that the system authorization program is all encompassing and that the outer perimeter of the organization's information technology resources has been defined.

The Process

The system inventory process begins with the system owner, who identifies general support systems and major applications for which he or she is responsible. This is best achieved with the assistance of the business manager, who identifies business processes and then the information technology that supports them. A three-step approach identifies business functions, identifies supporting information technology resources, and then categorizes these resources as types of systems.

Next, systems are classified by determining their needs for protection based on disclosure, modification, destruction, or denial. Further guidance on how this is achieved is in Chapter 2. From this step, the sensitivity of the system is set. Then, a system inventory form is completed for each general support system and major application (see separate section for discussion) and is submitted to the CIO or CISO as his or her agent. Finally, the CIO approves the official system inventory for the entire organization.

Validation

The CISO should perform a sanity check on all submissions. For new inventory programs, it may be helpful to interview each business unit point of contact and system owner to validate input to gain assurance about the accuracy of their submissions. This is best achieved in a short face-to-face meeting between them to ensure that they follow organizational guidance, use sensitivity rankings appropriately, ensure forms are completed correctly, and ensure they have understood terms and definitions and have applied them properly. They must also be able to justify their rankings regarding data sensitivity and system criticality. In addition, the CISO must be sure to check that submitted information is consistent with previous years' submissions. Criticality information must be closely scrutinized because there is a temptation for each system owner to classify his or her system as mission critical. Although it is possible that all systems could be classified as mission critical, it is highly unlikely. Under normal conditions, not everything can be critical, and not every security impact can be categorized at the highest levels of sensitivity. Actually, someone with a view of the big picture must decide on the criticality of organization systems. Similarly, someone with knowledge of security impacts must be the judge of system sensitivity rankings.

The CISO must be careful not to punish the good guys or those who submit their inventory data on time, well ahead of the average. There may be a temptation to focus on inventory deficiencies of those who report their systems first, while paying progressively less attention to the information submitted by system owners late in the process. The CISO should maintain system owner cooperation. Those reporting first should be applauded for being diligent, and negative feedback should be apportioned equally, regardless of when inventory information is submitted.

Inventory Information

It may be tempting to collect a lot of information regarding the system using the system inventory form and process. However, to minimize the impact on system owners, the form should be used to capture only enough information to provide a snapshot of the system. Essential information that should be collected include the name of the system and an abbreviated description of the system and its environment (no more than three to four sentences); the status of the system (operational or in development); a list of systems to which it is connected; data sensitivity impacts; mission criticality ranking; and identification of system points of contact (owner, approving authority, and ISSO). The name of the individual authorizing the submission should also be indicated. Table 1.13 provides additional information on these essential data elements. An organization should also consider implementing a unique number or naming scheme for its systems to facilitate the identification process. Such a scheme should accommodate systems of varying types that belong to different business units at different stages of their life cycles, and its most important characteristic will be the fact that it is centrally issued and managed. A numbering system can also be used as a means for controlling the development and funding of systems. Without an official system designation, there will be no continued resources committed to the system.

Inventory Tools

Three tools are necessary for managing the inventory program: the inventory form, an inventory change form, and an organization inventory summary. These can be combined into an integrated inventory tool with controlled access, can be built using existing office automation software, or can even be based on the use of hard-copy forms. There does have to be centralized and controlled collection and validation of forms by a single authority. Templates for these forms are provided in Tables 1.14, 1.15, and 1.16, respectively.

Table 1.13 Inventory Data Requirements	
System name	• Official name
	• Approved abbreviation
	• Other cross-reference numbers
System description	• Specify what the system is intended to do
	• Identify the business function it supports
	• Indicate data flows
System environment	• Hardware
	• Software
	• Components
	• URLs
	• IP addresses
System status	• Stage of the system's life cycle
	• Operational
	• Development
Dependencies and interconnectivity	• Data flows
	• Hosting systems
	• Supporting systems
	• Supported systems
Sensitivity	• Consider all data processed
	• Ensure knowledgeable personnel are involved
	• Justify all determinations
	• Consider consequences of over- and undercategorization
Criticality	• Ensure the term *criticality* is understood
	• Ensure ramifications are understood, both positive and negative
Points of contact	• Include system owner and system security officer
Approval	• Management should sign off on each system inventory form

Using the Inventory

The inventory process can be helpful in gaining support for and participation in security initiatives. As stated previously, funding can be tied to the process. This is probably the benefit with the greatest potential for the CISO. The program can be used to support periodic reporting requirements (like FISMA) as well. The program can be beneficial in supporting the information needs of the information technology security oversight board, enterprise architecture team, and other management

Table 1.14   Sample Inventory Form

Owning Organization:		Office of Administration
Date:		April 1, 2005
Information System Name and Acronym:		General Disbursement System (GDS)
System Status:	Operational	Under Development
Accreditation Status:	Yes Date: <u>11/13/2012</u>	No Scheduled Completion Date: _____

Points of Contact:

Position	Name	Telephone
Information system owner	John Brown	202-123-4567
Information owner	John Brown	202-123-4567
Information systems security officer	Tom Green	202-123-5678
Primary system administrator	Jane Black	202-123-6789
Secondary system administrator	Bill White	202-123-7890
Designated approving authority	Mary Blue	202-123-8901

Type of Automated Information Resource	GSS (General Support System) MA (Major Application)
Associated URLs:	http://www.gds.xyz.com
Associated IP Addresses:	123.45.678.90
Technologies (i.e., Windows, Oracle, etc.):	Microsoft Windows 2003; Microsoft SQL Server; Microsoft IIS 6.0
Name(s) of System(s) the Information System Is Interfaced, Interconnected, or Shares Data With:	Resides on corporate intranet general support system; interconnected to the financial management system
Description of Data and Business Function:	General Billing System (GBS) data consists of financial information related to distribution of government funds. GBS is used to process disbursements of appropriated funds to state-level agencies
Mission Criticality:	Critical Noncritical
Criticality Justification:	GDS is essential to the performance of corporate funds disbursement operations, which directly support one of the company's major missions

Table 1.14 (continued) Sample Inventory Form				
Information Sensitivity:				
Protection Requirements	**High**	**Med**	**Low**	**Justification**
Confidentiality		X		The application is used to process department financial information that must be safeguarded from public access.
Integrity	X			System information is used in the disbursement of government funds and must be accurate.
Availability			X	Users access the system during normal hours only, and manual processes are available for use when required. The system can be down for 7 days without significant disruption.

Comments: The General Billing System (GBS) is currently scheduled for replacement by Universal Disbursement System within the next 12 months, at which time GBS will be retired.

_____   _____

Signature of Approving Official   Date

groups tasked with managing information technology resources. Also, the program supports compliance review and audit functions. One should not discount the value of such a system in gaining management support by avoiding the risk of embarrassment and erosion of credibility.

Disputes involving the inventory are a near certainty. One can anticipate disagreements over what constitutes a system; why a system should be added to or deleted from the inventory; ownership of and responsibility for systems; criticality of systems; and responsibility for reporting. I have found that the system inventory shrinks proportionally to the number of requirements associated with identifying a system. Once system owners understand requirements, they are prone to deactivate systems outright if possible or combine them with others when feasible. The CISO stands in the middle of all these disagreements, but the inventory process can be used to assist in resolving them rather than simply causing them. Such disputes need to be surfaced and addressed rather than left to fester while vulnerabilities are not addressed.

Maintenance

There needs to be a formalized, annual requirement to review, update, and authorize system inventory data. With an automated inventory system, input and registration

Table 1.15   Inventory Change Form

System Inventory Change Procedures

Background

Information recorded in the system authorization inventory may change between scheduled inventories. Changes to the inventory may surface due to changes in the type of information processed, software/hardware modification, or other changes to the processing environment of the system. Awareness of these changes by the CIO is necessary to permit maintenance of the appropriate level of security controls for systems in the inventory.

Responsibilities

Business unit security managers will complete one of the following forms to record system inventory changes and will submit it to the CISO for update of the organization systems inventory. The CISO will track changes to systems requiring system authorization to ensure compliance with federal guidelines.

Procedure

Business unit security managers will use the appropriate form (add, update, or delete) included below to update system inventory for their business unit and will forward it to the CISO for action.

Systems Inventory Form—System Addition

Business Unit:

Date:

Name of System:

Type of System: GSS or MA

Mission Critical: Yes or No

System Security Plan Date:

Risk Assessment Date:

ST&E Date:

Contingency Plan Date:

Security Certification Level (SCL): High, Moderate, or Low

System Inventory Form—Update System Information

Business Unit:

Date:

Name of System:

Nature of Change:

Reason for Change:

System Inventory Form—System Addition

Business Unit:

Date:

Name of System:

Mission Critical: Yes or No

Reason for Deletion:

Table 1.16 Inventory Summary

No	Name of System	System Type: GSS/MA	Mission Critical: Y/N	C&A: Y/N	C&A Date (actual or planned) (MM/DD/YY)	System Security Plan Date (MM/DD/YY)	Risk Assessment Date (MM/DD/YY)	ST&E Date (MM/DD/YY)
1	NUTRIA	MA	N	N	9/30/2012	5/6/2012	5/6/2012	6/11/2012
2	APOLLO	MA	N	N	9/30/2012	12/30/2012	12/30/2012	6/11/2012
3	HERMES	MA	N	N	9/30/2012	4/1/2012	4/1/2012	6/9/2012
4	JUPITER	GSS	Y	Y	8/11/2012	12/21/2012	12/21/2012	6/24/2012
5	MERCURY	MA	N	N	9/30/2012	12/26/2012	12/26/2012	6/11/2012

Chapter 1

can be continuous, reducing reliance on periodic data calls. This periodic review permits close scrutiny of changes to the inventory, which may affect total system count, number of critical systems, and identification of personnel and environment changes. It also can be used to trigger a review of security documentation like the system security plan or risk assessment and contingency plan. Periodic review will only be effective if the program owner—the CISO—locks down and tightly controls the system change process. This will establish requirements for justifying changes to the inventory and prevent manipulation and churning. Keeping the inventory up to date will be a continual challenge and needs continuing management support to be effective. The inventory system must also be simple to use and be responsive to organizational needs. When possible, the inventory process should be integrated into the system change management process. An inventory form should be submitted as part of the initiation phase of the SDLC, and inventory change forms should be updated as part of routine change management. All changes need to be fully approved on the submission side. The system owner needs to be informed, as does the ISSO as a minimum. This ensures the form is properly documented with the approval of the responsible manager. Inventory data should be updated any time that information submitted in inventory forms changes. This means that the system owner needs to establish a process for identifying these changes and for submitting an updated inventory form whenever there are changes in the system name, operating status, environment, connectivity, sensitivity, criticality, or responsibilities. The CISO should have a corresponding process to review inventory data regularly to ensure there is close scrutiny of increases and decreases in the number of systems in inventory, particularly changes in the number of systems considered mission critical. Monitoring this information is important because of the potential impact on resources.

Observations

Unless there is an accurate assessment of what composes an organization's general support systems and major applications, it will be impossible to have any degree of assurance that its information resources have implemented appropriate security controls. Therefore, it is of utmost importance to know what the organization's information resources are. The most effective approach to identifying information technology assets is to identify systems. A systems inventory process can help an organization specify information technology security requirements at the appropriate level of sensitivity with the right amount of detail. From an enterprise perspective, a system authorization program can only be effective when it has a comprehensive systems inventory as its foundation. Unless all information resources are identified, classified, and inventoried, the system authorization program has no place to begin and is certain to find a quick end.

Interconnected Systems

System authorization would be a much simpler process if there were no interconnections between systems to cause worry. In the days of centralized mainframe processing, it was an easy task to determine certification scope and the boundaries of the security perimeter. Since those days, however, the definition of what is to be certified has become clouded by the increasing interconnectivity between an increasing number of systems. Because these systems share sensitive information, system owners have to be concerned about them and about how security controls are implemented to protect their data. It is nearly always impractical to draw the scope large enough to include these interconnected systems into a single certification. Therefore, an alternative approach must be identified.

The Solution

The response to the problem of certifying the protection of data that passes from one system to the next has come to be addressed through the process of establishing memoranda of agreement between system owners to address the responsibilities and roles of each. First, a formal approach is necessary to ensure that the controls of a connecting system are equal to or exceed those established for the system to which it will be connected. Because system owners surrender direct control over data when data leaves the confines of their systems' security perimeters, security agreements provide system owners some assurance that owners of interconnected systems will provide a known level of protection to their data. Second, security authorization of an information system is a formal process that demands documentation of requirements and the implementation of corresponding controls. The development of formal agreements between system owners satisfies this need for documentation to provide assurance of protection.

Agreements in the System Authorization Process

System authorization provides a commonly accepted standard for security that can facilitate the process of interconnecting systems. The owner of an accredited system should ensure that all interconnected systems have also been accredited.

This includes accreditation for all data-sharing relationships (other than the exceptions listed in the following) to ensure requirements for protecting data that is passed between systems are established and that these standards are being met. The process used to certify and accredit interconnected systems should meet or exceed the standards in effect for the system to which they are connected. The system owner evaluating the security posture of the connecting system should review all system authorization documentation with a concentration on protection of data to ensure it is being protected at the same level as that of his or her own system.

Interconnectivity agreements between system owners are key elements of the security authorization process that are considered at several times during the process. The minimum security baseline review assesses the effectiveness of controls over data transmitted between connected systems. The risk assessment documents the value of assets associated with these incoming and outgoing data flows, identifies threats to this data, pairs identified vulnerabilities with the threats, and calculates corresponding risks. The certification test assesses controls designed to provide protection to this data. And, the remediation plan documents the weaknesses and provides mitigating controls for shortfalls in protective measures. The system security plan identifies memoranda of agreement and existing documents and planned controls that relate to developing and maintaining agreements for interconnected systems. Without addressing the security of data introduced into the system and transmitted out of it, the certification is incomplete. Therefore, it is important to identify all data flows with other systems as part of the risk assessment and to identify the sensitivity of the data, how it is being used, and how it needs to be protected. This information is best gleaned from the use of discovery tools, network diagrams, interviews, design documents, and review of existing memoranda of agreement, memoranda of understanding, service-level agreements, and contracts with other system owners and vendors. Once there is a full picture of where data comes from and where it is transmitted, a complete picture of control requirements can be established.

Trust Relationships

Trust relationships between systems that share data should be based on full knowledge of how the gaining system intends to use and protect that data. Trust relationships need to be based on a mutually beneficial agreement between owners of the two systems. This is normally an agreement between equals, with neither having a superior or inferior position relative to the other. However, system owners may in fact both be part of a common organization in a supporting or supported relationship. The trust relationship may also be between supporting vendors and supported customers.

Initiation

The agreement may be sought by either party, but under normal conditions it is initiated by the system owner who desires access to data processed by another system. The requesting owner must meet any requirements established by the owner of the system from which the data is to flow. The data owner normally makes the call on what security requirements must be met to protect the data. If the system has been previously accredited, then this is a relatively easy process. If not, then data protection requirements need to be established by some alternative process. Ideally, this will be based on a minimum security baseline assessment or risk assessment that is part of an established system authorization process.

A memorandum of agreement documents at a high level terms and conditions for the interconnection of two systems. This governs both one-way and two-way connectivity. The memorandum of agreement must then be supplemented with a more specific interconnection security agreement, which is used to detail security controls and procedures required relative to the agreement (e.g., incident response and reporting requirements). The memorandum of agreement is a formal contractual document, both parties must concur with it, and it must meet the standards each organization normally applies to formal agreements. A sample memorandum of agreement is provided as Appendix L, and Appendix M is a sample interconnection security agreement.

Memoranda of agreement and interconnection security agreements are critical documents to be reviewed in the system authorization process, whether for the system being certified or for systems with which it connects. Many times, memoranda of agreement and interconnection security agreements will be made with system owners in other organizations of the federal government or even in the same department, where both systems must meet common system authorization requirements as well as control requirements. In such cases, it may be tempting merely to seek the accreditation date for an interconnected system under the assumption that because the system has been accredited, this substantiates that that system can and should be fully trusted. This may not be the case, and both memoranda of agreement and interconnection security agreements as well as the actual system authorization packages for these accredited systems should be reviewed in detail to ensure that the data will be or is being adequately protected.

Time Issues

Getting memoranda of agreement and interconnection security agreements drafted, approved, and signed takes a great deal of time and effort. This is because they are legal documents, which obligate two parties in a contractual arrangement. The agreements must undergo detailed legal review by the general counsels of both organizations. Also, much prior coordination and negotiation must take place before the two organizations can agree on what controls will be provided and the details of the interconnection security agreement can be worked out. There are several things that can be done to speed up the process for implementing security agreements. First, a system must have its security in order before a request to connect with another system is initiated. The system should have already undergone certification and be accredited or have it fully planned prior to starting the process. This way, it is known what is required to protect the system's data, and there is a foundation for knowing what controls need to be considered for the system about to be interconnected. It is much simpler to begin with a written set of requirements that can be substantiated as accurate and complete through a comprehensive system authorization process that produces coherent supporting documentation.

System owners must ensure that agreements are in place before an interconnection is made. The owner of the system to which the request is made is in the best position to ensure that this takes place. Requiring a finalized agreement prior to connection not only prevents exposure to potential security risks but also provides a clearly defined benchmark that both parties can work toward. Once systems have been informally interconnected, it becomes much more difficult to formalize that arrangement. Should there be an urgent necessity to interconnect the systems, and there is insufficient time to adequately finalize an interconnection agreement, a documented interim agreement should be created to establish responsibilities and timetables for finalizing the interconnection agreement and conditions for terminating the connection should the agreement be broken. Review and approval of memoranda of agreement and interconnection security agreements should follow established organizational processes, which normally include legal review by the general counsel and contractual review by the procurement officer. In addition, information technology operations and the CISO should review all interconnection-related documentation. At a minimum, agreements should be signed by the system owner and also preferably by the accrediting official for all systems concerned.

There are several steps that can be taken to facilitate the agreement process to ensure that systems are able to retrieve critical data when they need it. Communications between the owner of the system requesting the connection and the owner receiving the request should be mutually open and can be expedited through face-to-face meetings to set expectations, avoid misunderstandings, and speed up the process. Wording of interconnection agreements should be simplified as much as possible to promote clarity, and involvement of the legal and contracting functions early in the process will promote the identification of requirements early in negotiations when they can still be effectively resolved. Ideally, agreements should be initiated during development whenever possible to permit integration of requirements for interconnection into the system development methodology employed by the organization. This allows for the systematic establishment of milestones for development, coordination, review, and approval of the agreement prior to placing the system into production.

The wording used in formal agreements should define the nature of the interconnection and of the data involved and should establish minimum standards for protective controls and for complying with these requirements. To ensure that these provisions are met, the agreement should include provisions for reporting on the status of security controls and for the right to inspect operations to ensure compliance. Because it is not possible to foresee all future developments, on-site validation of the security posture of interconnected systems should be included, even though there may be no real intent to exercise them at the time the agreement goes into effect. The agreement should also establish requirements for timely notification in the event of a security breach that could put the connected system at risk. Finally, there should be provisions for cancellation of the agreement for cause when its provisions have not been met.

Exceptions

The need for formal agreements between system owners is not warranted when individual users of a particular organization have been granted access to a system. In such a case, these users are governed by existing user-level rules (i.e., system access, incident reporting, etc.), and the agreement is between the individual user and the system owner rather than between organizations. Here, established rules of behavior suffice for communication of security requirements to protect system data.

Security rules need to be established and documented for all back-end connections, maintenance hooks, modem use, telecommuters, and other means of remote access to the system. However, the use of formal agreements between organizations solely for this purpose is seldom necessary. Instead, agreements with individual users in the form of rules of behavior or identification of security controls and rules in existing maintenance agreements, service-level agreements, and the like, are easier to maintain, and they monitor and serve the purpose.

In addition, major applications that reside on a general support system do not normally need to have a formal memorandum of agreement and interconnection security agreement. This is because in most cases both the owner of the major application and the general support system owner are in the same organization. Any service-level agreement establishing this relationship needs to specify security requirements that the general support system will provide to the major application.

Maintaining Agreements

One of the most difficult problems to be surmounted by system owners is keeping up not only with changes to their own systems but also with changes of interconnected systems. Those changes may be of equal or greater importance to the security of their own data and consequently must be assessed for their impact by the owning system. This is the most difficult aspect of maintaining the security of interconnected systems. Any time there is an incident or breach of security controls in System A, then the owner of System B needs to know about it so that he or she can assess the extent his or her own system had been affected. Language must be included in the memorandum of agreement to ensure that changes to connected systems and incidents affecting security controls are shared in each direction.

Agreements should be periodically reviewed to ensure their validity. However, as formal contracting documents, they should be written to expire when their conditions are no longer valid rather than on a specified anniversary date. This approach will prevent an unnecessary administrative burden for periodic renewal. Provisions should also be included in the agreement to permit either party to opt out should conditions for the interconnection change.

From the perspective of the CISO, the need for maintaining visibility of interconnected systems is a great concern since it is difficult to achieve and maintain. A process for mapping interconnected systems graphically will help the security manager visualize data flows across the enterprise and understand the potential impact of a security incident.

Interconnectivity agreements are essential in providing assurance that system data is adequately protected once it leaves the protective perimeter controlled by the system owner. Once system owners transmit data beyond their secure environment, they no longer have control over its protection. Formal agreements with interconnected systems help to ensure that the data is protected beyond the limits of the system owner's direct control. Likewise, the agreements provide reasonable assurance that the information that is being introduced into the system owner's system from outside the security perimeter has originated from a trustworthy system.

SUMMARY

Chapter 1 touched on the interrelationships of several essential system security authorization processes and how each can be implemented by the security professional in practical ways as part of an overarching risk management program. The chapter included a discussion of key elements necessary to construct a successful enterprise system authorization program and detailed how to plan for a system authorization project. The importance of the enterprise system inventory and identification of system security authorization roles and responsibilities was described. Processes for coordinating security for interconnected systems and integration of system authorization requirements into the SDLC were also detailed. Root causes for failures in system security authorization programs were highlighted. Finally, Chapter 1 provided an introduction to the NIST RMF and how it relates to an enterprise-wide risk management program.

SECURITY AUTHORIZATION OF INFORMATION SYSTEMS: REVIEW QUESTIONS

1. During which Risk Management Framework (RMF) step is the system security plan initially approved?

   A. RMF Step 1 Categorize Information System

   B. RMF Step 2 Select Security Controls

   C. RMF Step 3 Implement Security Controls

   D. RMF Step 5 Authorize Information System

2. Which organizational official is responsible for the procurement, development, integration, modification, operation, maintenance, and disposal of an information system?

   A. Information system security engineer (ISSE)

   B. Chief information officer (CIO)

   C. Information system owner (ISO)

   D. Information security architect

3. Which authorization approach considers time elapsed since the authorization results were produced, the environment of operation, the criticality/sensitivity of the information, and the risk tolerance of the other organization?

   A. Leveraged

   B. Single

   C. Joint

   D. Site specific

4. System authorization programs are marked by frequent failure due to, among other things, poor planning, poor systems inventory, failure to fix responsibility at the system level, and

   A. inability to work with remote teams.

   B. lack of a project management office.

   C. insufficient system rights.

   D. lack of management support.

5. In what phases of the Risk Management Framework (RMF) and system development life cycle (SDLC), respectively, does documentation of control implementation start?

   A. Categorization and initiation

   B. Implement security controls and development/acquisition

   C. Authorization and operations/maintenance

   D. Monitor and sunset

6. The tiers of the National Institute of Standards and Technology (NIST) risk management framework are

   A. operational, management, system.

   B. confidentiality, integrity, availability.

   C. organization, mission/business process, information system.

   D. prevention, detection, recovery.

7. National Institute of Standards and Technology (NIST) guidance classifies security controls as

   A. production, development, and test.

   B. people, process, and technology.

   C. system-specific, common and hybrid.

   D. technical, administrative, and program.

8. Which of the following specifies security requirements for federal information and information systems in 17 security-related areas that represent a broad-based, balanced information security program?

   A. Federal Information Processing Standard (FIPS) 199, Standards for Security Categorization of Federal Information and Information Systems

   B. FIPS 200, Minimum Security Requirements for Federal Information and Information Systems

   C. Committee on National Security Systems (CNSS) Instruction No. 1253, Security Categorization and Control Selection for National Security Systems

   D. Section 3541 Title 44 U.S.C. Federal Information Security Management Act of 2002

9. After a monthly change control board meeting at which the team determined the security impact of proposed changes to an application, what would be the team's next action?

   A. Prepare the plan of action and milestones based on the findings and recommendations of the security assessment report excluding any remediation actions taken.

   B. Prepare the security assessment report documenting the issues, findings, and recommendations from the security control assessment.

   C. Update the security plan, security assessment report, and plan of action and milestones based on the results of the change control board's security impact analysis.

   D. Assess a selected subset of the security controls employed within and inherited by the application in accordance with the organization-defined monitoring strategy.

10. When an authorization to operate (ATO) is issued, which of the following roles authoritatively accepts residual risk on behalf of the organization?

   A. Information owner

   B. Chief information security officer (CISO)

   C. Authorizing official (AO)

   D. AO or the AO's designated representative (DR)

Chapter 2

Information System Categorization

Categorization of the information system is based on an impact analysis. It is performed to determine the types of information included within the security authorization boundary, the security requirements for the information types, and the potential impact on the organization resulting from a security compromise. The result of the categorization is used as the basis for developing the security plan, selecting security controls, and determining the risk inherent in operating the system.

Certified Authorization Professional (CAP®) Candidate Information Bulletin,
November 2010

TOPICS

- Defining Sensitivity
- Data Sensitivity and System Sensitivity
- Sensitivity Assessment Process
- Data Classification Approaches
- Responsibility for Data Sensitivity Assessment
- Ranking Data Sensitivity
- National Security Information
- Criticality
- Criticality Assessment
- Criticality in the View of the System Owner
- Ranking Criticality
- Changes in Criticality and Sensitivity
- NIST Guidance on System Categorization

OBJECTIVES

As a Certified Authorization Professional (CAP®), you are expected to

- Categorize the system
- Describe the information system, including the security authorization boundaries
- Register the system

Introduction

If it were not for the data that they process, information technology hardware and software could be secured like any other piece of high-value property. We could protect them just as we would safeguard tools, typewriters, merchandise, and other types of physical property. But, in the case of an information technology system made up of hardware, software, and data, it is the data that places them in an altogether different category for which protection against a distinct set of threats must be provided. And, many of these threats (e.g., unauthorized access) do not pertain to other types of physical property. In terms of determining protection requirements, it is the sensitivity of data and the criticality of systems that are the primary drivers. This chapter explores data sensitivity as it relates to information technology systems and addresses the criticality or importance of computer systems to an organization's overall mission. It is imperative to determine data sensitivity and criticality to define requirements for protection of information. The most recent guidance of the NIST (National Institute of Standards and Technology) on information system security authorization refers to this process as categorization.

Defining Sensitivity

It is the data that a system processes that makes an information technology system sensitive. Unlike other pieces of equipment, it is not the value of the hardware or software that governs sensitivity ranking of an information technology system. Requirements for security have to be addressed in the context of the business requirements. Similarly, implementation of security controls for a system has to be grounded in the context of the sensitivity of the data that the system is used to process, transmit, or store.

Sensitivity is often thought of as that quality that makes it necessary to protect data from being seen by those who do not have a need to see it. This view is based on the consideration of data as "confidential," "secret," and "top secret" in national defense terms. However, this narrow view obscures the breadth of how we actually define sensitivity. Sensitivity is more than simply protecting the confidentiality of system data, although that is surely a key aspect of the definition of sensitivity and is perhaps the overriding factor in determining the sensitivity level of a large number of government and business systems. Rather, the sensitivity of a system must also be based on how prone system data is to risks to its integrity and to its availability.

This broader definition was first found in the Computer Security Act of 1987. This act, which has since been replaced by the Federal Information Security Management Act (FISMA), established minimum acceptable security practices for federal computer systems that do not process national defense (i.e., "classified") information. The act specifies that federal computer systems be protected against unauthorized modification or destruction, as well as unauthorized disclosure. The act therefore more broadly defines "sensitive" information, which is said to be any information, the loss, misuse, or unauthorized access to or modification of which could adversely affect the national interest or the conduct of federal programs, or the privacy to which individuals are entitled under section 552a of title 5, United States Code (the Privacy Act), but which has not been specifically authorized under criteria established by an Executive Order or an Act of Congress to be kept secret in the interest of national defense or foreign policy.

There is a common misconception that there exists a class of systems that is not sensitive based on the nature of the data the systems process. However, the federal government's view is that all federal systems are inherently sensitive and require protection to a lesser or greater extent. According to the NIST, the intent of the Computer Security Act was not to create two distinct categories of information: "sensitive" and "nonsensitive." Also, the act did not create a category of "nonsensitive systems" that do not require implementation of security controls. All federal systems are required to be protected by security controls that correspond with the actual importance of the information the system processes or to the government investment in the system. Office of Management and Budget (OMB) Circular A-130, which implements the Computer Security Act, also defines sensitivity to include all three of these important components. This means that information that has no requirement for protection against unauthorized disclosure, such as information on a Web site intended for public access, can still be categorized as sensitive because it may still need to be protected against modification and denial of service. In the federal sector, there has been an unfortunate tendency toward using limited information technology security resources to determine which systems should be labeled sensitive. This is not only wasteful but also unnecessary because all systems require some minimum level of protection and are therefore sensitive.

Data Sensitivity and System Sensitivity

The sensitivity of a system is based on the data that it processes. Simply stated, remove the data and the system is no longer sensitive. It may be of high value based on what it would cost to replace it, but it will not be sensitive by definition. Even though systems themselves are often referred to as sensitive, it is actually the data processed, stored, or transmitted by the system that makes it sensitive. It is possible to establish an overall sensitivity level for a system based on the aggregated sensitivity levels of data by security objective (i.e., confidentiality, integrity, availability). Federal Information

Processing Standard (FIPS) 199 refers to this as the "high-water mark" that is to be used in defining the security category of an information system. This categorization represents the worst-case potential impact relating to the system.

Sensitivity Assessment Process

The most practical approach to determining sensitivity is by assessing the data by each of the three security concerns: confidentiality, integrity, and availability, in no particular order. This assessment not only should include a determination of the applicability of the security concern but also should result in a relative ranking of the sensitivity against a predetermined standard, as well as an overall ranking of sensitivity based on a view of the combined sensitivity in all three impact areas. The relative importance of the following three security objectives will depend on the nature of the system and the data it processes.

- *Confidentiality*: The sensitivity of data must be assessed based on its need for protection against disclosure. One should identify the impact that unauthorized disclosure of the data would have on the organization. The level of confidentiality that data requires naturally depends on the nature of the information. The confidentiality of information that is widely available to the public requires no, or perhaps only minimal, protection from disclosure. On the other hand, protection against disclosure is a key consideration for personal information about employees or customers, trade secrets and other proprietary information, information regarding operational plans and procedures, or information that could otherwise result in a loss or embarrassment to the organization should it be disclosed. Of course, confidentiality is a primary consideration in the protection of national defense information or data classified in nature. Confidentiality protection also includes protection of the privacy of those to which data processed by the system pertains.

- *Integrity*: System data must be protected from the effects of unauthorized or inadvertent modification or alteration. This quality of data defines how severe a loss would be incurred if the data integrity was lost. Determining the appropriate level for data integrity requires consideration of the needs for protection of the information from unauthorized, unanticipated, or unintentional alteration or loss. The data integrity security objective also includes consideration of the security objectives of authenticity, nonrepudiation, and accountability, which are also sometimes used. For example, a system that processes financial information may result in it being targeted for unauthorized modification. Consideration should be given to how the system is employed in a business process. For example, when system data is not the sole source of input for a business process, data integrity needs are generally less than when the business process fully relies on system data for its performance.

■ *Availability*: Data must be protected from adverse consequences of denial of its use or its destruction. Should system data not be available, how severe a loss would the organization suffer? To determine the appropriate system need for availability, one must consider the need for its data to be available to users on a timely basis to avoid substantial losses or to meet mission requirements. Protection requirements for availability need to be based on the period of operation during which the system is most critical to the business function it supports. For example, if the system is used only the last 2 weeks of each quarter, consider the availability requirement only for that period.

Ideally, early in the system development life cycle (SDLC), the sensitivity of the data that the system will process will be determined. Because data sensitivity drives controls, this will permit the identification and employment of appropriate controls when it is most cost-effective. However, the system owner should continue to assess data sensitivity throughout the development/acquisition, implementation, and operations/maintenance phases to ensure that the adequacy of controls is maintained. Any change in the functionality of the system, in the user population, or in interfaces with other systems should trigger a review of system sensitivity.

Data Classification Approaches

The systematic definition of data sensitivity and protection needs normally results from the application of formal data classification schemes. FIPS 199 is one example of an approach required for the classification of U.S. government data. There is a common misconception that data classification schemes relate only to the need to protect data against unauthorized disclosure. Perhaps this is because use of the term *classification* is thought to relate only to classified (i.e., national security) information. However, a formal data classification process as used most currently addresses the three main system security objectives of integrity, availability, and confidentiality. A sample of a data classification scheme is provided in Table 2.1.

FIPS 199, *Standards for Security Categorization of Federal Information and Information Systems*, provides the government standard for categorization of information and information systems with the goal of providing appropriate levels of security according to risk level. It defines three levels of potential impact on an organization

Table 2.1 *Example of a Data Classification Scheme*		
Classification	**Definition**	**Examples**
Public	Information that can be disseminated to the public following management review	Marketing materials Public records
Internal use	Information related to the day-to-day operations of the company that is restricted to company employees and consultants only	Customer information Financial reports System configuration data Incident reports Personnel records
Restricted	Information that must be closely safeguarded and is restricted to use by fewer than 5% of employees of the company	Trade secrets Merger and acquisition information

or individuals should there be a breach of security (i.e., loss of confidentiality, integrity, or availability). Application of these three definitions must occur within the context not only of the system but also of the organization's mission and the national interest. The FIPS 199 security level of a system is used as an indicator of how severe the potential impact the risk could potentially be on an agency mission. The most significant aspect of the FIPS 199 categorization is to align security categories to recommended initial baseline sets of security controls according to NIST Special Publication (SP) 800-53.

Responsibility for Data Sensitivity Assessment

Because system owners are responsible for securing their information technology systems by defining and implementing necessary controls, it is the system owner who must be primarily interested in the sensitivity of the data the system processes. Many times, system owners are also responsible for defining the sensitivity of the data their system processes in terms of confidentiality, integrity and availability of the information, and performance of the functions of the data owner. However, in other cases systems process data that is the responsibility of another department or individual. Here, system owners must rely on the judgment of a data owner regarding the sensitivity of the data rather than making their own determination of the sensitivity of the data. For instance, the human resources department is in the best position to determine the sensitivity of an employee database rather than the mailroom manager whose mail application uses information from that database to distribute benefits information to each employee's home address. The data sensitivity determination must be made by someone who has knowledge of the process for identifying the confidentiality, integrity, and availability impacts on the data. That individual must know what those terms mean and how they apply to specific sets of data. This means that there has to be a process for making data owners aware of their responsibility for designating data sensitivity and for educating them in how to do this. Consultants are often relied on to facilitate the data sensitivity designation because of their familiarity and expertise with these processes as well as their independence. Although this approach can ensure consistency, data owners, because of their familiarity with the data and the nature of its use, should consider the consultant's work simply as a recommendation and must continue to exercise ultimate responsibility for the data sensitivity designation to ensure it is accurate, applicable, and reasonable.

When the system owner and the data owner are distinct entities, it is essential that they closely coordinate how the system processes the data to ensure that it is properly safeguarded. It is important to note that as the owner of the data, the data owner should review the system design and grant permission to the system owner to use or otherwise process data only when he or she is satisfied that the data is being properly protected. This is because once the data owner permits the data to be processed by the system, the data owner gives control over the protection of data to the system owner. In this case, the system owner becomes a custodian of the data.

Ranking Data Sensitivity

It is important to distinguish levels of sensitivity using well-defined categories. The most common means of expressing sensitivity is by use of such terms as "high," "moderate," and "low" or some similar scheme (e.g., red, amber, green; 1, 2, 3; etc.). The definitions for each sensitivity level need to be both clear and consistent for each security impact area. However, it is not enough simply to attach a ranking to the data. The data sensitivity assessment must document in writing the justification for ranking the data. Table 2.2 provides examples for describing various sensitivity rankings for a government system, which are taken from NIST SP 800-18. Samples of assessment justifications by impact area and by category of information are provided in Table 2.3.

Ranking sensitivity can be based on predefined criteria relating to the sensitivity of data according to category of information processed (i.e., public, national security,

Table 2.2 **Examples of Sensitivity Ranking Descriptions**

Ranking	Confidentiality	Integrity	Availability
High	The consequences of unauthorized disclosure or compromise of data or information in the system are unacceptable. Loss of confidentiality could be expected to affect national-level interests adversely, prevent mission accomplishment, or create unsafe conditions that may result in loss of life or other exceptional grave damage.	The consequences of corruption or unauthorized modification of data or information in the system are unacceptable. Loss of integrity could be expected to affect national-level interests adversely, prevent mission accomplishment, or create unsafe conditions that may result in loss of life or other exceptional grave damage.	The consequences of loss or disruption of access to system resources or to data or information in the system are unacceptable. Loss of availability could be expected to affect national-level interests adversely, prevent mission accomplishment, or create unsafe conditions that may result in loss of life or other exceptional grave damage.
Moderate	The consequences of unauthorized disclosure or compromise of data or information in the system are only marginally acceptable. Loss of confidentiality could be expected to affect agency-level interests adversely, degrade mission accomplishment, or create unsafe conditions that may result in injury or serious damage.	The consequences of corruption or unauthorized modification of data or information in the system are only marginally acceptable. Loss of integrity could be expected to affect agency-level interests adversely, degrade mission accomplishment, or create unsafe conditions that may result in injury or serious damage.	The consequences of loss or disruption of access to system resources or to data or information in the system are only marginally acceptable. Loss of availability could be expected to affect agency-level interests adversely, degrade mission accomplishment, or create unsafe conditions that may result in injury or serious damage.
Low	The consequences of unauthorized disclosure or compromise of data or information in the system are generally acceptable. Loss of confidentiality could be expected to affect agency-level interests minimally and have little to no impact on mission accomplishment.	The consequences of corruption or unauthorized modification of data or information in the system are generally acceptable. Loss of integrity could be expected to affect agency-level interests minimally and have little to no impact on mission accomplishment.	The consequences of loss or disruption of access to system resources or to data or information in the system are generally acceptable. Loss of availability could be expected to affect agency-level interests minimally and have little to no impact on mission accomplishment.

Chapter 2

Table 2.3 Examples of Justifications by Impact Area and Category of Information

Information Category	Confidentiality	Integrity	Availability
Personal information	Some groups within the institution collect private citizens' contact data concerning certain ongoing research projects. Departmental contact lists with addresses and phone numbers are also stored within the system. This information needs to be guarded against unauthorized access.	The integrity of contact information stored on the systems is important to ensure the ability to follow up with individuals.	The data is not time-sensitive in most circumstances. Current operations require the ability to retrieve any lost or corrupt data within 72 hours.
Research and development (R&D) information	Certain institutional servers contain information concerning ongoing tests and results of statistical research. These data are expected to be kept confidential until final results are released to appropriate parties.	Any unauthorized modification of R&D data would affect the reliability of institutional reporting and affect the institution's reputation in the research community.	R&D data are not time sensitive. An event that causes the data to be unavailable for 2 days or less would not affect the institution's mission.

financial, personal, etc.). Sensitivity can be ranked according to operational, contractual, regulatory, and legal requirements relative to its use. In determining appropriate protection measures, it is important to bear in mind that requirements for the protection of particular types of information are often provided by statute or according to organizational decision. Information required to be protected under statute includes, for example, privacy information (protected under the Privacy Act), financial information (protected under the Federal Manager's Financial Integrity Act), taxpayer information, and census data. In other cases, an organization may establish security requirements according to specific types of information. For example, some organizations have created internal labels of "restricted" or "official use only" for certain types of information that need to be protected from unauthorized disclosure. Table 2.4 provides a sample of information categories.

To ensure that mission or business-based information is appropriately identified, and to comply with FIPS 199, system owners must develop an information taxonomy or catalog of all information types processed, stored, or transmitted by the information system. This permits mapping of types of information to security objectives (e.g., confidentiality, integrity, availability) and impact levels (high, moderate, low). Determining the degree of detail needed is an important step in this process since broad categories may be too general to be useful, while attempts to record every element of information processed by the system may be unwieldy and may require frequent change. NIST SP 800-60 provides additional guidance on this process.

The Business Reference Model (BRM) provides an organized, hierarchical framework for describing the day-to-day business operations of the federal government. While there are many models for describing organizations (organization charts, location maps, etc.), the BRM uses a functionally driven approach to represent the business of an organization. The BRM is the first layer of the Federal Enterprise Architecture (FEA) and provides a good viewpoint from which to analyze data, service components, and technology. The BRM describes 39 lines of government business distributed among four business areas: purpose of government (missions or services to citizens); mechanisms the government uses to achieve its purpose (modes of delivery); support functions necessary to conduct government (support delivery of services); and resource management functions that support all areas of the government's business (management of resources). The BRM provides a structured approach to classifying information system data and may be useful to the system owner in the security categorization process.

Privacy data presents special concerns for the system owner. The E-Government Act of 2002 strengthened privacy protection requirements. Under its terms, federal

Chapter 2

Table 2.4 Examples of Information Categories	
Category	**Explanation and Examples**
Personal	Information that is related to the identity of a person (i.e., human resources, medical, and similar data). Includes all information covered by the Privacy Act of 1974.
Financial	Information related to the financial operations of an organization. Includes budgeting and accounting records.
Proprietary and trade secret	Commercial information received in confidence or trade secrets (i.e., contract bidding information, proprietary, and sensitive patent information).
Administrative	Information related to the internal administration of the organization that requires protection against disclosure. Category includes policies, procedures, guidelines, internal memoranda and messages, management decisions, and advance information concerning procurement actions.
Procurement sensitive	Advance information concerning procurement actions to include selection criteria, assessments of vendor qualifications, etc.
Investigative, intelligence, and security related	Information related to law enforcement investigations; intelligence-related information that is confidential; and security documentation to include security plans, contingency plans, emergency operations plans, incident reports, reports of investigations, risk or vulnerability assessments, certification reports.
Business partner information	Information, the protection of which is required by agreement or statute, that has come from another business partner and requires release approval by the owning organization.
Controlled research and development	Information related to novel technology; scientific information that is prohibited from disclosure to designated foreign governments or that may require an export license.
Mission critical	Information designated as critical to the organization mission and includes vital statistics information for emergency operations.
Operational information	Information that requires protection during operations; usually time-critical information.
Life critical	Information in which loss of integrity, availability, or confidentiality could result in loss of human life.
System configuration	Information related to the configuration and functioning of an information technology system. This includes network management information protocols, network and device addresses, implemented system and protocol addressing schemes, network information packets, device and system passwords, and device and system configuration information.
Public	Information that has been cleared for public release by official company authorities. This category includes information contained in official press releases and information posted on publicly accessible World Wide Web (WWW) sites.

agencies have specific responsibilities regarding the collection, dissemination, or disclosure of information on individuals. The OMB has defined privacy information as that which identifies individuals in a recognizable form, including name, address, telephone number, Social Security Number, and e-mail address. This public law has necessitated the broadening of the definition of *unauthorized disclosure* to encompass *any* sharing of privacy-protected information between federal government agencies where sharing is prohibited by privacy laws and policies. Agencies are now required to conduct a Privacy Impact Assessment (PIA) before developing an information system that contains personally identifiable information (PII), or before collecting PII electronically, and PIAs must be updated whenever changes in the manner in which an agency handles PII creates new privacy-related risks. Also, the law mandates annual reporting electronic privacy-related activities. Privacy impacts normally fall in the moderate range. System owners should review the categorization to ensure that the consequences of violations have been adequately factored into impact determinations.

The overall sensitivity of a system or its security categorization will be at least as high as the highest level of sensitivity of information used by the system. The security category of an information system that processes, stores, or transmits multiple types of information should be set as high as the highest impact level determined for each type of information for each security objective. This becomes the high-water mark for the system. However, data context must also be considered in determining the security categorization of a system. That is, the compromise of some system information may have low impact in the context of the system's primary function but may have a much greater impact on other systems to which the system is connected or other systems dependent on that specific data. These dependencies and connections must be factored into the sensitivity ranking of the system.

National Security Information

Classified or national security information provides an additional challenge. Systems that process this type of data must be certified and accredited using the National Information Assurance Certification and Accreditation Process (NIACAP) rather than NIST SP 800-37. The National Security Telecommunications and Information Systems Security Committee (NSTISSC), which formerly was an intergovernmental organization charged with setting policy for the security of national security systems, developed the NIACAP to provide minimal national standards for certifying and accrediting national security systems. NSTISSC has now been replaced by the Committee on National Security Systems (CNSS). While there is currently movement toward updating CNSS requirements for national security systems to more clearly map to NIST guidance, there is still a need for understanding of NIACAP and how it is used to ensure the protection of the government's most sensitive information systems.

NIACAP provides a standard set of system authorization activities, tasks, and documentation designed to certify that the information system meets documented accreditation requirements and continues to maintain them throughout its life cycle. The NIACAP approach to documenting accreditation requirements is the System Security Authorization Agreement (SSAA), which is akin to the NIST-based system security plan. NIACAP methodology is broken down into four phases: definition, verification, validation, and postaccreditation. The SSAA is created from the input gathered during initiation and continues to guide the system development activities by ensuring that all development adheres to requirements documented in the SSAA. Each step and component goes through certification analysis, and the results are fed into the SSAA. The SSAA then sets the required level of testing for the integrated system, including the various aspects of system validation—the peripherals and support activities that the system relies on and the mission functions it supports. Once the system is accredited, the SSAA provides the authority for system operations, and as the system or its operational environment changes, so does the SSAA.

The roles and responsibilities for authorizing an information system using NIACAP are almost the same as those required under NIST SP 800-37. However, the authorizing official is referred to as the designated approving authority (DAA), and the certification agent is referred to as the certifier and has responsibility for evaluating the system based on the security requirements documented in the SSAA.

Criticality

Criticality is a term that is often confused with sensitivity; unfortunately, they are often used interchangeably. Criticality is similar to sensitivity in that it is used to determine the nature and types of security controls necessary to protect a system. It differs, however, in that it relates to a system as a whole, whereas sensitivity relates to the data that the system processes and more often is used to determine the priority for implementation of security controls according to the importance or criticality of a system. The key aspect of criticality that must be remembered is that criticality is a statement of the importance of a system to the organization it supports. Criticality answers the question of how valuable a system is to the performance of an organization's operational mission. Criticality most often relates to the amount of time that an organization can tolerate the nonavailability of the system; therefore, it is directly related to the availability objective of the system. Hence, the difference between sensitivity and criticality is one of breadth; sensitivity addresses all three security objectives, while criticality generally places emphasis on system availability. However, it should be noted that criticality does not have to relate to availability only. For instance, it is possible that a critical system that is used to submit a consolidated report to Congress on a quarterly basis would be judged as low sensitivity for availability, but because of the need for assurance of the integrity of submitted data, it would still qualify as a critical system but based on data integrity and its importance to the organization.

Critical infrastructures and key resources (CI/KR) require special attention in accordance with the Critical Information Infrastructure Act of 2002 (Public Law 107-296). This legislation defines the term *critical infrastructure information* as information related to the security of critical infrastructure or protected systems not customarily in the public domain. Accordingly, the criticality of a system should be carefully determined when a loss of confidentiality, integrity, or availability would result in a negative impact on infrastructure components such as water, public health, emergency services, defense installations or the defense industrial base, telecommunications, transportation, agriculture and food, or other critical infrastructures.

Criticality Assessment

Definition of mission or business criticality is an approach to determining the importance of a given information system to the organization. A mission-critical system is a system that would have a "debilitating" impact on the mission of the overall organization if it is lost. Mission criticality defines how integral the general support system or major application is to carrying out the mission of the organization and must also be considered as part of the sensitivity assessment. Systems should be evaluated to be either mission critical or non-mission critical using the definitions provided in the following discussion. As part of the assessment, it should be recognized that the criticality of some systems may vary according to peak processing

Chapter 2

periods of operation. The mission criticality of such systems should be based on the period of operation when it is most essential for the supported business function to be performed.

- *Mission Critical*: A mission-critical system is one that is used or operated by an organization or by an agent of the organization that meets one or more of the following three characteristics:
  - − Is classified as a national security system under section 5142 of the Clinger–Cohen Act of 1996 (40 U.S.C. 1452); or
  - − Is used to process information classified by an executive order or an Act of Congress in the interest of national defense or foreign policy; or
  - − Processes any information for which the loss, misuse, disclosure, or unauthorized access to or modification of would have a debilitating impact on the mission of an agency.

- *Non-Mission Critical*: A non-mission-critical system is one that does not fit under any of the conditions for a mission-critical system defined previously and whose failure would not prevent the owning or using organization from accomplishing critical business operations. However, such a loss might result in either a short- or long-term impact on the efficiency of routine business operations.

In determining whether a system is mission critical, an important question to ask is whether the business process supported by the system can be accomplished through manual means, even if less efficient, or what the extent of the impact of the system being unavailable for 30 days or more would be. Another consideration in this determination is that if a major application has been determined to be mission critical and resides on a general support system, then the general support system must also be identified as mission critical. Conversely, a major application does not automatically qualify as mission critical simply by residing on a mission-critical general support system.

Criticality in the View of the System Owner

System owners tend to think their system is the most critical. When asked, they will almost always say that the continued survival of the organization depends on the availability of their system. Accordingly, their system is critical to the performance of the mission of the entire organization, not just their office. The problem is, in the grand scheme of things, not every system can be the most critical. Not every system can be restored first because recovery resources are limited, and priorities for restoration have to be established. Criticality definitions are important for making such decisions. Criticality is a matter of perspective, and an objective entity needs to be the honest broker to make fair assessment of the relative criticality between systems. This will be someone with higher perspective who has an objectively broad view of the whole organization, its mission, and its operations. This typically is not the system owner.

Ranking Criticality

Ranking of systems by criticality can be based on several key factors, each related to the importance of the system in terms of its impact on the overall mission of the organization. Criticality can be judged on factors such as

- The *financial* impact, or the dollar loss, that can accrue if the system is at risk or harmed, such as falling behind in a production schedule.

- The *operational* importance of the system (e.g., the system is critical to paying employees in a timely fashion).

- The importance of the system based on *health, life, or safety* considerations (e.g., the system is necessary to control airline traffic).

- The *breadth/scope* of impact/value/importance of the system is also useful in ranking criticality. For example, based on breadth of use, an employee time accounting system that supports the entire organization is more critical than a time accounting system used by a single business unit.

The business impact analysis is the methodology normally used to quantify the criticality of systems based on the amount of time that an organization can tolerate the nonavailability of a system. The business impact analysis process supports both disaster recovery/contingency planning requirements and system authorization needs. Therefore, it is a well-suited approach for conducting the criticality analysis. A sample business impact analysis is provided in Appendix H.

The findings of the criticality assessment should document the criticality of the system in relation to other systems in the organization. Most often, criticality will be expressed in two or more criticality tiers. These can be labeled as high-, moderate-, and low-criticality categories. Alternatively, systems may simply be defined as either critical or noncritical.

Changes in Criticality and Sensitivity

System criticality is based on how a system is used by an organization. Of course, this can change over time, and the utility of this categorization is not set in stone. When the scope, data, business process supported, or user population served change, for example, the criticality of the system is likely to change accordingly. There must be a process for ensuring that system criticality is considered when changes to the system's environment occur. There are three good ways to ensure that the criticality of a system is evaluated on either a periodic basis or when changes to the system occur. First, a criticality review should be a part of an annual review of the security plan for the system. Second, the change management program should be in tune with the need to evaluate system criticality when changes also take place. Third, assessment of system criticality should also be integrated into the system inventory processes, which review all systems annually. An annual criticality review should be conducted by an official with a more objective view of systems criticality, and the chief information security officer (CISO) is well situated to perform an objective reassessment of criticality.

When similar changes result in changes to data sensitivity, the system owner must update the system security plan and make changes in system inventory. Changes in sensitivity should trigger a reevaluation of security controls. For instance, NIST SP 800-53 employs enhanced controls for more sensitive systems. Hence, changes in sensitivity can lead to additional vulnerabilities that warrant consideration of reassessment of risks to the system. Also, the system owner should define processes that measure the impact of changes in system design, use, operations, and interfaces.

NIST Guidance on System Categorization

The first step of the Risk Management Framework (RMF) leads to categorization of the information system and the information it processes, stores, and transmits and includes an impact analysis. The following paragraphs summarize the manner in which NIST SP 800-37, Revision 1, addresses system sensitivity and criticality through the RMF categorization step.

Task 1-1: Categorize and Document the Information System

In this task, the system owner or information owner categorizes the information system and records the results of the security categorization in the system security plan. NIST guidance anticipates the use of a formalized approach to categorization based on NIST 800-60 or 800-59 and Committee on National Security Systems Instructions (CNSSI) 1253 for national security systems.

Primary Responsibility	Supporting Roles	SDLC Phase	References
System owner, IO/IS	RE(F), AO or AODR, CIO, CISO, ISSO	RE(F), AO or AODR, CIO, CISO, ISSO	FIPS Publication 199, NIST SPs 800-30, 800-39, 800-59, 800-60, CNSS Instruction 1253

AO, authorizing official; DR, designated representative; CIO, chief information officer; ISSO, information system security officer; IO/IS, information owner/steward; RE(F), risk executive (function).

■ System categorization must consider organization-wide activities, including the enterprise architecture and the information security architecture, to ensure the categorization reflects organization mission and business objectives.

■ Results of security categorization influence selection of system-level security controls and minimum assurance requirements for the system.

■ The system owner may decompose the system into multiple subsystems to more efficiently and effectively allocate security controls. This may include categorizing each identified subsystem (including dynamic subsystems).

■ Separate categorization of each subsystem does not change the overall categorization of the system but allows subsystems to receive a separate controls allocation rather than deploying higher-impact controls across every subsystem.

■ Smaller subsystems may be bundled into larger subsystems within the system with categorization of each aggregated subsystem, and allocation of security controls to the subsystems, as appropriate.

■ Document security categorization information in the system identification section of the security plan or include it as an attachment.

■ The risk executive (function) provides advice and relevant information to authorizing officials concerning the risk management strategy to guide authorization decision making. This includes organization risk assessment methodologies, risk mitigation approaches, organizational risk tolerance, approaches for ongoing risk monitoring, known existing aggregated risks, and additional sources of risk.

■ System-level security categorization must consider potential adverse impacts to organizational operations, organizational assets, individuals, other organizations, and the nation.

Task 1-2: Describe the Information System

Describe the information system (including the system boundary) and document the description in the system security plan. In this task, descriptive information about the system is documented in the system identification section of the security plan or in attachments to the plan or is referenced in other artifacts.

Primary Responsibility	Supporting Roles	SDLC Phase	References
Information system owner	AO or AODR, CISO, IO/IS, ISSO	Initiation	None

■ The level of detail provided in the security plan is determined by the organization and is typically commensurate with the security categorization of the information system.

■ Information may be added to the system description as it becomes available during the SDLC and execution of the RMF tasks.

■ A system description may include name; acronym; unique system number or code; information system owner (ISO); AO; owning organization; system location; version or release number; purpose, functions, and capabilities; missions/business processes supported; how the information system is integrated into the enterprise architecture and information security architecture; SDLC status; security categorization; information type(s); system boundary; applicable laws, directives, policies, regulations, or standards; architectural description; network topology; hardware and firmware; system and applications software; internal and external hardware, software, and system interfaces; subsystems; information flows/inputs and outputs; cross-domain devices/requirements; network connections; interconnected systems with identifiers; encryption techniques used; cryptographic key management information; system users (organizational affiliations, access rights, privileges, citizenship, etc.); type of ownership/operation (e.g., government owned, government operated; government owned, contractor operated; contractor owned, contractor operated; nonfederal); authorization date; authorization termination date; and incident response points of contact.

Task 1-3: Register the Information System

Register the information system with appropriate organizational program/management offices. The registration process begins by recording the system (and applicable subsystems) in the organization's system inventory.

Primary Responsibility	Supporting Roles	SDLC Phase	References
ISO	ISSO	Initiation	None

- System registration documents the existence of the information system, key system characteristics, and security implications of operating the system.

- System registration provides an effective management/tracking tool that supports security status reporting required by laws, executive orders, directives, policies, standards, guidance, or regulations.

- Dynamic subsystems may not be present throughout all phases of the SDLC and must be registered either as a subset of a defined system or an alternative registration method for dynamic subsystems must be implemented.

- Some information about dynamic subsystems (e.g., assumptions and constraints) is known prior to its inclusion in the information system, but detailed information may only be known when the subsystem is added.

SUMMARY

Sensitivity and criticality assessments are essential processes in categorizing system security and determining specific controls that are to be implemented to protect system data and in the prioritization of resources. Definition of data and system sensitivity permits the organization to identify protection requirements based on the nature of data that the system processes, and then it permits mapping of the system to predefined control sets or minimum security baselines (as addressed in Chapter 3). The criticality assessment allows the organization to define the relative priority of importance of information systems to permit efficient apportionment of protection resources. The determination of system criticality is a matter of perspective and must be done with an objective eye because decisions relating to funding, priority for support, restoration and recovery operations, application of controls, and crisis management are affected by the system's criticality ranking.

Chapter 2

INFORMATION SYSTEM CATEGORIZATION: REVIEW QUESTIONS

1. When attempting to categorize a system, which two Risk Management Framework (RMF) starting point inputs should be accounted for?

   A. Federal laws and organizational policies

   B. Federal laws and Office of Management and Budget (OMB) policies

   C. Federal Information Security Management Act (FISMA) and the Privacy Act

   D. Architectural descriptions and organizational inputs

2. Documenting the description of the system in the system security plan is the primary responsibility of which Risk Management Framework (RMF) role?

   A. Authorizing official (AO)

   B. Information owner

   C. Information system security officer (ISSO)

   D. Information system owner

3. The registration of the system directly follows which Risk Management Framework (RMF) task?

   A. Categorize the system

   B. Describe the system

   C. Review and approve the system security plan

   D. Select security controls

4. When should the information system owner document the information system and authorization boundary description in the security plan?

   A. After security controls are implemented

   B. While assembling the authorization package

   C. After security categorization

   D. When reviewing the security control assessment plan

5. Information developed from Federal Information Processing Standard (FIPS) 199 may be used as an input to which authorization package document?

   A. Security assessment report (SAR)

   B. System security plan (SSP)

   C. Plan of actions and milestones (POA&M)

   D. Authorization decision document

Chapter 2

Chapter 3

Establishment of the Security Control Baseline

The security control baseline is established by determining specific controls required to protect the system based on the security categorization of the system. The baseline is tailored and supplemented in accordance with an organizational assessment of risk and local parameters. The security control baseline, as well as the plan for monitoring it, is documented in the security plan.

Certified Authorization Professional (CAP®) Candidate Information Bulletin,
November 2010

TOPICS

- Minimum Security Baselines and Best Practices
- Assessing Risk
- System Security Plans
- NIST Guidance on Security Controls Selection

OBJECTIVES

As a Certified Authorization Professional (CAP®), you are expected to

- Identify and document common (inheritable) controls
- Select and document security controls
- Develop security control monitoring strategy
- Review and approve security plan

Introduction

There are three distinct aspects to the selection of security controls for an information system. First, control selection relies on the results of the security categorization as described in Chapter 2. Then, based on the category of the system, the system owner makes use of a catalog of security controls accepted by the organization to provide a starting point for the selection process; this is known as a minimum security baseline (MSB). Finally, using this catalog, the system owner then chooses controls from the catalog and tailors them to meet the requirements for protecting the system. This final step relies on risk assessment to determine risks to the confidentiality, integrity, and availability of the data the system processes. This chapter describes the minimum security baseline establishment and use and the risk assessment process. In addition, an overview of the guidance of the National Institute of Standards and Technology (NIST) on security control selection is provided.

Minimum Security Baselines and Best Practices

A practical approach to securing information technology assets that an organization can take is the establishment of a minimum security baseline and best practices for security configurations of its information technology platforms and devices. Here, the organization draws a line in the sand and says, "All of our systems will implement this basic set of security controls." Other controls may be necessary, but at least these minimum security baseline controls will be in place. Through this baseline, the organization establishes a point of reference from which it can determine its security posture through compliance with implementation of minimum controls. It also provides the organization a starting point for assessing the validity of this control set for a given system through the risk assessment process, which is used to enhance control requirements, eliminate nonapplicable controls, or recommend alternative controls for each system. In short, a minimum security baseline is a set of standards that are applied enterprise-wide to ensure a consistent level of compliance.

Security Controls

According to Federal Information Processing Standard (FIPS) 199, *security controls* are defined as "the management, operational, and technical controls (i.e., safeguards or countermeasures) proscribed for an information system to protect the confidentiality, integrity, and availability of the system and its information." Agencies may find that even with the categorizing assistance of FIPS 199, it may be cost prohibitive or technically infeasible for the organization to implement generally accepted security controls. To make this problem more manageable, the organization should examine the nature of its information systems and create minimum security baselines that are responsive to the agency's risk needs. Similarly, authorizing officials, when addressing security authorization for individual systems, should determine whether large or complex systems can be effectively decomposed into more manageable components. The decomposition of large and complex systems into multiple components or subsystems facilitates accomplishment of system authorization activities, making them more cost-effective without diminishing the effectiveness of the exercise.

Chapter 3

Levels of Controls

A single set of controls in minimum security baseline form is not normally the answer for most organizations because of variables in system type (general support system or major application) and system sensitivity. Controls applicable to a general support system will be different for a major application and vice versa. Although management-level controls will be identical for both, as will many operational controls, many controls (i.e., incident response, integrity controls, and technical controls) will vary substantially. Because the minimum security baseline set is system nonspecific, it must be augmented by baseline security configuration standards for all technology components that make up the system. A separate set of technology-specific controls needs to be developed to ensure that industry-accepted leading security practices are employed as an extension of the minimum security baseline. These must exist for operating systems, databases, Web servers, networks, and routers, among others. Table 3.1 provides an example of platform security configuration standards.

Organizations may want to consider additional sets of security controls for more sensitive systems to provide a greater degree of protection and security in depth. Although this approach tailors control requirements to the elevated need for security a system may have, it creates additional complexity that must be considered and managed. NIST Special Publication (SP) 800-53 provides a good example of the application of controls according to system sensitivity. For instance, the three levels of controls pertaining to countering malicious code in NIST SP 800-53 according to system sensitivity are

- *Low Sensitivity*: The information system implements malicious code protection that includes a capability for automatic updates.

- *Moderate Sensitivity*: The information system implements malicious code protection that includes a capability for automatic updates. The organization centrally manages virus protection mechanisms.

- *High Sensitivity*: The information system implements malicious code protection that includes a capability for automatic updates. The information system automatically updates virus protection mechanisms.

Table 3.2 provides an example of a minimum security baseline for production input/output controls.

Selecting Baseline Controls

FIPS 200 provides minimum security requirements covering the 17 families of security controls applicable to most federal systems. These control families represent

Table 3.1 Example Best Practice Security Configuration

Test Number: 3
Test Name: SQL Servers

Site: Corporate Headquarters
Date: February 6, 2004

Resources required: All SQL servers.

Personnel required: Users with database administrator privileges for the network to be tested and a network security administrator.

Objectives: To determine if the database servers are configured correctly and securely.

Procedure description (summary): Review system settings on the SQL servers. Interview database administrators and network security administrators.

Step No.	NIST 800-26 Element ID	Procedure Description	Expected Results	Actual Results	Pass/ Fail/ NA
1	3.1.6	Verify all SQL patches, service packs, and hot fixes have been identified, installed, and tracked for each server.	All patches and service packs are up to date.	On both servers, auto update is used to install hot fixes. SQL versions are 8.00.760, which is current.	P
2	16.2.2	Is Secure Sockets Layer (SSL) or Transport Layer Security (TLS) protocol used for sensitive communications between servers and clients?	SSL or TLS is used for secure communication between the server and client.	SSL and TLS are not used because confidentiality is rated as low.	N/A
3	1.2.3	Ensure the "sa" and "probe" (SQL 6.5) accounts are secured with strong passwords and that the passwords are stored in a secure location. Note: The probe account is used for performance analysis and distributed transactions. Assigning a password to this account can break functionality when used in standard security mode.	The "sa" and "probe" accounts are secured with strong passwords, and the passwords are stored in a secure location.	On both servers, the "sa" account has a strong password, and the password is stored in a secure location. The probe account does not exist.	

Chapter 3

Table 3.2   Example of a Minimum Security Baseline

Production Input/Output Controls

8.1 Is there user support?

    8.1.1   Is there a help desk or group that offers advice? (NIST SP 800-18)

8.2 Are there media controls?

    8.2.1   Are there processes to ensure that unauthorized individuals cannot read, copy, alter, or steal printed or electronic information? (NIST SP 800-18)

    8.2.2   Are there processes for ensuring that only authorized users pick up, receive, or deliver input and output information and media? (NIST SP 800-18)

    8.2.3   Are audit trails used for receipt of sensitive inputs/outputs? (NIST SP 800-18)

    8.2.4   Are controls in place for transporting or mailing media or printed output? (NIST SP 800-18)

    8.2.5   Is there internal/external labeling for sensitivity? (NIST SP 800-18)

    8.2.6   Is there external labeling with special handling instructions? (NIST SP 800-18)

    8.2.7   Are audit trails kept for inventory management? (NIST SP 800-18)

    8.2.8   Is media sanitized for reuse? Federal Information System Controls Audit Manual (FISCAM AC-3.4, NIST SP 800-18)

    8.2.9   Is damaged media stored or destroyed? (NIST SP 800-18)

    8.2.10 Is hard-copy media shredded or destroyed when no longer needed? (NIST SP 800-18)

a broad-based, balanced foundation for selection of controls for system-level implementation. Although FIPS 200 is mandatory for government agencies and there are no provisions for waivers of its requirements, security controls themselves can be tailored and adjusted as described further in this chapter to more clearly meet the needs of the agency or of a particular information system. To be effective, agency-level minimum security baselines have to be realistic. They should be grounded in actual business needs based on a systematic review of risks to an organization's resources through a high-level risk assessment and as identified over an extended period of time (several years of operation). An initial high-level, enterprise-wide risk assessment will determine which assets need to be protected, what they need to be protected from, and to what degree the assets should be protected. This initial review should serve as the basis for selecting an industry-accepted minimum security baseline set in its entirety, in creating a wholly new set for the organization, or in customizing an existing minimum security baseline for use within the organization. Recently, NIST provided updated guidance on the security control selection process, which is described in detail at the end of this chapter.

Minimum security baselines can be developed from external sources, such as International Organization for Standardization 27002, NIST SP 800-53, and so on. For example, NIST SP 800-53 is currently employed government-wide as the accepted minimum security baseline standard. Table 3.2 provides an example. SP 800-53 provides graduated controls for systems at all levels of sensitivity. Minimum security baselines provide a comprehensive, integrated set of controls that is accepted by large numbers of organizations for use in setting standards for themselves. Because organizations are responsible for determining the appropriate level of security for their systems, they may consider developing minimum security baselines entirely on their own. In such cases, one of these common standards should be used as the starting point for developing a hybrid organization-specific set of minimum security baselines, or at least a review of the hybrid set should be made against at least two of the common standards. Any generally accepted minimum security baseline should be modified to incorporate business needs stemming from various other sources. This would include incorporation of controls mandated by regulatory requirements such as the Health Insurance Portability and Accountability Act (HIPAA) and the Gramm–Leach–Bliley Act (GLBA). In addition, baselines should be updated to incorporate recent guidance that has not yet been addressed into published baselines. For instance, the Office of Management and Budget (OMB) frequently publishes security-related requirements, which are not normally incorporated into NIST SP 800-53 until the next annual revision is released, or in some cases may not be included in an update at all because of their specific nature (e.g., the e-authentication requirements of M-04-04). Minimum baseline controls should take into account organization policies, management statements and strategies, contracts, laws, operational rules, legal obligations, privacy needs, proprietary and trade secret requirements, and other governing regulations. The authority for the minimum security baseline sets is an important consideration. When they have been approved by the highest management levels in the organization, which have directed their implementation, then they are far less likely to be questioned when the cost of implementing minimum controls is discovered. Management acceptance of the controls provides stronger justification for requesting resources for corrective actions. In addition, external auditors are more prone to accept as adequate the minimum security baselines fully underwritten by management as adequate and those that have been developed based on industry-accepted best practices.

The complexity and comprehensiveness of the controls set should be driven by the organization's ability to implement them and its commitment to enforcing compliance with them. Defining the minimum security baseline set too stringently will lead to the organization wasting resources in a quest to achieve unrealistic security goals. If the organization sets its control requirements too low, then the minimum security baseline approach will fail because the controls will not provide sufficient protection against common threats to its resources. If the organization establishes a program requiring a set of stringent controls that looks good on paper but fails to build an accompanying enforcement mechanism, the effects likely will be worse than having done nothing at all because a false sense of security on the part of management and a disregard of security by system owners will be the likely outcomes. Minimum security baselines need to be sufficiently detailed to allow their application across the entire organization and also must be specific enough to be clearly understood by those charged with their implementation. For cases when a system owner considers the baseline to be inapplicable to his or her system (perhaps the system has already been certified under a more stringent set of standards), a formal exception process should be available to document and approve noncompliance with the baseline standard. However, this process only applies to application for exemption of compliance with the minimum security baseline set in its entirety. Addressing nonapplicability of individual baseline controls is part of the normal certification process described in the following discussion.

To ensure that a set of controls is identified that can adequately protect the largest proportion of its systems, an enterprise risk assessment needs to be conducted. This broad-based approach will provide a solid foundation for constructing the right set of minimum security baselines. At a high level, the risk assessment will assess the assets to be protected and probable threats that may have an impact on the resources. The assessment should then focus on identification of the controls that will provide protection to organization assets, irrespective of existing, in-place controls. Although the application of minimum security baselines is assessed as part of the certification of each system, the minimum security baseline set must be continually evaluated and updated on an enterprise-wide basis. Significant changes in the organization's processing environment, user community, business operations, or operating locations may very well necessitate changes in the minimum security baselines. The enterprise information security function should also review all system-level system authorization documentation to identify trends that may affect the minimum security baseline set. For example, findings that show numerous privileged users have not been screened to the appropriate level of trust will indicate that a reassessment of the organization's standards for personnel security is warranted; review of certification results may show that systems in development are not ready to be placed into production due to lack of system security controls, and this makes it likely that a lack of integration of security into the system development life-cycle methodology exists. Perhaps there will be recommendations for updating the organization's minimum security baseline based on reviews of remediation plans over several review cycles. The minimum security baseline must be adjusted over a period of time—perhaps 2 to 3 years—in which incidents are measured and the threat list is updated to provide a current picture for control implementation.

Minimum security baselines must be developed to ensure that the control requirements for the organization are specified across the entire control spectrum. They must address management controls, operational controls, and technical controls. The importance of minimum security baseline cross-reference numbers must be emphasized because they form the basis for the identification of controls and weaknesses in other system authorization documentation.

Use of the Minimum Security Baseline Set

With respect to use of the minimum security baseline with individual information systems, it serves as the starting point for selection of security controls specific to the system. The control selection process begins with the categorization of the system and selecting the control baseline applicable to the categorization of the system (high, moderate, or low). NIST SP 800-53 provides a "security control catalog" for systems at each level. The information system owner (ISO) must then apply a risk-based approach to his or her selection of specific controls considering effectiveness, efficiency, and constraints resulting from applicable laws, directives, executive orders, policies, standards, or regulations that are not addressed in the minimum security baseline control set (for instance, OMB memos, such as those included in Appendix A). This adjustment of controls is known as tailoring and results in refinement of the baseline control set to identify a set of system-specific controls that are based on an assessment of risk and local conditions, address organization- and system-specific threat information, cost-benefit analysis, special circumstances, and the availability of compensating controls. This revised control baseline is then documented in the system security plan along with justification for any refinements, adjustments, or variations from the initial minimum security baseline. The justification for tailoring of security controls should map to the recommendations of the risk assessment.

When performing a minimum security baseline assessment, it is important to use the baseline set in its entirety to record the system's compliance with the entire breadth of controls. Elimination of an entire section because it is not applicable to the system will merely give rise to questions that will have to be answered later. A better approach is to regard the minimum security baseline set as an inviolate whole. Individual controls that are not applicable to the system for whatever reason should be marked as such, and a justification of why they are not applicable should be provided. And, controls that are not achievable and for which the risk of not implementing them is being accepted also need to be fully justified.

Chapter 3

Common Controls

NIST SP 800-37 encourages the identification of common controls to promote efficiency in control implementation. To reduce the cost of control implementation, agencies are encouraged to identify controls that are applicable to multiple systems. This means the protection of an information system may rely on security controls that have been implemented by other system owners or other authorities outside of his or her area of responsibility. Examples are policy-related controls, awareness training, or perimeter security controls that protect all systems within the operating environment. Common controls may apply to all systems of the organization, all systems at one location, all systems using a particular technology or service, or common systems at multiple sites. Common controls are developed by agency-level officials, most commonly the chief information security officer (CISO) and his or her staff, and are documented in organizational policy or procedures. These provide direction to ISOs regarding which controls will be implemented outside the information owner's control. The results of assessments of common controls must also be shared with the system owner, who relies on those controls so that he or she can determine the impact of weaknesses in common controls and can formulate a plan for addressing them.

In many cases, controls that would normally be categorized as common controls also require implementation action at the system level. Such controls are classified as hybrid controls since they have characteristics of both common controls and system-specific controls.

All controls must be clearly identified in the security plan for the information system. These include system-specific, common, and hybrid controls. The security plan should specify the category for each control.

Observations

The employment of minimum security baselines provides an organization with a mechanism for ensuring that a minimally acceptable security posture is established. They provide a benchmark for system owners to aim to achieve. However, minimum security baselines are only a starting point, and their effectiveness can only be ensured if they are tailored to the specific needs of an information system. As long as this condition can be met, and as long as they can be applied to the entire organization, adoption of minimum security baselines is a viable part of the system authorization process. Establishment of minimum security baselines, which have as their foundation generally accepted security practices, provides a convincing argument that the organization has exercised due care in the implementation of security controls to protect its information systems.

Assessing Risk

This section describes risk assessment as part of an overall system authorization process. It is therefore not intended to be an in-depth exploration of risk assessment. In the context of the overall system authorization process, risk assessment determines or verifies requirements for minimizing risks to the system. These requirements are expressed as controls, and risks are expressed in terms of vulnerabilities paired with threats.

According to NIST SP 800-30, "risk is a function of the likelihood of a given threat-source's exercising a particular potential vulnerability and the resulting impact of that adverse event on the organization." This chapter describes the steps involved in assessing risk through the identification of paired threats and vulnerabilities and the likelihood and the impact of their occurrence.

Risk assessment can range from highly complex efforts resulting in very precise quantitative results to a simple exercise conducted by a lone, knowledgeable individual. Normally, the complexity of the risk assessment is driven by the time it requires and by the resources available to perform it. However, the primary driver should actually be the level of precision demanded by the system being analyzed.

The risk assessment information described is consistent with recent guidance provided by NIST in SP 800-37, Revision 1, pertaining to application of the Risk Management Framework to information systems, in particular to Task 2-2 regarding the assessment of risks when selecting security controls (described further in this chapter). In addition, this updated guidance also provides a framework for linkage of information system risks to mission/business processes and organization-level risks (see Chapter 1).

Background

In judging how risk assessment can be effectively integrated into an enterprise system authorization program, it is a good idea first to look at issues that have hampered full-scale acceptance of risk assessment for information technology systems over the years.

Chapter 3

■ *Scalability*: In the past, risk assessment came in one size, one flavor: big. Although there may have been an appetite for a sundae, only a banana split could be ordered—and an expensive banana split at that. Every system that was thought for various reasons to need risk assessment received the banana split treatment. Systems that were not considered to be worthy of the banana split treatment were simply not subjected to risk assessment at all. One size fit all, and it was expensive. Because security budgets were small, risk assessment efforts normally incorporated only a small number of systems each year and made little provision for updating these assessments once they were initially completed. Of course, in a centralized, mainframe-based processing environment, focusing on the primary information technology resources generally worked fine because all systems processed in the same environment. However, with decentralization, all bets were off. Risk assessment methodology needed to change to accommodate the move away from centralized processing. But, for a long time it did not and still to some degree has not. In many circles, a risk assessment methodology most appropriate for a data center or enterprise-wide application is still being shoehorned into use for an office automation system, local-area network (LAN), or an application with limited functionality and applicability. A more cost-effective and practical approach tailors the risk assessment level of effort to the sensitivity of the system that calls for it.

■ *Terminology*: Another problem with old-school risk assessments is that no one could understand them other than those who wrote them. Their use of odd terminology (annual loss expectancy (ALE), single loss expectancy (SLE), etc.), their complicated formulas, and their heft convinced managers that risk assessment was more magic than science. This led them to discount the usefulness of risk assessment reports, and if used at all, managers would only make use of the safeguard recommendations that they understood and had resources to address. So, nothing ever happened other than being able to say that a risk assessment of the system had been conducted.

■ *Automated Tools*: Tools were developed to support the laborious task of analyzing risk, and they greatly eased the process. However, most organizations were unable really to take ownership of the automated process because a great deal of knowledge of information technology security theory and practice was required to use them, and paid consultants were most often called on to use the tools. With the coming of the facilitated risk assessment process (FRAP) and other approaches that aimed at ease of application, many organizations got risk assessment religion again because these new methodologies offered practical approaches to assessing information technology systems in an understandable way. Although these methodologies still required outside help to learn how to perform them, they proved to be relatively inexpensive and led to more systems being assessed than before their advent.

Risk Assessment in System Authorization

The level of effort required to conduct a risk assessment of a given system must fit the situation. Because this has not always been the case with system authorization, a new approach is warranted. System security authorization has traditionally been hindered or at least has not been effectively supported by realistic risk assessment efforts and methodologies. The risk assessment must present a realistic and concise picture of which assets need to be protected, which events threaten those assets, which vulnerabilities in security controls are of concern, and which safeguards should be considered for implementation. The risk assessment must successfully unveil these things clearly; if it cannot, the results of the risk assessment will be discounted, and the effort will have failed.

As part of a system authorization process that emphasizes tailoring effort to need (i.e., matching supply to demand) to be cost effective, the risk assessment must be cleanly integrated into the overall system authorization process to be worthwhile. Asset identification must be tied to the system description and environment definition; vulnerability assessment must be connected to minimum security baselines as a start; and safeguard recommendations must match remediation plans.

When implemented as part of a comprehensive system authorization process, the primary purpose of the risk assessment is to refine minimum security baseline controls to fit the need for the system's protection. This means that the relationship between system assets, threats, and vulnerabilities is used to tailor the initial set of controls established for the system to ensure it provides adequate protection for system resources. The risk assessment in this context looks for minimum security baseline controls that are applicable, and it identifies and justifies additional or alternative controls necessary above those called for in the minimum security baseline. For instance, the system may be subject to federal directives that call for controls that are not in the standard minimum security baseline. Using this approach, the risk assessment serves as the foundation for defining how the system should be protected. It can also be used to document risks that management should accept so that corrective action is not wasted on the mitigation of costly risks that have little realistic impact on the system. The results of the risk assessment must identify and justify recommendations for risks that should be accepted, and the system authorization process must ensure that these are carried forward into the plan of action and milestones.

The Risk Assessment Process

The risk assessment process consists of nine distinct steps: system characterization, threat identification, vulnerability identification, control analysis, likelihood determination, impact analysis, risk determination, control recommendations, and results documentation. Each step depends on the results of the previous step. Steps in the risk assessment process are defined in the following sections.

Step 1: System Characterization

The first step in the risk assessment process is system characterization. Activities performed during this step include definition of the system type (general support system, major application, enterprise, facility, business unit, process, etc.), establishment of the system scope, definition of system functions and purpose, development of the system boundaries, and identification of assets and information associated with the system.

System characterization is actually the starting point of the overall system authorization process in that it is the central element of the scoping exercise and system inventory process. The process of defining the system type, scope, functions, and boundaries is covered in Chapter 1, and definition of information processed by the system is addressed in Chapter 2.

System assets such as hardware, software, data, facilities, and people related to the operation of the system must be identified and documented during this step. Mainframes, servers, workstations, and attached devices and peripherals that make up the system need to be documented in the process—if not in the risk assessment itself, then in the security plan. Operating system software, application programs, databases, and utilities must be considered in asset identification. The particular data files processed by the system as well as input and output data in all forms need to be addressed. The physical facilities where processing and system use takes place need to be included as system resources, as does the user population—internal, external, and system administration. Other asset groups that should not be overlooked are intangibles such as organization or product reputation and credibility. The primary groups of information technology system assets that the risk assessment must consider are identified in Table 3.3.

Information required for the system characterization step may be gathered via questionnaire, interview, automated analysis tool, and document review. The results of this step allow for a complete picture of the information system environment and delineation of its boundaries

Step 2: Threat Identification

Threat identification should document threats that apply to the system as well as the potential motives that might lead to attacks. However, the step should concentrate

Table 3.3 Examples of Asset Groups
• Application software • Data • Database programs • Documentation (plans, procedures, hardware/software documentation) • Environmental systems (fire detection/suppression, temperature/humidity controls, drainage systems) • Facilities • Hardware and equipment • Intangibles (credibility, reputation, trust) • Operating system software • Personnel • Security software • Security systems (badge system, access control systems, closed-circuit TV systems) • Telecommunications equipment (cabling, routers, switches, gateways, bridges, etc.) • Utility programs

only on those threats that are realistic in the context of the system's purpose and functionality. For example, if the system does not process confidential information, then threats related to the disclosure of information will not apply. To make the threat identification process easier to perform, categorizing threats can be helpful. Normally, threats are labeled as environmental or human, internal or external, and intentional or accidental. The methodology must include a master list of threats that can be pared down to fit the system's environment. Table 3.4 provides an example of a threat list.

Sources of information that relate to this step include the history of attacks on the system itself; threat experiences from interconnected systems, from systems with similar functionality and purpose, and from systems operating the same technologies; data from other government agencies; threat information from intelligence agencies; and threat reports gleaned from open media sources. The output of the threat identification step is a threat statement that contains a list of threat sources that could potentially exploit vulnerabilities in system security controls.

Step 3: Vulnerability Identification

The goal of the vulnerability identification step is to create a list of system vulnerabilities (i.e., flaws or weaknesses) that might be exploited by the potential threats identified in the previous risk assessment step. Methods for determining vulnerabilities vary depending on whether the system is in development or in operation. NIST maintains a database of hundreds of known vulnerabilities, and it can be used for this step. Vulnerabilities may also be determined by assessment of security controls against the

Threat Classification	Specific Threat	Primary Impacts		
		Confidentiality	Integrity	Availability
Natural	Aircraft accident			•
	Earthquake			•
	Electrical interference/ disruption			•
	Extreme temperatures			•
	Fire			•
	Flood			•
	Hurricane			•
	Lightning			•
	Tornado			•
	Windstorms			•
	Winter storm			•
Environmental	Hazardous material incident			•
	HVAC failure			•
	Hardware/software failure	•	•	•
	Illness/epidemic			•
	Power outage/failure			•
	Radiological incident			•
	Rodent/insect infestation			•
	Structural fire			•
	Substance abuse	•		•
	Transportation accident	•	•	•
Man-made	Administrative error	•	•	•
	Bomb threat			•
	Computer virus		•	•
	Disgruntled employee or citizen incident	•	•	•
	Errors/omissions (user)	•	•	•
	Industrial espionage	•		
	Intentional modification of data		•	
	Management error/ omission	•	•	•

Table 3.4 Example of a Threat List

Threat Classification	Specific Threat	Primary Impacts		
		Confidentiality	Integrity	Availability
	Theft of assets	•		•
	Unauthorized access to client facilities	•	•	•
	Unauthorized access to client system/data	•	•	•

Table 3.4 (continued) Example of a Threat List

HVAC, heating, ventilation, air-conditioning

minimum security baseline and then against existing controls paired with identified threats. These include weaknesses in management, operational, and technical controls. Any control that does not provide protection in the manner for and to the extent to which it was designed is classified as a vulnerability, and if it can be paired with a realistic threat, then it is also a risk. The minimum security baseline or some other set of control requirements serves as a reference point for judging the effectiveness of controls. This can show the weakness of and the lack of controls. Vulnerability scanning tools provide additional data on control effectiveness and should be used as well. Where the minimum security baseline lacks detail, industry standard best practices can be used to identify and evaluate technology-specific vulnerabilities. This ensures that the risk assessment identifies vulnerabilities in controls that exceed the minimum security baseline. In addition, findings from previous risk assessments and system or organization audits can highlight vulnerabilities applicable to the system. Other sources of information that are helpful in identifying vulnerabilities include results of previous risk assessments, audit findings, and results of security reviews and tests.

Vulnerability identification is only useful in the context of threats to the system. Pairing realistic threats to actual vulnerabilities results in identification of risks that management must address. How does one go about determining these pairings? There are a number of good sources from which to start this exercise, but the key is to be consistent. There may be multiple pairings for each threat and for each vulnerability. For instance, a breech in the wall of a server room causes a physical access vulnerability as well as an increased vulnerability to fire and smoke penetration of the room.

Step 4: Control Analysis

The fourth step in the risk assessment process is an analysis of current system protective controls as well as planned controls that have had resources (time and

Chapter 3

funding) applied or allocated to them. The idea here is to note the controls that are now in place (or will be in place in the near term) so that they are not included in the controls recommended in Step 8 of the process. This process must lead to the identification of both technical (safeguards built into hardware, software, and firmware) and nontechnical (procedures, policies, and practices) controls, as well as types of controls (i.e., preventive, detective, etc.). The output of the control analysis is a list of current or planned controls for the information system intended to mitigate the likelihood of a vulnerability occurring and to reduce its potential impact.

Step 5: Likelihood Determination

The next risk assessment step results in a determination of the likelihood of the threat/vulnerability pair's occurrence. To determine the likelihood of the occurrence of a given threat/vulnerability pairing, factors such as threat motivation and capability, nature of the vulnerability, and effectiveness of current controls must be assessed. Likelihood can be expressed in either quantitative or qualitative terms. For most systems, it will be sufficient to use "high," "medium," and "low" terminology relative to each security impact category (confidentiality, integrity, availability). On the most sensitive systems, actual frequencies by measurement of increments of time (i.e., annual expectancy) may be necessary. The result of this step is a likelihood rating for each threat/vulnerability pair.

Step 6: Impact Analysis

Step 6 in the risk assessment process is analysis of the impact of threat/vulnerability pairings should they occur. This step identifies the effect of a successful exploitation of a vulnerability on the ability of the agency to accomplish its mission. This is a function of the criticality of the system and the sensitivity of the data (see Chapter 2). Note that the focus here is on the high-level agency mission impact rather than on the impact on the operation of the system or the impact on the organizational subelement the system supports. As with the likelihood determination, results of impact analysis can be expressed in either quantitative or qualitative terms, but for most systems, it is sufficient to use high, medium, and low terminology for each security impact category (confidentiality, integrity, availability). Highly sensitive, highly critical systems may require measurement of impact in potential dollar loss. The results of the impact analysis is an impact rating for each threat/vulnerability pairing that takes into consideration of confidentiality, integrity, and availability impacts.

Step 7: Risk Determination

The objective of Step 7 is to determine the seriousness of the risk to the organization. In this step, risk is calculated for each threat/vulnerability pair by assessing the impact and likelihood of losses to data confidentiality, integrity, and availability. NIST SP 800-30 details a risk assessment process, which assigns a numerical score for high, moderate, and low impacts and the probability of occurrence for each of these three security components. Potential scores for each threat/vulnerability pair range from 0 to 300, with scores below 100 considered to be low risks, scores over 200 to be high risks, and all scores in between judged to be moderate risks. This is one practical approach that can be performed by a system owner without difficulty (if he or she has a few hours to concentrate on the task without the phone ringing). Such an approach easily lends itself also to automation. Use of this approach allows one to readily identify the most significant risks to the system as starting points for safeguard selection and implementation of corrective actions. A sample risk matrix is provided in Table 3.5.

The results of the risk determination step will be a listing of risks along with their risk level, similar to the matrix shown in Table 3.5.

Step 8: Control Recommendations

Step 8 in the risk assessment process recommends appropriate controls that are needed to protect the system. To determine what is appropriate, a cost-benefit analysis is conducted on all recommended controls to ensure that the cost of implementing the control is justified by the reduction in the level of risk. The goal of this step is to recommend controls that will reduce the risk to the system and its data to an acceptable level. Recommendations must be specific to the system, detailed enough to allow them to be understood, and practical enough to make them cost effective. If controls are too costly, hamper system use, or do not provide adequate return on investment, the recommendation should consider management's role in accepting risk. Cost-effectiveness of controls should be a key consideration in the selection process, but one cannot forget the overriding principle of asset protection in the process. Because the use of a minimum security baseline is the foundation of the system authorization process described in this volume, the primary focus of the risk assessment is to verify the adequacy of minimum security baseline controls and to recommend changes: additional controls, alternative controls, or decreased controls. Even in this context, risk assessment continues to perform its traditional role of

Chapter 3

Table 3.5 Example of a Risk Matrix

| Question | Vulnerability | Threat | Status I, P, NI, Accept Risk | Availability (Denial of Service) | | Integrity (Destruction and Modification) | | Confidentiality (Disclosure) | | Risk Factor | Risk |
				Likelihood High = 1 Med = 0.5 Low = 0.1	Impact High = 100 Med = 50 Low = 10	Likelihood High = 1 Med = 0.5 Low = 0.1	Impact High = 100 Med = 50 Low = 10	Likelihood High = 1 Med = 0.5 Low = 0.1	Impact High = 100 Med = 50 Low = 10	High (201–300) Med (101–200) Low (1–100)	
166	11.2.4 Integrity verification programs are not used by the application to look for evidence of data tampering, errors, and omissions (NIST SP 800-18)	Data integrity loss/ modification	NI	0.1	50	1	100	0.1	50	110	Moderate
170	11.2.8 Penetration testing is not performed on the system (NIST SP 800-18)	Hacking/social engineering	NI	0.5	50	0.5	100	0.5	100	125	Moderate

		NI	1	100	1	100	0.5	100	250	High
177	12.1.5 There are no software and hardware testing procedures and results (NIST SP 800-18)	Data integrity loss/modification	NI	1	100	1	100	0.5	100	250	High
178	12.1.6 There are no standard operating procedures for all the topic areas covered in this document (NIST SP 800-18)	Human threats	NI	0.5	50	0.5	50	0.1	50	55	Low
190	13.1.2 Employee training and professional development is not documented and monitored (FISCAM SP-4.2)	User errors/omissions	NI	0.5	50	0.1	10	0.1	10	27	Low

Chapter 3

determining control requirements through safeguard selection. That is, risks serve as the primary drivers for control recommendations.

The results of the control recommendations step is a list of recommended controls. This also includes quantifying control costs in either qualitative (e.g., high, moderate, or low) or quantitative terms (i.e., dollars and man-hours).

This step is often confused with Step 4. However, this step focuses on recommending additional controls to reduce the residual risk to an acceptable level, whereas Step 4 documents controls that are already in place or are in the process of being implemented. Step 4 is necessary to prevent the waste of resources by identifying the same control twice.

Step 9: Results Documentation

The results documentation step of the risk assessment process is to document the formal report or briefing that outlines the threats and vulnerabilities, measures the risk, and provides recommendations for control implementation. The output of this step is the risk assessment report or report on risk. It is the policy of many organizations to include the risk assessment as an appendix to the system security plan.

Conducting the Risk Assessment

The risk assessment team should include members of the organization who have knowledge of the value of information technology assets, threats to them, the posture of and vulnerabilities in security controls, and the information technology security program and operations. These personnel can provide the most current data necessary to calculate risks to the system. The involvement of these individuals is particularly important when outside consultants are engaged to perform the risk assessment. The use of consultants can be beneficial when the organization lacks risk assessment expertise or when it cannot afford to dedicate its own experts to the effort. Consultants can also provide a degree of independence that organizational personnel cannot, and on those grounds, their recommendations may be easier for management to accept.

A successful risk assessment effort depends on current and reliable data. This is done by asking the right questions of the right people, by being aware of the most current sources of information, and by having knowledge of the system being assessed. The most valuable information is gained from personnel using the system from organization management, from reports generated by the system, from audits and incident reports, and with external data from local, regional, and national sources. The user community of the system is most familiar with current practices, system operations, system security features, and weaknesses in controls. System management personnel who are most aware of the sensitivity of the system can provide a historical view of incidents, threats, and vulnerabilities. Of course, personnel can only be valuable sources of risk-related information if the right questions are asked by risk assessment team members skilled in interview techniques. The team should prepare an interview matrix that first identifies the type of information needed mapped to the general identification of who can best provide this information. A sample interview matrix is provided in Table 3.6.

In coordination with the system owner, this matrix can be fleshed out to include the names of specific personnel that need to be interviewed. For each type of information sought, a standard interview questionnaire should be prepared to guide the interviewer, particularly if the person conducting the interview is not overly familiar with the system being analyzed. However, this should only be a guide, and interviewers must know the meaning of the questions they are asking and must have general knowledge of the system to be able to relate the questions to the specific system being analyzed. Advance knowledge of the system should be based on a review of documentation requested early in the risk assessment effort. System descriptions, data descriptions, design documents, policies and procedures, user manuals, organization charts, building layouts, audits and inspections, process flows, hardware/software inventories, and network diagrams should be requested in advance to allow the risk assessment team to familiarize itself before interviews begin. In addition to interview results, this documentation will provide the primary information for system description, asset identification, and system connectivity descriptions. It is critical that risk assessment team members have access to and make use of such data. Otherwise, organization personnel being interviewed will have to take longer than necessary to describe the system, wasting valuable time and lengthening the disruption of their work. Team members must understand the importance of limiting disruption of normal activities only within reason. To limit the amount of time required for data collection, facilitation can be effectively employed. The FRAP approach greatly speeds up the collection of good risk assessment data and minimizes the impact of the collection effort on the hosting organization.

It may be impossible to obtain all information helpful in analyzing risk to the system. It is important to know, however, when enough information has been obtained to avoid a prolonged effort chasing peripheral information with little value to the primary objective at hand. Therefore, the team needs to know what information

Chapter 3

Table 3.6 Example of an Interview Matrix	
Position	**Interview Topics**
System owner	• System description
	• System sensitivity
	• System criticality
	• System interconnectivity
	• Security drivers
	• Security incidents
	• Threats/vulnerabilities
	• Management controls
	• Operational controls
System administrator	• Security incidents
	• Threats/vulnerabilities
	• Operational controls
	• Technical controls
ISSO	• Threats/vulnerabilities
	• System sensitivity
	• Security incidents
	• Management controls
	• Operational controls
	• Technical controls
Database administrator	• Operational controls
Application programmer	• Operational controls
	• Technical controls
Facility manager/physical security	• Operational controls
	• Technical controls
User	• Operational controls
	• Technical controls
Personnel security officer	• Operational controls
Executive management	• System criticality
	• Threats/vulnerabilities

is essential and cannot be omitted in the interest of time, lack of cooperation of personnel, or paucity of documentation. The minimum essential information for the risk assessment relates to asset, threat, and vulnerability identification. The data-gathering effort should focus on those three main areas of information as the basis for further analysis. The team should not cease data collection activities until it has enough data to understand what the system is designed to do, the kind of data it processes, how it works, system inputs and outputs, hardware and software components, the user community, and facilities where the system resides and is used. Historical threat-related data is essential for determining threat impacts and likelihood. In all likelihood, this will be obtained through interviews. Finally, a complete inventory of vulnerabilities in security controls should be considered essential to the data collection effort.

Often, it is not possible to collect all information needed during the scheduled data collection period, and follow-up telephone coordination must be conducted after the fact. However, a face-to-face interview is far more effective and fruitful because it permits the analyst to probe into initial answers to identify associated issues, and every effort should be made to try to obtain information firsthand. For instance, when the person being interviewed nervously states that system security controls are reviewed "periodically," follow-up probing may reveal that the most recent review was conducted 18 months previously. Only in a personal interview can the impact of nonverbal communications be assessed.

When conducting risk assessments of large and complex systems, the use of automated tools can ease the effort substantially. Tools such as OCTAVE® and RiskWatch® standardize data collection, automate the risk assessments described, and produce reliable quantitative results.

Risk Categorization

Depending on the needs the user may have, risks can be categorized according to the assets to which they relate, by related threat, by vulnerability, by associated safeguard, by threat impact, or by threat frequency. The only limitation is the ease with which the collected risk assessment data can be generated into lists. Housing risk assessment data in a relational database provides the greatest degree of flexibility in categorizing risks.

Documenting Risk Assessment Results

The risk assessment report documents all activities performed during the risk assessment. The report should not be so complex that it cannot be easily understood by a reader not familiar with the system. It should define terms and definitions as well as the methodology used in conducting the assessment. The level of detail contained in the report needs to correspond to the sensitivity of the system. The report should allow the results to be used by management in selecting controls that are most appropriate to the sensitivity of and risks to the system, allowing implementation of controls that are cost effective. Therefore, risks must be ranked specific to the system according to their severity to allow the most cost-effective controls to be chosen. Because executive management is the target audience of the report, the report should make extensive use of risk summary information and graphics to highlight information. A sample risk assessment format is provided in Appendix N.

Using the Risk Assessment

The results of the risk assessment should provide the system owner and authorizing official sufficient information to identify potential problems before they occur so that mitigation activities may be planned or undertaken as needed throughout the life of the system. A system-level risk assessment should support the assessment requirements of the certification phase and the accreditation phase, as well as the mitigation and evaluation requirements of the continuous monitoring phase.

Overview of NIST Special Publication 800-30, Revision 1

The initial public draft of NIST SP 800-30, Revision 1, Guide for Conducting Risk Assessments, was published by NIST in September 2011 to provide updated guidance for conducting risk assessments. It was developed in partnership with the Department of Defense, the intelligence community, NIST, and the Committee on National Security Systems and consequently provides updated risk assessment guidance applicable to all communities of the federal government.

Since NIST SP 800-39 now serves as the authoritative source for comprehensive risk management guidance, the initial public draft of SP 800-30 changes the original risk management guideline focus of SP 800-30. It now focuses entirely on the subject of assessing risk, the second step in the risk management process described in NIST SP 800-39. This step addresses assessment of risk in the context of the overall organization.

The update does not change the primary purpose of the risk assessment, which remains the identification of

- *Threats* to organizations (i.e., operations, assets, or individuals) or threats directed through organizations against other organizations or the nation;
- *Vulnerabilities* internal and external to organizations;
- *Harm* (i.e., adverse impact) to organizations that may occur given the potential for threats exploiting vulnerabilities; and

- *Likelihood* that harm will occur.

And as before, the process results in a determination of risk, which is the degree of harm and likelihood of harm occurring.

The updated version describes a three-step risk assessment process of preparation, execution, and maintenance activities. It also describes how to apply the process with all three tiers of the risk management hierarchy (*organization, mission/business process,* and *information system* levels) as part of an overall risk management process. It is constructed as a practical, "how to" guide to risk assessment as a useful set of templates, tables, and assessment scales is provided to facilitate ease of use in performing risk assessment activities.

Five of the risk assessment steps described in the previous version (threat identification, vulnerability identification, likelihood determination, impact analysis, and risk determination) have been included as risk assessment tasks in the update, and all are now part of the *conduct risk assessment* step of the process. However, the system characterization step has now been replaced by five new tasks in the step to *prepare for risk assessment*. Finally, a new step in the process (*maintain risk assessment*) consisting of two tasks has been added to the process. The process described in Revision 1 is summarized in the following table:

Summary of Risk Assessment Tasks (NIST SP 800-30, Revision 1, September 2011)		
Task	**Title**	**Description**
Step 1: Prepare for Risk Assessment		
1-1	Identify purpose	Identify the purpose of the risk assessment in terms of the information the assessment is intended to produce and the decisions the assessment is intended to support.
1-2	Identify scope	Identify the scope of the risk assessment in terms of organizational applicability, time frame supported, and architectural/technology considerations.
1-3	Identify assumptions and constraints	Identify the specific assumptions and constraints under which the risk assessment is conducted.
1-4	Identify information sources	Identify the sources of threat, vulnerability, and impact information to be used in the risk assessment.
1-5	Define risk model	Define (or refine) the risk model to be used in the risk assessment.

Chapter 3

Step 2: Conduct Risk Assessment

2-1	Identify threat sources	Identify and characterize the threat sources of concern to the organization, including the nature of the threats and, for adversarial threats, capability, intent, and targeting characteristics.
2-2	Identify threat events	Identify potential threat events, relevance to the organization, and the threat sources that could initiate the events.
2-3	Identify vulnerabilities and predisposing conditions	Identify vulnerabilities and predisposing conditions that affect the likelihood that threat events of concern result in adverse impacts to the organization.
2-4	Determine likelihood	Determine the likelihood that threat events of concern result in adverse impact to the organization, considering (a) the characteristics of the threat sources that could initiate the events; (b) the vulnerabilities and predisposing conditions identified; and (c) organizational susceptibility reflecting safeguards/countermeasures planned or implemented to impede such events.
2-5	Determine impact	Determine the adverse impact to the organization from threat events of concern considering (a) the characteristics of the threat sources that could initiate the events; (b) the vulnerabilities and predisposing conditions identified; and (c) organizational susceptibility reflecting the safeguards/countermeasures planned or implemented to impede such events.
2-6	Determine risk	Determine the risk to the organization from threat events of concern considering (a) the impact that would result from the events and (b) the likelihood of the events occurring.

Step 3: Maintain Risk Assessment

3-1	Monitor risk factors	Conduct ongoing monitoring of the factors that contribute to changes in risk to organizational operations and assets, individuals, other organizations, or the nation.
3-2	Update risk assessment	Update existing risk assessment using the results from ongoing monitoring of risk factors.

Observations

For the purpose of system authorization, risk assessment must validate the applicability of the minimum set of security controls chosen for the system to determine if they are appropriate. The results should therefore substantiate the need for additional controls, alternative controls, or fewer controls. The findings of the risk assessment allow prioritization of corrective actions recorded in the remediation plan to allow resources to be applied to mitigate the highest-risk weaknesses cost effectively. Performance of risk assessment as a part of an integrated system authorization allows the definition of how and in what order it will be performed and allows its results to be cleanly incorporated into other security documentation. These features permit the risk assessment to serve as a practical process rather than black art.

System Security Plans

Security plans are necessary because they provide a single reference for defining how a system needs to be secured and how it is secured. A good security plan facilitates the review of system security controls to determine its current security posture. The security plan permits the identification of resources required to secure the system, and the plan documents controls that work as well as those that do not. All this information needs to be identified in writing rather than stored in someone's head, as is often the case. Well-written security plans support oversight, planning, budgeting, and compliance requirements for the system. However, security plans addressed in this section relate to information technology systems, and these plans should not be confused with program-level plans that are often mistakenly referred to by the same name.

Applicability

In the federal government, security plans are required. But, does the fact that they predominate in government circles translate to them being impractical for nongovernment systems? As you might expect, my answer is no. Security plans both inside and outside government can be helpful in implementing controls at the system level to form a coherent security architecture. They can also be used to drive development efforts, and finally in both public and private sectors security plans serve to integrate controls not only enterprise-wide but also at the system level, where integration is necessary to ensure there are no gaps in control boundaries. OMB Circular A-130's categorization of system-level controls into management, operational, and technical control categories is practical for application with all systems, making this approach useful to the masses.

Responsibility

Now that I have stated my case that security plans are useful and important, the next issue to resolve is who should develop them. Obviously, it should be someone who is familiar with the system—what it is designed to do, how it operates, how it is constructed, and how it is secured. The system owner, as with everything else related to the system, is responsible for security planning, which includes documenting the plan. However, the owner may want to delegate this task to his or her information system security officer (ISSO), assuming that an ISSO has been appointed for the system. The plan will take both time to prepare and detailed information gathering, and the ISSO will probably be more available to perform such duties. The system owner may want to consider using contractors to develop the security plan, particularly if he or she requires them for multiple systems. This ensures consistency. However, the time necessary to train contractor personnel and to familiarize them with the systems will extend the duration of the initiative, as will the effort required to approve their methodologies, to supervise them, and to review their work.

Plan Contents

A well-written security plan provides all the information necessary to describe the security posture of a system against a set of control requirements. The contents of the security plan normally must include the following categories of information related to the design, operation, and security of an information system:

- *System Description*: The security plan describes what the system does and the business process it supports. It defines the system environment in a clear and understandable way, using both text and graphics as necessary. This will include a listing of system hardware components and software products that make up the system and how they are configured. The plan will document data flows into and out of the system and interconnections with other systems. The system description will include a description of the organization and user community that is supported. This will identify the locations and sites where the components and users are situated. Means of access must be described, such as dial-up, VPN (virtual private network), wireless, dedicated connection, and the like. The system description should specify the operational status of the system and planned changes to the system environment. Process flowcharts can be helpful in defining data input and output. The type of data processed by the system should also be included in the plan. Components and products whose primary function is to protect system data should be given emphasis in the system description. Firewalls, secure gateways, antivirus products, intrusion detection systems, and vulnerability scanning tools need to be highlighted. For the user community, the clearance level, category of clearance, and need-to-know levels should be defined. Facilities where equipment and users are located also should be described from a security perspective.

- *Description of Controls*: The purpose of a good system description is to allow all necessary controls to be described in the plan. Controls can be taken from a number of sources, such as NIST Special Publications 800-18 and 800-53 and International Organization for Standardization 27002. These are addressed elsewhere in Chapter 3. The description of controls must include control requirements and the implementation status of each control. Details for each control should identify if controls are fully in place or not. Controls that have not been implemented need to be justified in full, and plans for future implementation need to be stipulated. When using a standard set of controls to format the plan, controls that are not applicable to the system should be specified as such and should be identified with a justification of why the control does not apply. This is superior to merely deleting the nonapplicable control. Once again, the control must be described in terms of the system to include the "who," "what," "why," "where," "when," and "how." For example, it is not adequate to state that changes to an operational system will be documented. Rather, the security plan should specify that the system administrator will record all changes in operating system software as specified in the system's change control procedures document. Security control documentation contained in the system security plan need not be quantified. That is, it is normally unnecessary to state that the control is green, amber, or red, or that there is a high, medium, or low degree of compliance. The standard for the control is either met or not met. Controls that have not been implemented should be categorized as planned and should strictly map to remedial actions identified in the plan of action and milestones (Chapter 4).

- *System Security Roles and Responsibilities*: The plan is used to document the roles and responsibilities for security of the system. The name, title, office, major organization, address, phone number, and e-mail address for each individual named in this section of the plan must be provided. Ideally, the plan will identify the system owner, security officer, system administrator, line of business security manager, database administrator, approving authority, user population, and developer involved in the maintenance of the system. Other roles referred to in Chapter 1 should be considered for inclusion in the security plan.

- *Security-Related Business Drivers*: The plan should include a section that identifies external requirements that drive security controls. This section should identify all legal, operational, contractual, regulatory, and statutory requirements that call for protection of the system or its data. When necessary, the specific requirements should be annotated for each source. For example, the security plan of a system that processes data that is governed by the Privacy Act of 1974 not only should cite that reference, but also should specify that the confidentiality of such data will be protected by output labeling controls.

■ *Information Categories*: All categories of information processed by the system should be included in the plan following the guidance provided in Chapter 2. For each category, a brief description of the severity of impacts should be documented. Associated with the category of information is the sensitivity of information, which must be specified in the plan. This information is drawn from the system inventory (Chapter 1) and from the system sensitivity review described previously in this chapter. The security plan should fully document why the system needs to be protected in terms of its confidentiality, integrity, and availability requirements.

■ *Interconnectivity*: Next, the plan needs to document the system's interconnectivity and dependencies with respect to other systems. The plan should explain data input and output flows (both automated and manual), whether they are one-way or two-way flows, trust relationships, types of connections, and the status of formal agreements between connected systems. Whenever possible, these data flows should be graphically depicted. Refer to Chapter 1 for a discussion of coordinating security for interconnected systems. For general support systems, a listing of applications that are hosted on the system should be provided.

■ *System Certification Level*: The security plan should also be used to document decisions made regarding the certification level of effort that is necessary to provide adequate assurance of security controls. Although this will have to be determined prior to conducting the security test and evaluation, the security plan as the document of record in the certification process should also contain this information. This decision will be based primarily on the sensitivity of the system, but also may be based on internal and external exposures to threats. External exposures include the means of user access, the nature of back-end connections, and the number of users. Internal exposures include user clearance-level access approval and need to know for information processed on the system. Internal exposures are only a concern when dealing with information that is highly sensitive to disclosure. Table 3.7 provides a sample for documenting the certification level of effort to match assurance level to the sensitivity and criticality of the system.

■ *Rules of Behavior*: Rules of behavior were mandated by OMB A-130, and they are a good way for ensuring that users of all types acknowledge their responsibilities for securing the system. Hence, they are normally signed and dated by a user and are maintained on file as long as the user's account is active. Automated acknowledgment is an efficient alternative to signed, hard-copy documents as long as an audit trail exists. The rules of behavior serve as a basis for security awareness training and provide a basis for disciplinary action when rules are violated. The rules must be specific to the system to address all responsibilities that apply. Likewise, they need to be specific to the actual role the individual plays with regard to system operations. These rules of behavior can be considered agreements

Table 3.7	Example of Security Level of Effort Matrix	
Concern	**Ranking**	**Justification**
Data Sensitivity		
Confidentiality	Low	The consequences of unauthorized disclosure or compromise of data are generally acceptable. The loss of confidentiality could be expected to affect company-level interests and have some negative impact on business operations.
Integrity	Moderate	The consequences of corruption or unauthorized modification of data are only marginally acceptable. Loss of integrity could be expected to affect company-level interests adversely and degrade business operations
Availability	Low	The consequences of loss or disruption of access to system resources or to data are generally acceptable. The loss of availability could be expected to affect company-level interests and have some negative impact on business operations.
Certification Level		
Certification level (based on sensitivity "high-water mark")	Moderate	Moderate intensity, demonstration-based, independent assessment that includes: • Demonstrations to verify security control correctness and effectiveness • Functional testing • Penetration testing • Regression analysis and regression testing • Low certification level verification techniques

between the user and the system owner regarding proper use of the system. When a user understands his or her role in the protection of the system, he or she will be more likely to exercise security responsibilities. And, because users are one of the primary sources of threats to information systems, rules of behavior establish ground rules that can minimize many of the threats users pose. Appendixes I and J provide sample rules of behavior for a general support system and for a major application, respectively.

■ *Plan Development Information*: The security plan should document details regarding who developed the plan, when it was developed, the methodology used in its development, the duration of the project to develop the plan, who provided input for the plan's development, source documentation used in developing the plan, and the authority for developing the plan. This information serves as a historical reference point for future evaluation of the plan, update activities, and related efforts.

To demonstrate how the information that forms the security plan is normally presented, a sample security plan in outline form is provided in Appendix K.

What a Security Plan Is Not

One common misconception relating to security plans is that they are meant to serve as the repository for all security-related information for a system. They become gigantic in scale while becoming ever more difficult to create and impossible to use in the process. The purpose of the plan is not to prove the existence of controls. The plan should be brief and usable. It should not become a repository for security procedures or similar documentation. This is the purpose of the security handbook. The plan should merely cross-reference procedures, not include them or duplicate them. Consider using hyperlinks for such documents. On the other hand, controls must be completely described relative to the system. Only the controls of the simplest systems should be described in yes/no responses, such as for a self-assessment questionnaire. Complete answers should be documented to describe fully how the control has been implemented for the system. Who is responsible for it? When is it used? How is it implemented? What is its purpose? These questions should be answered for each and every control protecting the system or that is planned for implementation.

The purpose of the system security plan is to provide an overview of the security posture of the system. It is important to remember that the plan is a summary, or else it can evolve into a security procedures manual developed by an overzealous contractor. On the other hand, it needs to provide enough information to describe controls to allow one to understand how requirements are being met (or are failing to be met). A lack of time or emphasis is not a good excuse for a plan that does not meet this standard.

Plan Initiation

The security plan can be initiated at almost any time in the system authorization process, but it certainly needs to be finalized before the accreditation decision is made. However, remedial action should not be closely tied to completion of the plan. If vulnerabilities are identified, they should be addressed immediately rather than waiting for the plan to be finalized. Vulnerabilities can be uncovered at any time during the process, such as when preparing the security plan, conducting a baseline security assessment, or executing a security test and evaluation. There is nothing to be gained in waiting on security documentation to be completed before proceeding with corrective action, and a plan of action and milestones is not a prerequisite for remediation. Through this we see that the security plan is related to all the other documentation in the system authorization process. It should be considered a summary or overview document that brings together information from these other documents: risk information from the risk assessment, control data from the security test and evaluation, and remediation information from the plan of action and milestones.

When a security plan is prepared as part of certification, it may be necessary to prepare a draft plan early during the certification effort to define security controls, then perform interim updates following the risk assessment, and then again after the certification test is performed. However, this could result in extra, unnecessary effort and could become confusing and easily forgotten. As an alternative, it may be far more practical to wait until the conclusion of the certification process to prepare the plan. That way, one is not burdened with the need to update the plan continually at major milestones in the project.

Information Sources

As we have seen, information necessary to complete the security plan is derived from several processes completed at various stages of the entire certification methodology. Therefore, the security plan should be completed as one of the final steps in certification, or at least finalization of the plan should occur late in the process. When the plan is completed near the end of certification, then its construction should take no more than a few man-hours to consolidate the required information in a desired format. This act of consolidation and formatting should be performed by an individual who has been involved with the certification of the system and who is familiar with the information. Usually, the ISSO, system owner, or a dedicated analyst fulfills this role and prepares the system security plan. If the plan is developed apart from an overall certification process, then data collection for the effort can be expected to require from as little as 2 days for a simple system to several weeks for a complex one. Table 3.8 presents a work plan for such a project. Security plan data collection is primarily the responsibility of the system owner, who often delegates this task to the ISSO for the system or to a contractor charged with developing or updating the plan. The information necessary for the development of the plan is identified in the previous paragraphs. This information is most often recorded in existing system and organization documentation, such as requirements and design documents, system administration guides, technical architecture documentation, user guides, facility management documentation (i.e., evacuation plans, maintenance procedures), recovery plans, backup procedures, in-/out-processing procedures, and so on. When documentation such as this is not available, those charged with developing the plan must

Table 3.8 Example of a Work Plan for Security Plan Development Project			
Activity/Task	Duration	Start Date	End Date
Project preparation	5 days	Jan. 20, 2012	Jan. 24, 2012
Prepare data collection tools	2 days	Jan. 20, 2012	Jan. 21, 2012
Locate existing documentation	3 days	Jan. 22, 2012	Jan. 24, 2012
Data collection and analysis	15 days	Jan. 20, 2012	Feb. 7, 2012
Schedule interviews	2 days	Jan. 20, 2012	Jan. 21, 2012
Conduct interviews	5 days	Jan. 27, 2012	Jan. 31, 2012
Conduct minimum security baseline assessment	5 days	Jan. 27, 2012	Jan. 31, 2012
Collect follow-up information	2 days	Feb. 3, 2012	Feb. 4, 2012
Data analysis	3 days	Feb. 5, 2012	Feb. 7, 2012
Documentation	7 days	Feb. 10, 2012	Feb. 18, 2012
Prepare and submit inventory forms	1 day	Feb. 10, 2012	Feb. 10, 2012
Prepare draft system security plan	4 days	Feb. 11, 2012	Feb. 14, 2012
Prepare minimum security baseline assessment	2 days	Feb. 17, 2012	Feb. 18, 2012
Security plan submission	0 days	Mar. 19, 2012	Mar. 19, 2012
Receive comments to draft security plan	5 days	Mar. 19, 2012	Mar. 25, 2012
Develop final security plan	4 days	Mar. 25, 2012	Mar. 28, 2012
Address comments	2 days	Mar. 25, 2012	Mar. 26, 2012
Prepare final security plan	2 days	Mar. 27, 2012	Mar. 28, 2012
Submit final security plan for signature	0 days	Mar. 28, 2012	Mar. 28, 2012
Security plan approval	0 days	Mar. 31, 2012	Mar. 31, 2012

identify individuals who have knowledge of the system and its design, operations, and security and should then schedule and conduct interviews with these individuals to obtain the information.

Security Plan Development Tools

The security plan development process can be expedited through the use of automated tools. Such tools can facilitate the collection and organization of data related to system environment, operational status, data sensitivity, and control status in particular. Whatever tool is chosen, it must provide the user the flexibility to modify its parameters to suit the particular needs of the system and preferences of the preparer of the plan. The result must drive the tool, rather than the tool driving the result.

Many times, a boilerplate template, sample plan, or plan from a similar system may be used to create an initial system security plan. This can save time and may ensure completeness. It can, however, lead to inaccuracies and can limit thoughtful consideration of system controls and the system's environment. When using such helper documents, care must be taken to remove superfluous facts contained in the sample or template, and careful proofreading and review for inaccuracies is essential. The information in the plan must be precisely tailored to the system. This ensures it is not overly vague and generic. Wherever possible, individuals responsible for the control should be identified by position, the steps involved in operating the control should be listed, and details of when and where the control is employed should be provided. For example, the description of a control that calls for periodic review of audit trails should specify that the ISSO conduct a review of operating system audit records on a weekly basis to identify security-related events.

Plan Format

There is nothing wrong with having several formats for security plans depending on the nature of the system for which the plan is written. In fact, NIST guidance calls for differences between plans for general support systems and major applications. However, the organizations should define formats that are permissible for use. While plan formats should be somewhat flexible, the contents of the plan should be fairly standard (see Appendix K). Minimum requirements for information required to be included in the plan must also be clearly defined in organization system authorization guidelines.

Plan Approval

The approval of the plan should begin with the signature of the individual who prepared the plan. At times, this will be the certification agent acting at the behest of the system owner. The system security officer should then review and approve the plan before it goes to the system owner. Because it will be part of the system authorization package, certification will include analysis and validation of the plan by the certification authority, and accreditation will result in the designated approval authority's approval of the plan.

Plan Maintenance

The security plan is a living document, and effort should be made to update it throughout the system authorization process and during the effective life cycle of the system. The plan should be constructed before the system goes into production to aid in

Chapter 3

the documentation of protection requirements during system design and implementation. Meeting system authorization requirements throughout a system's life cycle is addressed in Chapter 1. After the system goes live, the plan needs to be reviewed yearly to ensure it is current. Changes in the system's operating environment, changes in risks to the system, and changes in controls protecting the system should be cause for updating the plan. The annual review should seek to evaluate all such changes to determine if a plan update is warranted. The reviewer, normally the ISSO, should document in the plan that a review has been performed and should indicate the date of the review. If changes are necessary, they can be written in with pen with the initials of the individual authorizing the change. This works well as long as the changes are fairly minor in nature. For more significant changes, new pages should be inserted, with each page bearing the date of the change. In addition, a change information page in the front of the security plan should be annotated to document the date, purpose, and page numbers of all changes for both minor and major changes.

Because the security plan is so critical and so tied to other report inputs, care must be taken to ensure it is kept up to date in response to system changes and to updates in associated documentation. This can be facilitated by including the date on each page, as well as by including in the plan format an approval page, a review page, and a change information page. The approval page provides a place to record the signatures of the ISSO, system owner, and perhaps the approving authority on initial development of the plan. The review page allows the security reviewer to record when the plan was reviewed for currency. The change page is used to record the date and nature of changes made to the document. Examples of these pages are included in Tables 3.9, 3.10, and 3.11.

Plan Security

Because security plans document the status of security controls protecting a system, it allows one to see "warts and all." Consequently, plans need to be closely safeguarded. Access to electronic versions of the security plan should be limited based on the need to know, as is access to printed copies of the plan and associated working papers. Although it may be desirous to display security plans prominently on a bookshelf because of the effort that went into them, this practice should be avoided in the interest of confidentiality. Sensitivity labeling should be used copiously, and a good rule of thumb is that, once they are prepared, do not let plans out of your building. Armed with a copy of your well-written security plan, a bad guy will have more than enough information to penetrate your system's security controls successfully.

| Table 3.9   Security Plan Approval Sheet |

System owner:

_____   _____   _____
Name: Signature   Date

Security officer:

_____   _____   _____
Name: Signature   Date

Security reviewer:

_____   _____   _____
Name: Signature   Date

| Table 3.10   Security Plan Review Page |

This security plan has been updated and approved on the following dates to account for the latest changes. This plan must be reviewed annually.

Approval Date	Name of Security Officer	Signature of Security Officer

Chapter 3

Table 3.11 Security Plan Change Information Page			
Issue	**Date**	**Pages Affected**	**Description**

Plan Metrics

In establishing a program for security planning, it is important to know how to measure its effectiveness. Security planning is effective if the following criteria are achieved:

- *Documented Plans*: Plans are documented for each system rather than being merely concepts in someone's mind or being unwritten practices routinely performed off the top of one's head.

- *Use of Defined Formats*: Security plans are documented following a pre-scribed format that makes it easy to determine their completeness and the security posture of the system. Basic information requirements are most easily established and enforced through reliance on the development and use of standard security plan templates.

- *Approved Plans*: Security plans have been provided to those entities that they affect, are approved by those responsible for the security of the system, and have been reviewed and appropriately updated within the past year.

- *Consistent Plans*: Security plans relate to, support, and complement other documentation for the system. The information they present directly maps to risk assessment, certification testing, remediation planning, and contingency planning documents that relate to the system. For example, the sensitivity rankings the plan reflects are consistent with those documented in the system inventory and risk assessment.

- *Documented Implementation Planning:* Plans are constructed to serve as a basis for improving security controls. That is, the plan clearly identifies controls that need to be added or how controls need to be upgraded to reduce residual risks. The plan will accurately describe actions to be taken to address deficiencies, identify responsibilities for those actions, and provide milestones for completion of actions.

Resistance to Security Planning

Given the advantages that security plans provide system owners, one must ask why they are not prepared more reliably or why their use is not more widespread. The primary reason is a failure by system owners to give priority to documentation tasks in general. This may be due to shortage of manpower or skills or because of more pressing issues that occur day to day that prevent the system owner from focusing on strategic initiatives like security planning. However, without resolving strategic issues such as this, resolution of tactical issues also may not be possible either. In other words, security planning operates on both strategic and tactical levels.

Observations

A well-constructed security plan provides the security manager an effective instrument for meeting security oversight, planning, budgeting, and compliance requirements. Because these requirements can be applied to all systems, security plans are both feasible and practical for commercial and government systems alike. The management, operational, and technical controls taxonomy that has been effectively applied in the federal government is a workable approach for categorizing controls for nongovernment systems as well. In addition, as discussed in Chapter 3, security plans can serve as effective mechanisms for integrating security into system development efforts. The security plan provides a path for implementing an organization's security architecture, in that a security planning process implemented across the breadth of an organization can produce mutually supporting system-level plans that integrate security controls across multiple systems. The information provided in this chapter is consistent with updated guidance published by NIST in Special Publication 800-37, Revision 1, and in particular Tasks 1-2, 2-2, 2-3, 2-4, 3-1, 3-2, and 6-4.

Chapter 3

NIST Guidance on Security Controls Selection

The second step of the Risk Management Framework results in the identification of an initial set of baseline security controls for the information system based on its security categorization. The tailoring, adjustment, and supplementation of the security control baseline as necessary is then undertaken to address risks according to an organizational assessment of risk as well as local conditions. The following paragraphs summarize the guidance of NIST SP 800-37, Revision 1, in addressing system sensitivity and criticality through the Risk Management Framework categorization step.

Task 2-1: Identify Common Controls

The security controls provided by the organization as common controls are identified for the system and are recorded in the system security plan.

Primary Responsibility	Supporting Roles	SDLC Phase	References
CIO or CISO, ISA, CCP	RE(F), AO or AODR, ISO, ISSE	Initiation	FIPS Publications 199, 200, NIST SPs 800-30, 800-53, CNSS Instruction 1253

AO, authorizing official; CCP, common control provider; CIO, chief information officer; CNSS, Committee on National Security Systems; I DR, designated representative; SO, information system owner; ISSE, information system security engineer; SDLC, system development life cycle; ISA, information security architect; RE(F), risk executive (function).

- CCPs may double as ISOs if the common controls reside within an information system.

- ISOs help identify common controls to ensure they provide adequate protection.

- When the common controls are not sufficient, system owners supplement the common controls with system-specific or hybrid controls to protect the system.

- System owners can either document common controls in their security plans or make reference to the security plans of CCPs.

- Common control identification and selection may be deferred until a later phase in the SDLC.

■ Common controls not associated with a particular information system will be assigned to one or more senior organizational officials for authorization.

■ CCPs are responsible for documenting common controls in a security plan; ensuring common controls are developed, implemented, and independently assessed for effectiveness; documenting assessment findings in a security assessment report; producing a plan of action and milestones for all common controls that are less than fully effective; ensuring authorization for the common controls from the designated authorizing official; and continuously monitoring effectiveness of controls.

■ Security documentation for common controls will be made available to system owners whose systems inherit the controls.

■ CCPs must keep security documentation current since it typically supports multiple systems.

■ Authorizing officials will use security documentation for common controls to make risk-based decisions in the authorization process for their information systems.

■ CCPs must be able to communicate rapidly changes in the status of common controls that may adversely affect the protection they render to systems relying on them.

■ Organizations should employ automated management systems to enhance the ability to communicate common control status rapidly.

■ Arrangements should be made to obtain timely information on the effectiveness of common controls provided by external entities.

Task 2-2: Select Security Controls

Select the security controls for the information system and document the controls in the system security plan. Security controls are selected according to the security categorization of the information system.

Primary Responsibility	Supporting Roles	SDLC Phase	References
ISA, ISO	AO or AODR, IO/IS, ISSO, ISSE	Initiation	FIPS Publications 199, 200, NIST SPs 800-30, 800-53, CNSS Instruction 1253

■ The security control selection process begins by choosing a set of baseline security controls.

■ The baseline controls are then tailored by applying scoping, parameterization, and compensating control guidance.

- This is followed by supplementing the tailored baseline security controls with additional controls or enhancements to address unique system needs. This is based on a review of documentation, including the system security plan, concept of operations, and risk assessment as well as local conditions (i.e., operation environment, organization-specific security requirements, specific threat information, cost-benefit analyses, or special circumstances).

- The final requirement of control selection is to specify minimum assurance requirements.

- The system owner must document in the system security plan his or her decisions (e.g., tailoring, supplementation, etc.) made during the security control selection process to provide a sound rationale for them.

- The security plan must provide an overview of security requirements for the system that are sufficiently detailed to allow a determination whether the controls selected meet those requirements.

- The security plan must describe each control in enough detail to allow them to be implemented in a compliant manner.

- System owners should begin planning for continuous monitoring during the security control selection process with the development of a monitoring strategy.

- The monitoring strategy development can include monitoring criteria and monitoring frequency for specific controls.

- For systems in which subsystems may be added or removed, the system owner will include in the security plan descriptions of the subsystems; security controls employed in the subsystems; constraints and assumptions regarding the functions of the subsystems; dependencies of other subsystems on the security controls of the subsystems; procedures for determining that the subsystems conform to the security plan, assumptions, and constraints; and the impact of the subsystems and their security controls on other existing security controls protecting the system.

- Not all subsystems are security relevant. Inclusion of a subsystem may have an impact on the system or other subsystems but not necessarily an impact on the security of the system or other subsystems.

- Changes in system boundaries that exceed the anticipated limits of the security plan may not be allowed or may require reassessment prior to approval.

- When security services are provided by external providers, the system owner must define the external services provided and how they meet established security requirements and must obtain assurances that the risk to organizational operations and assets is acceptable.

- The system owner must also consider that a complex information system with multiple subsystems may have common vulnerabilities that permit exploitation by a common threat source, which may negate the redundancy possibly relied on to mitigate risk.

- The impact resulting from a security incident in one subsystem might also have an impact on other subsystems of a complex information system.

Task 2-3: Develop Monitoring Strategy

A continuous monitoring strategy will be developed for each information system to allow determination of the effectiveness of security controls over time as well as the impact of any proposed or actual changes to the system and its environment of operation.

Primary Responsibility	Supporting Roles	SDLC Phase	References
ISO or CCP	RE(F), AO/AODR, CIO, CISO, IO/S, ISSO	Initiation	NIST SPs 800-30, 800-39, 800-53, 800-53A, CNSS Instruction 1253

- The monitoring strategy allows understanding of the system's security state over time.

- Strategy should stress use of automated tools to facilitate near-real-time risk management.

- Strategy includes monitoring of inherited controls; configuration management/control processes; security impact analysis of proposed or actual changes; assessment of selected controls employed; and security status reporting to management officials.

- Strategy identifies security controls to be monitored; frequency of monitoring; and control assessment approach.

- Strategy defines how changes are monitored; how security impact analyses are conducted; and status reporting requirements.

- Criteria for selecting controls to monitor will reflect the criticality of the system.

- Prioritize monitoring on controls that are volatile, critical, or listed in the plan of action and milestones.

- The frequency for monitoring inherited controls depends on the provider's trustworthiness.

- A risk assessment can be used to select controls to be monitored and to establish the frequency of monitoring.

Chapter 3

- The AO or AODR approves the strategy usually as part of security plan approval.

- A control monitoring strategy is required throughout the system's life cycle.

- Strategy accounts for security controls of dynamic subsystems that did not exist at the beginning of the SDLC.

- Monitoring strategy for dynamic subsystems balances risk by not requiring reauthorization of the system each time a new subsystem is added or removed and not compromising the accepted risk posture of the complex system.

Task 2-4: Approve Security Plan

The system security plan is reviewed and approved. An independent review of the security plan followed by proper approval establishes that the plan is complete and consistent and satisfies the stated security requirements for the information system.

Primary Responsibility	Supporting Roles	SDLC Phase	References
AO or AODR	RE(F), CIO, CISO	Development/ acquisition	NIST SPs 800-30, 800-53, CNSS Instruction 1253

- The security plan review also determines if the security plan properly identifies the potential risk the organization would incur if the controls identified in the plan were implemented as intended.

- The independent review may result in recommendations for changes to the system security plan.

- If the security plan is deemed unacceptable, it is returned to the system owner or CCP for corrective action.

- If the security plan is acceptable, the authorizing official approves the plan.

- Acceptance of the security plan is an important milestone in the risk management process and in the SDLC.

- The authorizing official's approval of the security plan serves as agreement to the system-specific, hybrid, and common security controls selected for the system.

- Authorizing official approval of the security controls for the system completes the security controls selection step of the Risk Management Framework.

- Approval of the security plan also establishes the level of effort required to complete the remaining steps in the Risk Management Framework.

- The approved system security plan provides the security specification for acquisition of the information system, subsystems, or components.

SUMMARY

This chapter stressed the importance for organizations to define specific security control requirements for their information systems through development of a catalog of security controls known as a minimum security baseline. From this, they must establish a security control baseline for each system according to its security categorization and then tailor and supplement this control set to accommodate specific requirements for the system using a formalized risk assessment process. Chapter 3 also provided an overview of the most current NIST guidance on selection of security controls and how organizations and specifically system owners can apply Step 2 of the Risk Management Framework to identify common controls, select security controls, develop a monitoring strategy for their systems, and then document and approve control selection in the security plan for the system.

Chapter 3

ESTABLISHMENT OF THE SECURITY CONTROL BASELINE: REVIEW QUESTIONS

1. An organization's information systems are a mix of Windows and UNIX systems located in a single computer room. Access to the computer room is restricted by the use of door locks that require proximity cards and personal identification numbers (PINs). Only a small percentage of the organization's employees have access to the computer room. The computer room access restriction is an example of what type of security control relative to the hardware in the computer room?

    A. Managerial

    B. System specific

    C. Technical

    D. Inherited

2. Why is security control volatility an important consideration in the development of a security control monitoring strategy?

    A. It identifies needed security control monitoring exceptions.

    B. It indicates a need for compensating controls.

    C. It establishes priority for security control monitoring.

    D. It provides justification for revisions to the configuration management and control plan.

3. An information system is currently in the initiation phase of the system development life cycle (SDLC) and has been categorized high impact. The information system owner wants to inherit common controls provided by another organizational information system that is categorized moderate impact. How does the information system owner ensure that the common controls will provide adequate protection for the information system?

A. Supplement the common controls with system-specific or hybrid controls to achieve the required protection for the system.

B. Ask the common control provider for the system security plan for the common controls.

C. Consult with the information system security engineer and the information security architect.

D. Perform rigorous testing of the common controls to determine if they provide adequate protection.

4. An effective security control monitoring strategy for an information system includes

A. monitoring the security controls of interconnecting information systems outside the authorization boundary.

B. active involvement by authorizing officials in the ongoing management of information system-related security risks.

C. the annual assessment of all security controls in the information system.

D. all controls listed in NIST SP 800-53, Revision 3.

5. A large organization has a documented information security policy that has been reviewed and approved by senior officials and is readily available to all organizational staff. This information security policy explicitly addresses each of the 17 control families in NIST SP 800-53, Revision 3. Some system owners also established procedures for the technical class of security controls on certain of their systems. In their respective system security plans, control AC-1 Access Control Policy and Procedures (a technical class security control) must be identified as what type of control?

A. Fully inheritable

B. Hybrid

C. System specific

D. Inherited

Chapter 3

Chapter 4

Application of Security Controls

The security controls specified in the security plan are implemented by taking into account the minimum organizational assurance requirements. The security plan describes how the controls are employed within the information system and its operational environment. The security assessment plan documents the methods for testing these controls and the expected results throughout the systems life-cycle.

Certified Authorization Professional (CAP®) Candidate Information Bulletin,
November 2010

TOPICS

- Security Procedures
- Remediation Planning
- NIST Guidance on Implementation of Security Controls

OBJECTIVES

As a Certified Authorization Professional (CAP®), you are expected to

- Implement selected security controls
- Document security control implementation

Introduction

Once security controls for a system have been selected based on the categorization of system information, these controls are implemented to ensure the protection of the system and its data. The system owner or common control provider (CCP) has the lead responsibility in the application of specified security controls, but normally rely on project teams, information system security officers (ISSOs), and security engineers to carry out day-to-day implementation tasks. The resources necessary to implement controls in accordance with the security plan are often problematic, and this requires the system owner or CCP to coordinate resource requirements with the organization's senior leadership, including the chief financial officer (CFO) as soon as security controls can be accurately quantified. To facilitate early planning, security controls are normally applied in the development or acquisition phase of the system development life cycle (SDLC) for a new or updated system. The early identification of control requirements allows the system owner or common control provider to communicate resource requests efficiently. During this task, security procedures are documented in accordance with the security plan to provide detailed instructions on how a control is implemented and maintained. When security control changes to an operational system are anticipated, the system owner or common control provider uses a plan of action and milestones (POA&M) to track the application of necessary controls to ensure timely implementation. This chapter describes the processes for developing procedures and for satisfying control implementation requirements through remediation. In addition, National Institute of Standards and

Technology (NIST) guidance on the security controls implementation step of the Risk Management Framework is highlighted.

Security Procedures

Security procedures play a prominent part in the minimum security baseline set. They are an important type of control that documents the security practices and processes that have been implemented to protect the system. Although system-level security procedures can be regarded as another type of security control, their development is key to the successful implementation of a system authorization program. This is because the program can foster the development of critical controls not only by identifying and increasing the visibility of the need for documented procedures, but also by providing tools and techniques to aid in their development. This section addresses security procedures specific to individual systems, as well as those considered to be common controls that are applicable to multiple systems at either the business unit or the enterprise level.

Purpose

Procedures are important to the security of information technology systems because they serve as the connection between people (who protect) and assets (which are protected). It has been said that the greatest risk to an information system is the people who are authorized to use it. Security procedures reduce the risk posed by people by providing users instructions in how to use the system securely, how to perform security-related tasks and functions correctly, and how to administer security controls properly. This allows secure practices to be repeatable over time and to be passed on from one user to the next, permitting alternates to be able to step in and assume the duties when necessary. Security procedures also provide a basis for training in the secure use of the system, and they ensure that security policies and standards that are applicable to the system are translated and applied to the system. An additional benefit from the perspective of the security manager is that security procedures allow measurement of the level of compliance with and the adequacy of security. Reviewing compliance with security procedures demonstrates the degree to which system users and managers perform security-specific tasks.

The Problem with Procedures

The lack of security procedures is one of the more persistent problems in implementation of security at the system level. System administrators are busy, with much

Chapter 4

competition for their time. Security is but one of these competitors. Consequently, system administrators do not place much emphasis on documentation, particularly on the processes they already know how to do, because they do them routinely with their eyes closed. System administrators are "doers" by nature and specialize in knowing how to do things. For many, doing does not include putting down in writing the steps involved in doing something. This mind-set fails to give credence to needs for continuity of operations, cross training of replacements and backups, and compliance measurement goals. Management must understand the importance of security procedures and be forceful in ensuring that procedures specific to its systems are developed and maintained.

Responsibility

The system owner is normally the official responsible for developing and approving system-specific procedures. This is because system owners have the most knowledge of the system and know what procedures are needed and what they need to address. However, the owner may need to call on someone like a system administrator actually to draft the procedures due to the administrator's more intimate knowledge of the process to be documented (i.e., backing up system data). Also, the system owner is in the best position to create procedures because they must apply to all users of the system irrespective of their location, business unit or organization, position, rank, or status. Because procedures are considered mandatory and noncompliance should be grounds for disciplinary action, users should be required to acknowledge their understanding and acceptance of them as a condition of use. This can be enforced through the use of an initial system access request approval process, which includes an acknowledgment form for the user's signature. Key procedures or elements of procedures that warrant emphasis and reinforcement through stricter oversight can be integrated into the rules of behavior for the system.

Procedure Templates

Management can facilitate the creation of security procedures by being proactive and developing approved procedure templates for system owners to use in developing their procedures for their systems. Table 4.1 provides a sample of procedures that should be prepared for each system.

It should be pointed out that care must be exercised in the use of "canned" procedures of this sort to ensure that they are properly modified to fit the organization's environment and do not establish overly complex processes that have no prospect

Table 4.1 Sample Procedures List	
Procedure	**Type of Procedure**
Account setup	System specific
Account termination	System specific
Audit trail retention and storage	System specific
Audit trail review	System specific
Authorization to process	Common
Configuration management and change control	Common
Contingency planning and testing	Common
Data backup	System specific
Data entry/integrity/validation controls	System specific
Emergency evacuation	Common
Incident response	Common
Interconnecting systems	Common
Malicious software prevention	Common
Media protection	Common
Nondisclosure of information/confidentiality	Common
Password compromise	System specific
Password issuance	System specific
Password reset	System specific
Personally owned computers and software	Common
Personnel background screening	Common
Personnel in-processing	Common
Personnel sanctions	Common
Personnel termination and transfer	Common
Physical access authorization	Common
Portable computers/controlling laptops	Common
Position sensitivity designation	Common
Privacy impact assessment	Common
Property accountability	Common
Remote access	System specific
Risk assessment	Common
Risk management (plan of action and milestones)	Common
Security awareness and training	Common
Security controls review	Common

continued

Chapter 4

Table 4.1 (continued) Sample Procedures List	
Procedure	**Type of Procedure**
Security planning	Common
System maintenance	Common
Third-party security	Common
User accounts review	System specific
Visitor controls	Common
Vulnerability scanning	Common

of being followed. The creation of a security procedures library can assist the entire organization in complying with minimum security requirements. NIST Special Publications (SPs) 800-26 and 800-53 minimum security baselines require a large number of procedures for both general support systems and major applications. An organization will be well served to create templates that permit system owners to tailor them to their own needs. The easiest way to build such a library is for the chief information security officer (CISO) to collect, review, and sanitize procedures drafted by system owners across the organization. This also permits the development of procedure templates for different types of systems by function, by business unit, and by level of protection necessary.

Process for Developing Procedures

The organization should establish a standard approach for creating procedures to ensure standardization of content and format. Steps involved in this process ensure that requirements for procedures are routinely identified; that responsibilities for their development are assigned; that new procedures are reviewed and approved by appropriate operational and security personnel; that a procedure is disseminated to those charged with its implementation and compliance; and that procedures are maintained. Table 4.2 depicts the steps involved in the development of security procedures.

Style

Procedures may be several pages in length or may only be a few sentences. Generally, procedures should be written to be as concise as possible because use and maintenance of extensive, complex, and overly wordy procedures can be problematic. It is clearly possible to go overboard with procedures by thinking that more is better, but breadth is more important than heft. Ideally, system-specific procedures should be grouped into a consolidated security manual to make it easier to access and use them

Table 4.2 Procedure Development Process	
Task 1	Identify the need for a new or updated security procedure as a result of an audit or the system certification process or through routine self-assessment.
Task 2	Create or update the procedure by the organizational element responsible for performing the process being documented in the procedure.
Task 3	Review of the procedure by the task lead, who supervises the element, creating/updating the procedure. The task lead ensures the procedure accurately documents the process in its entirety and reflects the manner in which it should be performed. If additional content or corrections are required, the task lead returns the material for corrective action.
Task 4	The information system security officer (ISSO) responsible for the performance of the procedures reviews the updated or newly created procedure to ensure adequate security controls are included in the procedure. If additional security-related content or corrections are required, the ISSO returns it to the prior task lead for corrective action.
Task 5	The updated or newly created procedure is reviewed by the organizational information system security staff to ensure adequate security controls are included in the procedure. If additional security-related content or corrections are needed, it is returned to the ISSO for action.
Task 6	The updated or newly created procedure is reviewed by the system owner. If the system owner desires changes, he or she contacts the ISSO for action.
Task 7	Once the system owner approves the procedure, it is maintained by the division that created it. Any updates to the approved procedure should follow this approval process.

when needed and to facilitate updating individual procedures as necessary. Therefore, such a handbook should be constructed in a modular fashion with the authority, date of release, applicability, and scope of each clearly indicated on each individual procedure. Ideally, posting individual procedures on Web pages indexed by topic is the best solution because this facilitates ease of use as well as ease of updating.

Many organizations use the system security plan as the repository for security-related procedures, applying the principle that all security-related information should be consolidated into a single document. Although in principle this makes sense based on ease of use, from a practical standpoint the approach diminishes the usability of the security plan and weakens the plan's ability to meet its primary purpose: documenting the security posture of a system. When detailed procedures are included in the plan, the overall status of system security is obscured. This is an unnatural blending of operational information with management information that is difficult to maintain. An additional reason for avoiding this practice is that it is an unnecessary addition to the certification package and is difficult to include, and this risks delays

Chapter 4

in the development of the system authorization package. The security plan should merely make reference to individual security procedures as it addresses specific plan topics, but there is little value in including the procedures as part of the plan.

Formatting

First, procedures need to be documented. For the reasons stated, it is not sufficient for the system administrator or other user to "have them in their head." If procedures are not written down, they do not exist (particularly from an auditor's perspective). The formatting of the procedures should be fully consistent with organizational standards to link them to the authority of organizational management, as well as to ensure consistency and comprehensiveness. A sample security procedure is provided in Appendix O. As stated, procedures should be developed individually according to topic. The format of each procedure should include the subject or title of the procedure and should address the purpose of or justification for the procedure; its scope (what it applies to); responsibility (who must implement, enforce, and comply with it); applicability (individuals or organizational elements to which it applies); when it is to be employed (routinely, periodically, occasionally, as required, or during emergencies); and the process itself. Each procedure should be affixed with a date and should bear the signature of the individual responsible for the procedure, usually the system owner. The content of the procedure should permit the reader to understand how to do something. To promote this level of understanding, maximum use of bullet lists of tasks and activities to be performed, steps, graphs, figures, tips, and reminders is warranted. Screen shots of system-based processes should be incorporated into the procedures to promote clarity as well as brevity.

Access

It does no good to spend countless hours developing, coordinating, publishing, and updating an intricate set of security procedures if they are not available when they are needed by those who need them. To ensure that they will be available when they are needed, they should be backed up, and a copy should be stored at an off-site location. It might be good for those to whom the procedures pertain to be required to maintain a copy at home as long as copies can be kept secure. Although there may be a need for some users to have procedures in printed form (e.g., data entry personnel), this should be discouraged because of the difficulty of updating the procedures. A better solution for access is to post the procedures in a protected format on a shared directory on the network or on the company intranet. The CISO should establish a procedures library to serve as a repository for various security procedures developed by system owners. This will provide examples for organizations that are in the process of developing their own system-specific procedures.

Maintenance

Procedures should be reviewed annually to determine if they are current. The process for conducting such a review itself should be documented. Update of procedures should be built into the change management process, the incident response process, and in any other process that may result in changes to how things are done. A procedure update is enhanced when a change information sheet as depicted in Chapter 3 is included as a part of the procedure and is used to record the date and a brief description of each change. The identification of the approver of each of the changes should also be recorded. Users should be encouraged to submit requests for changes when they are observed, and such requests should themselves be subject to the change management process. This ensures that each change is fully documented for historical purposes and approval is recorded.

Common Procedures

System owners should not have to be responsible for developing procedures relating to controls that are outside their area of responsibility; they have enough to do. Instead, procedures that are common to several systems in a business unit should be addressed at the business-unit level and at the enterprise level for controls that apply to all or most systems in the organization. Controls in the areas of facility physical security, environmental protection, personnel security, incident response, and security awareness and training should generally be addressed as common controls, and those functions should be responsible for developing procedures for them. However, this does not take the system owner entirely off the hook. Even though there is an enterprise procedure, there may still be a need to write a system-specific procedure. The common procedure has to be made specific to the information technology system by identifying who is responsible for implementing, complying, and using it at the system level. This system-level augmentation must describe how the procedure is implemented on the system and under what conditions it must be followed. Table 4.1 identifies both common and system-specific procedures generally applicable to information technology systems.

Procedures in the System Authorization Process

Security procedures fall into the category of security controls, and they have a direct impact on the security of a system and an indirect impact on the overall system

Chapter 4

authorization program. The ways that procedures affect system authorization processes and documents is that

- They are established as requirements in the minimum security baseline for an organization.
- The existence/nonexistence of procedures is to be documented in the system security plan.
- Vulnerabilities related to lack of or failure to comply with procedures are included in the risk assessment.
- They are evaluated as part of security testing.
- Weaknesses relating to security procedures are documented and tracked in the remediation plan.

These various system authorization processes and documentation are designed to record the need for, existence of, effectiveness of, and weaknesses in security procedures just as with all controls necessary for the system's protection.

Observations

The purpose of security procedures is to describe tasks to be performed and actions to be taken in securing a system. Procedures provide the detailed steps, assign specific responsibilities, and provide aids in the implementation and maintenance of security controls. The consequences to the system owner of not having documented procedures is a lack of consistency in controls implementation and maintenance, a lack of repeatability in their administration by system users, and the risk of failure to comply with minimum control requirements. In addition, the documented procedures ensure that there is no major loss of knowledge when a key user is absent. Procedures are the primary means for the system owner to address the significant threat of user errors and omissions affecting his or her system in that they translate control requirements into specific user tasks that can be performed, measured, enforced, and taught.

Remediation Planning

System authorization is more than merely an exercise in documenting security controls and assessing security weaknesses. The purpose of an effective system authorization program is to ensure that sensitive information resources are protected and to point out shortfalls when they are not. As stated previously, certification is an assessment exercise rather than a mitigation activity. However, one must understand that certification does not stand alone, and that mitigation of risks is essential to the success of the entire system authorization process. What is needed following assessment is a plan for mitigation of risks. A risk remediation plan is necessary to provide a consolidated, easy-to-use road map for correcting security weaknesses. Also known as a POA&M, risk mitigation plan, remediation plan, or system risk management plan, the risk remediation plan provides a source document for tracking the correction of deficiencies and improving a system's security. The development of a risk remediation plan assumes that an assessment has been completed, at least temporarily, and that deficiencies in security controls have been adequately documented.

There are two perspectives to be taken in addressing remediation plans: that of the system owner, who is only concerned in mitigating risks to one system, and that of the approving authority or upper management, who must be concerned about risk to multiple systems. To aid the system owner in his or her task of mitigating risks, the risk remediation plan must classify corrective action by risk level and resources required. This allows him or her to focus remediation efforts first on those risks that are the most severe and second on those that can be fixed with relatively little effort ("low-hanging fruit"). This narrow perspective of these two factors fully supports the needs of the system owner, who normally does not have to be concerned with competition between systems for resources.

Contrast this with the perspective of the executive manager who is responsible for corrective actions for many systems across the entire organization, all of which compete for resources necessary to get well. Because of this, upper-level managers must have an additional qualifier that tells them the relative importance of systems or criticality (see Chapter 2). If managers know that the accounts receivable system is more critical than the property inventory system, then they can emphasize the mitigation effort toward the more critical system, giving it priority for resources. Therefore, each risk remediation plan should reflect the criticality of the system to permit management of the risk mitigation effort at a high level across multiple systems. A simple high, medium, or low categorization is sufficient for this purpose or perhaps a binary approach in which a system is critical or it is not.

The following information on planning for remediation of system weaknesses supports Tasks 4-4, 5-1, and 6-3 of the Risk Management Framework (RMF) described in NIST SP 800-37, Revision 1.

Chapter 4

Managing Risk

The purpose of risk management is to identify potential problems before they occur so that risk-handling activities may be planned and invoked as needed across the life of the system. Risk management provides an approach for organization management to ensure that cost-effective, risk-based security is implemented as required by the Federal Information Security Management Act and other federal legislation.

The results of the risk assessment (see Chapter 3) should provide organization management sufficient information to permit them to decide on a strategy for how to respond to each risk to an information system. However, there may not always be adequate controls available to mitigate known risks. In these cases, the risk assessment must acknowledge the risk, document it so that the authorizing official can clearly understand it, and then conduct research into appropriate, cost-effective controls that can be implemented at a later time. According to NIST SP 800-30, a variety of response options is available, and the authorizing official, based on the recommendations of his or her staff and the system owner, must determine the most effective approach for addressing each risk.

The authorizing official may choose to assume the risk as part of the system authorization decision. Risk avoidance is an alternative that requires action to be taken to avoid occurrence of the risk. Risk limitation aims to limit residual risk by limiting the exposure to it. Risk transference is most commonly implemented in the private sector, where insurance is used to transfer the risk to another entity. Risk planning is used in many industries outside government, and it focuses on accepting that risk is inherent to normal operations, and there will be a certain amount of loss that can always be expected. This results in appropriate operational and financial planning to absorb the loss.

Mitigation of risks requires the authorizing official to evaluate and prioritize risks and then to implement controls recommended in the risk assessment effort accordingly. Because the elimination of all risk is normally impractical or impossible, it is the responsibility of the authorizing official to use the least-cost approach to implementing the most appropriate controls to decrease the mission risk to an acceptable level, with minimal adverse impact on the organization's resources and mission.

Applicability of the Remediation Plan

It is indeed a rare occasion when at the conclusion of a certification a system is found to have no security weaknesses. Normally, there are between 10 and 50 issues to be resolved, ranging from the severe (malicious software found to be present) to the relatively mundane (time that a visitor departed the server room not recorded in the visitor log). This being the case, practically every system then needs a risk remediation plan to correct these weaknesses.

Responsibility for the Plan

System owners have ultimate responsibility for mitigating risks to their systems and must plan for the correction of deficiencies in security controls. This is achieved by developing a usable plan that guides implementation of new controls or improvement of existing controls over time. Although many others may use the plan to guide corrective action or monitor progress in improving system security, system owners initially need to develop and maintain ownership of the plan. Often, system owners will delegate this responsibility to the ISSO or another worker, and this is fine as long as system owners understand that they are the official ultimately accountable for implementing corrective action to improve the security of the system.

Whoever is assigned responsibility for maintaining the risk remediation plan must be careful not to update the plan based on inaccurate or incomplete information. He or she should accept updated information only from bona fide sources, preferably only from the individual assigned responsibility for implementing the corrective action, always being sure that the individual is held accountable for the status information provided. And, the system owner as owner of the mitigation effort must be sure to hold the risk remediation plan gatekeeper accountable as well.

Risk Remediation Plan Scope

The risk remediation plan should include all vulnerabilities that have been identified during certification testing of the system. In addition, other weaknesses that have been identified from other sources (i.e., financial audit, Inspector General (IG) inspection, privacy impact assessment, prior material weaknesses that relate to the system) should be included in the plan. It should provide a comprehensive list of all vulnerabilities irrespective of vulnerability, threat, or safeguard category or risk level. Management controls should be included alongside technical controls alongside operational controls. Vulnerabilities ranked as high risk should be identified along with those ranked lower. The primary principle is that they all are included in a single plan to make corrective action easier to manage. They may vary, however, in the level of detail offered for each. For instance, it may be worthwhile to group types of vulnerabilities together if it makes them easier to manage. Low-severity

Chapter 4

vulnerabilities identified during a vulnerability scan may be easier to manage as a single risk remediation plan issue as long as details relating to their description and remediation are readily available, preferably as an attachment to the certification test. Risks that have been or are likely to be accepted by the approving authority should also be included in the risk remediation plan so that they can be tracked.

Plan Format

The risk remediation plan at a minimum must identify a weakness, a fix, a milestone, and a responsible person for each identified risk to the system. Although one could have a plan without them, without these four elements the plan would not identify what the problem to be solved is, how the problem can be solved, who will solve it, and the deadline for solving the problem. These are the essential data fields and are depicted in Table 4.3. Additional information, while not essential, can make the plan a more useful tool. When determining what information should be included in the plan, do not lose sight of the requirement for the plan to be usable. Following is a discussion of the data elements that should be included in the risk remediation plan:

- *Cross-Reference Numbering*: A simple cross-reference numbering system helps identify the plan entry and serves as a sort of shorthand to facilitate identification. Ideally, this number would map to entries in the risk assessment, security testing, and the security plan. A reference can be included along with each weakness to answer the question of why there is vulnerability. Inclusion of NIST SP 800-53, Federal Information System Controls Audit Manual (FISCAM), International Organization for Standardization 27002, or the like controls cross-reference numbers, for example, or perhaps an organization policy or procedure number provides a basis for better understanding both the vulnerability and the corrective action. The responsibility column can be expanded to record both the primary and the secondary players as well as both direct and indirect responsibilities. For example, the plan can specify that the system owner will be responsible for reviewing the facility access list (a direct responsibility), while the facility manager (who is only indirectly related to system operations) will be responsible for updating the access list once he or she receives an update from the system owner.

- *Weakness*: Vulnerabilities in system controls should be specified here. Whenever possible, the weakness should be described using the same language used in certification testing or source. However, the description of the weakness should only be described to the degree necessary to be clear without revealing sensitive information.

- *Risk Ranking*: It is helpful if the risk ranking for each weakness is also included for each weakness listed in the plan so that the relative need for

corrective action can be readily noted. In addition, sorting the risk remediation plan by risk further aids in the effort to emphasize those corrective
actions that have the greatest need for attention. The ranking reflected in the
risk remediation plan is obtained from the risk assessment (Chapter 3). The
ranking must be specific to the system, must be relative to the nature of the
system depending on its sensitivity and criticality, and must not be established simply based on a generic template. One challenge for the security
manager is to determine the risk ranking of weaknesses that are added
to the remediation plan from external audits, reviews, and inspections. To
achieve this, the weakness should be mapped to the control to which it is
most closely associated and should assume the risk ranking of that control.

- *Corrective Actions*: Corrective actions can be broken down into more
  detailed subtasks that have their own responsible individuals and milestones. This will facilitate completion of mitigation activities by showing
  dependencies and fixing responsibility more clearly. Resources necessary
  for implementing corrective actions can also be identified in the plan to help
  estimate costs and manpower. Costs to purchase or license software and
  buy hardware and the man-hours required for their implementation and
  operation or to develop policies, plans, and procedures can be detailed in
  this resources column. Finally, the plan should provide space to record the
  status of corrective action, which allows the document to be current.

- *Responsibility for Corrective Action*: The risk remediation plan should be
  very specific with respect to responsibilities for corrective action. Rather
  than identifying an organization, the plan should state the name of an individual, and a name is better than just entering a generic position title or job
  title. It will be easier to determine who has responsibility for corrective action
  if you can read, "Joe, the system administrator" rather than simply "system
  administrator." It is much easier to hold people accountable if you identify
  them by name because by nature individuals are more responsive if they are
  identified in the plan by name. In fact, the first fight in coordinating the plan
  will be defending the decision to choose particular individuals as responsible for corrective actions specified in the plan. Early on, it may be difficult
  to identify a specific person for each task or milestone, but that should be
  the end goal. As the plan matures with use, these identities should become
  known and should be documented in the plan.

- *Resources Required*: Record in this column the resources (man-hours,
  dollars, etc.) required to complete action to correct the weakness.

- *Scheduled Completion Dates*: Document the initial date that the information
  system owner (ISO) has agreed to for completion of milestones and remediation of the weakness.

- *Milestones with Completion Dates*: Milestone dates may be difficult to project in the initial version of the plan. However, as the plan matures, milestone

Chapter 4

Table 4.3   Remediation Plan Contents

ID	Weakness	POC	Resources Required	Scheduled Completion Date	Milestones with Completion Dates	Status	Comments	Risk Ranking
1	1.2.3 Log-ons are cached on security-sensitive servers.	J. Doe	24 man-hours		Prevent log-ons from being cached on sensitive servers.	Ongoing		Low
2	2.1.5 Security alerts and security incidents are not analyzed and remedial actions are not taken. (FISCAM SP 3-4, NIST SP 800-18)	G. Cross	8 man-hours	5/30/2012	Develop a process for analyzing alerts and security incidents and for taking appropriate remedial action.	Ongoing		Moderate
4	6.1.3 Sensitive functions are not divided among different individuals. (OMB Circular A-130, III; FISCAM SD-1; NIST SP 800-18)	G. Cross	4 man-hours	9/30/2012	Develop a process for ensuring that sensitive functions are divided between different individuals.	Completed	Procedure # 27-A finalized on 4/15/2012.	Low
7	10.1.4 The system boot time is not set to 0 seconds.	J. Doe	8 man-hours	9/30/2012	Set system boot time to 0 seconds.	Ongoing		Low

#	Finding	Responsible	Effort	Target Date	Action	Status	Result	Risk
8	15.1.7 Password complexity has not been enabled.	J. Doe	2 man-hours	9/30/2012	Modify the system to accept only passwords that contain case-sensitive alphanumeric and special characters.	Completed	System modified to enforce password complexity on 4/11/2012.	Low
9	16.1.3 Access to security software is not restricted to security administrators. (FISCAM AC-3.2)	J. Doe	4 man-hours	5/30/2004	Restrict access to security software to security administrators only.	Completed	System modified on 4/12/2004 to limit access to security administrators.	Moderate
10	17.1.1 The audit trail does not provide a trace of user actions. (NIST SP 800-18)	J. Doe	4 man-hours	4/30/2004	Modify audit trail to ensure that it provides a trace of user log-ons, log-offs, password changes, and file deletions.	Completed	Audit trail modified to record recommended events on 4/12/2004.	High

Chapter 4

dates should become increasingly more specific and realistic. From "within the next 6 months" should evolve into "no later than June 30." Again, it is easier to keep mitigation on schedule when precise dates are established. Measuring success is easier with fixed dates as well. The CISO should provide basic guidance on milestone dates. For instance, high-risk weaknesses have to be corrected within 30 days, those ranked as moderate in 60 days, and low risks in 90 days or when resources are available. Although the CISO can provide a framework for corrective action dates such as these, it should always be the system owner who decides the actual milestone date. This is because the system owner has the best idea of resources available, knowledge of competing priorities, knowledge of the system, and primary accountability for the security of the system. Within reason, the system owner should be given free rein to determine when the corrective action must be completed, but the CISO must review each system-level plan to ensure that dates entered are realistic and are consistent with the risk the weakness poses. The CISO should be prepared to slap the hands of any system owner who approves a milestone 5 years in the future. An actual date of completion should be provided as applicable. In such cases, reference should be made to where evidence is located to substantiate that the weakness is closed.

■ *Changes to Milestones*: This field is necessary to allow changes in implementation timelines to be recorded. Changes in dates specified in this column must be justified and may require approval by the authorizing official according to agency policy.

■ *Source*: Reflect in this column where the weakness was initially identified, for example, a self-assessment, certification testing, or an external audit.

■ *Status*: This field is used to indicate whether corrective action is ongoing or has been completed.

These are the primary columns that need to be included in the risk remediation plan. Because of the usefulness of sorting each of these data fields, the use of a spreadsheet tool is ideal. A sample risk remediation plan is provided in Appendix Q. Office of Management and Budget (OMB) Memorandum 02-01 and NIST SP 800-37 provide guidance on the data elements that should be included in the POA&M that is used by government organizations to plan for and manage risks to information systems.

Using the Plan

Like the security plan, the risk remediation plan is a living document. It needs to be used and updated to reflect the current status of the mitigation effort as it evolves. It should serve as the primary tool in the facilitation of correction of security weaknesses as well as for management oversight. The plan should also serve as a record of action taken. Once a weakness has been addressed and corrective action has been completed, the plan needs to be updated to record this activity, and the action should be marked as completed. However, it should always remain a part of the plan and not be removed when completed. By keeping both open and closed issues in the plan, this more effectively allows measurement of progress toward a goal. This is particularly true with significant vulnerabilities that require subdivision into multiple tasks and activities with varying kinds and degrees of resources involved. In this case, the plan should show corrected and pending tasks together. Also, risks that management chooses to accept rather than correct should remain in the plan to allow the plan to function as a clearing-house document for addressing all risks to the system. If it is demonstrated that the costs of mitigating a risk do not warrant correction, then the plan is the place to document this acceptance (as well as in other more formal documentation, such as the accreditation letter). This allows management to manage risks using a common plan.

In general, this discussion has concentrated on system-level remediation plans that are used to measure progress of corrective action for an individual system. These should not be confused with program-level remediation plans that document weaknesses and corrective actions applicable to the entire enterprise. However, when taken together, system-level plans of action and milestones also document the security of the entire enterprise. To do this, a tool for managing collected remediation plans is necessary to provide a means of performing trend analysis to identify common controls and other solutions that apply to multiple systems. When selecting tools to perform this function, do not forget to address access controls and auditing controls to ensure the integrity of the information. Only system owners or their designated ISSOs should have the capability of adding, updating, or inactivating remediation plan data for their own systems. To maintain a record of all actions related to an entry, entries for which corrective action is complete should never be deleted. Instead, they should be deactivated so that they are still available for historical purposes. Although the security manager should have access to this remediation plan data, it should be limited to view access only.

When to Create the Plan

Because it is so important to risk mitigation efforts, consideration should be given to creating a risk remediation plan whenever vulnerabilities are first identified, irrespective of the status of other system authorization documentation. Naturally, the plan is prepared following a certification test after weaknesses have been verified. However, to support management needs for elevating the visibility of the mitigation effort, the plan can be prepared based on the results of a minimum security baseline assessment, a risk assessment, a vulnerability scan, development of a security plan, on receipt of results of an audit or inspection, or following an incident in which new weaknesses become known. When a risk remediation plan already exists for the system, additional vulnerabilities identified on these occasions should be appended into the existing remediation plan to allow a central repository for corrective action information. This avoids the confusing problem of having multiple remediation plans pertaining to a single system. The sooner corrective action is initiated, the sooner the security of the system will begin to improve. Early development of the risk remediation plan supports this goal.

The plan is a highly valuable tool in mitigating weaknesses in a system's security controls. It should be the focal point of regular, periodic meetings in which progress toward correcting vulnerabilities is evaluated and measured. The plan should be in a continuous state of update, refinement, and completion. Feedback from those involved in executing the plan must be integrated into the plan in a controlled manner. A keeper of the plan should be appointed to be solely responsible for approving additions and updates and for enforcement (with an iron hand) of version control. The plan will change not only as tasks are completed, but also tasks will lead to identification of other tasks and subtasks that will need their own milestones, resources, and responsible points of contact. In addition, it is doubtful that the system will remain static throughout the risk mitigation period, so the system owner will need to be prepared to update the plan to include addressing impacts stemming from changes to the system's environment, from security incidents, and from results from periodic vulnerability scans. Each of these will probably have an impact on ongoing mitigation efforts, and the plan must document these impacts in measurable tasks.

To be useful, the plan must be logically organized, should resist excessive detail, and must provide the information necessary to track actions through to their completion. It should not be forgotten that the plan is a management document, and its primary purpose is to track the status of corrective action. Anything falling short of this objective is inadequate, and anything going beyond this goal is excessive and unnecessary. The plan should comprise high-level summary information that links to more specific data as necessary. It is possible for recommended corrective actions to be overly detailed and therefore too restrictive. The manager should be open to and should in fact seek solutions that best suit his or her system's environment rather than unthinkingly accepting courses of action recommended by outsiders.

Continued reliance on solutions that have always been used and are thought to be time tested could result in unnecessary costs and time and might turn out to be over-kill. The corrective action should be written to give the system owner and his or her staff some latitude in identifying novel solutions that fit a precise need.

In all likelihood, the risk remediation plan will never be entirely completed. Because of ever-changing operating conditions, security needs are identified, changed, expanded, or eliminated in a continuing cycle. The system owner will find that he or she will probably never have sufficient resources to mitigate all the risks that are identified. The risks that remain after safeguards have been implemented may be too expensive to correct, or corrective action may be impractical given the current status or nature of the system. Though they cannot be mitigated, they must still be addressed, and the risk remediation plan is the mechanism for doing this. The plan documents these residual risks for the approving authority's acceptance and approval.

The risk remediation plan should have a close relationship with the organization's capital planning process. The resources identified in the plan should be fully integrated into the planning, programming, and budgeting system. Entries in the organization's budget request that are based on the risk remediation plan are particularly well documented and have an increased chance of being supported. Labor hours projected in the plan can be consolidated and serve to scope projects for budgeting purposes.

The organization's audit function will without doubt be a key user of the risk remediation plan because it can play a role in assessing firsthand the status of corrective action. As an independent entity, an auditor can assess risk remediation plan activities to see that they are complete and effective and to validate that due diligence has been performed.

The ISSO looks to the risk remediation plan with the aim of improving system security. System owners use it to manage the correction of deficiencies so that their system is as secure as possible. Organization management relies on the plan to prove that they have exercised due diligence. The organization information technology security manager makes use of the plan as one of many to determine trends, to identify resource requirements, to consolidate mitigation efforts organization-wide, and to monitor the status of corrective action on a broad base to establish and manage compliance with security standards. The organization information technology staff relies on the remediation plan to integrate corrective actions into the strategic information technology plan. And, the approving authority uses the plan to gain assurance that he or she is accepting no more risk than is absolutely necessary.

Chapter 4

The costs identified in the plan only have to be detailed enough to allow planning for budgeting and resourcing requirements. Normally, measuring costs by rough order of magnitude (in tens of man-hours and in thousands of dollars) offers sufficient precision. Of course, as corrective actions are refined, costs can be more precisely defined as necessary. Consultants are often a good source for providing costing information because they have a good perspective on resource costs based on their experience in implementing corrective actions across many types of organizations.

Risk Mitigation Meetings

Periodic meetings at which the risk remediation plan serves as the focal point need to be held frequently enough to maintain visibility of the mitigation effort. Systems with substantial weaknesses in either severity or number of corrective actions should meet perhaps weekly until the most significant weaknesses are mitigated fully or in part. Less-significant systems or those with only minor issues to resolve need not meet as frequently or with decreasing frequency as progress is made. It is important, at least in the beginning, to go through each weakness and corrective action in the plan to ensure it is understood and to establish a baseline for follow-on activities. If the weakness is unclear, a call for additional information should be channeled to the appropriate source (for example, the certifying agent for weaknesses and the ISSO or system administrator for corrective actions). This exercise also builds a team mentality toward problem solving and provides a forum for further specific corrective actions necessary, as well as milestones, schedules, resources, and priorities. This meeting should be chaired by the system owner to give emphasis to its importance and should be attended by all those who have responsibility for the corrective actions being discussed. It is obvious that this should be distributed more broadly than the ISSO or else it would be a very small meeting.

In addition, the CISO should conduct periodic meetings with elements of the organization to review progress in mitigating risks. This can be with individuals or groups of system owners according to mission needs, and risk remediation plans should be the focus of such meetings.

Observations

You have heard it said, "Don't fix what ain't broke." The goal of system authorization is to identify what is "broke" and to ensure that corrective action to fix what is broke is applied where needed. The risk remediation plan identifies what is broken;

moreover, it provides a road map for correcting identified weaknesses in a logical and cost-effective way. The risk remediation plan along with the accreditation letter (with which it goes hand in hand) are the two most important documents generated by the system authorization effort. Although the accreditation letter documents the approving authority's authorization for the system to process and his or her acceptance of residual risks, the risk remediation plan documents the plan for mitigating these risks to the minimum extent possible. Both of these documents must be totally synchronized.

Assessment of security controls is an important part of the system authorization methodology, but assessment must be followed by remediation of any identified vulnerabilities. This ensures that system security is improved sufficiently to meet minimum standards applicable to the system. It provides a means of tracking the status of corrective action to ensure that these minimum standards are met and establishes a baseline from which to monitor the system to ensure minimum standards *continue* to be met. Without mitigation, the organization is caught in an endless loop of assessing without ever getting around to solving security problems. Therefore, the entire system authorization methodology must point toward the risk mitigation process with an aim toward improving security. The risk remediation plan is ideally suited to meet this need and is the capstone of the system authorization methodology.

NIST Guidance on Implementation of Security Controls

Once the security controls set has been documented for the system in the security plan, the system owner may begin implementation of the controls accordingly. The third step of the Risk Management Framework results in implementation and documentation of security controls identified for the information systems. The following paragraphs summarize the guidance of NIST SP 800-37, Revision 1, for the security controls implementation step in the Risk Management Framework.

Task 3-1: Implement Security Controls

The system owner or CCP is responsible for implementing the security controls that are specified in the security plan for the system. Ideally, this task is performed during development or acquisition of a new or modernized information system.

Primary Responsibility	Supporting Roles	SDLC Phase	References
ISO or CCP	IO/IS, ISSO, ISSE	Development/ acquisition, implementation	FIPS Publication 200, NIST SPs 800-30, 800-53, 800-53A, CNSS Instruction 1253, Web: scap.nist.gov

CCP, common control provider; CNSS, Committee on National Security Systems; FIPS, Federal Information Processing Standard; ISO, information system owner; IO/IS, information owner/steward; ISSE, information system security engineer.

■ Implementation of security control must be consistent with the organization's enterprise architecture and information security architecture.

■ Security controls need not be allocated to every subsystem.

■ Best practices should be used when implementing security controls within the system to include system and software engineering methodologies, security engineering principles, and secure coding techniques.

■ The system owner must ensure mandatory configuration settings are implemented on information technology products according to federal and organizational policies such as the Federal Desktop Core Configuration.

■ Information system security engineers must adhere to a sound security engineering process to capture and refine information security requirements and ensure their integration into information technology products and systems.

■ As much as possible, organizations should employ information technology products that have been tested, evaluated, or validated through approved, independent, third-party assessment.

■ The system owner must satisfy minimum assurance requirements in the security controls implementation.

■ Assurance requirements guide activities of security control developers and implementers to increase the level of confidence that security controls are properly implemented.

■ Additional assurance measures should be considered for high-value systems and those that may be targets for advanced cyberattacks.

■ The implementation effort must address integration of common and system-specific controls and interfaces between them.

■ Information system security engineers and ISSOs must coordinate with CCPs to determine the most appropriate way to apply common controls to the system.

■ Particular management and operational controls may not require formal integration into information technology products, services, and systems.

- Implementation of certain types of operational and technical controls may require additional components, products, or services to enable the system to utilize common controls fully.

- When the system owner has deferred the selection of common controls, this should be revisited during control implementation to determine if they are appropriate at this point in the SDLC.

- The system owner should assess the adequacy of common controls by referring to the authorization packages prepared by CCPs.

- The system owner must identify compensating or supplementary controls if common controls do not meet the security requirements for the system, including those that have unacceptable weaknesses.

- System owners may begin conducting initial security control assessments during system development and implementation. These activities are also referred to as developmental testing and evaluation.

- Conducting security control assessments during the development and implementation phases of the SDLC permits early detection of deficiencies and provides a cost-effective approach for corrective action.

- Because of their potential impact on risk acceptance, it may be necessary to refer certain issues identified during security control assessments to authorizing officials for early resolution.

- Initial security control assessment results should be used later in system authorization to save time and avoid repeating some assessment activities.

Task 3-2: Document Security Control Implementation

Document the security control implementation in the security plan by providing a functional description of how each control is implemented to include planned inputs, expected behavior, and expected outputs. Security control documentation must describe how system-specific, hybrid, and common controls are implemented to meet system security requirements.

Primary Responsibility	Supporting Roles	SDLC Phase	References
ISO or CCP	IO/IS, ISSO, ISSE	Development/ acquisition, implementation	NIST SP 800-53, CNSS Instruction 1253

- Functional description of security control implementation must include planned inputs, expected behavior, and expected outputs primarily as related to technical controls employed in the system.

Chapter 4

■ Documenting the implementation of security control should include a record of decisions made prior to and following system deployment.

■ The level of effort for documenting system security controls implementation should be commensurate with the sensitivity and criticality of the system.

■ To increase the overall efficiency and cost-effectiveness of documenting security control implementation, the system owner should reference existing documentation (from vendors or other organizations that have employed the same or similar systems), use automated tools, and maximize communications.

■ Documentation must describe how a security requirement is met by the control in sufficient detail to permit assessment.

■ System owners should use vendor-provided functional specifications for technical security control mechanisms to facilitate their assessment and monitoring.

■ System owners should obtain security control implementation information for certain management and operational controls from appropriate organizational entities, including facilities, human resources, and physical security offices.

■ Documentation of security controls implementation should record how organizational security requirements reflected in the enterprise architecture and information security architecture have been satisfied.

SUMMARY

Chapter 4 addressed the implementation of security controls documented in an approved security plan for an information system to ensure the protection of the system and its data. The importance of the system owner and CCP in this process has been fully addressed. Both system-specific and common security procedures were highlighted to show their importance in providing detailed instructions on how a security control is implemented and maintained. Then, the process for remediation of gaps or weaknesses in security controls was described to show how they are tracked to ensure timely implementation. Finally, this chapter described current NIST guidance on the security control implementation tasks of the Risk Management Framework.

APPLICATION OF SECURITY CONTROLS: REVIEW QUESTIONS

1. When determining the applicability of a specific security control, the security professional should utilize which type of guidance?

    A. Categorization guidance

    B. Selection guidance

    C. Scoping guidance

    D. Remediation guidance

2. When making a determination regarding the adequacy of the implementation of inherited controls for their respective systems, an information system owner (ISO) can refer to the authorization package prepared by which of the following?

    A. Information owner/steward (IO)

    B. Information system security engineer (ISSE)

    C. Information systems security officer (ISSO)

    D. Common control provider (CCP)

3. The initial security plan for a new application has been approved. What is the next activity in the Risk Management Framework (RMF)?

    A. Develop a strategy for the continuous monitoring of security control effectiveness.

    B. Assemble the security authorization package.

    C. Implement the security controls specified in the security plan.

    D. Assess a selected subset of the security controls inherited by the information system.

Chapter 4

4. Which role has the supporting responsibility to coordinate changes to the system, assess the security impact, and update the system security plan?

   A. Information system security officer (ISSO)

   B. Information system owner (ISO)

   C. Common Control Provider

   D. Senior agency information security officer

5. Who is primarily responsible for the development of system-specific procedures?

   A. The system owner

   B. The information systems security officer (ISSO)

   C. The system architect

   D. The system administrator

Chapter 5

Assessment of Security Controls

The security control assessment follows the approved plan, including defined procedures, to determine the effectiveness of the controls in meeting security requirements of the information system. The results are documented in the security assessment report.

Certified Authorization Professional (CAP®) Candidate Information Bulletin, November 2010

TOPICS

- Scope of Testing
- Level of Effort
- Assessor Independence
- Developing the Test Plan
- The Role of the Host
- Test Execution
- Documenting Test Results
- NIST Guidance on Assessment of Security Control Effectiveness

OBJECTIVES

As a Certified Authorization Professional (CAP®), you are expected to

- Prepare for security control assessment
- Establish security control assessment plan
- Determine security control effectiveness
- Develop initial security assessment report
- Perform initial remediation actions
- Develop final security assessment report and addendum

Introduction

The purpose of security controls testing is to evaluate the effectiveness of security controls protecting an information system. The process for achieving this result is also referred to as security controls assessment, security assessment review, or security test and evaluation (ST&E). Certification testing is necessary to provide assurance that implemented controls meet a predetermined set of standards. Testing as part of the system certification process seeks to answer the question, "Are controls doing what they are intended to do?" Also, certification testing determines if required controls are in place, have been implemented correctly, and are operating as intended. Certification testing also results in identification of specific actions necessary to ensure that the protection requirements of the system are met. This includes actions to improve existing controls or to implement additional controls to counter established risks. The objective of certification testing is not to record quality of protection but merely to express if a requirement is being met or is not being met. Finally, security controls testing provides assurance that information recorded in security plans, risk assessments, contingency plans, and elsewhere is accurate and complete. Generally, there are two activities involved in certification testing: assessment of security controls and documentation of the results of testing. This chapter also provides highlights of the guidance of the National Institute of Standards and Technology (NIST) on security controls assessment as described in NIST Special Publication (SP) 800-37, Revision 1.

Scope of Testing

The scope of certification testing should be driven by the entire range of control requirements applicable to the system. These requirements, as described in previous chapters, stem from minimum security baselines adopted by organizations and from adjustments in controls determined by means of a risk assessment process. Normally, control requirements that are documented in the security plan for the system will comprise the scope of certification testing. As stated in Chapter 3, the security plan documents the broad range of controls protecting the system, both those that have been implemented and those planned for future implementation. That plan also identifies weaknesses in controls. Using the security plan as a start, a test plan is developed by the certification test team to validate that controls in the plan are in place as specified, to validate areas of weakness described in the plan, to identify additional areas of weakness, to document the status of planned controls, and to validate that controls identified as not applicable do not in fact apply. In addition, certification testing validates controls for which management has accepted risk to determine if cause still exists to warrant continuation of this acceptance.

The scope of certification testing normally addresses all NIST SP 800-53 control families with the purpose of uncovering design, implementation, and operational flaws in those controls. The extent of testing must be driven by the need for determining the adequacy of security mechanisms in enforcing the security policy relative to the target system. The scope will also be broad enough to allow an assessment of the accuracy and completeness of the system's security documentation.

Chapter 5

Level of Effort

When considering needs for and approaches to certification testing, system owners need to consider the sensitivity and criticality of the system. According to NIST SP 800-37 (p. 25), organizations are authorized to tailor system authorization activities to the level of effort and rigor that is suitable for the information system being tested. The organization may create a specific methodology based on the criticality of systems or a combination of factors that include need for integrity, availability, and confidentiality along with exposure the system's environment presents. It is important to tailor the level of effort of certification testing to the needs of the system to ensure testing is cost-effective. The level of effort established will drive the size of the testing team, the rigor of the testing, and the amount of documentation required. A comparison of levels of effort for systems categorized at three levels of risk is provided in Table 5.1.

Table 5.1 Certification Levels of Effort	
Certification Level	**Elements of Testing**
Low	Low-intensity, checklist-based, independent security review that includes • Interview of personnel • Review of system-related security policies, procedures, documents • Observation of system operations and security controls
Moderate	Moderate-intensity, demonstration-based, independent assessment that includes • Low certification level verification techniques (if appropriate) • Functional testing • Regression analysis and regression testing • Penetration testing (optional) • Demonstrations to verify security control correctness and effectiveness
High	High-intensity, exercise-based, independent assessment that includes • Low and moderate certification level verification techniques (if appropriate) • System design analysis • Functional testing with coverage analysis • Regression analysis and regression testing • Penetration testing (Red Team optional) • Demonstrations and exercises to verify security control correctness and effectiveness

Costs should not be overlooked in determining the scope of testing. The size and complexity of the system to be tested are the primary cost drivers. The level of human interaction required to perform testing and the feasibility of selecting an accurate sample for testing are additional cost factors for consideration. Costs for testing must be quantified to ensure that they are commensurate with the sensitivity and criticality of the system being tested.

The aggressiveness of testing to be conducted depends on the risk assessment and the need to ensure that testing activities are in line with the risks to the system. According to NIST SP 800-37, the rigor and intensity of testing should be guided by risk assessments to implement a risk-based security controls assessment cost-effectively.

Assessor Independence

The level of effort determination may also drive the decision on the level of independence required for the certification team. The certification team must normally be independent of the system owner. How independent must the team be? Certification testing is different from the routine self-assessments conducted by the system owner on a regular basis. Certification testing is different in that it is not performed as often, is more rigorous, and is conducted by an independent entity. For our purposes, independence requirements call for testers to be independent of the influence of the system owner. A practical approach will be to permit testing of low-risk systems by personnel assigned to the approving authority's organization but not from the system owner's; for moderate-risk systems, by personnel assigned to the organization but not to the approving authority's organization; and for high-risk systems, by personnel from outside the organization. It is nearly impossible to achieve perfect independence because testers have to have some familiarity with the system and must be funded by the organization in some manner. Application of the common-sense test can avoid extended and pointless discussions about the relative existence of independence of a certification team. Independence can also be achieved by using internal or external auditors; however, their use in this fashion should not be allowed to conflict with their primary auditing responsibilities to the organization.

Independence is most often achieved through the use of independent contractors skilled and experienced in certification testing or ST&E procedures. And, in many cases, certification testing will be performed by contractors who have been engaged

Table 5.2 Planning Estimates for Testing	
Certification Level	**Duration of Testing**
Low	One to two days
Moderate	Three to five days
High	Five to ten days

to perform certification testing for the system or a group of systems. In some cases, these contractors are tasked to perform all certification tasks relating to the system and prepare or update all documentation, including the security plan, risk assessment, and certification report. Although this approach has the advantage of achieving consistency in project execution and work products, it presents a disadvantage in that the same team completes all tasks, lessening the opportunity for independent oversight of their work.

The team performing certification testing should be composed of the certifying agent, the host, and test team members. The certifying agent is responsible for coordinating requirements for the team to include testing methodology, tools, travel, support requirements, and documentation. Much of this coordination needs to be made with the host, who is a representative of the system owner. Test team members are selected by the certifying agent and are responsible to the agent for performance of testing functions. These functions include preparation of the test plan, performance of testing, and documentation of test results. The number of test team members is dependent on the size and complexity of the system being tested, as well as the amount of time available to perform testing and the methodology being used. Table 5.2 provides planning estimates for various levels of testing. With few exceptions, testing should be performed by a minimum of two analysts. This permits comparison of findings, ensures full coverage of control requirements, and allows an additional perspective to be brought into play. In simple systems that are well known to the tester, a second analyst may be dispensed with in the interest of minimizing costs.

Team members need to be fully knowledgeable of the system, its processes, its functions, its purpose, and its user community. In addition, team members need to have specialized skills in the technologies that make up the system to include operating system, database, and application software and other platforms as necessary (i.e., firewalls, switches, routers, etc.). When tools are used in support of testing, team members should be skilled in their use and know their limitations and must be able to understand their output sufficiently to permit identification of false positives. They must have not only these technical skills but also people skills because they will have to work closely with hosting personnel throughout the duration of testing.

Finally, they must have the requisite credentials to perform the tests. Security clearance, access, background screening, and professional certifications fall into this category. The certifying agent should ensure that the host approves the qualifications and credentials of all team members before testing is initiated.

Developing the Test Plan

In planning for the certification testing task, the certifying agent must consider a multitude of tasks, requirements, and issues that affect successful completion of testing. These should be documented in a certification test plan. Table 5.3 provides an outline of a certification test or ST&E plan. The plan serves to guide all involved in the test to include those performing testing and those supporting testing. Therefore, to effect coordination and to ensure optimum cooperation, the plan should be prepared well in advance and be forwarded to all who will be performing a role in the certification test. It should be stressed that all controls are subject to testing, not just technical controls. Naturally, the types of tests to be performed and the types of evidence required will vary greatly between technical, operational, and management controls. Nevertheless, test standards and procedures should be prepared for all controls within the scope of the certification. Testing officials should use NIST SP 800-53A as a guide for developing test procedures. It provides standardized test procedures for each of the security controls included in NIST SP 800-53. Assumptions applicable to the certification test also need to be included in the test plan. Assumptions may address general issues, like availability of personnel to assist in testing, or specific concerns, such as the availability of a particular platform for testing in light of a planned deployment schedule.

Beyond identification of steps to test individual controls, the test plan must also include provisions for other areas that are critical to the protection of the system. Testing must include an assessment of the system boundary as described in the system security plan, as recorded in the risk assessment, and as reflected in the accreditation boundary. All must be identical, and any variation must be recorded in the test results. To ensure accuracy, the information contained in the system security plan should be compared against current system operation, design, and configuration as part of testing. The test plan needs to allow for development of an awareness of the system's operating environment as a basis for understanding the risks to the system. Finally, the test plan should provide for the evaluation of plans that support the information system, such as the incident response plan, disaster recovery plan,

Chapter 5

Table 5.3 Certification Test Plan Outline	
Section	**Description**
Purpose	Describes the purpose of the test plan
Objectives	Describes the objectives of certification testing
Memoranda of understanding	Specifies all memoranda of understanding with interconnected, hosting, or hosted systems
Responsible organizations/ personnel	Identifies the host organization and host personnel
Assumptions	Specifies any assumptions on which the test plan is based
Scope	Defines the scope of testing (i.e., components, locations, etc.)
Testing requirements	Provides a high-level description of areas that testing will focus on (i.e., categories of controls to be tested)
Testing approach	Provides an overview of how testing will be performed
Tests to be used	Makes reference to the specific tests that will be used to test each control found in the appendix
Schedule	Identifies the proposed start and end dates and times that testing will be performed
Test team composition	Identifies the names and positions of personnel assigned to the certification test team
Test team roles and responsibilities	Specifies the roles and responsibilities for each test team member
Other supporting organizations	Identifies the role that will be played by other elements in support of testing
Remediation plan	Describes the process for managing the correction of weaknesses identified through certification testing
Appendix: Controls and tests	For each control applicable to the system, a specific protocol for testing is stipulated

and the contingency plan to ensure that they are up to date and meet the protection needs of the system in its current operating environment.

The plan must include a detailed description of the testing methodology that will be used. It must address the support that is required from the hosting organization. It must clearly state the roles and responsibilities of those involved and must specify personnel to be involved in the exercise, if not by name then at least by position. This includes individuals to be interviewed, those required to demonstrate system controls, and those to provide documentation. If the team needs access to the system or its components, this should be specified in the plan so that it can be coordinated by the host in advance. Also, documentation necessary to perform testing (i.e., configuration standards, records of changes, system access lists, training records, etc.) should be identified in the plan to allow the host sufficient opportunity to locate and gather them prior to the initiation of testing. Identify particular facilities in the plan that will need to be accessed as well. If only a sampling of servers, workstations, wiring closets, or storage rooms will be selected for testing, provide the host the approximate number, type, IP address range, and so on to allow adequate preparation. The plan should detail the testing schedule and allow sufficient time for test preparation, actual test execution, and posttest feedback. If automated tools are to be used, they need to be identified in advance, and the plan should document requirements and coordination for their use. The plan should also detail administrative, logistics, and travel requirements. Finally, and most important, the plan must specify the scope of what will be tested, how it will be tested, and the results expected from testing for each control.

The plan must address structured testing of all controls within the scope of the project and must map directly to the previously developed scope statement. The plan should be jointly developed by the system owner and the certifying agent to the maximum extent possible to ensure openness and facilitate efficient performance of control testing. This is aided by providing the plan to the host as far in advance as possible and by gaining early agreement on the plan. For each control to be tested, the specific standard that is to be met must be documented. This should be written in the form of "expected results" or criteria for success and should make specific reference to a regulatory requirement or to a best practice. In addition, the plan should establish the type of evidence required to prove findings (i.e., scan result, screen shot, documentary evidence, etc.). If special tools are required to test the control, they should also be specified in the plan. Examples of certification test plan entries are provided in Table 5.4 and Table 5.5.

Preparation of the certification test plan should include a review of existing documentation related to the system. The certification agent should work with the system owner to identify documentation that will be helpful in preparing for certification testing. The system security plan serves as the starting point for developing the plan since it documents specific requirements for the system's security controls as well as the status of implementation of those controls. If the system security plan is out of date or does not accurately reflect the system's controls or functionality, the certifying agent will have to locate other documentation to obtain this information to create an effective test plan. Security procedures specific to the system, often documented

Chapter 5

Table 5.4 Sample Certification Test Plan Entry

Question	Vulnerability	ST&E Actions	Expected Results	Pass/Fail	Actual Results Summary	Document Reference
Personnel Security						
64	6.1 Are duties separated to ensure least privilege and individual accountability?					
65	6.1.1 Are all positions reviewed for sensitivity level? (FISCAM SD-1.2, NIST SP 800-18)	Verify by inspection and interview with management that the system-related positions are reviewed for sensitivity level on an annual basis. (FISCAM SD-1.2)	All positions are reviewed by the system owner for sensitivity level annually.			

| 66 | 6.1.2 Are there documented job descriptions that accurately reflect assigned duties and responsibilities and that segregate duties? (FISCAM SD-1.2) | Review several job requirements and descriptions and interview management and personnel regarding system support and user positions. (FISCAM SD 1.2) | All reviewed job descriptions are accurately documented to reflect assigned security-related duties and responsibilities. |
| 67 | 6.1.3 Are sensitive functions divided among different individuals? (OMB Circular A-130, III, FISCAM SD-1, NIST SP 800-18) | Determine if multiple steps in the process or key functions are performed by the same individual, for example, data entry and data validation or data entry and supervisory authorization. Observe tasks performed by SA and security administrator. | Sensitive functions are divided between at least two different individuals. |

Chapter 5

Table 5.5   Sample Certification Test Entry

Question	Vulnerability	ST&E Actions	Expected Results	Pass/Fail	Actual Results Summary	Document Reference
73	6.2 Is appropriate background screening for assigned positions completed prior to granting access?					
74	6.2.1 Are individuals who are authorized to bypass significant technical and operational controls screened prior to access and periodically thereafter? (OMB Circular A-130, III, FISCAM SP-4.1)	Review personnel security records for a minimum of two system administrators and security administrators to ensure that their records were screened prior to their access being granted.	Background screenings for assigned positions are completed prior to granting access and periodically thereafter.	P	A review of the records of four Nutria System users revealed that all four have undergone SF86 Public Trust investigations.	Interview with personnel security officer; personnel records of four system users. These were H. Snow, B. Crow, D. Glow, and R. Roe.

				P		
75	6.2.2 Are confidentiality or security agreements required for employees assigned to work with sensitive information? (FISCAM SP-4.1)	Verify personnel records of at least five system users to ensure that confidentiality agreements have been signed.	Nondisclosure agreements for all records of personnel reviewed are signed and maintained on file.	P	A review of five user files maintained by the office of primary responsibility revealed that all five users had signed confidentiality agreements.	Review of five personnel records maintained by the office of primary responsibility. These were J. Doe, H. Snow, B. Crow, D. Glow, and R. Roe.
76	6.2.3 When controls cannot adequately protect the information, are individuals screened prior to access? (OMB Circular A-130, III)	Review records of background screening for at least three users with elevated system privileges and user access dates to determine if screening was concluded prior to their being granted access.	Individuals (i.e., system administration personnel) are screened prior to being granted access when controls cannot adequately protect the information.	P	All Nutria System users checked were found to have been screened prior to being granted access to the system.	Review of five personnel records and user access files pertaining to B. Crow, D. Glow, and R. Roe maintained by the office of primary responsibility.

Chapter 5

in the system's concept of operations (CONOPS) document are also useful in developing the test plan.

Procedures employed to test individual controls need to be comprehensive and complex enough to determine if the control meets the test standard and thereby determine if there are vulnerabilities in system controls. The types of testing that can be considered for employment in certification testing include

- *Inspection*: Inspection is the physical review or examination of a control, such as review of a security setting or software version number.
- *Demonstration*: Demonstration includes evaluation through operation, movement, or adjustment under specific conditions to determine the control's capability of satisfying a stated requirement.
- *Test*: A test is the collection, analysis, and evaluation of controls by means of hands-on measurement under specified test conditions.

Documenting specific steps to be followed in testing each control ensures the test adequately if the control standard is being met, aids the test team in test execution, permits the host to know in advance how the control will be tested, and provides historical data to allow understanding of testing procedures after testing has been concluded. These test scripts may have to be very detailed, down to the keystroke level, in the case of technical controls.

The plan should also document procedures for addressing findings that require immediate resolution, such as discovery of malicious software, identification of child pornography, or other evidence of criminal wrongdoing. Provisions should be made to suspend testing pending resolution of issues such as these. It should be stipulated in the plan that incidents of this nature will be reported in accordance with policies and following procedures of the owning organization. Also, it is a good idea for the testing team to work with the owning organization to correct weaknesses on the spot whenever possible. This practice not only builds goodwill but also limits the need for follow-up monitoring in the remediation plan. There is little for the test team to gain from playing "gotcha" during certification testing. Therefore, provisions for correcting weaknesses as they are discovered need to be recorded in the plan to assure the system owner that the team will play fair and does in fact seek the improvement of the system's security controls.

The test plan as developed and submitted to the host for approval must be constructed to permit its use in that same format for documenting the results of testing. That is to say, the test team should initiate testing with the same test plan that the host has approved and should actually use it for the duration of the certification test. The plan should therefore provide adequate space for documenting the actual test results. For controls that meet standards, the results must document how standards have been met, and for controls that do not meet standards, the results must record how or why they failed. An additional column for recording whether the control passed or failed allows the reader to see quickly which controls were lacking. When evidence of testing is required, the plan must specify the type of evidence that is necessary and the format for documenting it. This includes written procedures, screen shots, tool-generated output, and so on. Normally, such documentary evidence is best presented as an appendix to the test report once it has been compiled. Also, the test plan must provide space for recording information about when individual or groups of controls are tested, who conducted the testing, where controls were tested, and what components were involved.

The Role of the Host

The hosting organization is responsible for ensuring that certification testing is performed in a timely and efficient manner. This is done by making arrangements to have required personnel available to supplement the test team when they are needed. Requirements for personnel that have been documented in the test plan will be coordinated with the certifying agent. Personnel necessary for interviews, for assisting with performing tests, for running test scripts, for demonstrating practices, and for escorting test team members must be identified in advance, and personnel must be instructed about what is expected of them. The system owner should provide the test plan to all personnel involved to ensure they are aware of their roles in the test. The host should make a concerted effort to collect in advance all documentation required by the test team that has been specified in the test plan to avoid causing delays once the test team begins testing. The host is responsible for providing logistical support to the test team for the duration of testing. Network access, access to a phone and fax machine, reproduction support, and meeting rooms all fall into this category. Finally, access to facilities where testing will be conducted requires prior coordination between the test team and the hosting organization to ensure test team members can get to where they need to be without difficulty. However, testing should not require special access to be granted, and the host should ensure that normal access rules are followed in processing physical access for the team. Unescorted access should be arranged only when it is warranted and has been justified by the test team

Chapter 5

director. The host should also be involved in daily coordination meetings held while testing is under way.

Test Execution

Using the prepared and approved plan, the test team conducts the test. Results of testing should be immediately recorded into the plan as tests are performed one after the other. Deviation from conditions specified in the plan should be documented as they are observed. If specific components cannot be tested, this fact should be explained, and any exceptions should be clearly noted. Individuals involved in the testing should be specified by name, including those who provided assistance to the testing team.

It is useful to rank findings according to risk. This can be handled by including a column in the test results table that maps to risk assessment findings or by addressing it elsewhere in the results report, such as in an executive summary. The report should include charts to summarize findings by risk level and by control type. The process for ranking findings also must be fully described in the results report. Results should be ranked as either meeting standards (pass) or not meeting standards (fail). There is little value in ranking the degree to which a control passes or fails. Rather, the ranking should be based on the degree of risk attaching to the control.

When technical controls are tested, it is advisable to have an authorized system user from the owning organization who has been approved by the host to enter commands to execute test scripts. This avoids having to grant the member of the certification test team access to the system, protects the owning organization against inadvertent errors, and protects the team members from claims that they have caused damage to the system. If this is not possible, a second team member along with someone from the owning organization should be present as witnesses. This helps achieve one of the main objectives of testing: the avoidance of disruption of normal operations. System crashes, accidental disclosures, and data integrity losses can be avoided or at least limited through thorough preparation and coordination. Knowledge of the system and of tools used will help achieve this objective. Resources and operations that are off-limits must be known to the team in advance. And, system management must be aware of any plans to use social engineering, vulnerability scanning tools, or physical or logical penetration techniques. Assessing blame for problems can quickly deteriorate to a condition where testing can no longer be continued.

To avoid this, escalation procedures must be established to provide a controlled process for identifying and resolving problems quickly and completely to allow testing to get back on track.

Conducting testing after normal hours of operation should be considered carefully and must be well coordinated in advance. Testing during normal operating hours is preferable because the capability to respond to unexpected problems is greater, and the organization's staff is normally better prepared to respond to issues that may arise. They also have more depth and can better afford to accommodate testing during normal hours of operation, whereas after operating hours, testing can more easily lead to crippling disruptions of service. After-hours testing can also place additional stress on the staff of the owning organization, which may hamper its cooperation with the test team.

Assessors should attempt to gain as much information about the system as possible preliminary to security controls testing. This will normally include accessing and browsing publicly accessible information about the agency, organization, or perhaps even the system undergoing assessment. Such public source data gathering can be focused specifically on newsgroup postings, domain records, Web sites, and so on. In addition, sniffers can be used to monitor network traffic.

It is always a good idea to provide interim results to permit system owners to get a head start on remediating problems whenever possible. The certification testing team should conduct a briefing immediately following the conclusion of testing to provide system management/operations personnel an opportunity to know their security posture and to take immediate action. In addition, if a "war-stopper" is encountered (e.g., evidence of criminal activity), testing should be halted until the issue is resolved. Should testing cause a system crash or other adverse effect on the production environment, all testing should be terminated immediately and should not be resumed until the situation has been stabilized, investigated, and resolved. The certification test team chief should immediately brief management on the incident.

Automated scanning tools can benefit the testing effort because they can detect evidence of the most currently identified vulnerabilities; also, they are easy to use, save time, and standardize output. Automated scanning that is normally considered for certification testing includes network scanning, vulnerability scanning, penetration testing, password cracking, audit log reviews, and file integrity checking. Advantages and disadvantages relative to the use of each of these are shown in Table 5.6.

Chapter 5

Table 5.6	Strengths and Weaknesses of Automated Testing Tools	
Type of Tool	**Strengths**	**Weaknesses**
Network scanning	Fast; efficient scanning of hosts	Does not determine risk level of discovered vulnerabilities; significant expertise required to interpret results
Vulnerability scanning	Reasonably fast; highly automated; freeware tools available	High false-positive rate; generates large amount of traffic; often fails to identify latest vulnerabilities
Penetration testing	Replicates activities/tools of an actual attacker; verifies vulnerabilities	Requires significant expertise; labor intensive
Password cracking	Quickly identifies weak passwords; easy implementation; low cost	Potential for abuse
Automated log review	Provides historical data	May filter out important information
File integrity checking	Reliable means for determining compromise; highly automated; low cost	Does not detect compromises that occurred prior to installation; need for updating checksums; need for protection of checksum values
Virus detectors	Excellent prevention/eradication of viruses; low-to-medium cost	Require constant updating; false-positive issues; limited response to fast-replicating viruses

When using automated tools, caution must be taken to avoid disruption of operations or damage/loss to data. To limit the potential for harm to the system, specific files may be temporarily modified to test potential vulnerabilities. However, be sure to record all modified files that will be kept and the penetration testing team's log files so that the system may be restored. User files such as .rhosts or .forward might be created or modified to attempt shell access on a UNIX host. Windows resource kit executables and operating system programs such as rcp.exe, rsh.exe, and net command may also be used. Use caution when using UNIX programs such as mail, netstat, telnet, and crontab to gather information, expand user privileges, or gain access to other hosts. Permission should be obtained before installation of executables on machines that can be used to grant remote access, elevate system privileges, and so on. Finally, unless a system owner has specifically requested it, denial of service and buffer overflow attacks should not be exploited.

In addition to automated testing tools, social engineering, war dialing, and war driving are testing techniques that are frequently used in certification testing. Social engineering tests how users protect sensitive information for which they have access, but requires experience and skill to be effective. War dialing is an effective way to identify unauthorized modems that allow connectivity to the system, but it is slow and may be subject to legal and regulatory issues. War driving is an effective approach to identifying unauthorized wireless access points but requires computing, networking, and radio engineering expertise and can cause legal issues if another organization's wireless signals are intercepted.

The certification team must take sufficient time to ensure that the results of automated scanning are integrated seamlessly into the test results report and are consistent with other report findings. Scan findings should map to individual control requirements specified in the minimum security baseline and to the certification test plan. If this is not possible, then a new control requirement must be added. This will necessitate an update of the risk assessment to determine threat pairing, the security (i.e., confidentiality, integrity, availability) impact and probability, and the risk factor. Once this has been done, the results of the scan can be clearly documented in the plan of action and milestones (POA&M) and in the security plan.

Systems that employ firewalls pose particular challenges for certification testing. Because of their importance to the security of the system, all aspects and functions of the firewall need to be addressed when performing certification testing, to include configuration controls and firewall policy implementation and management. Testing should encompass the firewall functionality at all OSI (Open System Interconnection) layers. Firewalls that operate at multiple layers provide more effective and comprehensive security and more granular configuration. Firewalls are normally tested by comparing documented firewall policies against the configuration actually implemented. This is the fastest and easiest means of testing. Alternatively, more rigorous testing includes the use of tools to assess the configuration of the firewall by attempting to perform operations that should be prohibited. The goal of firewall testing is to ensure that the firewall is configured exactly as described in the documented policy and that it is functioning as expected.

There are normally controls that the system owner will identify in advance as not in place for any number of reasons. It is not necessary to conduct testing on controls of this nature. There is no need to prove to the system owner that controls are truly not in place; he or she already knows this, and the methodology is not designed to measure qualitatively how well or how poorly controls have been implemented. However, these preidentified, failing controls must be documented in the test results

Chapter 5

report for this report will serve as the basis for the remediation plan, and it needs to include all control weaknesses, whether they have undergone testing or not.

As a general principle, the scope of certification testing should include all controls that are defined in the system security plan. Of course, this assumes that all controls that are necessary for the system have been documented in the security plan. If that is not the case, additional controls found in the risk assessment need to be tested even though they are not documented in the security plan. However, as stated previously, there is little need to test controls that the system owner has reported as not in place. Controls of this nature are not tested, permitting more time to be spent on testing other system controls that actually need testing. Although they will not undergo testing, controls that have not been implemented still need to be recorded in the certification test results report as failing so that they can be included in the remediation plan.

Documenting Test Results

The results of certification testing are documented by the certification agent to record the extent to which security controls have been correctly implemented, are operating as intended, and are producing the desired outcome. Once certification testing has been completed, the test team should gather and analyze the results of all control tests and collectively record the results of testing. This should be done by completing the previously submitted and approved test plan. Raw data collected during testing should be transformed into documented test results immediately following the conclusion of testing while it is still fresh and while test team members are still available. The team should coordinate closely to compare observations and validate their individual findings. The results of automated technical testing must be evaluated to ensure they are accurate and free from duplication and false-positive findings. Scan results should be reviewed and integrated into the test results by the responsible test member. According to the test plan, each control should be annotated as either pass or fail, the actual findings recorded in detail, and sources and processes used to validate the status of the control. A sample certification test results matrix is provided in Appendix P.

The POA&M is normally generated or updated as a result of certification testing. This activity is the responsibility of the information system owner (ISO) but is often performed by the certifying agent as part of certification testing activities. The POA&M is used to identify all weaknesses in system security controls and provides a road map for actions to correct each deficiency. The POA&M should include the status of planned controls so that the certifying official can accurately assess the risk to the system and make appropriate recommendations. Chapter 4 addresses the use of the POA&M for remediation planning, and an example POA&M is provided in Appendix Q. Following the completion of certification testing, adjustments will need to be made to the system security plan. Primarily, changes in the status of security controls identified as part of testing will need to be updated in the plan. It is the system owner who is responsible for updating the system security plan following testing. However, the certifying agent normally documents the need for plan updating as an entry in the POA&M.

The test results report should include an additional section that describes who conducted testing (i.e., the names of team members); who assisted in testing (from the hosting organization); where testing was conducted (an overview of locations, platforms, components, and subsystems included in the scope of testing); a summary of the process for conducting testing; and starting and ending times of the test. In addition, the test results report should detail any case where deviations from the test plan took place. For instance, if a particular server could not be tested or a procedure could not be demonstrated, this should be documented with a recommendation that follow-up testing be conducted. In this case, if the functionality of a control cannot be verified, it must be recorded as a failure. Testing may also reveal that a listed control is not applicable to the system or that there are other controls not in the test plan that may be necessary to secure the system. These deviations to the test plan should be recorded, and recommendations for additional controls should be emphasized.

Also, the test results report should rank test results (i.e., prioritize the significance of each control that failed to meet standards) and describe the process for ranking weaknesses found. This is most effective when based on risk assessment findings, rather than on the subjective view of the test team. The report should be written to map findings to specific risks previously identified in the risk assessment report, using the same ranking definitions. The report also needs to summarize, perhaps in an executive summary, a high-level view of testing results. This provides a snapshot of areas of concern, the most significant findings, and, for benchmarking purposes, the security of the system relative to other like systems, connected systems, or similar organizations.

Chapter 5

NIST Guidance on Assessment of Security Control Effectiveness

In this step of the Risk Management Framework, the security control assessor formally assesses security controls to determine if they are correctly implemented, are operating properly, and meet the system's security requirements. Security control assessments are guided in large part by the detailed instructions found in NIST SP 800-53A. This section summarizes NIST SP 800-37, Revision 1, guidance on testing of security controls effectiveness.

Task 4-1: Prepare for Controls Assessment

Develop, review, and approve a plan for assessing security controls protecting the system. A security assessment plan documents the objectives for the security control assessment, details how to conduct such an assessment, and records assessment procedures.

Primary Responsibility	Supporting Roles	SDLC Phase	References
SCA	AO or AODR, CIO, CISO, ISO or CCP, IO/IS, ISSO	Development/ acquisition, implementation	NIST SP 800-53A

AO, authorizing official; CCP, common control provider; CIO, chief information officer; CISO, chief information security officer; DR, designated representative; ISSO, information system security officer; SDLC, system development life cycle.

- The security assessment plan records the type of assessment being conducted. This may include developmental testing and evaluation, independent verification and validation, assessments supporting security authorizations or reauthorizations, audits, continuous monitoring, and assessments related to remediation activities.

- Security control assessments conducted in parallel with system development/acquisition and implementation permit early identification of weaknesses and cost-effective corrective action.

- Issues identified during security assessments may be referred to AOs for early resolution as necessary.

- Results of security control assessments performed during system development and implementation can also be used during the security authorization process to avoid delays or repetition of assessment activities.

- The system owner must ensure the security assessment plan is consistent with organizational security objectives, reflects the use of tools, techniques, procedures, and automation that support continuous monitoring and near real-time risk management, and that resources for the assessment are cost-effective.

- Approval of the security assessment plan establishes appropriate expectations for the assessment and establishes the level of effort for accomplishing it.

- Security assessment plan approval ensures sufficient resources are applied to meet the objective of determining security control effectiveness.

- For security controls external to the system, the system owner should obtain a security assessment plan developed by the external provider.

- Technical expertise and the level of independence required are key considerations for system owners in selecting security control assessors.

- System owners must ensure security control assessors have the skills and technical expertise necessary to assess all system-specific, hybrid, and common controls.

- Security control assessors must have knowledge of and experience with specific hardware, software, and firmware components of the system.

- An independent assessor must be able to conduct an impartial assessment of security controls employed within or inherited by a system.

- Independent assessors must be free from any perceived or actual conflicts of interest related to system development, operation, and management or determination of security control effectiveness.

- Other organizational elements or external (public or private-sector) entities may be used to provide independent security control assessment services.

- The independence of contracted assessment services depend on the non-involvement of the system owner in the contracting process or the system owner's inability to unduly influence the contractors charged with conducting the security controls assessment.

- The AO is responsible for defining the amount of independence required based on the system security categorization and risk to the organization.

- Independent assessors are used to perform security control assessments in support of both initial and subsequent security authorizations.

Task 4-2: Assess Security Controls

Conduct an assessment of the system's security controls in accordance with the assessment procedures defined in the security assessment plan from Task 4-1.

Chapter 5

Security control assessments determine if controls are implemented correctly, are operating as intended, and meet system security requirements.

Primary Responsibility	Supporting Roles	SDLC Phase	References
SCA	ISO or CCP, IO/IS, ISSO	Development/ acquisition, implementation	NIST SP 800-53A

- Security control assessments will be conducted as early as possible in SDLC, preferably during the development phase.

- Developmental testing and evaluations are intended to validate that required security controls are correctly implemented and are consistent with the established information security architecture.

- Developmental testing and evaluation activities include design and code reviews, application scanning, and regression testing.

- Deficiencies identified early in system development can be resolved more quickly and cost effectively prior to proceeding to subsequent SDLC phases.

- The objective of security control assessment is to identify the security architecture and security controls up front and to ensure that the system design and testing validate their implementation.

- The system owner relies on the technical expertise and judgment of security control assessors to use assessment procedures defined in the security assessment plan and to provide specific recommendations for corrective action to reduce or eliminate vulnerabilities.

- Assessor findings should provide an unbiased, factual representation of the weaknesses and deficiencies discovered during the assessment.

- The use of automation to conduct security control assessment should be maximized to increase the speed and overall effectiveness and efficiency of assessments and to support ongoing monitoring of system security posture.

- Iterative development (e.g., agile development) typically includes iterative assessment with each cycle.

- Assessment of security controls in commercial off-the-shelf (COTS) information technology products used with a system may also be conducted iteratively.

- Organizations may choose to initiate security controls assessment prior to the complete implementation of all security controls listed in the security plan since incremental assessment may be more efficient or cost-effective.

- The system owner ensures assessors have access to the system and all security controls, as well as to all documentation, records, artifacts, test results, and other materials needed to assess the controls.

- Assessors will have the required degree of independence as determined by the AO.

- The independence of assessors employed during continuous monitoring, while not mandatory, permits the reuse of assessment results should reauthorization be required.

- If security controls are provided by an external provider, the system owner ensures that assessors have access to the system and its security controls as well as to appropriate information needed to perform the assessment.

- The system owner should obtain any information related to previous assessments conducted by the external provider and should reuse this information whenever possible.

- For the risk management process to be as timely and cost effective as possible, organizations should reuse previous assessment results whenever reasonable and appropriate.

- On the same basis, organizations should also reuse assessment results from programs that test and evaluate security features of commercial information technology products.

- If the system developer has conducted a prior assessment, the security control assessor may include those results in the assessment if appropriate.

Task 4-3: Prepare Security Assessment Report

Prepare a security assessment report to document the issues, findings, and recommendations from the security control assessment. The security assessment report is prepared to document the results of the security control assessment, including recommendations for correcting any security control weaknesses.

Primary Responsibility	Supporting Roles	SDLC Phase	References
SCA	ISO or CCP, ISSO	Development/ acquisition, implementation	NIST SP 800-53A

- The security assessment report is one of the key documents in the security authorization package developed for authorization of a system.

- The assessment report records the assessor's determination of the effectiveness of all security controls protecting the system based on the assessor's findings.

- The security assessment report is an important factor in an AO's determination of risk to the organization.

Chapter 5

■ The level of detail of the security control assessment will be driven by organizational or federal policies as well as the type of assessment (e.g., testing and evaluation, self-assessments, independent verification and validation, independent assessments supporting the security authorization process or subsequent reauthorizations, assessments during continuous monitoring, assessments subsequent to remediation actions, independent audits/evaluations).

■ The security assessment report is an evolving document that includes results from all relevant phases of the SDLC. Hence, security control assessments performed during system development are recorded in an interim report that is later included in the final security controls assessment report.

■ It may be beneficial to develop an executive summary from the detailed findings generated during a security control assessment to provide the AO an abbreviated version of the assessment report that focuses on the highlights of the assessment and summarizes key findings and recommendations.

Task 4-4: Conduct Remediation Actions

Conduct initial remediation actions relative to security controls based on the findings and recommendations documented in the security assessment report and reassess remediated controls as appropriate.

Primary Responsibility	Supporting Roles	SDLC Phase	References
ISO or CCP, SCA	AO or AODR, CIO, CISO, IO/IS, ISSO, ISSE, SCA	Development/ acquisition, implementation	NIST SPs 800-30, 800-53A

ISSE, information system security engineer.

■ The findings generated during the security control assessment should serve as the basis for mitigating risks to the system according to organizational priorities.

■ The system owner reviews assessment findings to determine their severity or seriousness (i.e., the potential adverse impact on the organization) and whether they are worthy of further investigation or remediation.

■ System owners and CCPs, in collaboration with selected organizational officials, may decide that particular findings present no significant risk to the organization.

■ On the other hand, they may decide that certain findings are significant and require immediate remediation.

- An updated risk assessment in response to the results of the security control assessment along with inputs from the risk executive (function) help to determine and prioritize initial remediation actions.

- The involvement of senior agency leadership may be necessary to ensure resources for mitigation are allocated, prioritizing systems supporting the organization's most critical and sensitive missions or correcting deficiencies posing the highest risk.

- When weaknesses in security controls are corrected, the controls must be reassessed to ensure they are effective.

- Original assessment results should never be changed, but assessors will update the security assessment report to include findings from reassessments.

- The system security plan must be updated to reflect the findings of the security control assessment and remediation efforts.

- The updated security plan reflects the actual state of the security controls after the initial assessment and reflects any corrective actions taken to address recommendations.

- When the assessment is completed, the security plan accurately lists and describes the security controls implemented (including compensating controls) and residual vulnerabilities.

- System owners and CCPs may prepare an addendum to the security assessment report for transmission to the AO in response to the initial findings of assessors and may describe initial remediation actions taken in response to findings or provide perspective on the findings. This addendum does not change or influence the initial findings but is considered by AOs in their risk-based authorization decisions.

- AOs may employ an issue resolution process to determine appropriate actions to take to address security control weaknesses identified during the assessment. This process can help address vulnerabilities, false positives, and other factors that may be useful to AOs in determining the security state of the system and to ensure only substantive items are incorporated in the plan of actions and milestones.

Chapter 5

SUMMARY

Certification testing is the crown jewel of the system authorization process. Because of its importance in the overall system authorization program, certification testing must be well planned, conducted by knowledgeable professionals, and well documented. The certification test determines if all technical and nontechnical controls designed to protect the system have been implemented and meet a predetermined set of standards. Certification testing identifies weaknesses in a system's controls from an objective point of view and serves as the basis for remediation efforts. The certification test also serves as a quality control process to validate the results of other security processes, such as the security plan, risk assessment, and contingency plan. Most important, certification testing serves as the basis for the decision by the accrediting official to authorize or not authorize the system. The documented results of the certification test along with the recommendations of the certifying agent provide the ISO and the accrediting authority assurance of the effectiveness of security controls and all other information that he or she needs to make this decision.

ASSESSMENT OF SECURITY CONTROLS: REVIEW QUESTIONS

1. An initial remediation action was taken by the information system owner (ISO) based on findings from the security assessment report (SAR). What is the next appropriate step based on the Risk Management Framework (RMF)?

    A. ISO documents the remedial action in the security plan.

    B. Include the remediation action taken by information system owner as an addendum to the SAR.

    C. Information system security officer (ISSO) documents the remediation action and informs the ISO.

    D. Remedial action taken is sent for review to the ISSO.

2. Which of the following control families belongs to the management class of security controls?

    A. Media protection

    B. Configuration management

    C. Access control

    D. Risk assessment

3. Prior to completion of the security assessment report (SAR), what type of analysis is performed when agile, iterative development, is used?

    A. Regression analysis

    B. Interim assessment

    C. Incremental assessment

    D. Executive assessment

Chapter 5

4. In the case of a complex information system, where a "leveraged authorization" that involves two agencies will be conducted, what is the minimum number of system boundaries/accreditation boundaries that can exist?

    A. Only one.

    B. Only two, because there are two agencies.

    C. At least two.

    D. A leveraged authorization cannot be conducted with more than one agency involved.

5. Who determines the required level of independence for security control assessors?

    A. Information system owner (ISO)

    B. Information system security manager (ISSM)

    C. Authorizing official (AO)

    D. Information system security officer (ISSO)

Chapter 6

Information System Authorization

The residual risks identified during the security control assessment are evaluated and the decision is made to authorize the system to operate, deny its operation, or remediate the deficiencies. Associated documentation is prepared and/or updated depending on the authorization decision.

Certified Authorization Professional (CAP®) Candidate Information Bulletin,
November 2010

TOPICS

- System Authorization Decision Making
- Essential System Authorization Documentation
- NIST Guidance on Authorization of Information Systems

OBJECTIVES

As a Certified Authorization Professional (CAP®), you are expected to

- Develop plan of action and milestones (POA&M)
- Assemble security authorization package
- Determine risk
- Determine the acceptability of risk
- Obtain security authorization decision

Introduction

The authorization or accreditation phase of the system security authorization process consists of activities associated with making the security accreditation decision and formal documentation of that decision. The purposes of the accreditation phase are to evaluate the remaining known vulnerabilities in the information system and to determine whether the risk of its operation is acceptable to the organization. The guidance of the National Institute of Standards and Technology (NIST) on system authorization or Step 5 of the Risk Management Framework is also highlighted in this chapter.

System Authorization Decision Making

The culminating event in the system authorization process is accreditation, or the approval by a senior management official for the system to process. The act of signing an accreditation letter for the system is the physical substantiation of upper-level management involvement in ensuring the security of the system. The accreditation letter fixes responsibility for the operation of the system. It is the end link in the chain of accountability. Risk Management Framework tasks that relate to the information found in this chapter are Tasks 5-2, 5-3, and 5-4.

By requiring a signature, management involvement at least to this extent must occur. Authorizing officials (AOs) may be totally removed from the system authorization process up to this time, but they are indispensable in this, the final step in the process. This is a function that AOs should never delegate to someone else. With his or her signature, the approving authority indicates that he or she has considered the risks to operating the system and has decided to allow the system to begin processing or to continue processing. To ensure that the security of the system is given thoughtful consideration by the approving authority and to provide assurance that the approving authority is aware of risks to system processing, ample documentation in the form of the system authorization package accompanies the accreditation letter. I suppose that there might be an approving authority out there somewhere who would sign an accreditation letter without having had the system first certified. However, this not only would be risky but also would not meet the requirements for exercising due care. From another angle, however, this is exactly what happens every day when systems go into production or continue to operate without a system authorization process being implemented. In such cases, responsibility for security is not fixed except at the highest level of the organization. Of course, we attempt to cushion the impact of not assigning security accountability with talk that "security is everyone's responsibility." However, such evasion does little to really improve security.

The System Authorization Authority

The act of accreditation establishes accountability for system operation and is a function of ownership of the system. The accrediting authority, while not being the actual, direct owner of the system, owns the business process that the system supports and owns the resources on which the system derives its sustenance. Being in the ownership chain while being removed from the day-to-day operations of the system puts the approving authority in a good position to oversee the security of the system from a higher perspective in the context of the broader mission of the organization. The approving authority should be able to see the "big picture." Because the approving authority controls the "purse strings," he or she holds a commanding position with respect to the manner in which risks will be mitigated or accepted.

Authorization Timing

Authorization to process should occur during the implementation phase of the system's life cycle. Any system currently in development should not be allowed to go into production until it has been accredited based on certification of its security posture. For legacy systems, the accreditation decision should be a priority, with emphasis given to the most critical systems first.

The Authorization Letter

The authorization letter, which documents system accreditation, must be clearly and carefully worded to reflect the desires of the approving authority with respect to security of the system. It should state the authority of the individual to accredit the system or should specify who appointed him or her to that position. It should provide a background of the system authorization process on which the accreditation decision is being made (i.e., who performed it, over what period of time, the locations, for what purpose, using what methodology, and over what resources). The statement should declare its purpose—to document management's decision to permit the system to process in a stated security environment. It needs to specify the duration of the authorization, not normally more than 3 years. It is essential that the statement document, either in the document itself or in an attached or associated document like a risk mediation plan, states the specific risks that are being accepted as part of the accreditation. If the approving authority establishes conditions of authorization processing in light of residual risks, the accrediting statement is the place to document them. Often, the statement includes additional information such as approved mode of operation, identification of data types, sensitivity levels, criticality categorization, risk level, and certification level to classify the accreditation according to predetermined standards. An example of an accreditation letter is provided in Appendix S.

Approving authorities must understand that there may be both personal and operational consequences to their accreditation decision. Accreditation not only will affect the security of the system in an operational way but also will affect the responsibility, accountability, credibility, and reputation of the approving authority in a personal sense. However, system accreditation should be considered a normal management function, and there are no special rules for punishing malfeasance or negligence in this area any more so than in any other normal management function. However, the Computer Security Act of 1987 requires that systems processing federal data be authorized to process by a management official, and failure to do so constitutes a violation of a federal directive. As an example, failure to authorize an operational system to process demonstrates that management has not exercised due care in protecting the system in the event of a security incident.

Suppose the approving authority does not wish to authorize processing. Perhaps the risks of continued operation are too great, or perhaps the system's design is inadequate and data will be compromised should the system be allowed to go into production. The approving authority can deny and perhaps should deny accreditation on any number of grounds: potential disclosure of customer data; lack of assurance of integrity of payment data; inability to meet customer uptime demands; potential loss of financial resources; potential impact on health, safety, and welfare; loss of credibility and embarrassment; or inability to establish trust with an interconnected system. The approving authority's denial of accreditation is just as important as an approved accreditation. It will certainly be treated more expeditiously and with more emphasis. The reason for the nonaccreditation decision should be clearly stated so that corrective action can be initiated. Of course, it is within the authority of the approving authority to say "forget the whole thing," to cut losses and retire the system immediately, or to stop development altogether. But, that is an exception. However, the potential for this provides justification for applying the system authorization methodology to the system's life cycle.

Authorization Decisions

There are generally three possible outcomes resulting from an accreditation decision: full accreditation, interim accreditation, and denial of accreditation. Full accreditation permits an information system authority to operate (ATO) is granted by the AO when risks to the organization's operations, assets, or individuals are acceptable. Interim authority to operate (IATO) is granted in the case of systems having risks that are not acceptable but there is a compelling need for the system to operate. Denial of authorization to operate applies to systems presenting unacceptable risks that are so significant that they should not be allowed to operate or continue to operate.

Because of operational necessities, full accreditation is often granted even though there are significant weaknesses in system security controls, particularly with respect to legacy systems. In such cases, conditions for continued operation are normally specified by the AOs. Such conditional accreditation permits the system to operate under certain conditions for the full term of a normal accreditation. For instance, the system will be permitted to continue to process but only if compensatory controls are employed until necessary controls have been fully implemented. An interim accreditation, on the other hand, limits the length of time the system is permitted to operate in a degraded mode, usually a 6-month period. If at the end of that 6-month period prescribed corrective action has not been taken or completed, the accreditation expires, and the system must cease processing. Interim accreditation must be

Chapter 6

used judiciously because there will be a great temptation to extend the temporary approval to process for another interim period ad infinitum. Interim accreditation may be appropriate for an operational system to allow it to continue to operate following a change to its processing environment or in response to a serious incident. Or, an interim accreditation may be considered for a system in development that must meet a strict implementation date but that does not yet meet all conditions for full accreditation. Compensatory controls should be considered in addressing the most significant risks. They compensate for the lack of normal controls by providing equal or greater protection temporarily until the residual risk can be permanently mitigated. For example, the approving authority may require that audit trails be reviewed on a daily basis until background checks on all administrative users can be completed. Similar to compensatory controls are operational restrictions, which temporarily limit actions that can be performed until residual risks can be mitigated. For example, if the trust level of a connected system cannot be fully established, sharing data with that system will be suspended. An example of an interim accreditation letter is provided in Appendix T.

Designation of Approving Authorities

Because of the importance of their role in making decisions that may have an impact on the entire organization, a policy that clearly defines the role and responsibilities of individuals appointed as approving authorities is especially important. Such a policy should define the minimum level of authority of position that the approving authority must hold. The policy should require that each approving authority be a senior management official who has authority over and responsibility for the information technology system and the business process it supports and who manages the resources required to support both. In every case, the approving authority must be able to commit necessary resources for remedial action or correction of deficiencies (not necessarily all deficiencies but a clear majority of them). If total responsibility for all mitigation activities was a requirement, then the president or chief executive officer (CEO) would probably be required to serve as the approving authority in every case. It is sensible to set aside facility-related corrective actions as an example because this will in most cases fall outside most approving authorities' span of authority. The policy should also implement separation of duties by restricting system owners from being approving authorities for their own systems; by restricting chief operating officers (COOs) from being approving authorities for any system that does not directly support the chief information officer (CIO) function; and restricting individuals in information technology from security positions.

Table 6.1 Approving Authority Matrix			
Approving Authority	Business Unit	System Name	Reaccreditation Due Date
John Hanson	Office of Administration	Zeus	July 15, 2013
		Prometheus	April 30, 2012
Catherine Bulloch	Office of the Chief Financial Officer	Apollo	August 2, 2012
		Mercury	January 31, 2013
		Bacchus	September 30, 2014
Vernon Van Fleet	Research Department	Eros	February 10, 2012
Ray Horner	Office of Information Technology	Corporate LAN	November 12, 2014
		Corporate Intranet	June 30, 2013
		Corporate Internet	June 30, 2013

LAN, local-area network.

Most organizations will find it necessary to appoint several individuals to serve as approving authorities because they are normally organized according to distinct lines of business. It is important to assemble an approving authority matrix that indicates the approving authorities in association with the systems for which they are responsible. A viable system inventory process (as shown in Table 6.1) will facilitate identification of individuals performing as approving authorities.

Approving Authority Qualifications

Not everyone is qualified to be an approving authority, just as not everyone is qualified to serve as a senior manager in an organization. The qualities of integrity, competence, common sense, involvement, and initiative required to lead a major organizational element are the same qualities necessary to function effectively as an approving authority. According to federal system authorization guidance found in NIST Special Publication (SP) 800-37, the approving official must have budget authority over the system that is to be accredited as well as responsibility for the process supported by the system. The approving authority must also have solid knowledge of operations of his or her line of business and the broader organization as well and must understand the necessity of implementing appropriate corrective actions. This means that the approving official must know security to some extent. Certainly, it does not need to be at the level of an experienced practitioner, but the approving authority must be familiar with the principles of risk management and certification testing. Development of a presentation specifically for those serving as approving authorities is time well spent

Chapter 6

by the chief information security officer (CISO) and can reap benefits when provided to newly appointed approving authorities and periodically thereafter.

The duties of the approving authority entrust the position with substantial authority, which must be judiciously exercised. An approving authority who chooses to flex his or her muscles by refusing to authorize processing can not only be aggravating to the system owner but also can hamper future compliance. The authority to take a live system off-line through deaccreditation should not be taken lightly, and decisions of this nature should be taken only when there are no compensatory controls available or no ways that operations can be restricted to minimize risks temporarily. Of course, when a severe incident has occurred, temporary cessation of operations may be warranted until the extent of damage is known, but this should not immediately provoke deaccreditation.

For the accreditation process to be effective, it must be tied to the budget process, and the approving authority more than anyone should understand the connection between these two processes. Funding for a new project should be made contingent on security authorization of the system. Likewise, continued funding for an operational system should also be associated with reaccreditation of the system.

Authorization Decision Process

The process for documenting the accreditation decision begins with a completed, approved certification package for the system. The system authorization package may be assembled by the system owner, the CISO and staff, or the AO's designated representative (DR). As described further in this chapter, the package includes only documentation germane to the certification effort, but normally includes the system security plan, the security assessment report, the plan of action and milestones (POA&M), and the certification statement. The package needs to be signed by the certifying agent and must be reviewed by the system owners and their staffs for completeness, accuracy, feasibility of recommendations, and applicability of findings. Once this has been done and all comments and questions have been addressed to his or her satisfaction by the certifier, the system owner will document his or her concurrence with the findings and recommendations of the certification package. This concurrence should also address any open issues identified in the remediation plan. The system owner should update the risk mitigation plan and fine-tune tasks, responsibilities, and schedules for corrective action. The system owner should signify his or her concurrence and the plan for corrective action in a written endorsement of the package for the approving authority. The system owner should also prepare an accreditation letter for the approving authority's signature. The package should be routed through standard review channels to ensure that all affected parties have an opportunity to comment on the findings of the certification. This may include the general consul, CISO, chief financial officer (CFO), and chief of staff. Because this approval process touches on individuals not previously involved in the system authorization process, one must ensure that documentation is clearly written and easily understood and that terms used are well defined. If the approving authority or other reviewers involved in the approval process wish to dig deeper into findings and recommendations, supporting documentation must be readily available. Screen shots made during the certification test; the risk ranking methodology; references to documentation reviewed during the certification process; and details of mitigation plans must be easily referenced during the review.

The basis of the accrediting official's decision is the degree of risk to the organization's operations, assets, or personnel stemming from vulnerabilities in the system's protective controls. The accrediting official must judge which vulnerabilities are of greatest concern to the organization and which can be tolerated without creating unreasonable enterprise-level risk. The POA&M submitted as part of the accreditation package must be considered in this decision. The accreditation official should make it a practice to consult with the system owner, certifying agent, certification authority, CISO, or any other informed official in making the final risk determination.

The AO must establish what the acceptable level of risk to the agency is. This determination is usually based on his or her knowledge of the organization's mission, operations, and assets; on information he or she receives in consultation with other agency officials as noted; and perhaps on information documented in an enterprise-level risk assessment. In any case, the AO must consider all factors possible to determine the trade-off between security considerations and mission/operational requirements. As stated previously, the accreditation statement is used to document the AO's decision to include the rationale for his or her risk acceptance decision.

Time is almost always an issue with approval of system authorization packages. This is because it is an important decision that plays a large role in expenditures of resources and has long-term implications for system security. Consequently, management normally involves a number of offices in the preliminary review, requiring them to make recommendations to the approving authority within their areas of responsibility. The need to minimize the number of preliminary approvers in the interest of timeliness must be balanced against the need to be thorough in protecting the interests of the approving authority.

Chapter 6

With so many eyes potentially reviewing the package, there is a tendency for reviewers to pick it apart at many levels. Therefore, every mistake, typo, misstatement, incomplete statement, or error contributes to delays in final approval of the documents. Preparers must be very, very careful to spell names correctly and to designate organizational elements, position titles, name assignments, and system descriptions correctly. Although this seems comparatively trivial from a security point of view, such errors are easily spotted by staff members and provide them grounds for rejecting the system authorization package. It is best to get it right the first time.

The system owner should offer to meet with the approving authority early on to explain the system authorization package in the interest of speeding up the process. The hour it takes to explain the certification process, findings and recommendations, and residual risks can go a long way in ensuring the approving authority prioritizes his or her accreditation decision and speeds the approval process. Such a presentation should attempt to portray data graphically to ease understanding in the shortest amount of time. The presentation can benefit from providing the approving authority a comparison with like systems and organizations to help explain the consequences of approval or disapproval, as does a description of system dependencies.

System owners should continually press for resolution. If the approving authority has the package, he or she should be prodded weekly until a decision is made; if the package is in the hands of reviewers, they should be encouraged to complete their reviews speedily because the security of the system is at stake; and if the package has been returned for corrective action, then the system owner should facilitate resolution as rapidly as possible. Perhaps the biggest mistake the system owner can make is to assume that the package is progressing toward approval. It is far more realistic to assume that it has been delayed somewhere along the way, needing intervention to help get it back on track.

Actions Following Authorization

Once the approving authority has approved the system authorization package and has accredited the system, the system owner should safeguard the signature page with his or her life. It should be maintained on file in hard copy as part of the system authorization package, and it should be scanned into an electronic format as well. The system owner must ensure the package is readily available when required by auditors, owners of interconnected systems, or others having a need to verify the security of the system. Also, the authorization of the system to operate should be registered in the system inventory system, and the master organization accreditation plan and schedule should be updated to show when the next periodic recertification and reaccreditation will be required based on this date.

In most organizations, reorganizations, reassignments, terminations, promotions, mergers, and acquisitions occur with great regularity and affect the identity of the responsible approving authority. There is normally no need to reaccredit a system based solely on a change in the responsible approving authority. However, that is a decision that the approving authority must make and should be considered and planned for by the CISO and system owners. The completeness, currency, and usability of the system authorization package will play a key role in the approving authority's decision on the need for reaccrediting the system, as will the security awareness of the individual newly assigned to that role. When the approving authority changes, the CISO and system owner should provide him or her with a briefing or at least a memo outlining the current accreditation with the objective of informing the approving authority of risks to the system, resource concerns, and the status of any ongoing corrective action.

Observations

The authorization decision is an important one for at least two reasons: It demonstrates that due care has been exercised in the protection of the system, and it establishes accountability for the security of the system with a high-level official of the organization. System security authorization is a highly effective approach to ensure that those in upper-level management are involved in the security of information technology resources, and it makes them directly accountable from a security perspective for the decision to allow a system to go into production or to continue to operate. AOs who understand the importance of the system authorization process and the important role that they play in the process can also play a significant role in the implementation of the organization's overall information technology security program.

Essential System Authorization Documentation

What sort of documentation should be included in the certification package? The answer is driven by the definition of what information is required by the approving authority to make an informed decision about the security of the system. The list of major documents required for inclusion in the certification package varies by

Chapter 6

Table 6.2 DITSCAP and NIACAP Documentation	
Example of DITSCAP Documentation	**Example of NIACAP Documentation**
• Mission need statement • System architecture analysis • Software design analysis • Network connection rule compliance analysis • Integrity analysis of integrated products • Life-cycle management analysis • Vulnerability assessment • Security test and evaluation • Penetration test results • TEMPEST and red-black verification • COMSEC compliance validation • System management analysis • Site accreditation survey • Contingency plan evaluation • Risk-based management review • Certification authority's recommendations • Accreditation decision	• System security authorization agreement (SSAA) • Security test and evaluation (ST&E) • Penetration testing results • TEMPEST and red-black verification • Communication Security (COMSEC) compliance validation • System management analysis • Site evaluation • Contingency plan evaluation • Risk management review • System certification statement • Authorization to operate

DITSCAP, Department of Defense Information Technology Security Certification and Accreditation Process; NIACAP, National Information Assurance Certification and Accreditation Process.

methodology. As shown in Table 6.2, several formal system authorization methodologies have lengthy lists that require a multitude of documentation to substantiate that security has been adequately implemented. The documentation required by these methodologies records the results of the certification process but also includes extensive evidence of implemented controls if not the actual controls themselves. The logical question that results is, What form of proof is necessary to substantiate to the approving authority that controls are adequate? And, is an assessment report that documents and provides evidence of the existence of a control sufficient? For example, does the approving authority need to see the configuration management plan for the system as part of the system authorization package to be convinced, or is it sufficient to have an independent certifier review the plan and attest that it exists and that it meets requirements? The answer lies in the definition of the purpose of certification. Certification is an assessment exercise and not a remediation exercise. Certification is designed to assess whether the controls implemented to protect a given system meet a set of predefined requirements. Certification is not intended to assess and to remediate weaknesses found during the assessment. This is the reason that many certification programs fail; they lose sight of what they are intended to do.

So, getting back to the original question of what documentation needs to be included in the certification package, one must decide how much evidence the approving authority needs. NIST SP 800-37 has refined the contents of the certification to the system security plan, the risk assessment report, the security test and evaluation report, the POA&M, and the certification statement. By comparison, this was quite a departure from the list associated with most previous methodologies. But, this revision refocused requirements for documentation to match the purpose of the effort—to assess controls. By reducing the amount of documentation to five primary documents, requirements increased for the system security plan and the certification test to be more descriptive and complete based on solid evidentiary and testing requirements for each control. To eliminate the need for inclusion of a technical architecture document, the security plan's system description and environment had to be more complete. To remove the disaster recovery plan from the package necessitated detailed findings in the certification test report and system security plan on the contents and effectiveness of various aspects addressed in the plan (i.e., identification of a recovery strategy, specification of an alternate processing site, documentation of critical resources required for recovery, etc.). And, if actual procedures were not to be included as proof of their existence, then the certification test needed to relate specifically the extent to which procedures supporting each NIST SP 800-18 topic had been prepared, with any weaknesses documented in the POA&M.

The approving authority is responsible for making the decision regarding the operation of the system. As such, he or she can require that any and all controls be fully implemented before processing is authorized. The approving authority can decide to accredit the system either based on direct observation and proof that required controls have been implemented (a time-consuming process) or based on an assessment that documents the status of controls. The decision on what belongs in the certification package should take into consideration the nature of the role of the approving authority. One should not expect the approving authority to be or to become a security expert as part of his or her accreditation responsibilities. Rather, the objective should be on the certifying agent to prepare and present reliable and objective evidence regarding the existence of controls, with emphasis on the responsibility of the certifying agent, who is (or should be) an expert in information technology security and who holds a trusted position as an independent evaluator of the system.

Normally, the approving authority is a member of the executive leadership of the organization, and for him or her, time is a luxury. Because time is at such a premium, the certification should be complete but should also be summarized to facilitate ready understanding of security issues that affect the decision to accredit the system. For

Chapter 6

instance, the approving authority needs to be aware of the weaknesses in security controls for the system. However, this does not mean that the approving authority needs to be informed of each buffer overflow vulnerability detected. Instead, vulnerabilities should be summarized to the extent that the approving authority knows that technical vulnerabilities in database controls exist. Corrective actions proposed should also be presented in summarized fashion. On the other hand, the approving authority should be able to acknowledge specifically which residual risks he or she needs to accept to accredit the system.

The purpose of system authorization documentation is to record the security of the information technology system and to present information to the approving authority to provide a basis to make an informed decision on the operation of the system. Further, it provides a historical record for auditing purposes and documents that management has exercised its due diligence responsibilities. The system authorization package records which activities were performed in the process of certifying and accrediting the system, when they were performed, who performed them, the purpose for which they were performed, and the results of the system authorization activities. The system authorization documentation must record all findings, vulnerabilities, requirements, and recommendations relating to the security of the system that result from system authorization activities.

Authority

Under the authority of senior leadership, the CISO, acting in his or her capacity as system authorization program manager, should be the individual granted the authority to define minimum requirements for the contents of certification packages. This decision should not be left to approving authorities or business unit managers because of the potential for other officials to add requirements without understanding the need to keep the system authorization process clean and simple. The CISO must be on guard for violations of this nature, knowing full well that the more things are added to the certification process the greater the likelihood that nothing will ever get certified. Therefore, the CISO should establish a process for spot-checking certification packages for compliance with program requirements. Certification package guidance should be available in the organization's policy library, where it can be easily accessed by system owners initiating certification activities. This guidance may be posted on the organization's information technology security Web site and could include templates for all documents that have to be included in the package along with samples to assist in developing the documents. The most current template versions should be available to avoid the wrath

Table 6.3   Authorization Package Contents
• System security plan
• Risk assessment (which includes a minimum security baseline assessment, and which may be an attachment to the system security plan)
• Certification test plan and results report (might also be referred to as a security assessment report)
• Remediation plan (or plan of action and milestones)
• Certification statement

of a system owner who has just completed his or her certification package using out-of-date templates.

System Authorization Package Contents

So, to be properly informed, the approving authority normally needs only documentation that describes the system and its environment, that identifies the controls that are required to protect the system, and that gives the status of those controls. The security plan provides that information. The approving authority must be made aware of the assets that need to be protected, the threats to those assets, the vulnerabilities in controls implemented to protect system resources, and necessary safeguards to reduce risks to the system and its operations. A risk assessment is designed to provide such information. The approving authority must have a record of the results of testing of security controls to ensure that they perform as required and all functions of the certification test and an accompanying certification statement. Finally, the approving authority must also have information that describes what must be done to address weaknesses in security controls. This information requirement is satisfied by a remediation plan or POA&M. Table 6.3 depicts the essential documentation that should be included in the system authorization package.

Excluded Documentation

Care must be taken to avoid making the system authorization process a paperwork exercise. This can be avoided by carefully scrutinizing what should be excluded from the package. Normally, there is a wide variety of documentation that should be prepared for the development or operation of an information technology system. Although it may be tempting, it is neither practical nor necessary to include much of it in the certification package. A minimalist point of view should be taken when deciding what documentation should be included in the package. This perspective rules out a substantial amount of documentation that, although necessary and worthwhile for the operation of the system, is not required to provide assurance of the security of

Chapter 6

the system and does not belong in the certification package. Its inclusion can merely result in delays in submission of the package for the period that it takes to accumulate the superfluous information. This documentation can be omitted from the package because the documents that are included in the package should be written to report clearly on the security posture rather than to prove the security posture. Following this line of thinking, procedures, life-cycle methodologies, contingency plans, emergency plans, configuration management plans, service-level agreements, appointment orders, security clauses of governing contracts, audit reports, hardware/software documentation, templates and forms, maintenance records, access lists, notification lists, and interconnection agreements generally do not belong in the package. Exceptions should possibly be considered in the case of a system with a higher level of sensitivity or criticality, which is being certified at a higher level of scrutiny. But, even in such cases as this, the inclusion of additional documentation in the certification package should be based on written guidance from the CISO that specifies circumstances warranting these exceptions and defines specifically what supplemental documentation is to be included.

The Certification Statement

The certification statement is prepared by the certifying agent to provide an unbiased and independently developed summary document that assures the authorizing authority that the system has been properly certified. The statement summarizes activities involved in the certification process and at high-level documents findings, recommendations for remediation, and identification of residual risks. The essential elements of the certification statement should include the following:

■ The identification of the system being certified

■ The purpose of the certification and why it was performed

■ The inclusive dates of certification testing

■ The locations involved in testing

■ Organizations involved in the certification (i.e., owning business units)

■ The identity of the team conducting the certification and its authority for performing the certification

■ The operating status of the system (in development, in operation)

■ Reference to primary source documents by name and with date (i.e., security plan, risk assessment)

■ The certification level at which the certification was performed

- A summary of weaknesses found in security controls
- A summary of recommendations for corrective actions
- Specific residual risks for which acceptance is recommended

Transmittal Letter

Once the package has been constructed, a concise memorandum should be prepared for transmittal of the package to the accrediting authority. This document will in very brief terms describe why the package has been prepared, what it contains, and what is to be done with it. This document should state what action is to be taken, state who is responsible for taking the action, and give a deadline for taking action. This transmittal memo ties the certification together and establishes requirements for its handling. An example of a transmittal letter is presented in Table 6.4.

Administration

Although the original of the certification package is submitted to the accrediting authority for review and approval, a copy must be retained by the system owner. This copy should be held until the original has been approved and returned by the AO. The package will be maintained until it is replaced by an updated package whenever an update is required (either periodically or after changes to the system). Normally, both hard-copy and electronic versions of the package need to be maintained to facilitate its update when required. Final versions of all files should be burned onto a CD and stored securely to ensure the unalterable copy is maintained. The package must be labeled according to the sensitivity of information it contains—usually quite sensitive because it describes in detail vulnerabilities in system controls. Hence, the documentation should be securely handled and stored to prevent unauthorized disclosure of any sensitive information it contains. The CISO should consider establishing a central repository for all system authorization documentation. This will allow him or her not only to maintain a record copy for ease of access but also to use the repository as a knowledge base for other system owners who may benefit from using approved documents as examples for developing documentation for their own systems.

Observations

The system authorization package is designed to provide to the AO necessary information to make an informed decision regarding the secure operation of the system.

Table 6.4   Example Transmittal Memo

Subject: Security Authorization of the Nutria System

From: Chief Information Technology Security Officer

To: Ron Noteworthy

System Owner—Nutria System

Finance and Accounting Office

Under my direction, a team of security analysts has completed a certification review of the Nutria System in accordance with Office of Management and Budget Circular A-130, Appendix III; *Security of Federal Automated Information Resources*; applicable National Institute for Standards and Technology (NIST) guidelines; and the XYZ Agency System Security Authorization Program.

The results of the security certification effort and supporting evidence for accrediting the system are provided in the attached Nutria System certification package. Please review the contents of this certification package, which includes a system security plan, minimum security baseline assessment, risk assessment report, security test and evaluation (ST&E) results report, plan of action and milestones, and certification statement. Comments and questions regarding these reports should be returned to Robert Inkwell, in the office of the chief information security officer. Please note that your review need only address findings and content of the deliverables. Completion of corrective actions stipulated in the certification package is not required at this time. However, monitoring of the status of necessary corrective actions will begin on notification that the system has been authorized for operation. Please provide comments to the attached deliverables within 5 business days. If we do not receive comments by April 19, 2012, we will assume you concur and will generate a final certification package for the system.

Following review of the certification package, I request that you coordinate with the responsible authorizing official for approval and signature of the attached accreditation memo to accredit the system for continued operation. This authorization serves as the authorizing official's formal declaration regarding the level of implementation of security controls and the need for any additional controls to ensure that the system is adequately protected. On approval, a copy of the signed accreditation memo should be returned to Enterprise IT Security.

Attachment: Nutria System Authorization Package

The purpose of the package is to inform, not to overwhelm. Therefore, it should contain only the documentation necessary to allow this senior management official to decide if the system should be allowed to operate or to continue to operate. If a package is properly prepared, it will contain the system security plan, risk assessment, certification test report, remediation plan, and certification statement.

NIST Guidance on Authorization of Information Systems

The fifth step in the Risk Management Framework leads to authorization by an approving authority or other senior agency executive for an information system to operate based on the risks the system poses to organizational operations and assets. Step 5 also covers requirements for the accompanying risk acceptance decision made by that management official. This section summarizes NIST SP 800-37, Revision 1, guidance on the authorization of an information system.

Task 5-1: Prepare Plan of Action and Milestones

Prepare the POA&M to track weaknesses based on the findings and recommendations of the security assessment report, excluding any remediation actions previously taken.

Primary Responsibility	Supporting Roles	SDLC Phase	References
ISO or CCP	IO/IS, ISSO	Implementation	OMB Memorandum 02-01, NIST SPs 800-30, 800-53A

CCP, common control provider; ISO, information system owner; ISSO, information system security officer; IO/IS, information owner/steward; OMB, Office of Management and Budget; SDLC, system development life cycle.

- The POA&M is one of three key documents in the security authorization package along with the security plan and security control assessment.

- The POA&M describes the actions that are planned to correct any weaknesses in security controls noted during the assessment and to address residual vulnerabilities.

- At a minimum, the POA&M identifies actions to be taken either before or after the system is implemented, resources required, milestones, and the scheduled completion dates for milestones.

- The AO uses the POA&M to monitor progress in correcting weaknesses identified in the security control assessment.

- POA&Ms record the results of the security control assessment and are developed according to applicable laws, executive orders, directives, policies, standards, guidance, or regulations.

- Weaknesses remediated during the assessment or prior to the submission of the authorization package to the AO need not be entered in the POA&M for the system.

Chapter 6

- Organizations must define a strategy for developing POA&Ms to facilitate prioritized mitigation of risk that is consistent throughout the organization.

- Such a strategy ensures that POA&Ms are based on the security categorization of the system, specific weaknesses in security controls, importance of the weaknesses, and the organization's proposed risk mitigation approach to remediation.

- Risk assessment informs the prioritization process for weaknesses identified in the POA&M.

Task 5-2: Prepare Security Authorization Package

Assemble the security authorization package and submit the package to the AO for an authorization decision.

Primary Responsibility	Supporting Roles	SDLC Phase	References
ISO or CCP	ISSO, SCA	Implementation	None

SCA, security controls assessor.

- The security authorization package is made up of the security plan, the security assessment report, and the POA&M.

- The AO uses the information in the authorization package to make risk-based authorization decisions regarding an information system.

- The authorization package for systems inheriting common controls must include or make reference to the security authorization package for the common controls.

- When security controls are provided by an external provider, the system owner must ensure the information the AO needs to make an authorization decision is made available by the provider.

- In addition to the documentation noted, information can be included in the package at the request of the responsible AO.

- The security authorization package must be protected in accordance with federal and organizational policies to prevent unauthorized disclosure.

- Automated support tools should be used in preparing and managing package contents to facilitate ongoing maintenance and update of system security status information for use by AOs.

- Effective updating of the security plan, security assessment report, and POA&Ms on an ongoing basis is essential to providing near-real-time risk management and ongoing authorization and facilitates more cost-effective and meaningful reauthorization actions.

- Organizations must ensure strict version control is maintained as key authorization package documents are updated.

- The use of automated tools permits the AO and other agency officials to maintain awareness of the security state of the system to include the ongoing effectiveness of its security controls.

Task 5-3: Conduct Risk Determination

The AO in collaboration with the CISO determines the risk to the organization based on an assessment of information provided by the system owner or CCP on the current security state of the system and on recommendations for addressing residual risks.

Primary Responsibility	Supporting Roles	SDLC Phase	References
AO or AODR	RE(F), CISO	Implementation	NIST SPs 800-30, 800-39

RE(F), risk executive (function).

- Formal and informal risk assessments are used to provide information on threats, vulnerabilities, and potential impacts and as the basis for risk mitigation recommendations.

- The risk executive (function) provides information to the AO for consideration in determining risk resulting from the operation and use of the system.

- The criticality of the mission or business functions supported by the system and the organization-wide risk management strategy are essential risk-related information.

- The organization level risk management strategy typically describes how risk is assessed within the organization (i.e., tools, techniques, procedures, and methodologies), how assessed risks are evaluated as to severity or criticality, known existing aggregated risks from organization systems and other sources, risk mitigation approaches, the organization risk tolerance level, and how risk is monitored over time.

- The AO's final risk determination must consider information provided by the risk executive (function) and the information in the security authorization package.

- Additionally, the risk executive (function) uses system-related security risk information to formulate and update the organization-wide risk management strategy.

Task 5-4: Perform Risk Acceptance

Determine if the risk of operating the system to organizational operations, organizational assets, individuals, other organizations, or the Nation is acceptable.

Chapter 6

Primary Responsibility	Supporting Roles	SDLC Phase	References
AO	RE(F), AODR, CISO	Implementation	NIST SP 800-39

- The explicit acceptance of risk for an information system is the responsibility of the AO and cannot be delegated to other officials within the organization, including the AO's DR.

- The AO must consider many factors when deciding if the risk to the organization is acceptable. Balancing security considerations with mission and operational needs is crucial in arriving at an acceptable authorization decision.

- After reviewing all of the relevant information and in consultation with other organizational officials, the AO issues an authorization decision for the system and the common controls it inherits.

- The AO's decision is based on the security authorization package and any input received from key organizational officials (e.g., the risk executive [function]).

- The authorization package provides relevant information regarding the security posture of the system, including effectiveness of the security controls protecting it.

- The risk executive (function) provides organization-level risk guidance to AOs that may be relevant and affect the authorization decision. This might include organizational risk tolerance, specific mission and business requirements, dependencies among information systems, and other types of risks not directly associated with a particular system.

- Information received from the risk executive (function) is documented and becomes part of the security authorization decision.

- Security authorization decisions are provided in the form of an authorization decision document to system owners and CCPs and are shared with interested parties within the organization as appropriate.

- The authorization decision document records the authorization decision, the terms and conditions for the authorization, and the authorization termination date.

- The security authorization decision informs the system owner whether the system is authorized to operate.

- The terms and conditions for the authorization describe any specific limitations or restrictions placed on the operation of the system that must be followed by the system owner or CCP.

- The authorization termination date is established by the AO and specifies when the security authorization expires.

- An authorization termination date may be excluded if continuous monitoring efforts provide the AO with information necessary to conduct ongoing risk determination and risk acceptance activities.

- Federal or organizational policies establishing maximum authorization periods must be adhered to in establishing authorization termination dates. Whatever the term of the authorization may be, the system owner must establish a continuous monitoring strategy to assess a subset of the system's security controls throughout the authorization period.

- The continuous monitoring strategy allows all security controls designated in the respective security plan to be assessed at least once during the period of authorization. This also includes any common controls deployed external to the system.

- The concept of ongoing authorization provides for the use of security control assessments conducted by qualified assessors independent of the development, maintenance, or operation of the system to reauthorize the system if that practice meets the needs of the AO.

- The authorization decision document will be attached to the original security authorization package for transmission to the system owner.

- When the system owner receives the authorization decision document and original authorization package, he or she acknowledges receipt and implements the terms and conditions of the authorization notifying the AO.

- The organization must implement a process to ensure authorization documents for both systems and for common controls are available to appropriate organizational officials for reference as needed.

- Authorization documents, in particular information dealing with system vulnerabilities, will be marked and protected in accordance with federal and organizational policies and will be retained in accordance with the organization's record retention policy.

- The AO will verify on an ongoing basis that the terms and conditions established as part of the authorization are being adhered to by the system owner.

Chapter 6

SUMMARY

This chapter has detailed the system authorization domain of the Certified Authorization Professional (CAP®) Common Body of Knowledge (CBK®) as well as Step 6 of the NIST Risk Management Framework. The chapter explained how residual risks that are identified during the security control assessment are evaluated by senior agency management officials to decide if an information system is to be authorized to operate or to deny permission to operate according to the risk it poses to agency operations and information. The chapter covered requirements for formal documentation of the authorization decision. In addition, the chapter provided an overview of NIST's current guidance on Step 5 (system authorization) of the Risk Management Framework.

INFORMATION SYSTEM AUTHORIZATION: REVIEW QUESTIONS

1. System authorization is now used to refer to which of the following terms?

    A. System security declaration

    B. Certification and accreditation

    C. Security test and evaluation

    D. Continuous monitoring

2. What key information is used by the authorizing official (AO) to assist with the risk determination of an information system (IS)?

    A. Security authorization package (SAP)

    B. Plan of action and milestones (POA&M)

    C. Security plan (SP)

    D. Interconnection security agreement (ISA)

3. When an authorizing official (AO) submits the security authorization decision, what responses should the information system owner (ISO) expect to receive?

    A. Authorized to operate (ATO) or denial authorization to operate (DATO), the conditions for the authorization placed on the information system and owner, and the authorization termination date

    B. Authorized to operate (ATO) or denial authorization to operate (DATO), the list of security controls accessed, and an system contingency plan

    C. Authorized to operate (ATO) or denial authorization to operate (DATO) and the conditions for the authorization placed on the information system and owner

    D. A plan of action and milestones (POA&M), the conditions for the authorization placed on the information system and owner, and the authorization termination date

Chapter 6

4. What should the system owner use to prioritize mitigation actions when developing the plan of action and milestones (POA&M)?

    A. Budget constraints

    B. Risk assessment results

    C. Continuous monitoring strategy

    D. Recommendations of the information owners

5. According to NIST SP 800-39, when an organization responds to risk by eliminating the activities or technologies that are the basis for the risk, that organization is

    A. accepting the risk.

    B. avoiding the risk.

    C. transferring the risk.

    D. mitigating the risk.

Chapter 7

Security Controls Monitoring

After an Authorization to Operate (ATO) is granted, ongoing continuous monitoring is performed on all identified security controls as well as the political, legal, and physical environment in which the system operates. Changes to the system or its operational environment are documented and analyzed. The security state of the system is reported to designated officials. Significant changes will cause the system to reenter the security authorization process. Otherwise, the system will continue to be monitored on an ongoing basis in accordance with the organization's monitoring strategy.

Certified Authorization Professional (CAP®) Candidate Information Bulletin,
November 2010

TOPICS

- Continuous Monitoring
- NIST Guidance on Ongoing Monitoring of Security Controls and Security State of the Information System

OBJECTIVES

As a Certified Authorization Professional (CAP®), you are expected to

- Determine security impact of changes to system and environment
- Perform ongoing security control assessments
- Conduct ongoing remediation actions
- Update key documentation
- Perform periodic security status reporting
- Perform ongoing risk determination and acceptance
- Decommission and remove system

Introduction

In the first years following the enactment of the Federal Information Security Management Act, government agencies placed great emphasis on certifying and accrediting their information systems reportable to the Office of Management and Budget (OMB) and expended large sums in ensuring the agency had achieved the OMB goals of 100% certification and accreditation of all systems in its information systems inventory. Unfortunately, in many organizations at that time certification and accreditation constituted the entire information security program. Although system authorization is important, obtaining authorization to operate is clearly not the end of the process. It must be remembered that system authorization consists of more than the initiation, certification, and accreditation phases. The continuous monitoring phase provides assurance that an information system remains secure following authorization to operate. Information included in this chapter maps to Risk Management Framework (RMF) Tasks 6-1 through 6-7, also highlighted in the chapter.

Continuous Monitoring

After the system has been accredited, the system owner still needs to track corrective actions to their completion, keeping the approving authority informed with periodic updates as directed. Or, when additional resources are required, the system owner should demand to brief the approving authority so that the approving authority can be appraised of resource issues. Completed corrective actions have to be documented and reported to the approving authority to provide assurance that residual risks have been addressed. This may be done as they are mitigated individually or after they have all been completed. Although accreditation is tied to a particular date based on conditions at a particular point in time, the security posture of the system must continue to be managed. Compliance reviews need to take place using frequent self-assessments, and automated tools need to detect vulnerabilities and malicious software. Incidents must be reported, investigated, tracked, and resolved to ensure security controls continue to function as designed and as implemented at the time of accreditation.

Changes in the environment must be monitored and assessed for their impact on security controls. Because of change, systems need to be evaluated to determine if reaccreditation needs to take place. As discussed previously, the approving authority needs to be aware of the identification of new threats identified, evolving risks, changes in data sensitivity and criticality, and changes in the operating environment to make a conscious decision to require the system to be recertified irrespective of where the system is in the cycle for periodic recertification. Consolidation of systems may also require a reevaluation of system accreditation status, in that multiple accredited systems when combined may need to be reaccredited as a single, redesigned system.

Configuration Management/Configuration Control

The configuration management/configuration control processes are essential for ensuring the security of an information system. Without sound configuration management, it is nearly impossible to maintain a secure system. A structured approach to managing, approving, and documenting changes affecting an information system is critical to the continuous assessment of the security posture of an information system. The objective of configuration management and control is to document all proposed or actual changes to an information system and to assess the impact of these changes on the security of the system. An information system will typically be in a constant state of evolution while in operation due to hardware, software, and firmware upgrades as well as possible modifications to the system environment. Documenting these changes and assessing the potential impact on the security of the system on an ongoing basis are essential aspects of maintaining the security authorization. Formal processes are required for describing all changes to the system, evaluating the impact of the changes on system operations and security, testing all modifications related to the change in a controlled environment, formally approving the change prior to its implementation, and having a controlled means for making the change in the production environment. The system owner is responsible for assessing the impact of the change on his or her system, the process it supports, and the data it processes. However, the information system security officer (ISSO), the chief information officer's (CIO's) information technology (IT) staff, and the staff of the information security function can provide support in the impact assessment.

The primary concern of the system owner should be the impact that changes to an information system may have on security controls protecting the system. System changes may affect controls that are currently in place or may produce new vulnerabilities that require additional controls. These impacts need to be known in advance of the change so that appropriate actions can be taken before vulnerabilities are experienced. The depth and complexity of the impact assessment should be in line with the sensitivity of the system. Depending on the urgency of the system change, corresponding actions to update security controls should be taken prior to the change being effected or at least should be addressed in the remediation plan (plan of action and milestones, POA&M), depending on the magnitude of the risk associated with the change.

Security Controls Monitoring

A critical aspect of the security system authorization process is the postaccreditation period during which the security controls protecting an information system are monitored continuously. This requires a process for analyzing the impacts of changes to the system, a process for assessment of selected controls, and security status reporting to appropriate organization officials.

Continuous monitoring of security controls helps to identify potential security-related problems that arise external to the system or that were not identified during the security impact analysis conducted during the configuration management and control process. The system owner must select an appropriate set of security controls to be monitored based on the organization's priorities and the importance of the system to the organization. Controls to be monitored must address management, operational, and technical controls and should address system-specific, common, and hybrid controls. There may not be a need to monitor 100% of the system's security controls, but the selected set must be representative of their importance to the protection of the system. The information system owner (ISO) should strive to test every control at least every 3 years and the most critical controls continuously. The controls that the system owner selects should be coordinated with the authorizing official (AO), his or her designated representative (DR), or the chief information security officer (CISO).

Once the selected set of controls has been determined, then the system owner must assess controls using approved methods and procedures. These are normally pre-scribed from an organizational perspective by the IT security function. However, the National Institute of Standards and Technology Special Publication (NIST SP) 800-53A provides assessment procedures to guide the system owner in determin-ing how selected controls will be continuously monitored. At the discretion of the system owner, requirements for continuous monitoring may also be satisfied by means of occasional security reviews, self-assessments, security test and evalu-ation, and security audits. Controls must be assessed to determine the extent to which they are implemented correctly, are operating as intended, and are pro-ducing the desired outcome of meeting the security requirements of the system. The system owner's plan and procedures for performing continuous monitoring of security controls must be documented and available for review by the AO.

Should the results of security controls monitoring indicate that the selected controls are not effectively applied and degrade the security of the system, corrective actions must be initiated and the plan of action and milestones must be updated to permit management and tracking of corrective actions.

Status Reporting and Documentation

The objective of the status reporting and documentation task is to ensure the ISO updates the security plan and POA&M for the system, and that the security status of the system is reported to the AO.

The system security plan should contain the most up-to-date information about the information system, and all changes to the system need to be reflected in the security plan. The ISO has the discretion of determining the frequency of security plan updates. Updates should be conducted frequently enough to capture significant changes to the system but not so frequently that they generate unnecessary paper-work. Organization policy normally requires that the plan be updated at least annually. Plan updates are important to the AO and others in guiding their decisions for future security system authorization activities.

In addition, the POA&M must be kept up to date in response to changes in information system security controls. The POA&M is used by the AO and the CISO's staff to monitor progress in correcting weaknesses in security controls, those that were previously identified as part of the system's system authorization, as well as those identified during continuous monitoring. The frequency of the POA&M update is at the discretion of the system owner but should be frequent enough to provide an accurate status of the progress in remediating known weaknesses.

The results of security monitoring should presented to the AO or his or her DR periodically to ensure that he or she continues to have confidence that the residual risk of operating the system is within acceptable limits. Reporting may include submission of POA&Ms for review, a summary of continuous monitoring activities and findings, and the results of security impact assessment of proposed or actual changes to the system. System status reporting is normally at the discretion of the AO or his or her DR. OMB currently requires quarterly and annual submission of system-level security status information. Status reports are used by the AO and others to determine if the changes to the system warrant reauthorization based on updated certification testing. Because they describe or allude to vulnerabilities in protective controls, security status reports should be safeguarded appropriately from unauthorized or inadvertent disclosure.

Key Roles in Continuous Monitoring

There are several important roles involved in the continuous monitoring phase. First, the system owner plays the central role in that he or she is responsible for operating the system and ensuring that standard configuration management procedures are followed. In addition, the system owner must implement controls that allow continuous monitoring of system security controls and must then review the results of such monitoring for adverse impacts on the effectiveness of security controls. The ISSO acts under the authority of the system owner to monitor the security posture of the system and immediately reports discrepancies to the system owner. The CISO provides oversight of the activities of the system owner, who performs trend analyses to identify problems that may have an impact on the security of multiple systems, and from an enterprise perspective reports to AOs and system owners on organization-wide risks. Finally, the AO reviews reports on systems security and determines whether to continue to authorize operation of systems.

Reaccreditation Decision

The AO's decision to require an information system to undergo reaccreditation will be made based on security status reporting and documentation and on the recommendations of his or her DR and IT security staff. He or she should consider several primary issues in making this decision. First, the official must determine if any changes to the system have affected the security controls or have introduced new vulnerabilities that expose the system to actual threats. If this is the case, then he or she must also establish if the organization-level risk has been affected. If not, grounds for reaccreditation of the system are not present. However, if the answer to both of these considerations is affirmative, or if the organization-specified time period (normally 3 years) for reauthorization has passed, then the system must be reaccredited. This begins with the initiation phase of a new security authorization process for the system.

NIST Guidance on Ongoing Monitoring of Security Controls and Security State of the Information System

The final step in the RMF focuses on continuous monitoring of system security controls for effectiveness, documentation of changes to the system, performance of security impact analyses of system changes, and providing status information to designated officials on the security posture of the system. This section summarizes NIST SP 800-37, Revision 1, guidance on the continuous monitoring step of the RMF.

Task 6-1: Analyze Impact of Information System and Environment Changes

This task results in a determination of the security impact of proposed or actual changes to the system and its environment of operation. Changes in hardware, software, or firmware associated with operational information systems are constant, with continual modifications to the surrounding environments where the systems reside and operate. An effective approach to managing, controlling, and documenting these changes is essential to effective security control monitoring.

Primary Responsibility	Supporting Roles	SDLC Phase	References
ISO or CCP	RE(F), AO or AODR, CISO, IO/IS, ISSO	Operation/maintenance	NIST SPs 800-30, 800-53A

AO, authorizing official; CCP, common control provider; DR, designated representative; ISO, information system owner; IO/IS, information owner/steward; RE(F) risk executive (function); ISSO, information system security officer; SDLC, system development life cycle.

■ The system owner or CCP must establish strict configuration management and control processes in support of monitoring activities.

■ Record any relevant information about specific changes to hardware, software, or firmware, including version or release numbers, descriptions of new or modified features and capabilities, and security implementation guidance.

■ Also record any changes to the operational environment for the system, such as modifications to hosting networks and facilities, mission/business use of the system, and threats, and changes to the organizational risk management strategy. All of these may have an impact on the effectiveness of existing security controls protecting the system.

■ The system owner or CCP uses this information to assess the potential impact of the changes on security controls. Documenting proposed or actual changes to a system or its operational environment followed by an analysis of the potential impact those changes may have is a crucial element of security control monitoring and ongoing maintenance for the system's authorization.

■ System changes should not be undertaken before an assessment of the impact of such changes is accomplished.

■ The use of automation to manage changes to the information system or its environment of operation facilitates security impact analysis.

■ The purpose of a security impact analysis is to determine the extent to which proposed or actual changes to the system or its operational environment can affect (or have affected) the system's security posture.

■ Changes to a system may have an impact on system-specific, hybrid, and common controls currently in place, may produce new vulnerabilities, or may require new or different security controls in response.

■ When a security impact analysis indicates that proposed changes can affect the security of the system, corrective actions must be initiated, and appropriate security documentation must be revised and updated accordingly.

- The system owner must consult with appropriate organizational officials and entities such as the configuration control board, CISO, or ISSO before implementing any changes to the system or its operational environment.

- The authorizing official uses the revised security assessment report in collaboration with the CISO and risk executive (function) to decide if the system requires reauthorization due to the change.

- The majority of routine changes to information systems can be managed through the organization's continuous monitoring program, avoiding the need for continual system reauthorization, instead relying on ongoing authorization and near-real-time risk management.

- Security impact analysis is a key aspect of ongoing assessment of risk.

- The risk executive (function) is responsible for notifying the authorizing official of any significant changes in the organizational risk posture.

Task 6-2: Conduct Ongoing Security Control Assessments

In this task, a selected subset of the technical, management, and operational security controls protecting the information system is assessed in accordance with the monitoring strategy defined by the system owner. The system owner is responsible for assessing all security controls employed within and inherited by the system during the initial security authorization. Following initial authorization, a subset of the security controls is assessed on an ongoing basis as part of continuous monitoring.

Primary Responsibility	Supporting Roles	SDLC Phase	References
SCA	AO or AODR, ISO or CCP, IO/IS, ISS	Operation/maintenance	NIST SP 800-53A

ISSO, security controls assessor.

- Selection of the security controls to be monitored and the frequency of monitoring will be based on the system owner's (or CCP's) monitoring strategy that has been approved by the authorizing official and the CISO.

- Assessors who conduct ongoing security control assessments must have the degree of independence that has been determined by the authorizing official.

- Assessor independence during continuous monitoring permits the reuse of assessment results when reauthorization is required, thereby providing efficiencies into the process.

- Organizations can use assessment results for the current year to satisfy the annual Federal Information Security Management Act (FISMA) security control assessment requirement.

- To satisfy this annual FISMA requirement, organizations can draw on security control assessments conducted for system authorization (either ongoing authorization or formal reauthorization), continuous monitoring activities, or system testing and evaluation as part of the SDLC process or an audit.

- As much as possible, existing security assessment results should be reused as long as they are valid and are supplemented with additional assessments as needed.

- This is critical to the establishment of a cost-effective, integrated security program able to produce necessary evidence to substantiate the security status of a system.

- Using automated tools to perform security control assessments permits increased frequency and volume of assessments consistent with the organization's monitoring strategy.

Task 6-3: Perform Ongoing Remediation Actions

The system owner will conduct remediation actions in response to the results of ongoing monitoring activities, based on risk assessment, and to address outstanding issues recorded in the POA&M. Assessment information produced during continuous monitoring is provided to the system owner and CCP in an updated security assessment report, which they use to initiate remediation actions.

Primary Responsibility	Supporting Roles	SDLC Phase	References
ISO or CCP	AO or AODR, IO/IS, ISSO, ISSE, SCA	Operation/maintenance	NIST SPs 800-30, 800-53, 800-53A, CNSS Instruction 1253

CNSS, Committee on National Security Systems.

- Security control assessors may be employed to provide recommendations for potential remediation actions.

- A formal or informal risk assessment should be used to guide decisions regarding remediation efforts.

- Security controls modified, enhanced, or added during continuous monitoring must be independently reassessed to ensure appropriate corrective actions are taken to eliminate weaknesses or to mitigate an identified risk.

Task 6-4: Perform Key Updates

Update the security plan, security assessment report, and POA&M based on the results of the continuous monitoring process. The system owner must update the security plan, security assessment report, and POA&M on an ongoing basis to facilitate near-real-time management of risk associated with operation of the system.

Primary Responsibility	Supporting Roles	SDLC Phase	References
ISO or CCP	IO/IS, ISSO	Operation/maintenance	NIST SP 800-53A

- The security plan will be updated to reflect any modifications to security controls based on remediation efforts performed by the system owner (or CCP).

- The security assessment report will be updated to reflect additional assessment activities conducted to determine the effectiveness of security controls in response to modifications to the security plan and to security controls.

- The POA&M will be updated to report progress in addressing weaknesses, to record vulnerabilities identified in security impact analysis or security control monitoring, and to describe how those vulnerabilities will be addressed.

- Documentation update supports ongoing authorization and near-real-time risk management by raising awareness of the current security state of the system (and the common controls inherited by the system).

- The system owners, CCPs, and authorizing officials are responsible for determining the frequency of updates to risk management-related information in accordance with federal and organizational policies.

- The accuracy and timeliness of updates to information about the security posture of the system are critical due to their influence on ongoing security-related actions and decisions by authorizing officials and other agency officials.

- The use of automated tools and effective organization-wide security program management enables authorizing officials to have ready access to the current security state of the system, facilitating near-real-time risk management, continuous monitoring, and ongoing authorization.

- Care must be taken when updating security plans, security assessment reports, and POA&Ms to ensure the integrity and availability of original information needed for oversight, management, and auditing.

- There must be an effective method to track changes to information over time by means of strict configuration management and control to ensure the transparency of information security activities, to establish accountability for security-related actions, and to better understand trends in the enterprise information security program.

Task 6-5: Report Security Status

The security status of the system, including the effectiveness of its security controls, will be reported to the AO and other officials on an ongoing basis according to the organization's monitoring strategy.

Primary Responsibility	Supporting Roles	SDLC Phase	References
ISO or CCP	ISSO	Operation/maintenance	NIST SP 800-53A

- Security status reporting can be driven by events (e.g., changes to system or environment changes or system compromise), according to a time schedule, or both.

- Security status reports provide the authorizing official and other senior agency leaders essential information about the security posture of a system.

- Security status reports describe the ongoing monitoring activities undertaken by the system owners and CCPs.

- Security status reports also address vulnerabilities in the system that are identified during security control assessment, security impact analysis, and security control monitoring and communicate how the system owner intends to deal with them.

- The format, scope, and complexity of security status reports are at the discretion of organizations, which are granted significant latitude and flexibility in determining their reporting needs.

- The goal of security status reporting is cost-effective and efficient ongoing communication with senior leaders about the security of a system with respect to its impact on organizational missions and business functions.

- At the very least, security status reporting should include a summary of key changes to security plans, security assessment reports, and POA&Ms.

- The effectiveness and timeliness of security status reporting may be enhanced though the use of automated management tools.

- Security status reports should be submitted frequently enough to transmit significant information about a system but not so frequently to create an unnecessary burden.

- The authorizing official uses the security status reports in collaboration with the CISO and risk executive to determine if a formal reauthorization of the system is necessary.

- Appropriate marking must be applied to security status reports, and they will be protected in accordance with federal and organizational policies.

- Organizations may use security status reports to help satisfy FISMA reporting requirements related to documentation of remedial actions for security-related weaknesses.

- Security status reporting is not intended to require the time, expense, and formality associated with the initial approval to operate. Reporting should be conducted as cost effectively as possible to meet reporting objectives.

Task 6-6: Perform Ongoing Risk Determination and Acceptance

Actions associated with this task include ongoing review of reported security posture of the system by the authorizing official according to the monitoring strategy to determine if the risk to the organization remains acceptable.

Primary Responsibility	Supporting Roles	SDLC Phase	References
AO	RE(F), AO or AODR, CISO	Operation/maintenance	NIST SPs 800-30, 800-39

- The authorizing official consults with the CISO and risk executive to determine whether the current system risk is acceptable and provides appropriate direction to the system owner.

- Automated tools may be used to capture, organize, quantify, visually display, and maintain security status information, enhancing an organization's ability to perform near-real-time risk management of its overall risk posture.

- An organization's ability to make risk-based decisions may be enhanced by the use of metrics and dashboards to consolidate data from automated tools and provide it to decision makers in uncomplicated format.

- To maintain adequate security, it is essential to determine how changing conditions affect the mission or business risks associated with the system.

- Authorizing officials conduct ongoing risk determination and risk acceptance to maintain the system security authorization over time.

- When required, formal reauthorization actions must follow federal or organizational policies.

- The authorizing official is responsible for conveying updated risk determination and acceptance results to the risk executive (function).

Task 6-7: Information System Removal and Decommissioning

A decommissioning strategy will be implemented to permit execution of required risk management-related actions when a system is removed from service.

Primary Responsibility	Supporting Roles	SDLC Phase	References
ISO	RE(F), AO or AODR, CISO, IO/IS, ISSO.	Disposal	NIST SPs 800-30, 800-53A

- The system owner must implement all security controls relating to information system removal and decommissioning, including media sanitization and configuration management and control as appropriate.

- Decommissioning requires updating organizational tracking and management systems to indicate specific system components are removed from service.

- Update security status reports to reflect the new status of the system.

- Notify users and application owners hosted on the decommissioned system as appropriate and review any security control inheritance relationships and assess them for impact.

- The decommissioning task also applies to subsystems removed from an information system or decommissioned.

- Assess the effects of subsystem removal or decommissioning with respect to the overall operation of the owning system.

In addition to the foregoing NIST SP 800-37, Revision 1, guidance on continuous monitoring, NIST published NIST SP 800-137, *Information Security Continuous Monitoring for Federal Information Systems and Organizations*, in September 2011. Its purpose is to help organizations develop an information security continuous monitoring (ISCM) strategy and the implementation of an information security continuous monitoring program. The program according to NIST is designed to provide "awareness of threats and vulnerabilities, visibility into organizational assets, and the effectiveness of deployed security controls" and describes a six-step process for implementing information security continuous monitoring consisting of definition of the program strategy; establishment of the program; program implementation; analysis and reporting of findings; response to findings; and review and update of the continuous monitoring strategy and program.

SUMMARY

Continuous monitoring activities are established to ensure that security controls continue to provide required protection, to ensure that the configuration of the system is maintained and changes are controlled during all phases of the system's useful life, and that changes to the system's environment are assessed for their impact on security. The impact of these potential or actual changes must be assessed in a structured manner to allow for appropriate mitigating controls to be identified and implemented in response to changes. Continuous monitoring includes activities related to the update of the system security plan and the POA&M for the system. Finally, continuous monitoring results in the development and submission of regular status reports to the AO to provide him or her confidence in the protection of the system over time, permits observation of progress in correcting identified weaknesses in security controls, and serves as a basis for making decisions regarding reaccreditation of the system in response to changes in the system's security controls, in system functionality and design, or in its operating environment. The effectiveness of the system authorization process with respect to a given system can only be established when it is accompanied by ongoing efforts to monitor the security of the system and subject it to appropriate management review as provided through continuous monitoring activities.

SECURITY CONTROLS MONITORING: REVIEW QUESTIONS

1. An effective continuous monitoring program can be used to

    A. meet the Federal Information Processing Standard (FIPS) Publication 200 requirement for monthly risk assessments.

    B. meet an organization's requirement for periodic information assurance training of all computer users.

    C. replace information system security audit logs.

    D. support the Federal Information Security Management Act (FISMA) requirement for annual assessment of the security controls in information systems.

2. According to the Risk Management Framework (RMF), which role has a primary responsibility to report the security status of the information system to the authorizing official (AO) and other appropriate organizational officials on an ongoing basis in accordance with the monitoring strategy?

    A. Information system security officer (ISSO)

    B. Common control provider

    C. Independent assessor

    D. Senior information assurance officer (SIAO)

3. During an annual assessment, numerous high-risk findings are discovered on a critical organizational system. The system's Federal Information Processing Standard (FIPS) 199 rating is "high" integrity, "high" confidentiality, and "low" availability. The organization has a very low risk tolerance. What is the *best* decision that should be made in this situation?

A. The authorizing official should deny operation of the system until risk is reduced to an acceptable level.

B. The information system owner should resolve issues as quickly as possible while keeping the system up.

C. The security control assessor should implement immediate compensating controls.

D. The chief information security officer should scope and tailor the weak controls to ensure proper function.

4. Which National Institute of Standards and Technology Special Publication (NIST SP) 800 series document is concerned with continuous monitoring for federal information systems and organizations?

A. SP 800-26

B. SP 800-64

C. SP 800-137

D. SP 800-144

5. Which of the following are phases of the National Institute of Standards and Technology (NIST) Risk Management Framework?

A. Categorize, select, implement, authorize

B. Assess, certify, accredit, manage

C. Prepare, execute, authorize, monitor

D. Assess, mitigate, authorize, monitor

Chapter 8

System Authorization Case Study

The purpose of this chapter is to provide an overview of how a major U.S. government department set about establishing and implementing an effective system authorization program. This case study illustrates the system authorization concepts and principles described in this book. Because I was contracted by the department to serve as its on-site system authorization program manager and oversaw its fiscal year 2003 and 2004 system authorization efforts as certification and accreditation project manager, I have an ideal perspective from which to describe the events recorded in this case study. In that capacity, I was in a position to assess the advantages and disadvantages of courses of action taken, the costs and benefits of approaches used, and lessons learned from this experience.

Situation

At the end of fiscal year 2002, the department had received a failing score in its level of compliance with Federal Information Security Management Act (FISMA) standards. The FISMA scorecard indicated that the department's information technology security program had performed very poorly, particularly in the area of system authorization, then referred to as certification and accreditation. Although department management had published system authorization guidance and had documented a certification and accreditation policy, neither had been effectively enforced, and less than 10% of the department's mission-critical systems and practically none of its noncritical systems were accredited. To that point, most of the department's certification and accreditation efforts had wisely been focused on life safety systems, which were being effectively managed; high standards for certification testing were being maintained; and effective tracking of risk mitigation was being accomplished.

Action Plan

The department chief information security officer (CISO) under the direction of the chief information officer (CIO) was tasked with meeting the recently established FISMA guidance, which called for executive branch organizations to accredit all of their mission-critical systems no later than October 1, 2003, and 90% of all department systems by July 1, 2004, to achieve an acceptable score. This meant that virtually all department general support systems and major applications would have to be certified and accredited, and this called for a concerted effort to meet this aggressive timetable. This newly assigned CISO constructed a strategy for meeting these milestones that included the following components:

- Update the department certification and accreditation process and establish a more responsive certification and accreditation oversight capability. This included a decision to implement National Institute of Standards and Technology (NIST) guidance related to certification and accreditation processes. Key objectives in the step were to achieve consistency in the development of certification and accreditation documentation and to develop a risk remediation process to document and correct weaknesses.

- Achieve certification and accreditation in two stages: First, concentrate efforts on mission-critical general support systems and major applications, targeting them for completion in fiscal year 2003; second, focus on non-mission-critical systems with a goal of accrediting 100% of all systems by June 30, 2004. The decision to achieve the final goal in 2 years rather than 1 year ensured that quality would not be sacrificed in the performance of project tasks.

- Provide system owners department-managed and department-funded certification and accreditation support on a nonreimbursable basis on request. The CIO would create a dedicated certification and accreditation capability at the department level to augment ongoing business unit-level efforts to speed up the work rate.

■ Build on current certification and accreditation efforts. This meant continued reliance on current efforts of major subordinate organizations relative to the most sensitive (high-sensitivity) systems and on certification and accreditation work currently under way on other systems with the provision that their results would comply with the updated methodology as fully as possible.

■ Simultaneously develop and integrate the department's incident response, contingency planning, compliance management, and vulnerability scanning capabilities with the certification and accreditation program.

Lessons Learned

There were numerous significant lessons that were learned during the execution of the project, which are instructive in the implementation of system authorization programs in general. These included

■ *Data Collection*: The gathering of data necessary to complete system authorization documentation became the biggest challenge to maintenance of the project schedule. Coordinating the availability of personnel to be interviewed by system authorization team members and the slow pace of document collection often resulted in 1- to 3-week delays in established timetables. To counter this, analysts were required to communicate with system owners daily via phone, e-mail, or in person and to record these communications. They were instructed to escalate issues that could cause delays to the organization information system security officer (ISSO) and to the project manager for assistance in resolving them. Finally, the project manager reported regularly to the CISO any scheduling difficulties; the project manager would enlist the assistance of the responsible major subordinate element CIO.

■ *Project Schedule*: From start to finish, the project spanned a period of 13 months. Availability of personnel proved to be a major consideration in trying to stay on schedule, and progress was limited during the months of July and most of November, December, and January by large numbers of personnel being away on vacation during the holidays and summer. The most productive months for accomplishing work proved to be February, March, April, May, August, and September. We found that there is little depth on government staffs, and the schedule had to accommodate the availability of a single worker in many cases.

■ *Methodology Development*: The effort expended to ensure that the system authorization methodology was well thought out, was coordinated with subordinate organizations, and was compliant with NIST guidance was time well spent. The department developed documented system authorization processes that were well integrated and permitted flexibility while ensuring consistency of format and methodology; these processes were simple to understand and to employ. In addition, the CISO provided an overview presentation on the new methodology to the NIST staff to increase assurance that the methodology would be technically acceptable and would not be discredited at a later date.

■ *System Inventory*: The project revealed significant flaws and inaccuracies in the system inventory. Systems on the list were found to be nearing retirement, in the early stages of development, not qualified to be a system, or previously certified within the scope of another system. Continual coordination and negotiation with ISSOs, system owners, and the CISO were necessary to justify and verify additions and deletions from the system inventory. Such coordination was required when it appeared logical to combine the certifications of several systems into a single system authorization package. This was continually sought as a means of achieving economies of scale. The general rule used in determining if such combining was warranted was to consider system ownership, system environment, and security environment. If all three of these tests could be satisfied and if combining was considered cost-effective, then a single certification package would be prepared for multiple systems. A combined system authorization package would seek first to describe the controls common to all the combined systems. However, care would be taken also to ensure that each system in the combined package was properly described and variances in controls would be fully addressed for each system specifically. This approach, though it caused deviations from the formatting in standard templates, proved to be well worth the trouble because it resulted in significant savings of time and effort required in the certification.

■ *Level of Effort*: The project also proved the value in scaling the level of effort to the sensitivity of the system being certified. By focusing the project on systems that were less sensitive, the existing vigorous certification process that incorporated robust security testing and full documentation was maintained for the most sensitive systems, using contractors who were most familiar with these systems because they had been performing certifications of this nature on these specific systems for many years. Other low- and moderate-sensitivity systems could then be subjected to the new abbreviated certification treatment in either of two forms: SCL-1 (security certification level) for simple, low-sensitivity systems, and SCL-2 for more sensitive systems categorized as having a moderate level of sensitivity. This permitted the effort to be scaled in terms of the level of detail required in each of the documents in the certification package.

■ *Use of Specialized Services*: As the project began, 42 systems were identified as having certification activities initiated but had not as yet been completed. These systems required that only certification testing be performed and a remediation plan be prepared for each. This permitted the project manager to design an adjunct project for assignment to a specialized contractor who could select analysts skilled in this single discipline to focus their efforts on a single aspect of the overall system authorization methodology and to coordinate with a single organization within the department for its completion. This subproject allowed the department to certify these 42 systems in approximately 6 weeks.

- *Expertise*: Contractors who were hired to perform system authorization services were placed under the control of a senior subject matter expert who was responsible for selecting and training all team members and ensuring that each met established standards of quality. The team was tasked with providing dedicated system authorization work and was not redirected to perform any other types of tasks for the duration of the project.

- *Centralized Support*: The provision of centralized system authorization services to subordinate organizations by the CIO proved to be an advantage in that the subordinate element did not have to concern itself with whether the services would meet department standards. This was implied. This permitted these organizations to shield themselves from the responsibility for compliance of work products delivered by the system authorization team.

- *Type Certification*: An additional way that was found to economize was to perform a type certification of enterprise architecture, budgeting, training, and travel software used throughout the department. Executive agents for these software products were named and were assigned responsibility as system owners. This eliminated the need for each user organization to certify its instance of the software individually.

- *Travel Consolidation*: Savings in time and funds were realized by developing a consolidated plan for out-of-town travel and then closely monitoring adherence to it. This plan identified all potential travel requirements for multiple contractors and projected potential costs to identify when travel could be combined to reduce costs. For instance, a team traveling to a destination for data collection would be assigned to conduct a certification test for another system while there to preclude another team having to travel there solely for that specific purpose. Possible alternatives to on-site data collection were identified to eliminate travel costs. If documentation could be obtained by mail, pouch, or transmission and if interviews could be effectively conducted via conference call, then remote data collection would be strongly considered. However, this did not prove to be practical for complex systems with significant security issues and risks. This practice also was not considered for certification test activities, which were required to be conducted on site in all cases.

Chapter 8

■ *Cooperation*: The project manager was able to make use of the fact that requirements applicable to the program stemmed from sources that department managers readily recognized, increasing the credibility of program efforts. Because system authorization compliance was established in federal law (FISMA) and compliance oversight was being driven by the Office of Management and Budget (OMB) and exercised by the Office of the Inspector General, the program was immediately recognized throughout the department as a substantial government initiative that could not be avoided.

■ *Training*: To ensure that program participants would be able to understand their roles and to equip them to expedite implementation of the program further, specialty training was provided to ISSOs, system development personnel, and designated approving authorities. Training ranged from as little as 1 hour for approving authorities to 12 hours for system developers. In addition, information technology security personnel assigned to the dedicated system authorization team were provided with 40 hours of hands-on training in the department's methodology during their first week of assignment.

■ *Deliverable Review*: Another schedule-related problem was the time required for deliverable review and final approval. Two weeks were planned for draft deliverable review and another 2 weeks for final accreditation. Approximately one-third of the systems failed to meet this schedule, however. Much effort had to be extended to follow up with organizations to determine the status of their review and approval efforts, requiring frequent requests for assistance to the CISO and CIO.

These were the most immediate lessons learned in execution of the project, but there were several others for which the significance developed less rapidly. These longer-term observations are described in the following paragraphs.

Tools

In the early stages of the project, tools were not considered for use. However, as the number of analysts declined over the term of the project, coupled with the sheer volume of collected data, the project team rapidly concluded that an automated tool could be useful in organizing data, ensuring consistency of results and speeding the data collection and deliverable preparation process. A number of tools were considered, each having its own strengths and weaknesses. Because the department's selection of an automated tool turned on the availability of funding, the reduction of the budget for the project demonstrated that the most practical alternative would be the development of a homegrown software solution. Using a spreadsheet-based risk assessment tool that had been previously developed by a contractor for one of the department's major subordinate organizations, the project team began modifying and expanding this risk assessment tool to support data collection for all the major processes of the system authorization methodology. The goal was to develop a single tool that would integrate the minimum security baseline assessment, the risk assessment, the certification test, the remediation plan, and the system security plan, as well as be capable of generating charts and graphs to summarize findings for these deliverables and for a certification statement.

The tool was designed to map precisely to the department's system authorization process. It included a NIST Special Publication (SP) 800-26-based questionnaire, which could be extracted and sent to system owners for completion prior to data collection interviews, with the results easily imported back into the tool. Analysts could also use the questionnaire to identify vulnerabilities in system controls during data collection interviews with systems personnel and during observations. The risk assessment methodology detailed in NIST SP 800-30 was also incorporated into the tool. From the NIST SP 800-26, minimum controls that were not implemented or that were only partially implemented populated the vulnerability list. From this list, the analyst would select the most applicable threat for each vulnerability by using a pull-down menu. Should there be a need to pair the vulnerability with more than a single threat, the analyst could choose to select a threat group (i.e., human threats) or could duplicate the vulnerability as often as necessary to ensure that all reasonable threat/vulnerability pairs were identified. For instance, failure to have true floor-to-ceiling walls in the server room would be paired with the threat of unauthorized physical access as well as with the threat of fire and smoke.

Once threat/vulnerability pairs were identified, the tool permitted the analyst to select appropriate values for threat likelihood and impact according to each security concern (i.e., confidentiality, integrity, availability). The range of values was taken directly from NIST SP 800-30, and the software limited entry to exact values specified in drop-down menus. From these six variables, the tool would then calculate the risk factor, which ranged from 3 to 300 points, and would translate the sum into a quantitative risk ranking. Scores from 3 to 100 ranked as low risk; moderate risk ranged from scores of 101 to scores of 200; and scores greater than 200 were ranked as high risk.

The analyst, based on his or her knowledge of the system and its environment, could then add additional threat/vulnerability pairs. This provided a mechanism for evaluating the adequacy of controls specified in the minimum security baseline and to document additional or alternative controls required to protect the system, as well as controls that were not applicable to the system or for which risk should be accepted. The use of the tool deferred safeguard selection until after security testing had been performed and was integrated into the remediation plan development process.

The tool then allowed the analyst to generate certification test plan input specific to the system that showed controls reported to be implemented, not implemented, or partially implemented or for which risk had been accepted. The certification test plan also reflected the risk ranking for each applicable control not fully implemented. The certification test plan generated from the tool also included a procedure for testing each control and the expected results or minimum criteria for determining if a control had been fully implemented. The certification test plan incorporated a set of industry standard best practice configurations for common technologies that the analyst could select from according to the system environment. Standards for Windows NT, Windows 2000, Solaris, Oracle, SQL Server, IIS, and Linux were documented in the tool. Other less-frequently encountered platforms had to be added manually to the plan by the analyst based on leading practices identified by the project team.

Analysts used the tool-generated plan to perform the certification test and to record pass/fail findings to document whether control requirements had been met. The certification test results report that documented certification test findings also included findings from the vulnerability scan conducted as part of the certification test. After reviewing these results of the scan for accuracy, they would be integrated into the tool by either mapping them to the most applicable minimum security baseline control or appending them to the controls list with a new control number. Typically, scan findings ranked as high or moderate (or their equivalents) were entered as separate findings, while those ranked as low severity were grouped to keep the results report brief. However, scan results produced by vulnerability assessment tools utilized were included in full in an appendix to the certification test results report.

The tool then generated a plan of action and milestones (POA&M) that included a list of weaknesses from the certification test. For each of these weaknesses, the analyst tailored certification test results to create specific corrective actions deemed necessary to mitigate the weakness, along with projected resources associated with the recommended corrective action (man-hours and funding) and estimated milestone dates for each corrective action. The tool incorporated the OMB-specified POA&M format with one key exception: A column was added to show the risk assigned to each weakness resulting from the risk assessment process. This permitted the system owner to see quickly which weaknesses were judged to be the most severe. Recommendations in the remediation plan might also include acceptance of risk as an alternative to full implementation of a control when the analyst considered the return on investment to be too low.

The final functionality of the tool permitted the results of the certification test to be fed into the text-based system security plan. Once this merge function was performed, the analyst could tailor the certification test findings to describe the level of implementation of each security control according to NIST SP 800-18 format.

An additional advantage of using a tool such as this was that all deliverables were fully synchronized. As the certification test was conducted, the minimum security baseline assessment was automatically updated with the results. And because all data was housed in a common storehouse, all templates could be updated consistently and could all be dated the same to facilitate ease of use.

Document Templates

Once all data had been entered in the tool and after the analyst had completed all system authorization processes, the draft deliverables for the system could be prepared using preestablished document templates. This set of Microsoft Word-based templates included the risk assessment, certification test plan and results report, and system security plan. The risk assessment template served as the starting point for describing the system, its environment, its assets, data sensitivity, general exposure levels, and certification levels. This same information was copied into the security plan template. The risk matrix section of the risk assessment was copied from the tool and pasted into the risk assessment template. The risk matrix listed each threat/vulnerability pair, threat likelihood and impact rankings for each of three security concerns, and the risk factor for each pair. This was the "meat" of the risk assessment. Graphics generated from the tool were also pasted into the template to show the relative number and percentages of high, moderate, and low risks relative to the system.

The certification test template was updated by the analyst to record certification test activities, dates, scope, and personnel involved as well as the certification test results appendix, which documented controls requirements, test procedures for each, expected results, the actual results, an indication if the certification test found the control to pass or fail, and reference to the evidence collected to substantiate each of the analyst's findings. Other appendices in the template included the platform-specific test procedures and results and vulnerability scanning results. The certification test template would be further updated with pie charts generated by the tool to show graphically the level of implementation of technical, operational, and management control categories plus the overall control implementation status.

The tool generated an initial remediation plan that included all 280-some controls listed in the minimum security baseline, irrespective of whether the control had been implemented. The analyst would begin with this version to pare it down to only those controls listed as having failed the certification test, including those for which risk had been accepted. The remediation plan would then be updated to include resources required, corrective action, and milestone information input by the analyst. The remediation plan was maintained in the original spreadsheet format based on an OMB requirement that they be submitted in that format.

The system security plan template as described previously was updated with information taken directly from the risk assessment and was further updated with control status merged into the template from the certification test section of the tool. This information was then customized by the analyst to describe in place or planned controls accurately according to NIST SP 800-18.

Templates for the certification agent's statement and a recommended accreditation letter for the approving authority's use were then updated to reflect the details specific to the system being certified to include certification scope, dates, results, and recommendations. The certification statement template was also updated to include a bar chart produced by the tool to show the relative number of high, moderate, and low risks to the system.

The final template used was a standard transmittal memo used by the department information technology security manager to provide instructions to the system owner regarding required actions and deadlines for providing comments to the deliverables in the system authorization package and for accrediting the system.

The draft version of the package was initially provided in hard copy with page updates provided in response to comments made by the system owner and with the final version of all files provided electronically in Microsoft Word and Excel format on a CD. However, it proved to be more efficient to convert initial drafts into Adobe files with a "draft" overprint and with distribution made electronically for system owner review. Then, after all comments had been received and addressed, the final system authorization package would be printed out and distributed in hard copy along with final versions of all files on CD. Because the package would contain vulnerability information, all files were page marked for sensitivity and were encrypted when transmitted outside the protected department network.

Coordination

For the project to be successful, the CISO had to emphasize the importance of gaining the full support and cooperation of its network of full-time information technology security managers or ISSOs. Each major subordinate organization in the department had the benefit of an assigned government employee dedicated to performing information technology security functions. Each of these individuals assisted in the project by identifying and categorizing systems to be certified and accredited by the centralized system authorization team, gathering resources for in-house system authorization efforts, facilitating the activities of the centralized system authorization team through identification of system owners, scheduling coordination interviews and data gathering, expediting the deliverable review process, assisting in problem resolution, and being the general "go-to" person for all communications with systems owners and organization management. The cooperation of this trained staff contributed mightily to the eventual success of the project as much as any single factor.

Role of the Inspector General

The department inspector general staff was tasked with ensuring compliance with FISMA requirements and would play a significant role in judging whether the department achieved its FISMA-mandated goals. It was clear that it would do little good to conduct certification activities based on inadequate guidance, that did not follow the prescribed standards, or that were performed based on a systems list that was inaccurate or incomplete. Therefore, the inspector general was given full access to system authorization guidance that had been developed to measure its compliance with FISMA requirements and NIST standards, and any issues for which there were questions a full explanation and justification were provided. The details of the project management plan were shared with the inspector general regularly to ensure that realistic milestones were set and to ensure that appropriate resources had been committed to the project; the inspector general reviewed the résumés and qualifications of contractor system authorization analysts. The project management staff coordinated systems inventory with the inspector general to validate the number, categorization, sensitivity, and criticality of systems being certified and the prioritization of the work effort. Finally, individual deliverables were checked by the inspector general to verify coherence, consistency, completeness, and compliance with standards. Overall, time expended in support of inspector general review activities, although time-consuming, provided a high degree of assurance that the project was being performed according to high standards.

Compliance Monitoring

Once all systems had been certified, the CISO was successful in establishing a quarterly compliance review process to ensure that security documentation was being properly maintained in response to changes in the system but primarily to ensure that plans for implementing corrective actions were being exercised. Certification and accreditation team members were charged with performing these reviews and utilized a compliance checklist to measure the adequacy of security documentation. The review also included a technical vulnerability scan using automated software. Weaknesses identified during the review were added to the POA&M for the system and would also be subject to quarterly review.

Measuring Success

The CISO required the project manager to track the status of work performed at all times. Information was documented to allow the project manager to track the status of work by organization supported, by type of system being certified, by types of deliverables completed, and by dates of work to be performed and work accomplished. Metrics for the project included risks to project costs to ensure the project budget was adhered to, associated travel expenses, technical risks that were related to the use of the designed methodology, and performance risks relative to delivery of work products. The project manager also tracked totals of work performed (i.e., security plans, risk assessments, etc.) by system count and reviewed content of deliverables to ensure adherence to minimum requirements. The measurements were included in weekly, monthly, and special-purpose reports, which allowed the CISO and other managers to respond before they could risk compromise to the project. As certifications were completed, the project management staff collected signed, hard-copy signature pages to be able to provide record documentation rapidly to substantiate proof of accreditation.

It was fortunate that all SCL-3 systems that required accreditation belonged to the same major subordinate organization. This eased accomplishment of coordination and oversight requirements. In addition, this organization had a stable of qualified contractors who were familiar with system authorization requirements, who had been previously cleared to work for the organization, and who had proved their trustworthiness to organization management.

Project Milestones

The establishment of extremely firm deadlines for completion of the project proved to be important in completing the project on time. Strict OMB submission dates driven by FISMA allowed equally firm deadlines for project tasks and milestones to be established and enforced. Department management was committed to the position that failure was not an option and maintained that stance throughout the project.

Getting an early start allowed the department to design a project that could be implemented over a period of two fiscal years. This permitted the department to fine-tune its methodology during the first year and to benefit from application of economies of scale during the second year. It also avoided the temptation to seek shortcuts, which would have diminished the effectiveness of the system authorization methodology and the quality of its results.

Interim Accreditation

Because of the aggressive nature of the schedule and because most of the systems requiring accreditation were already in operation, the CISO discouraged the practice of accrediting systems on an interim or temporary basis. FISMA guidelines stipulated that only fully accredited systems would be recognized for achieving system authorization program milestones. This presented no real obstacle because most of the department's systems had never been previously certified. Accreditation letters for these systems were closely reviewed to ensure that systems being fully accredited did in fact meet the conditions for full accreditation.

Management Support and Focus

The most critical discriminator in determining the difference between project success and failure was the level of support provided from the highest levels of government. This support began with the department secretary establishing his intent to comply fully with the mandate of Congress to certify and accredit all his systems; this support was amplified in the planning and pronouncements of the CIO and echoed by CIOs across the organization. This support was realized in provision of resources, continual monitoring of program status, and maintaining a high level of visibility for the effort. From the perspective of the project manager, there was never a question about the extremely high priority of the project, which facilitated the cooperation of managers across all lines of business deep into the organization. The success of the project demonstrated the effect of an organization focusing on a task and carrying it through to completion.

Results and Future Challenges

The department was able to achieve the goals that it established. All mission-critical systems were certified by the end of fiscal year 2003. And, fiscal year 2004 end, 96% of the department's IT systems had been certified and accredited. The inspector general had verified to the OMB that the department's inventory was correct, that the methodology met NIST standards, and that it was being implemented effectively with minor exceptions. These exceptions were the need for improving tracking of remedial actions and the need for adjustments in the formatting of security documentation (i.e., the wording of the accreditation letter and the inclusion of specific risks in the security plan). This allowed the department information technology security program to be removed from the list of material weaknesses.

To ensure that the system authorization program remains effective, the department has integrated the topic into its annual information technology security training and awareness program, has fine-tuned its inventory process to solidify the ownership of information technology systems, and has consolidated its compliance review process with privacy, Section 508 accessibility, capital investment, and enterprise architecture oversight requirements. The program has moved into this new post-certification phase in which the program manager now provides increased oversight of the security of systems in development, tracks changes to information systems and updates documentation, enhances the capabilities of existing automated tools and seeks software products to automate other project tasks, and schedules and manages recertification efforts.

SUMMARY

This case study documents how one of the government's largest departments developed and implemented a plan to meet FISMA standards. Through its efforts, the department experienced almost-complete success, increasing its FISMA score by four letter grades. This case study shows what can be achieved when there is a combination of concentrated effort with a clearly defined goal, full support from management, application of workable methodology, and a committed project team.

Chapter 8

Chapter 9

The Future of Information System Authorization

With the passage of the Federal Information Security Management Act (FISMA) and other federal legislation that mandated implementation of security controls to protect government information, compliance has become a primary business requirement for federal agencies that have generally accepted these mandated requirements. Likewise, private firms that have contractual relationships with the federal government are also meeting these security-related compliance requirements. Because of this compliance focus, the continued reliance on system authorization is certain, and with its gradual recognition as an effective means for managing security risk, its future at least for the next decade is ensured. The body of guidance that has been developed by the National Institute of Standards and Technology (NIST) has provided a solid foundation for a practical and simplified approach to system authorization, and NIST's commitment to system authorization gives reason to believe that it will stand the test of time.

Though certification has for the most part been restricted to the public sector and by companies doing business with the federal government, there is anticipation of increased acceptance by the commercial sector to demonstrate due diligence with respect to compliance with federal laws such as the Health Insurance Portability and Accountability Act (HIPAA), Graham–Leach–Bliley, Clinger–Cohen, and

Sarbanes–Oxley. However, the broadening impact of FISMA as an acceptable standard for security risk management drives demand for establishment of security programs that can demonstrate that private firms are able to exercise due diligence in their operations. This should result in steady acceptance of the NIST methodology and the one described in this book into usable approaches for private-sector firms and organizations. This will undoubtedly lead to changes in terminology and fine-tuning of processes to meet the needs of commercial industry more closely. Perhaps this will lead to even more streamlining and simplification of processes and greater flexibility in how system authorization is applied.

With the increasing breadth and depth of published guidance accompanied by more experience with established processes and practices, we can expect to see even flexible, integrated tools become available to implement federal mandates and automate the various complementary processes associated with system authorization and more successful integration of these processes through the use of expert systems. The day will soon come when a single automated tool will permit completion of self-assessments, development of the security plans, performance of the risk assessments, execution of certification testing, creation of remediation plans, and generation of periodic FISMA and other reports into a single, integrated, automated process. The process for which automation will reap the greatest reward is management of remedial actions. As more systems are brought into the scope of system authorization programs, as security-related incidents continue to occur, and as external drivers increase business needs for security, more and more weaknesses in system security controls will be identified, and an effective means of managing this ever-increasing set of corrective actions will increase in importance. Finally, there will be an increased emphasis on automating continuous monitoring to allow for better reporting of the system-level and organization-level security posture to provide a means for gaining and maintaining management support.

System security authorization will solidify its position as a key methodology for managing risk in government organizations by 2015, and expenditures for its implementation will generally stabilize as organizations become more adept in carrying out their system authorization responsibilities. However, an increasing emphasis on real-time assessment is expected to increase the need for its integration into certification tasks. Organizations will continue to seek increased efficiencies and capabilities in the implementation and maintenance of their system authorization programs. This should drive increased demand for the use of automation, as well as formalized training in system authorization processes and procedures.

As organizations become more familiar with system authorization, they will extend the reach of their programs to address smaller systems and systems in development more fully. The need for increased efficiency coupled with increasing competence in system authorization, accreditation boundary definition, and security controls selection will allow organizations to focus on security authorization of groups of systems, consolidation of systems, and emphasis on certification of common controls that support multiple systems. Because the entire federal government is moving toward a common standard for system authorization, it will become the primary prerequisite for the secure interconnection of systems since it provides a common, widely accepted standard for documenting the security posture of information systems as a basis for establishing trust between systems.

The federal government's current emphasis on cybersecurity will increase demand for security experts, including those who are experienced in security authorization of information systems. As demonstrated by the establishment of the Certified Authorization Professional (CAP®) certification and the Department of Defense certification directive, there will be increased demand for individuals and organizations that can perform certification tasks effectively. Efforts to "certify the certifiers" should meet with increased acceptance as the demand for value will increase the demand for those who can meet commonly accepted standards of performance and will weed out less-qualified performers, both individually and collectively. As with other industry certification efforts, commonly accepted standards of practice for system authorization will continue to mature, as will mechanisms for measuring the competence of individuals and organizations seeking credentials. For certification, NIST will play the lead role in providing the content for these minimum standards of practice, and an increasing number of industry recognized entities can be expected to develop credentialing programs that address system authorization practices and procedures. There will be continued refinement of the CAP® Common Body of Knowledge (CBK®) to keep up with NIST guidance and agency lessons learned. There will also be increasing availability of formal system authorization training offered by colleges and universities, both on campus and online, and shorter-duration learning opportunities such as boot camps and immersion sessions.

The broadening acceptance of system authorization as one of the government's primary methodologies for managing risk at the information system-level organizations can be expected to promote synergy with various other security processes, such as security awareness and training, incident response, contingency planning, and facility security. In each of these related areas, immediate access to risk information (nature and location of vulnerabilities, potential impacts from interconnection of systems, and threat/vulnerability trends) will allow the development of more realistic awareness presentations and identification of more targeted training requirements. The system authorization program will allow more effective implementation of security controls necessary to mitigate vulnerabilities that result from reported security incidents and events, and it will provide mechanisms for ensuring that corrective actions are thoroughly tracked. System security authorization processes support organization contingency planning efforts and facility physical security enterprise-wide through the application of oversight mechanisms offered by controls identification, risk determination, and controls implementation processes that the system authorization methodology offers to those information technology security-related functional areas.

We can expect over the next few years that there will be increased emphasis on control monitoring and configuration management or, in other words, increasing emphasis on continuous monitoring. Associated with this, as agencies complete initial authorization of their full system inventory and move toward maintaining secure systems through continuous monitoring, we can expect to see costs for periodic system authorization tasks decrease substantially. In addition, there should be increased international acceptance of system authorization now that NIST has mapped the NIST SP 800-53 security controls set to International Organization for Standardization (ISO) 27002 standards of practice. The potential for this is reinforced by NIST's stated commitment to updating that control set annually to counter emerging threats.

Within federal government agencies, the current high percentage of government systems now meeting FISMA requirements for system authorization will continue to be maintained as long as sufficient funding of agency information security programs remains stable. Stable funding will allow government agencies to become more efficient in how they address security requirements by increasingly focusing on implementation of system authorization as part of the system development life cycle. By refining their capabilities, agencies will have the necessary flexibility and agility to shift their strategies from triennial system authorization toward a more real-time approach that more closely meets the requirements of a highly dynamic environment. Today, only a few agencies attain consistently positive audit results relating to their system authorization processes. This demonstrates that even with the increased attention being paid to this area, agencies are still facing challenges in implementing effective system authorization programs. To improve this situation, there will need to be more standardization of system authorization processes; the current system authorization services community will need to become more accomplished in applying a program-level rather than simply a system-level perspective in their support of agency needs. In terms of terminology, the impact of NIST's promotion of "system authorization" has already resulted in fewer encounters with "certification and accreditation." However, by any name system authorization as a process of processes will continue to be an inherent part of NIST's Risk Management Framework, of government information security compliance requirements, and of security risk management in the federal government overall for many years to come.

System security authorization's place as a permanent information technology security methodology is ensured based on the fact that it has provided an approach for satisfying organizational requirements for both regulatory compliance and for managing risk for over 25 years. The system authorization methodology described in this volume represents a practical melding of both standards-based and risk-based approaches and is a proven management process for both public and private organizations that seek to ensure that practical, risk-based controls are identified, implemented, and continuously monitored.

Chapter 9

Appendix A

References

Clinger–Cohen Act of 1996 (Public Law 104-208, which amended Public Law 104-106, the Information Technology Management Reform Act of 1996), 1996.

Committee on National Security Systems (CNSS) Instruction No. 1253, Version 1, *Security Categorization and Control Selection for National Security Systems*, October 2009.

Computer Security Act of 1987 (Public Law 100-235), January 1988.

Department of Defense Instruction 5200.40, *Department of Defense Information Technology Security Certification and Accreditation Process (DITSCAP),* December 1997.

Department of Defense Instruction 8510.01, *Department of Defense (DoD) Certification and Accreditation (C&A) Process (DIACAP),* November 2007.

Director of Central Intelligence Directive 6/3, *Protecting Sensitive Compartmented Information within Information Systems,* June 1999.

Federal Information Processing Standard (FIPS) Publication 102, *Guideline for Computer Security Certification and Accreditation*, September 1983.

Federal Information Processing Standard (FIPS) Publication 199, *Standards for Security Categorization of Federal Information and Information Systems,* February 2004.

Federal Information Processing Standard (FIPS) Publication 200, *Security Controls for Federal Information Systems,* March 2006.

Federal Information Security Management Act of 2002 (Public Law 107-347), December 2002.

General Accounting Office GAO/AIMD-12.19.6, *Federal Information System Controls Audit Manual (FISCAM),* February 2009.

Information and Communications Enhancement Act of 2009 (Amendment to Chapter 35 of Title 44, USC), April 2009.

Information Technology Management Reform Act of 1996 (Public Law 104-106), August 1996.

Intelligence Community Directive 503, *Intelligence Community Information Technology Systems Security Risk Management, Certification and Accreditation,* September 2008.

International Information Systems Security Certification Consortium, *Certified Authorization Professional (CAP®) Candidate Information Bulletin*, November 2010.

International Organization for Standardization/International Electrotechnical Commission FDIS 17799, *Code of Practice for Information Security Management*, November 2004.

Internal Organization for Standardization (ISO)/International Electrotechnical Commission (IEC) 27002, Information Technology—Security Techniques—Code of Practice for Information Security Management, 2005.

National Computer Security Center (NCSC) Technical Guideline NCSC-TG-029, *Introduction to Certification and Accreditation*, January 1994.

National Institute of Standards and Technology (NIST) Interagency or Internal Report (NISTIR) 7358, *Program Review for Information Security Management Assistance (PRISMA),* January 2007.

National Institute of Standards and Technology (NIST) Special Publication 800-12, *An Introduction to Computer Security The NIST Handbook*, October 1995.

National Institute of Standards and Technology (NIST) Special Publication 800-18, Revision 1, *Guide for Developing Security Plans for Federal Information Systems*, February 2006.

National Institute of Standards and Technology (NIST) Special Publication 800-26, *Security Self-Assessment Guide for Information Technology Systems,* August 2001.

National Institute of Standards and Technology (NIST) Special Publication 800-30, Revision 1 (Draft), *Guide for Conducting Risk Assessments*, September 19, 2011

National Institute of Standards and Technology (NIST) Special Publication 800-30, *Risk Management Guide for Information Technology Systems,* July 2002.

National Institute of Standards and Technology (NIST) Special Publication 800-34, *Contingency Planning Guide for Information Technology Systems*, June 2002.

National Institute of Standards and Technology (NIST) Special Publication 800-37, *Guide for the Security Certification and Accreditation of Federal Information Systems,* May 2004.

National Institute of Standards and Technology (NIST) Special Publication 800-37, Revision 1, *Guide for Applying the Risk Management Framework to Federal Information Systems: A Security Lifecycle Approach,* February 2010.

National Institute of Standards and Technology (NIST) Special Publication 800-39, *Managing Information Security Risk: Organization, Mission, and Information System View*, May 2011.

National Institute of Standards and Technology (NIST) Special Publication 800-40, Version 2, *Creating a Patch and Vulnerability Management Program,* November 2005.

National Institute of Standards and Technology (NIST) Special Publication 800-41, Revision 1, *Guidelines on Firewalls and Firewall Policy*, September 2009.

National Institute of Standards and Technology (NIST) Special Publication 800-47, *Security Guide for Interconnecting Information Technology Systems,* August 2002.

National Institute of Standards and Technology (NIST) Special Publication 800-50, *Building an Information Technology Security Awareness and Training Program*, October 2003.

National Institute of Standards and Technology (NIST) Special Publication 800-53, Rev. 3, *Recommended Security Controls for Federal Information Systems and Organizations,* August 2009.

National Institute of Standards and Technology (NIST) Special Publication 800-53A, *Guide for Assessing the Security Controls in Federal Information Systems,* July 2008.

National Institute of Standards and Technology (NIST) Special Publication 800-55, Revision 1, *Performance Measurement Guide for Information Security*, July 2008.

National Institute of Standards and Technology (NIST) Special Publication 800-59, *Guide for Identifying an Information System as a National Security System,* August 2003.

National Institute of Standards and Technology (NIST) Special Publication 800-60, Revision 1, *Guide for Mapping Types of Information and Information Systems to Security Categories,* August 2008.

National Institute of Standards and Technology (NIST) Special Publication 800-61, Revision 1, *Computer Security Incident Handling Guide*, March 2008.

National Institute of Standards and Technology (NIST) Special Publication 800-64, Revision 2, *Security Considerations in the System Development Life Cycle*, October 2008.

National Institute of Standards and Technology (NIST) Special Publication 800-65, *Integrating IT Security into the Capital Planning and Investment Control Process*, January 2005.

National Institute of Standards and Technology (NIST) Special Publication 800-70, *Security Configuration Checklists Program for IT Products: Guidance for Checklists Users and Developer*, May 2005.

National Institute of Standards and Technology (NIST) Special Publication 800-83, *Guide to Malware Incident Prevention and Handling*, November 2005.

National Institute of Standards and Technology (NIST) Special Publication 800-88, *Guidelines for Media Sanitization*, September 2006.

National Institute of Standards and Technology (NIST) Special Publication 800-92, *Guide to Computer Security Log Management*, September 2006.

National Institute of Standards and Technology (NIST) Special Publication 800-100, *Information Security Handbook: A Guide for Managers*, October 2006.

National Institute of Standards and Technology (NIST) Special Publication 800-115, *Technical Guide to Information Security Testing and Assessment,* September 2008.

National Institute of Standards and Technology (NIST) Special Publication 800-122, *Guide to Protecting the Confidentiality of Personally Identifiable Information (PII)*, April 2010.

National Institute of Standards and Technology (NIST) Special Publication 800-128, *Guide for Security-Focused Configuration Management of Information Systems,* April 2011.

National Institute of Standards and Technology (NIST) Special Publication 800-137, *Information Security Continuous Monitoring for Federal Information Systems and Organizations,* September 2011.

National Security Telecommunications and Information Systems Security Instruction (NSTISSI) No. 1000, *National Information Assurance Certification and Accreditation Process (NIACAP)*, April 2000.

Office of Management and Budget, Circular A-11, *Preparation, Submission, and Execution of the Budget*, July 2007.

Office of Management and Budget, Circular A-123, *Management's Responsibility for Internal Control*, December 2004.

Office of Management and Budget, Circular A-127, *Financial Management Systems*, July 1993.

Office of Management and Budget, Circular A-130, Appendix III, Transmittal Memorandum #4, *Management of Federal Information Resources*, November 2000.

Office of Management and Budget, Memorandum M-00-13, *Privacy Policies and Data Collection on Federal Websites*, June 2000.

Office of Management and Budget, Memorandum M-00-15, *Guidance on Implementing the Electronic Signatures in Global and National Commerce Act*, September 2000.

Office of Management and Budget, Memorandum M-01-05, *Guidance on Inter-Agency Sharing of Personal Data-Protecting Personal Privacy*, March 2001.

Office of Management and Budget, Memorandum M-02-01, *Guidance on Preparing and Submitting Security Plans of Action and Milestones*, October 2001.

Office of Management and Budget, Memorandum M-03-22, *Guidance for Implementing the Privacy Provisions of the E-Government Act of 2002*, September 2003.

Appendix A

Office of Management and Budget, Memorandum M-04-04, *E-Authentication Guidance*, December 2003.

Office of Management and Budget, Memorandum M-04-15, *Development of Homeland Security Presidential Directive (HSPD)—7 Critical Infrastructure Protection Plans to Protect Federal Critical Infrastructures and Key Resources*, June 2004.

Office of Management and Budget, Memorandum M-05-04, *Policies for Federal Agency Public Websites,* December 2004.

Office of Management and Budget, Memorandum M-06-15, *Safeguarding Personally Identifiable Information,* May 2006.

Office of Management and Budget, Memorandum M-06-16, *Protection of Sensitive Agency Information,* June 2006.

Office of Management and Budget, Memorandum M-06-19, *Reporting Incidents Involving Personally Identifiable Information and Incorporating the Cost for Security in Agency Information Technology Investments,* July 2006.

Office of Management and Budget, Memorandum M-07-16, *Safeguarding Against and Responding to the Breach of Personally Identifiable Information,* December 2009.

Office of Management and Budget, Memorandum M-10-15, *Reporting Instructions for the Federal Information Security Management Act and Agency Privacy Management,* April 2010.

Office of Management and Budget, Memorandum M-10-22, *Guidance for Online Use of Web Measurement and Customization Technologies,* June 2010.

Office of Management and Budget, Memorandum M-10-23, *Guidance for Agency Use of Third-Party Websites and Applications,* June 2010.

Paperwork Reduction Act of 1995 (Public Law 104-13), May 1995.

Privacy Act of 1974 (Public Law 93-579), September 1975.

Appendix B

Glossary

Acceptable risk: A concern that is acceptable to responsible management due to the cost and magnitude of implementing countermeasures. [NIST SP 800-18]

Accountability: The security goal that generates the requirement for actions of an entity to be traced uniquely to that entity. This supports nonrepudiation, deterrence, fault isolation, intrusion detection and prevention, and after-action recovery and legal action. [NIST SP 800-30]

Accreditation: The official management decision given by a senior organization official to authorize operation of an information system and to explicitly accept the risk to organization operations (including mission, functions, image, or reputation), assets, or individuals based on the implementation of an agreed-on set of security controls. [NIST SP 800-37]

Accreditation boundary: All components of an information system to be accredited by designated approving authority and excluding separately accredited systems to which the information system is connected. [NIST SP 800-37]

Accreditation letter: The accreditation letter documents the decision of the authorizing official and the rationale for the accreditation decision and is documented in the final accreditation package, which consists of the accreditation letter and supporting documentation. [NIST SP 800-37]

Accreditation package: The evidence provided to the designated approving authority to be used in the security accreditation decision process. Evidence includes, but is not limited to, (1) the system security plan; (2) the assessment results from the security certification; and (3) the plan of action and milestones. [NIST SP 800-37]

Accrediting authority: See *Authorizing official.*

Adequate security: Security commensurate with risk, including the magnitude of harm resulting from the unauthorized access, use, disclosure, disruption, modification, or destruction of information. [OMB Circular A-130]

Allocation: The process an organization employs to determine whether security controls are defined as system-specific, hybrid, or common. The process an organization employs to assign security controls to specific information system components responsible for providing a particular security capability (e.g., router, server, remote sensor). [NIST SP 800-37]

AO: Authorizing official.

AODR: Authorizing official designated representative.

Application: The use of information resources (information and information technology) to satisfy a specific set of user requirements. [OMB Circular A-130, Appendix III]

Assessment: See *Security test and evaluation.*

Assurance: Grounds for confidence that the other four security goals (integrity, availability, confidentiality, and accountability) have been adequately met by a specific implementation. "Adequately met" includes (1) functionality that performs correctly, (2) sufficient protection against unintentional errors (by users or software), and (3) sufficient resistance to intentional penetration or bypass. [NIST SP 800-30]

Authorization: The risk management process of assessing the risks associated with an information system and, when necessary, mitigating vulnerabilities to reduce risk to an acceptably low residual level. [NIST SP 800-37] See also *Accreditation.*

Authorize processing: See *Accreditation.*

Authorizing official: Official with the authority to formally assume responsibility for operating an information system at an acceptable level of risk to agency operations (including mission, functions, image, or reputation), agency assets, or individuals. [NIST SP 800-37]

Availability: The security goal that generates the requirement for protection against intentional or accidental attempts to perform unauthorized deletion of data, or otherwise deny service or data, and protection against unauthorized use of system resources. [NIST SP 800-30]

Awareness: Awareness programs set the stage for training by changing organizational attitudes toward realization of the importance of security and the adverse consequences of its failure. [NIST SP 800-18]

Business impact analysis: An analysis of an information technology (IT) system's requirements, processes, and interdependencies used to characterize system contingency requirements and priorities in the event of a significant disruption. [NIST SP 800-34]

C&A: Certification and accreditation.

Categorization: See *Security categorization.*

Certification: A comprehensive assessment of the management, operational, and technical security controls in an information system, made in support of security accreditation, to determine the extent to which the controls are implemented correctly, operating as intended, and producing the desired outcome with respect to meeting the security requirements for the system. [NIST SP 800-37]

Certification agent: The individual, group, or organization responsible for conducting a system security certification. [NIST SP 800-37]

Certification level: A combination of techniques and procedures used during a certification and accreditation process to verify the correctness and effectiveness of security controls in an information technology system. Security certification levels represent increasing levels of intensity and rigor in the verification process and include such techniques as reviewing and examining documentation; interviewing personnel; conducting demonstrations and exercises; conducting functional, regression, and penetration testing; and analyzing system design documentation. [NIST SP 800-37]

Certification package: Product of the certification effort documenting the detailed results of the certification activities. The certification package includes the security plan, developmental or operational certification test reports, risk assessment report, and certifier's statement. [NIST SP 800-37]

Certification statement: The certifier's statement provides an overview of the security status of the system and brings together all of the information necessary for the designated approving authority to make an informed, risk-based decision. The statement documents that the security controls are correctly implemented and effective in their application. The report also documents the security controls not implemented and provides corrective actions. [NIST SP 800-37]

Certifier: See *Certification agent.*

CCP: Common control provider.

CEO: Chief executive officer.

CFO: Chief financial officer.

CIO: Chief information officer.

CISM: Certified information security manager.

CISO: Chief information security officer.

CISSP: Certified information systems security professional.

Clinger–Cohen Act of 1996: Also known as the Information Technology Management Reform Act. A statute that substantially revised the way that information technology resources are managed and procured, including a requirement that each agency design and implement a process for maximizing the value and assessing and managing the risks of information technology investments. [NIST SP 800-64]

CNSS: Committee on National Security Systems.

Common control: A security control that can be applied to one or more organization information systems and has the following properties: (1) The development, implementation, and assessment of the control can be assigned to a responsible official or organizational element (other than the information system owner); and (2) the results from the assessment of the control can be used to support the security certification and accreditation processes of an organization information system where that control has been applied. [NIST SP 800-37]

Common control provider: An organizational official responsible for the development, implementation, assessment, and monitoring of common controls (i.e., security controls inherited by information systems). [NIST SP 800-37]

Compensating security controls: The management, operational, and technical controls (i.e., safeguards or countermeasures) employed by an organization in lieu of the recommended controls in the low, moderate, or high baselines described in NIST Special Publication 800-53, which provide equivalent or comparable protection for an information system. [NIST SP 800-37]

Confidentiality: The security goal that generates the requirement for protection from intentional or accidental attempts to perform unauthorized data reads. Confidentiality covers data in storage, during processing, and in transit. [NIST SP 800-30]

Configuration control: Process for controlling modifications to hardware, firmware, software, and documentation to protect the information system against improper modifications before, during, and after system implementation. [Committee on National Security Systems (CNSS) Instruction 4009]

Contingency plan/planning: Management policy and procedures designed to maintain or restore business operations, including computer operations, possibly at an alternate location, in the event of emergencies, system failures, or disaster. [NIST SP 800-34]

Countermeasure: See *Safeguards.*

Criticality: See *Mission criticality.*

Data owner: See *Information owner.*

Denial of service: The prevention of authorized access to resources or the delaying of time-critical operations. [NIST SP 800-30]

Designated approving authority: See *Authorizing official.*

DITSCAP: Department of Defense Information Technology Security Certification and Accreditation Process.

DOD: Department of Defense.

Due care: Managers and their organizations have a duty to provide for information security to ensure that the type of control, the cost of control, and the deployment of control are appropriate for the system being managed. [NIST SP 800-30]

Dynamic subsystem: A subsystem that is not continually present during the execution phase of an information system. Service-oriented architectures and cloud computing architectures are examples of architectures that employ dynamic subsystems. [NIST SP 800-37]

External information system (or component): An information system or component of an information system that is outside the authorization boundary established by the organization and for which the organization typically has no direct control over the application of required security controls or the assessment of security control effectiveness. [NIST SP 800-37]

External information system service: An information system service that is implemented outside the authorization boundary of the organizational information system (i.e., a service that is used by, but not a part of, the organizational information system) and for which the organization typically has no direct control over the application of required security controls or the assessment of security control effectiveness. [NIST SP 800-37]

External information system service provider: A provider of external information system services to an organization through a variety of consumer-producer relationships, including but not limited to joint ventures; business partnerships; outsourcing arrangements (i.e., through contracts, interagency agreements, lines of business arrangements); licensing agreements; or supply chain arrangements. [NIST SP 800-37]

FIPS: Federal Information Processing Standard.

FISMA: Federal Information Security Management Act.

FY: Fiscal year.

General support system: An interconnected set of information resources under the same direct management control that shares common functionality. It normally includes hardware, software, information, data, applications, communications, and people. [OMB Circular A-130, Appendix III]

GLBA: Gramm–Leach–Bliley Act.

HIPAA: Health Insurance Portability and Accountability Act.

Hybrid security control: A security control that is implemented in an information system in part as a common control and in part as a system-specific control. [NIST SP 800-37]

IC: Information custodian

Information owner: An official having statutory or operational authority for specified information and having responsibility for establishing controls for its generation, collection, processing, dissemination, and disposal. [CNSS Inst. 4009]

Information security architect: Individual, group, or organization responsible for ensuring that the information security requirements necessary to protect the

Appendix B

organization's core missions and business processes are adequately addressed in all aspects of enterprise architecture, including reference models, segment and solution architectures, and the resulting information systems supporting those missions and business processes. [NIST SP 800-37]

Information system: A discrete set of information resources organized for the collection, processing, maintenance, use, sharing, dissemination, or disposition of information. [44 U.S.C., Sec. 3502; OMB Circular A-130, Appendix III]

Information system owner (or program manager): See *System owner.*

Information system security: A system characteristic and a set of mechanisms that span the system both logically and physically. [NIST SP 800-30]

Information system security engineer: Individual assigned responsibility for conducting information system security engineering activities. [NIST SP 800-37]

Information system security officer: Individual responsible to the (OA) operating agency ISSO, designated approving authority, or information system owner for ensuring that the appropriate operational security posture is maintained for an information system or a closely related group of systems. [CNSS Inst. 4009, Adapted]

Integrity: The security goal that generates the requirement for protection against either intentional or accidental attempts to violate data integrity (the property that data has when it has not been altered in an unauthorized manner) or system integrity (the quality that a system has when it performs its intended function in an unimpaired manner, free from unauthorized manipulation). [NIST SP 800-30]

Interconnection security agreement: An agreement established between the organizations that own and operate connected information technology systems to document the technical requirements of the interconnection. The interconnection security agreement also supports a memorandum of understanding or agreement (MOU/A) between the organizations. [NIST SP 800-47]

Interim accreditation: Temporary authorization granted by a designated approving authority for an information technology system to process, store, and transmit information based on preliminary results of security certification of the system. [NIST SP 800-37]

IO: Information owner.

IS: Information steward.

ISA: Interconnection Security Agreement.

ISACA: Information Systems Audit and Control Association.

ISO: Information system owner.

ISSA: Information system security architect.

ISSE: Information system security engineer.

ISSO: Information system security officer.

Likelihood: The probability that a potential vulnerability might be exercised within the construct of an associated threat environment. [NIST SP 800-37]

Major application: An application that requires special attention to security due to the risk and magnitude of harm resulting from the loss, misuse, or unauthorized access to or modification of the information in the application. [OMB Circular A-130, Appendix III]

Management controls: The security controls (i.e., safeguards or countermeasures) for an information system that focus on the management of risk and the management of information system security. [NIST SP 800-18]

Memorandum of understanding/agreement: A document established between two or more parties to define their respective responsibilities in accomplishing a particular goal or mission. In this guide, a memorandum of understanding/agreement defines the responsibilities of two or more organizations in establishing, operating, and securing a system interconnection. [NIST SP 800-47]

Minimum security baseline: A set of minimum acceptable security controls applicable to a range of information technology systems.

Minimum security baseline assessment: An evaluation of controls protecting an information system against a set of minimum acceptable security requirements.

Minor application: An application, other than a major application, that requires attention to security due to the risk and magnitude of harm resulting from the loss, misuse, or unauthorized access to or modification of the information in the application. Minor applications are typically included as part of a general support system. [NIST SP 800-37]

Mission criticality: The property that data, resources, and processes may have that denotes that the importance of that item to the accomplishment of the mission is sufficient to be considered an enabling/disabling factor. [NCSC-TG-029]

NCSC: National Computer Security Center.

National security information: Information that has been determined pursuant to Executive Order 12958 as amended by Executive Order 13292, or any predecessor order, or by the Atomic Energy Act of 1954, as amended, to require protection against unauthorized disclosure and is marked to indicate its classified status. [NIST SP 800-37]

National security system: Any information system (including any telecommunications system) used or operated by an organization or by a contractor of the organization, or by other organization on behalf of the organization: (1) the function, operation, or use of which involves intelligence activities; involves cryptologic activities related to national security; involves command and

Appendix B

control of military forces; involves equipment that is an integral part of a weapon or weapons system; or is critical to the direct fulfillment of military or intelligence missions (excluding a system that is to be used for routine administrative and business applications, for example, payroll, finance, logistics, and personnel management applications); or (2) is protected at all times by procedures established for information that have been specifically authorized under criteria established by an executive order or an act of Congress to be kept classified in the interest of national defense or foreign policy. [44 U.S.C., Sec. 3542]

Networks: Includes communication capability that allows one user or system to connect to another user or system and can be part of a system or a separate system. Examples of networks include local-area networks or wide-area networks, including public networks such as the Internet. [NIST SP 800-18]

NIACAP: National Information Assurance Certification and Accreditation Process.

NIST: National Institute of Standards and Technology.

OMB: Office of Management and Budget.

Operational controls: The security controls (i.e., safeguards or countermeasures) for an information system that primarily are implemented and executed by people (as opposed to systems). [NIST SP 800-18]

Operational status: For the purpose of identifying the operational status in the system security plan, the system is categorized as either (a) operational, system is currently in operation; (b) under development, system is currently under design, development, or implementation; or (c) undergoing a major modification, system is currently undergoing a major conversion or transition. [NIST SP 800-18]

Penetration testing: Security testing in which the evaluators attempt to circumvent the security features of a system based on their understanding of the system design and implementation. The evaluators may be assumed to use all system design and implementation documentation, which may include listings of system source code, manuals, and circuit diagrams. The evaluators work under no constraints other than those applied to ordinary users or implementers of untrusted portions of the component. [NCSC-TG-029]

Plan of action and milestones: A document that identifies tasks needing to be accomplished. It details resources required to accomplish the elements of the plan, any milestones in meeting the tasks, and scheduled completion dates for the milestones. [OMB Memorandum 02-01]

Policy: See *Security policy.*

Reaccreditation: The official management decision to continue operating a previously accredited system. [NCSC-TG-029]

Recertification: A reassessment of the technical and nontechnical security features and other safeguards of a system made in support of the reaccreditation process. [NCSC-TG-029]

Reciprocity: Mutual agreement among participating organizations to accept each other's security assessments in order to reuse information system resources or to accept each other's assessed security posture to share information. [NIST SP 800-37]

RE(F): Risk executive (function).

Remediation plan: See *Plan of action and milestones.*

Residual risk: Portion of risk remaining after security controls have been applied. [NIST SP 800-37]

Risk: The net mission impact considering (1) the probability that a particular threat source will exercise (accidentally trigger or intentionally exploit) a particular information system vulnerability and (2) the resulting impact if this should occur. Information technology-related risks arise from legal liability or mission loss due to

1. Unauthorized (malicious or accidental) disclosure, modification, or destruction of information
2. Unintentional errors and omissions
3. Information technology disruptions due to natural or man-made disasters
4. Failure to exercise due care and diligence in the implementation and operation of the information technology system. [NIST SP 800-30]

Risk analysis: See *Risk assessment.*

Risk assessment: The process of identifying the risks to system security and determining the probability of occurrence, the resulting impact, and additional safeguards that would mitigate this impact. This is part of risk management and synonymous with risk analysis. [NIST SP 800-30]

Risk executive (function): An individual or group within an organization that helps to ensure that (1) security risk-related considerations for individual information systems, to include the authorization decisions, are viewed from an organization-wide perspective with regard to the overall strategic goals and objectives of the organization in carrying out its missions and business functions; and (2) managing information system-related security risks is consistent across the organization, reflects organizational risk tolerance, and is considered along with other organizational risks affecting mission/business success. [NIST SP 800-37]

Risk management: The total process of identifying, controlling, and mitigating information system-related risks. It includes risk assessment; cost-benefit analysis; and the selection, implementation, test, and security evaluation of

Appendix B

safeguards. This overall system security review considers both effectiveness and efficiency, including impact on the mission and constraints due to policy, regulations, and laws. [NIST SP 800-30]

Risk mitigation: See *Risk management.*

Rules of behavior: The rules that have been established and implemented concerning use of, security in, and acceptable level of risk for the system. Rules will clearly delineate responsibilities and expected behavior of all individuals with access to the system. Rules should cover such matters as working at home, dial-in access, connection to the Internet, use of copyrighted works, unofficial use of federal government equipment, the assignment and limitation of system privileges, and individual accountability. [NIST SP 800-18]

Safeguards: Protective measures prescribed to meet the security requirements (i.e., confidentiality, integrity, and availability) specified for an information system. Safeguards may include security features, management constraints, personnel security, and security of physical structures, areas, and devices. Synonymous with security controls and countermeasures. [CNSS Inst. 4009, adapted]

SCA: Security control assessor (see *Certification agent*).

SCL: Security certification level (see *Certification level*).

SDLC: System development life cycle.

Security accreditation: See *Accreditation.*

Security authorization: See *Accreditation.*

Security categorization: The process of determining the security category for information or an information system. Security categorization methodologies are described in CNSS Instruction 1253 for national security systems and in FIPS 199 for other than national security systems. [NIST SP 800-37, Rec. 1]

Security category: The characterization of information or an information system based on an assessment of the potential impact that a loss of confidentiality, integrity, or availability of such information or information system would have on organizational operations, organizational assets, or individuals. [FIPS 199]

Security controls: See *Safeguards.*

Security control assessment: See *Security test and evaluation.*

Security control assessor: See *Certification agent.*

Security control inheritance: A situation in which an information system or application receives protection from security controls (or portions of security controls) that are developed, implemented, assessed, authorized, and monitored by entities other than those responsible for the system or application; entities either internal or external to the organization where the system or application resides. [NIST SP 800-37]

Security plan: See *System security plan.*

Security policy: The set of laws, rules, and practices that regulate how sensitive or critical information is managed, protected, and distributed. [NCSC-TG-029]

Security test and evaluation: The techniques and procedures employed during a certification and accreditation process to verify the correctness and effectiveness of security controls in an information technology system. There are typically two types of certification test activities (i.e., developmental and operational certification test) that can be applied during the certification phase depending on where the system is in the system development life cycle. [NIST SP 800-37]

Sensitive information: Information that requires protection due to the risk and magnitude of loss or harm that could result from inadvertent or deliberate disclosure, alteration, or destruction of the information. The term includes information whose improper use or disclosure could adversely affect the ability of an agency to accomplish its mission, proprietary information, records about individuals requiring protection under the Privacy Act, and information not releasable under the Freedom of Information Act. [NIST SP 800-18]

Sensitivity: An information technology environment consists of the system, data, and applications, which must be examined individually and in total. All systems and applications require some level of protection for confidentiality, integrity, and availability. This level of protection is determined by an evaluation of the sensitivity and criticality of the information processed, the relationship of the system to the organization's mission, and the economic value of the system components. [NIST SP 800-18]

Site accreditation: An accreditation in which all systems at a location are grouped into a single management entity. A designated approving authority may determine that a site accreditation approach is optimal given the number of information technology systems, major applications, networks, or unique operational characteristics. Site accreditation begins with all systems and their interoperability and major applications at the site being certified and accredited. The site is then accredited as a single entity, and an accreditation baseline is established. [NIST SP 800-37]

SP: Special Publication.

Subsystem: A major subdivision or component of an information system consisting of information, information technology, and personnel that performs one or more specific functions. [NIST SP 800-53]

System: See *Information system.*

System development life cycle: The scope of activities associated with a system, encompassing the system's initiation, development and acquisition, implementation, operation and maintenance, and, ultimately, its disposal, which instigates another system initiation. [NIST SP 800-34]

System interconnection: The direct connection of two or more information technology systems for the purpose of sharing data and other information resources. [NIST SP 800-47]

System owner: Official having responsibility for the overall procurement, development, integration, modification, or operation and maintenance of an information system. [CNSS Inst. 4009, adapted]

System security plan: Formal document that provides an overview of the security requirements for the information system and describes the security controls in place or planned for meeting those requirements. [NIST SP 800-18]

System-specific security control: A security control for an information system that has not been designated as a common security control or the portion of a hybrid control that is to be implemented within an information system. [NIST SP 800-37]

Tailoring: The process by which a security control baseline is modified based on (a) the application of scoping guidance; (b) the specification of compensating security controls, if needed; and (c) the specification of organization-defined parameters in the security controls via explicit assignment and selection statements. [NIST SP 800-37]

Technical controls: The security controls (i.e., safeguards or countermeasures) for an information system that are primarily implemented and executed by the information system through mechanisms contained in the hardware, software, or firmware components of the system. [NIST SP 800-18, adapted]

TG: Technical Guideline.

Threat: The potential for a threat source to exercise (accidentally trigger or intentionally exploit) a specific vulnerability. [NIST SP 800-30]

Threat agent: See *Threat source.*

Threat analysis: The examination of threat sources against system vulnerabilities to determine the threats for a particular system in a particular operational environment. [NIST SP 800-30]

Threat source: Either (1) intent and method targeted at the intentional exploitation of a vulnerability or (2) a situation and method that may accidentally trigger a vulnerability. [NIST SP 800-30]

Type accreditation: In some situations, a major application or general support system is intended for installation at multiple locations. The application or system usually consists of a common set of hardware, software, and firmware. Type accreditations are a form of interim accreditation and are used to certify and accredit multiple instances of a major application or general support system for operation at approved locations with the same type of computing environment. [NIST SP 800-37]

User representative: An individual who represents the operational interests of the user community and serves as the liaison for that community throughout the system development life cycle of the information system. [NIST SP 800-37]

VPN: Virtual private network.

Vulnerability: A flaw or weakness in system security procedures, design, implementation, or internal controls that could be exercised (accidentally triggered or intentionally exploited) and result in a security breach or a violation of the system's security policy. [NIST SP 800-30]

Vulnerability assessment: Formal description and evaluation of the vulnerabilities in an information system. [NIST SP 800-37]

Appendix B

Appendix C

Sample Statement of Work

Technical Requirements Section

2.1 Task Description

Certification and accreditation services for the ABC System.

2.1.1 Scope of Work

The XYZ Company requires the performance of computer security services on a major application operating in a time-shared and networked environment. Federal laws, regulations, and corporate standards applicable to security analyses, security plans, testing, and the certification and accreditation process will be followed. The certification and accreditation effort will identify and evaluate ABC System hardware and software assets, organizational personnel structure, and continuity of operations, emergency action, business resumption, and disaster recovery plans and procedures currently in effect for the system. Using this information, a preliminary contingency plan will identify roles and responsibilities, critical files, backup procedures, restoration procedures, off-site storage locations, and a list of hardware and software needed to restore the system. The contractor will assist XYZ Company staff personnel in providing training to personnel and in testing and implementing developed contingency plans.

2.1.2 Statement of Work

The contractor will complete this effort for the XYZ Company in five milestones, resulting in specific deliverables as described in Section 2.2.

2.1.2.1 Milestone 1: Work Plan and Presentation The contractor will conduct a review of the XYZ Company processing environment and the ABC System application environment to determine operational risks. Based on this review, the contractor will determine appropriate risk assessment, security planning, and certification testing approaches and methodologies to be used in completion of the task.

The contractor will prepare a project work plan and will present it to selected XYZ Company staff personnel.

2.1.2.2 Milestone 2: Risk Assessment The contractor will conduct a formal risk assessment of the ABC System operating environment to identify potential undesirable or unauthorized events; to identify risks that could have a negative impact on the integrity, confidentiality, or availability of information processed or stored by ABC System; to identify potential controls to reduce or eliminate the impact of risk events; and to establish responsibilities and milestones for the implementation of mitigating controls. The approach selected by the contractor should permit expeditious completion and should result in a qualitative measurement of risks.

The contractor will develop an ABC System risk assessment report to document the methodology, findings, and recommendations of this milestone.

2.1.2.3 Milestone 3: Security Plan Development Should it be found that the security plan for ABC System is inadequate or nonexistent, the contractor shall update or develop an ABC System security plan in accordance with National Institute of Standards and Technology Special Publication (NIST SP) 800-18. Based on documentation obtained during Milestone 1 and on risk assessment findings, the contractor will identify and request access to documentation related to ABC System. The contractor will interview cognizant XYZ Company personnel, physically inspect countermeasures protecting the system, and observe operations and demonstrations of security procedures. The contractor will compile necessary data to construct a system security plan for ABC System. Plan development will also include a preliminary estimation of the status of necessary safeguards (i.e., in place, not in place, planned, or not applicable). Concurrently, the contractor will prepare a plan for reviewing/testing the control measures protecting ABC System using the NIST SP 800-37 certification methodology.

The contractor will first prepare and submit a draft system security plan/test plan for ABC System to the XYZ Company client representative for review. Based on this review, the contractor will produce the final ABC System security plan.

2.1.2.4 Milestone 4: System Certification On approval of the ABC System security plan/test plan deliverable prepared in Milestone 3, the contractor will conduct system testing of safeguards for the ABC System. The contractor will make recommendations for improvements based on evaluation of the system test results and will incorporate recommendations into an action plan. Each safeguard shall be categorized as follows:

- *High Priority:* Corrective action should be taken prior to formal accreditation of the system.

- *Moderate Priority*: Corrective action should be taken irrespective of formal system accreditation.

- *Low Priority:* Corrective action should be taken as soon as it is practical and cost effective.

The contractor will prepare a certification report that will summarize the results of each step of this task. This report will be prepared for the XYZ Company management official responsible for accrediting ABC System. Preparation of certification statements and all worksheets and documentation required by Federal Information Processing Standard (FIPS) Publication 102 will be submitted for the certification of the system. The deliverables for Milestone 4 will be a draft and final certification report for the ABC System that includes the security plan, system testing documentation, and an action plan.

2.1.2.5 Milestone 5: Exit Briefing During this milestone, the contractor shall conduct an exit briefing, with no more than 10 XYZ Company staff in attendance. The presentation shall include a brief summary of the work performed and documents prepared and will answer XYZ Company staff questions. The contractor will prepare a written agenda identifying the task, project, contractor, and document titles. The deliverable for this effort will be an exit briefing agenda and presentation.

2.2 Deliverables

Deliverables are due as specified in the contractor's accepted proposal.

Any product delivered under this task order shall meet the conditions specified in the warranty section of the basic contract.

All written deliverables shall be identified with their delivery dates and an indication of whether they are draft or final. Draft copies requiring review shall be marked "DRAFT" and submitted to the client representative for comment on the deliverable

Appendix C

due date. The XYZ Company will have 10 working days to complete the review of each deliverable and either accept the deliverable through oral notification or reject the deliverable in writing. Once the draft document is reviewed and commented on by the client representative, the contractor shall incorporate client comments and produce a final document within 15 working days (unless the first draft is accepted by the XYZ Company).

All deliverables shall become the property of the XYZ Company. All working papers shall be delivered to the XYZ Company at the exit briefing and shall also become company property.

Deliverable product acceptance forms shall be submitted concurrently to the client representative and the XYZ contracting officer in conjunction with the final deliverable.

Except as specified in the following, all deliverables shall conform to the following generic guidelines:

- When printed reports are required: The contractor shall provide two paper (hard-copy) copies on 8½ × 11 inch white, single-sided, bound bond paper.
- When electronic copies are required: The contractor shall provide one copy on disk of the product. This copy must be verified and asserted as free of viruses.

To complete this task, the contractor must furnish the deliverables referenced in Section 2.1, as specified in the following list and subparagraphs to Section 2.2.

Deliverable Number	Milestone Number	Deliverable Description
1	1	Work plan
2	2	ABC System risk assessment report
3	3	ABC System security plan/test plan
4	4	ABC System certification report
5	5	Exit briefing

2.2.1 Work Plan (Deliverable 1)

2.2.1.1 Description The contractor shall present a project work plan briefing to designated XYZ Company personnel detailing project schedules, deliverable schedules (that incorporate dates/milestone objectives), and a management plan. The briefing shall be no more than 60 minutes long with the exception of questions or issues that may be initiated by XYZ Company staff, as described in Milestone 1.

2.2.1.2 Criteria for Acceptance The effort shall result in a project work plan and oral presentation that conform to the XYZ Company's stated intent for this project and that are acceptable to the XYZ Company.

2.2.1.3 Number of Copies In addition to the two work plan copies (stated in the previous chart), the contractor shall provide 10 paper copies of GBCbound presentation slides, as well as the foils (or software-based presentation).

2.2.2 ABC System Risk Assessment Report (Deliverable 2)

2.2.2.1 Description The contractor shall prepare a draft and final risk assessment report for ABC System, as described in Section 2.1. The documents will include formal accreditation recommendations.

2.2.2.2 Criteria for Acceptance The effort shall result in a risk assessment report that is acceptable to the XYZ Company.

2.2.2.3 Number of Copies The contractor shall submit an original and one copy of the draft and of the final report. A disk copy of the final report will also be provided.

2.2.3 ABC System Security Plan/Test Plan (Deliverable 3)

2.2.3.1 Description The contractor shall prepare an ABC System security plan/test plan as described in Section 2.1. The plan shall follow the format of NIST SP 800-18, which shall be used as a foundation for the analysis and presentation of essential security plan information. Plan development shall also include a preliminary estimation of the status of necessary safeguards (i.e., in place, partially in place, not in place, planned, or not applicable). The deliverable shall include plans for testing the adequacy of system security controls in accordance with applicable XYZ Company standards and NIST guidance.

2.2.3.2 Criteria for Acceptance The effort shall result in an ABC System security plan/test plan that is acceptable to the XYZ Company.

2.2.3.3 Number of Copies The contractor shall submit an original and one copy of the deliverable. A disk copy is not required.

Appendix C

2.2.4 ABC System Certification Report (Deliverable 4)

2.2.4.1 Description The contractor will document system testing results based on the approved system review/test plan prepared for the ABC System. The contractor will prepare a certification report containing test results, an action plan, and recommendations to the accrediting official. The certification report will be prepared in accordance with the Computer Security Act of 1987, federal statutes and regulations, and XYZ Company directives. Government comments to the draft deliverable will be reviewed and discussed with the XYZ Company client representative as necessary and will be incorporated into the final deliverable.

2.2.4.2 Criteria for Acceptance The effort will result in an ABC System certification report that is acceptable to the XYZ Company.

2.2.4.3 Number of Copies The contractor shall provide one typewritten original and one copy of the ABC System certification report deliverable to the XYZ Company. In addition, one electronic copy will be provided.

2.2.5 Exit Briefing Agenda and Presentation (Deliverable 5)

2.2.5.1 Description The contractor shall conduct an exit briefing to include a presentation of work performed and deliverables prepared during the task. The agenda will be prepared according to Milestone 5.

2.2.5.2 Criteria for Acceptance The effort will result in an exit briefing agenda and presentation that are acceptable to the XYZ Company.

2.2.5.3 Number of Copies The contractor will provide an original and 10 copies of the exit briefing agenda to the XYZ Company at the time of presentation of the exit briefing.

Appendix D

Sample Project Work Plan

Task	Duration	Start Date	End Date
Certify ABC System	52 days	10-Nov-13	9-Jan-14
Project preparation	2 days	10-Nov-13	11-Nov-13
Coordinate project with system owner	1 day	10-Nov-13	10-Nov-13
Obtain system inventory information	2 days	10-Nov-13	11-Nov-13
Set up project directory	1 day	10-Nov-13	10-Nov-13
Develop project plan	0 days	11-Nov-13	11-Nov-13
Project kickoff	5 days	11-Nov-13	17-Nov-13
Schedule kickoff briefing	2 days	11-Nov-13	12-Nov-13
Prepare kickoff briefing	1 day	12-Nov-13	12-Nov-13
Present kickoff briefing	1 day	17-Nov-13	17-Nov-13
Update project plan	0 days	17-Nov-13	17-Nov-13
Data collection	9 days	18-Nov-13	28-Nov-13
Collect documentation	4 days	18-Nov-13	21-Nov-13
Schedule interviews	4 days	18-Nov-13	21-Nov-13
Review documentation	1 day	24-Nov-13	24-Nov-13
Conduct interviews	5 days	24-Nov-13	28-Nov-13
Coordinate and perform vulnerability scan	5 days	24-Nov-13	28-Nov-13
Data analysis/deliverable preparation	12 days	1-Dec-13	16-Dec-13
Review and analyze collected data	1 day	1-Dec-13	1-Dec-13
Prepare draft risk assessment	2 days	2-Dec-13	3-Dec-13
Prepare draft security test and evaluation (ST&E) plan	1 day	4-Dec-13	4-Dec-13
Submit draft risk assessment and ST&E plan	0 days	4-Dec-13	4-Dec-13
Obtain and address comments to drafts	5 days	10-Dec-13	16-Dec-13
Security test and evaluation	6 days	5-Dec-13	12-Dec-13
Coordinate ST&E requirements	1 day	5-Dec-13	5-Dec-13
Conduct ST&E	2 days	11-Dec-13	12-Dec-13
C&A (certification and accreditation) package preparation	20 days	15-Dec-13	9-Jan-14
Prepare draft ST&E results report	2 days	15-Dec-13	16-Dec-13
Prepare draft plan of action and milestones (POA&M)	1 day	17-Dec-13	17-Dec-13
Develop system security plan	3 days	18-Dec-13	22-Dec-13
Compile C&A package	2 days	23-Dec-13	24-Dec-13
Submit C&A package	0 days	24-Dec-13	24-Dec-13

Task	Duration	Start Date	End Date
Obtain and address comments	10 days	25-Dec-13	7-Jan-14
Update and submit changes to C&A package	2 days	8-Jan-14	9-Jan-14
Project closeout			
Coordinate and present wrap-up briefing	3 days	12-Jan-14	14-Jan-14
Finalize project plan	1 day	15-Jan-14	15-Jan-14
Archive files	1 day	16-Jan-14	16-Jan-14

Appendix E

Sample Project Kickoff Presentation Outline

Title Slide

- Certification and Accreditation for the ABC System
- Kickoff Briefing
- December 15, 2004
- John Doe, Project Manager

Briefing Agenda

- XYZ Company C&A program overview
- ABC System C&A project overview
- Data collection tasks
- Questions

XYZ Company C&A Program Overview

- CISO-initiated C&A effort
- Permit lines of business to concentrate resources on remediation activities
- Scope
- Certify and accredit 50 XYZ Company systems in 2013

- C&A work to be performed according to OMB A-130 and NIST publications
- Focus on assessment and identification of weaknesses in security controls

ABC System C&A Project Objectives

- Prepare certification package for the system that includes
  - Risk assessment
  - Security testing and evaluation (ST&E) results
  - Plan of action and milestones
  - System security plan
  - Certification and accreditation statement
- Identify necessary security improvements
- Permit accreditation of the system by March 30

Deliverable Standards

- Risk assessment: NIST SP 800-30
- Security testing and evaluation (ST&E): NIST SP 800-53
- System security plan: NIST SP 800-18
- Certification statement: NIST SP 800-37
- Plan of action and milestones (POA&M): NIST SP 800-37

ABC System C&A Project Plan

- Conduct data collection to define the system and establish the certification boundary
- Review system security requirements and system documentation
- Develop draft risk assessment—submit to system owner for review
- Draft ST&E plan and procedures—submit to system owner for review

- Conduct testing of system security controls
- Prepare and submit draft certification package that includes the risk assessment, ST&E results, security plan, POA&M, certification statement, and accreditation statement

Project Organization

- Acme Consulting has organized a team of three security professionals for this effort:
    - Project management: John Doe
    - Data collection tasks: Hank Johnson
    - Other project tasks: Bill Black
- All personnel have appropriate personnel security screening/clearance.

Immediate Objective

- Data collection to permit development of ABC System:
    - Risk assessment
    - Security test and evaluation plan
    - Obtain data through
        - Interviews
        - Observation
        - Documentation review
- Vulnerability scanning

Documentation Review

Collect and review the following types of information concerning the system:

- Completed annual security controls test results
- System inventory submission

- Governing external regulations
- Mission statement
- Operating procedures
- Previous security analyses/audits and incident reports
- System application architecture/design or flowcharts
- User manuals
- Memoranda of understanding
- Vendor contracts/service-level agreements
- Configuration management plan
- Disaster recovery/contingency plan

Interviews

Interview personnel who have knowledge of system name security controls/operations (each interview should take 60–90 minutes):

- System management
- System security
- System administration
- Database administration
- Applications programming
- Systems programming
- Facility management
- Personnel

Vulnerability Scanning

- Nonintrusive
- SANS Institute Top 100 vulnerabilities

- Use of various public domain tools
- Full advance coordination

Other Data Collection Goals

- Limit interference with daily operations
- Objectively review system security controls
- Provide on-the-spot suggestions on best practice improvements
- Identify points of contact for follow-up questions/information

Project Schedule

- Data collection: January 10–14
- Follow-up data collection: January 20–21
- Submit draft risk assessment: January 28
- Submit ST&E plan: February 4
- Conduct ST&E: February 14–18
- Submit C&A package: March 4

Administrative Requirements

- Facility/office access: normal duty hours only
- Space requirements
- Work area
- Meeting room
- Interview area
- Phone/fax access
- Reproduction support

Next Steps

- Identify system points of contact
- Arrange data collection interviews
- Obtain written documentation
- Confirm date for ST&E

Other Comments

- Scope does not include development of contingency plan, configuration management plan, or detailed procedures.
- Anticipate need to expedite review of deliverables and approval of C&A package.
- User-level access to the system will not be required.

Team Contact Information

- John Doe
- Office phone: (123) 245-7890
- E-mail: john.doe@xyz.com
- Team will operate out of Room 13B, XYZ Corporate Headquarters Building.

Questions

Sample Project Wrap-Up Presentation Outline

Title Slide

Briefing Agenda

- Project objective
- Tasks and deliverables
- Findings
- Recommendations
- Next steps
- Questions

ABC System C&A (Certification and Accreditation) Objective

- Prepare certification package for the system that prospectively includes
  - Risk assessment
  - Security testing and evaluation (ST&E) results
  - Plan of action and milestones
  - System security plan
  - Certification and accreditation statement

- Identify security improvements necessary
- Permit accreditation of the system by March 30th

ABC System C&A Project Tasks and Deliverables

- Conducted data collection between January 10 and 14 to define the system and establish the certification boundary
- Reviewed system security requirements and system documentation
- Developed draft risk assessment and submitted it on January 28
- Conducted testing of system security controls between February 14 and 18
- Prepared and submitted a draft certification package on March 4 that included the risk assessment, ST&E report, security plan, plan of action and milestones (POA&M), certification statement, and accreditation statement
- Addressed XYZ Company comments and submitted the final certification package on March 8

Project Findings

- The security plan documented the sensitivity of the system as moderate.
- The risk assessment verified the validity of the minimum security baseline selected for the system (International Organization for Standardization [ISO] 17799) and identified 26 weaknesses in applicable controls (3 high, 11 moderate, and 12 low).
- Certification testing verified the adequacy of technical and procedural controls currently implemented on ABC System servers.
- The POA&M recorded corrective actions, resource requirements, responsibilities, and milestones for each of the 26 identified weaknesses in system controls.

Recommendations

- Mitigate high-severity vulnerabilities over next 30 days
- Mitigate moderate-severity risks over next 60 days

- Mitigate low-severity risks when resources are available
- Accept the risks specified in the certification report

Next Steps

- Complete plan of action and milestones
- Monitor corrective action
- Obtain approval of accrediting official

Questions

Appendix G

Sample System Inventory Policy

Statement of Policy

Subject:	System Inventory Policy	File code:	Q14-05-008
Function:	Information Services	Release date:	5/24/12
Issued by:	Chief Information Officer	Supersedes:	N/A
Approved by:	Chief Executive Officer	Reference:	N/A
Applicability:	Worldwide	Total pages:	2

Purpose

This document establishes system inventory policy for the XYZ Company, including all of its affiliates and subsidiaries. This policy governs the inventory of information systems in use throughout the company to ensure they are protected according to their sensitivity, criticality, and risk level.

Definition

System: A discrete set of information resources organized for the collection, processing, maintenance, use, sharing, dissemination, or disposition of information.

Policy

The XYZ Company will implement and maintain a process for identifying and classifying information systems according to the sensitivity of the information that they process, transmit, or store and according to the criticality of the system to the corporation as a whole. The system inventory process will be designed to support the corporation certification and accreditation process through the identification of all general support systems and major applications that require accreditation by a senior management official. The system inventory process will be automated as fully as possible, and the ability to add, modify, and delete inventory information will be strictly limited to those demonstrating a need to know.

The chief information security officer will develop inventory process requirements, ensure they are implemented within the process, and manage the inventory system. The system inventory will be verified quarterly or no less than annually in accordance with guidelines published by the office of the chief information security officer.

Applicability

This policy applies to all XYZ Company information systems in use at all corporate locations (corporate, group, local) worldwide.

Authority and Responsibility

This policy is issued by authority of the chief information security officer. It is the responsibility of general management at each level within the organization (corporate, group, local) to ensure compliance with this policy.

Document History

Q14-05-008   Released
01   5/24/10
02   6/16/11

Appendix H

Sample Business Impact Assessment

XYZ Corporate Intranet Business Impact Analysis (BIA)

Organization	Date BIA Completed		Confidentiality	Integrity	Availability	System Criticality
IT Operations	**1-Sep-05**	**BIA POC** **Bill Black**	Moderate	Moderate	Moderate	Mission Critical

System description The XYZ Corporate Intranet is a collection of predefined HTML templates into which information stored in a relational database is contextually extracted based on how the visitor navigates through the site. The site is publicly available to everyone within the XYZ Company intranet domain.

The XYZ Corporate Intranet Web site system (http://XYZnet.com) is located in Room 1005 of the corporate headquarters building. The system consists of two servers: INTRANET1.XYZ.COM—production server and INTRANET2.XYZ.COM—hot standby and testing server.

All servers run MS Windows NT 4.0 Service Pack 6a and Security Rollup Package. Servers also run Internet Information Server (IIS) 4.0 with the IIS lockdown tool and the latest patches and hot fixes. Microsoft SQL 7.0 Server is used as the database engine for the system. The SQL servers have SP-3 installed along with the appropriate hot fixes. The system consists of two Compaq Proliant ML370 servers with 4x700MHz P-III processors and 1024 MB RAM with approximately 96 GB of disk space in a RAID5 configuration.

Recovery Priority	Critical Resource/ Function	Critical Role	Department	Maximum Allowable Outage	Business Impact	
					Impact	Comments
1	Servers (primary and secondary)	System administrator	IT operations	72 hours	High	The consequences of loss of system resource or to data or information in the system are only marginally acceptable.
	Hardware					
	Operating system					
	Servers (primary and secondary)					Impact to resource would adversely affect the XYZ corporate mission.
	Hardware					
	Operating system					
	Security					
	Data archive					
2	Web application— HTML code	Web programming team	IT operations	72 hours	High	Impact to resource would adversely affect XYZ corporate mission.
3	Database software—SQL	System administrator/ Web programming team	IT operations	72 hours	High	Impact to resource would adversely affect XYZ corporate mission.
4	Web services software—IIS	Web programming team	IT operations	72 hours	High	Impact to resource would adversely affect XYZ corporate mission.
5	Content management system	Web programming team	IT operations	1 week	Low	Impact to resource would affect upload to primary (production) Web server.

Appendix H

Sample Rules of Behavior (General Support System)

XYZ Company Local-Area Network (LAN) Rules of Behavior

- I will comply with XYZ Company policies, regulations, and guidelines regarding the protection, handling, printing, duplication, processing, transmission, distribution, and destruction of sensitive information designated "restricted."

- I will not knowingly introduce any malicious code into the XYZ Company LAN, and I will not attempt to bypass or circumvent network security features or mechanisms.

- I will protect all passwords issued to me and will not disclose them to anyone. I understand that password sharing or the use of another user's ID and password is prohibited. I will change my password when I suspect that it may have been compromised.

- I will protect sensitive information from unauthorized access, disclosure, modification, misuse, copying, damage, destruction, or theft.

- I will immediately notify the system security officer when I no longer require access to the XYZ Company LAN because of transfer, completion of project, retirement, or termination of employment.

- I will not copy or remove copies of software licensed to the XYZ Company without proper authorization, and I will not import or use unauthorized software, firmware, or hardware in the work environment.

- I will only access XYZ Company LAN resources for which I am authorized.

- I will not embed passwords in log-on scripts.

- ■ I will report all security incidents, including password compromises, violations of software licensing agreements, and computer viruses, to the system security officer and my supervisor.

- ■ I will use the XYZ Company LAN for processing, transmission, and storage of official company-related or authorized work only.

- ■ I will not relocate XYZ Company LAN equipment or software without proper authorization.

- ■ On final checkout or departure from the company, I will not have in my possession or in my home any sensitive information in any form or any government-owned equipment, software, storage media (e.g., diskettes), user manuals, or system documentation.

I understand that failure to comply with any or all of the above security requirements could result in the loss of my system privileges, other administrative sanctions, and civil or criminal penalties.

I acknowledge receipt of and understand my responsibilities and will comply with the rules of behavior for the XYZ Company LAN.

Name	Signature	Date

Annual Update: _____ _____
Signature   Date

Annual Update: _____ _____
Signature   Date

Annual Update: _____ _____
Signature   Date

Appendix J

Sample Rules of Behavior (Major Application)

ABC Application Rules of Behavior

- I will comply with XYZ Company policies, regulations, and guidelines regarding the protection, handling, processing, transmission, distribution, and destruction of sensitive unclassified information designated "restricted."

- I will not knowingly introduce any malicious code, and I will not attempt to bypass or circumvent security features or mechanisms.

- I will protect all passwords issued to me and will not disclose them to anyone. I understand that password sharing or the use of another user's ID and password is prohibited. I will change my password when I suspect that it may have been compromised.

- I will protect sensitive information from unauthorized access, disclosure, modification, misuse, damage, or theft.

- I will immediately notify the security officer for my area when I no longer require access to the ABC Application because of transfer, completion of project, retirement, or termination of employment.

- I will only access ABC Application resources for which I am authorized.

- I will report all security incidents, including password compromises, anomalous system behavior, and illegal activity to the security officer and my supervisor.

- On final checkout or departure from the XYZ Company, I will not have in my possession or in my home any sensitive ABC Application information in any form.

I understand that failure to comply with any or all of the above security requirements could result in the loss of my system privileges, other administrative sanctions, and civil or criminal penalties.

I acknowledge receipt of and understand my responsibilities and will comply with the rules of behavior for the ABC Application.

_____   _____   _____
Name   Signature   Date

                        Annual Update: _____   _____
                                                        Signature   Date

                        Annual Update: _____   _____
                                                        Signature   Date

                        Annual Update: _____   _____
                                                        Signature   Date

Appendix K

Sample System Security Plan Outline

The following sample system security plan outline is based on guidance contained in National Institute of Standards and Technology Special Publication 800-18.

Security Plan Outline

System Identification
  System name
  Responsible organization
  Information contact(s)
  Assignment of security
  Operational status
  General description/purpose
  System environment
    Technical description
    Principal system components
    Security software
  System interconnection/information sharing
  Applicable laws or regulations affecting the system
  General description of information sensitivity
    Confidentiality
    Integrity
    Availability
  System risks (summarized from risk assessment)

System Controls
    Management controls
        Risk assessment
        Planning
        Systems and services acquisition
        Certification, accreditation, and security assessments
    Operational controls
        Personnel security
        Physical and environmental protection
        Contingency planning
        Configuration management
        Maintenance
        System and information integrity
        Media protection
        Incident response
        Awareness and training
    Technical controls
        Identification and authentication
        Access controls
        Audit and accountability
        System and communications protection

Appendix L

Sample Memorandum of Understanding

The following sample memorandum of understanding is based on guidance contained in National Institute of Standards and Technology Special Publication (NIST SP) 800-47.

Memorandum of Understanding

Introduction

This memorandum will record the formal agreement between the Acme Corporation and the Ajax Company with regard to interconnection between the Zeus System, operated by the Acme Corporation, and the Athena System, owned by the Ajax Company, to include the development, management, operation, and security of the connection. This agreement is designed to govern the relationship between these two named entities and their personnel in the absence of common management authority.

Background

It is the intent of the agreeing parties to interconnect the two named information systems to permit the exchange of training-related data. The Acme Corporation requires access to the Ajax Company's Athena System to permit the update of personnel training records, and the Ajax Company requires access to the Acme Corporation's Zeus System for the purpose of accessing training reports. The expected benefit of the interconnection is to expedite the processing of training information within prescribed timelines. Each information technology system is described as follows:

Zeus System

- Function: Training management system.

- Location: Acme Corporation Headquarters, Anywhere, New Jersey.

- Description of Data: Moderately sensitive data consisting of personnel training data, which includes training attended, dates of training, and completion status by employee name. Personal Social Security numbers are not used or stored by the system.

Athena System

- Function: Employee training repository.

- Location: Ajax Company Headquarters, Smallplace, Pennsylvania.

- Description of Data: Moderately sensitive data that consists of employee training information, which includes training attended, dates of training, and completion status by employee name. Personal Social Security numbers are not used or stored by the system.

Communications

To ensure the successful management and operation of the interconnection, frequent communications are essential. The parties agree to maintain open lines of communication between personnel at both the managerial and the technical levels. All communications described in this agreement will be documented in writing unless otherwise noted.

To support the management and operation of the interconnection, the owners of the Zeus System and the Athena System agree to designate points of contact for their respective system. To safeguard the confidentiality, integrity, and availability of the connected systems and the data they store, process, and transmit, the parties agree to provide notice of the following events within the time frames indicated:

- *Security Incidents*: Points of contact will immediately notify their designated counterparts by telephone or e-mail when a security incident is detected so that the receiving party may take action to determine if its system has been compromised and to permit taking appropriate security precautions. The system owner will receive formal notification in writing within three business days after detection of the incident.

- *Disasters and Other Contingencies*: Points of contact will immediately notify their designated counterparts by telephone or e-mail in the event of a disaster or other contingency that disrupts the normal operation of one or both of the connected systems.

- *Material Changes to System Configuration*: Planned technical changes to the system architecture will be reported to the point of contact prior to their implementation. The initiating party agrees to conduct a risk assessment based on the new system architecture and to modify and re-sign the interconnection security agreement (ISA) within 1 month of implementation.

- *Additional Interconnections*: The initiating party will notify the other party at least 1 month before it connects its information technology system with any other information technology system, including systems that are owned and operated by third parties.

- *Personnel Changes*: The parties agree to provide notification of the separation or long-term absence of their respective system owners or technical leads. In addition, both parties will provide notification of any changes in point-of-contact information. Both parties also will provide notification of changes to user profiles, including users who resign or change job responsibilities.

Interconnection Security Agreement

The technical details of the interconnection will be documented in an ISA. The parties agree to work together to develop the ISA, which must be signed by both parties before the interconnection is activated. Proposed changes to either system or the interconnecting medium will be reviewed and evaluated to determine the potential impact on the interconnection. The ISA will be renegotiated before changes are implemented. Signatories to the ISA shall be authorizing officials for each system.

Security

Both parties agree to work together to ensure the joint security of the connected systems and the data they store, process, and transmit, as specified in the ISA. Each party certifies that its respective system is designed, managed, and operated in compliance with all relevant federal laws, regulations, and policies.

Cost Considerations

Both parties agree to share the costs of the interconnecting mechanism and media equally, but no such expenditures or financial commitments shall be made without the written concurrence of both parties. Modifications to either system that are necessary to support the interconnection are the responsibility of the respective system owner's organizations.

Timeline

This agreement will remain in effect for 1 year after the last date on either signature in the signature block below. After 1 year, this agreement will expire without further action. If the parties wish to extend this agreement, they may do so by reviewing, updating, and reauthorizing this agreement. The newly signed agreement should explicitly supersede this agreement, which should be referenced by title and date. If one or both of the parties wish to terminate this agreement prematurely, they may do so on 30 days' advanced notice or in the event of a security incident that necessitates an immediate response.

Signatory Authority

I agree to the terms of this memorandum of understanding.

(Organization A Official)   (Organization B Official)

_____   _____

(Signature Date)   (Signature Date)

Acme Corporation   Ajax Company

Appendix M

Sample Interconnection Security Agreement

The following sample interconnection security agreement is based on guidance contained in National Institute of Standards and Technology Special Publication (NIST SP) 800-47.

Section 1: Statement of Requirements

The requirements for interconnection between the Acme Corporation and the Ajax Company are for the express purpose of exchanging data between the Zeus System, owned by the Acme Corporation, and the Athena System, owned by the Ajax Company. The Ajax Company requires the use of the Acme Corporation's personnel training database, and the Acme Corporation requires the use of the Ajax Company's training data repository. The expected benefit is to expedite the processing of employee training data within prescribed timelines.

Section 2: System Security Considerations

General Information/Data Description

The interconnection between the Zeus System and the Athena System is a two-way path. The purpose of the interconnection is to deliver personnel data to the Acme Company's training management branch and to deliver training information to the Acme Corporation's personnel office.

Services Offered

No user services are offered. This connection only exchanges data between the Zeus System and the Athena System via a dedicated connection.

Data Sensitivity

The sensitivity of data exchanged between the Zeus System and the Athena System is considered high based on its need for protection against disclosure.

User Community

All Acme Corporation users with access to the data received from the Ajax Company are U.S. citizens with a valid and current Acme Corporation background investigation. All Ajax Company users with access to the data received from the Acme Corporation are U.S. citizens with a valid and current Ajax Company background investigation.

Information Exchange Security

The security of the information being passed on this two-way connection is protected through the use of encryption mechanisms that meet federal requirements. The connections at each end are located within controlled access facilities, guarded 24 hours a day. Individual users will not have access to the data except through their system's security software inherent to the operating system. All access is controlled by authentication methods to validate the approved users.

Trusted Behavior Expectations

The Acme Corporation's system and users are expected to protect the Ajax Company's data, and the Ajax Company's system and users are expected to protect the Acme Corporation's data, in accordance with all applicable federal laws.

Formal Security Policy

Policy documents that govern the protection of the data are the Acme Corporation's computer security policy and the Ajax Company's information technology security policy and standards.

Incident Reporting

The organization discovering a security incident will report it in accordance with its incident reporting procedures. In the case of the Ajax Company, any security incident will be reported to the network operations center located in the company data center.

Audit Trail Responsibilities

Both parties are responsible for auditing application processes and user activities involving the interconnection. Activities that will be recorded include event type, date and time of event, user identification, workstation identification, success or failure of access attempts, and security actions taken by system administrators or security officers. Audit logs will be retained for one (1) year.

Section 3: Connectivity Drawing

Section 4: Approval

Signatory Authority

This interconnection security agreement (ISA) is valid for one (1) year after the last date on either signature below. At that time, it will be updated, reviewed, and reauthorized. Either party may terminate this agreement on 30 days' advanced notice in writing or in the event of a security incident that necessitates an immediate response.

Acme Corporation   Ajax Company

_____ _____   _____ _____

Signature   Date   Signature   Date

Appendix M

Appendix N

Sample Risk Assessment Outline

The following risk assessment outline is based on guidance contained in National Institute of Standards and Technology Special Publication (NIST SP) 800-30.

Executive Summary

I. Introduction

- Purpose
- Scope
- System description

Describe the system components, elements, users, field site locations (if any), and any other details about the system to be considered in the assessment.

II. Risk Assessment Approach

Briefly describe the approach used to conduct the risk assessment including

- Project participants
- The process used for information gathering (i.e., interviews, automated tools, questionnaires, etc.)
- The methodology for identifying, evaluating, and pairing threats and vulnerabilities; for ranking risks; and for specifying risk-mitigating controls

III. System Characterization

Characterize the system, including hardware (server, router, switch); software (e.g., application, operating system, protocol); system interfaces (e.g., communication link); data; and users. Also, include a connectivity diagram or system input and output flowchart to show the scope of the risk assessment.

IV. Threat Statement

Compile and list the potential threats and associated threat actions applicable to the assessed system.

V. Risk Assessment Results

List the findings (threat/vulnerability pairs), which include

- Finding cross-reference number with a brief description of observation
- A discussion of the threat/vulnerability pair
- Specification of likelihood of occurrence and evaluation (e.g., high, medium, or low likelihood)
- Impact identification and evaluation (e.g., high, medium, or low impact)
- Risk rating based on the risk-level matrix (e.g., high, medium, or low risk level)
- Recommended controls or alternative options for reducing the risk

VI. Summary

Provide a report of the findings and summarize them, the associated risk levels, the recommendations, and any comments necessary to facilitate understanding.

Sample Security Procedure

Procedure 3-7: Incident Response
Satisfies Security Requirements (National Institute of Standards and Technology Special Publication **[NIST SP] 800-53**): Controls IR-1 to IR-7

Responsibility for Implementation and Enforcement

- Group name: IT Operations
- Person's name: Joe Doaks
- Title: ABC System information system security officer (ISSO)
- Phone: (123) 456-7890
- E-mail: joe.doaks@xyz.com

References

XYZ Company Policy 37, Computer Incident Reporting

Applicability

A security incident occurs whenever XYZ Company information is compromised, when there is a risk of compromise of such information, when recurring or successful attempts to obtain unauthorized access to the ABC System are detected, or where misuse of the system is suspected.

Reporting Process

The ISSO manages a reporting process as part of the security incident reporting procedure for ABC System users to keep them informed of security-relevant activity that they may observe on the ABC System. This reporting process shall not use the ABC System itself to report security-relevant activity about the system.

The reporting process includes

- Description of the incident
- Identification of the individual reporting the security incident
- Identification of the loss, potential loss, access attempt, or misuse
- Identification of the perpetrator (if possible)
- Notification of appropriate security and management personnel, and support to civilian authorities, when required
- Reestablishment of protective controls, if required
- Restart of operations if the system had been shut down to facilitate investigation

Tasks

The ISSO will perform the following tasks in the implementation of this procedure:

- Monitor and react to system security warning messages and reports
- Immediately report security incidents through the appropriate security and management channels
- Submit an analysis of the security incident to the appropriate XYZ Corporate incident response team for corrective and disciplinary actions
- Perform an initial evaluation of security problems and, if necessary, temporarily deny access to affected systems

- Ensure that the system administrator evaluates, reports, and documents ABC System security problems and vulnerabilities
- Partially or completely suspend operations if any incident is detected that affects security of operations
- Ensure that all cases of actual or suspected compromise of passwords are investigated
- Ensure that occurrences within the ABC System that may affect the integrity and security of the data being processed are investigated
- Assist the investigating officials in analyzing actual or suspected compromises of information, if applicable

Appendix P

Sample Certification Test Results Matrix

Question	Vulnerability	ST&E Actions	Expected Results	Pass/Fail	Actual Results Summary	Document Reference
9	1.2.1 Are final risk determinations and related management approvals documented and maintained on file? Federal Information Security Controls Audit Manual (FISCAM SP1)	Review current risk assessment report.	Program officials understand the risk to their system and determined it to be acceptable.	P	Final risk determinations and related management approvals are documented and maintained on file.	ABC System risk assessment, dated August 6, 2003
10	1.2.2 Has a mission/business impact analysis been conducted? (National Institute of Standards and Technology Special Publication [NIST SP] 800-30)	Review current mission/business impact analysis.	A mission/business impact analysis has been conducted on the system by the system owners and presented to management.	F	A mission/business impact analysis has not been conducted.	Interview with program manager, February 1, 2005

#	Question	Test Procedure	Expected Result		Result	Evidence
11	1.2.3 Have additional controls been identified to mitigate identified risks sufficiently? (NIST SP 800-30)	Review current risk assessment to determine whether additional controls have been identified to mitigate identified risks sufficiently.	Program officials have ensured that additional safeguards are identified and implemented.	P	Additional controls have been identified to mitigate identified risks sufficiently.	ABC System risk assessment, dated August 6, 2003
13	2.1.1 Have the system and all network boundaries been subjected to periodic reviews? (FISCAM SP 5.1)	Review written procedures for conducting reviews and documentation showing evidence that periodic reviews have been conducted.	An independent security review has been performed once annually.	P	The system and all network boundaries are subjected to annual periodic reviews.	ABC Information System security plan, dated January 11, 2005
14	2.1.2 Has an independent review been performed when a significant change occurred? (Office of Management and Budget [OMB] Circular A-130, III FISCAM SP-5.1; NIST SP 800-18)	Review written procedures for conducting independent reviews and documentation showing that reviews have been conducted.	System security controls have been reviewed following major configuration changes.	P	An independent review was conducted in July 2003. The review that led to the development of this report was performed in February 2005. There were no significant changes in the ABC processing environment between those dates.	ABC Information System security plan, dated January 11, 2005

Appendix Q

Sample Risk Remediation Plan

Quarter 2 FY 2012

System Name	System Criticality	Confidentiality	Availability	Integrity	If no weakness, provide a reason
XYZ System	Non-Mission Critical	Moderate	Low	High	N/A

ID	Weakness	POC	Resources Required	Scheduled Completion Date	Milestones With Completion Dates	Actual Completion Date	Status/Comments	Risk Level
1	1.2.2 A mission/business impact analysis has not been conducted.	System Owner	16 Man/Hrs	9/30/2012	Prepare a business impact analysis in accordance with NIST SP 800-34.			Low
2	4.1.7 The vulnerability scan performed on the Unix server detected one medium risk (telnet Daemon is running) and one low risk vulnerability (XDMCP service detected).	System Owner	8 Man/Hrs	6/30/2012	Address the identified medium risk and low risk vulnerabilities by reviewing the necessity for using Telnet and XDMCP services, and remove them if possible.			Mod
3	6.1.4 Critical system support functions are divided between the System Administrator, Application Programmer, and DBA. However, the Application Programmer is granted permission to perform system modifications, testing and production system updates.	System Owner	8 Man/Hrs	4/30/2012	Establish procedures and implement mechanisms that require the functions of system modification, testing, and update of the production system to be performed by a minimum of two personnel.			High

Appendix R

Sample Certification Statement

ABC System Certification Statement

Background

Between April 18 and April 22, 2011, a security test and evaluation (ST&E) was conducted on the ABC System operated by the XYZ Company, located in Dusty Junction, Arizona. The ST&E was performed by an independent assessment team under the direction of the undersigned certifying agent at the direction of the chief information security officer, XYZ Company, and was conducted in accordance with Office of Management and Budget (OMB) Circular A-130, Appendix III, *Security of Federal Automated Information Resources*, and XYZ Company policy on accreditation. The purpose of the ST&E was to demonstrate, through selected verification techniques and verification procedures documented in the ABC System ST&E plan (dated April 1, 2009) and ST&E report (dated May 1, 2010), that necessary security controls that are identified in the ABC System security plan (dated November 11, 2009) are implemented correctly, meet minimum security requirements, and are effective in their applications, and that the controls adequately mitigate risks described in the ABC System risk assessment report (dated November 21, 2009). The certification effort provides the designated approving authority (DAA) with important information necessary to make an informed, risk-based decision regarding the operation of ABC System.

Summary of Findings

The results of the certification effort are summarized in Figures R.1 and R.2.

There were 58 vulnerabilities found in ABC System controls. These were ranked according to risk as shown in Figure R.1. Based on these findings, the ABC System

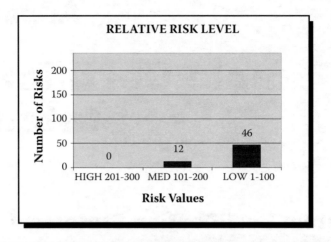

Figure R.1   **Relative risk level.**

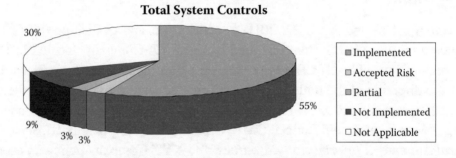

Figure R.2   **Total system controls.**

is categorized as having a moderate level of risk. This corresponds to the moderate security category identified in Federal Information Processing Standard (FIPS) 199.

The results of the risk assessment of ABC System indicated that the primary risks to system resources related to unauthorized acts committed by authorized system users and system intrusion, fraud, and spoofing. Unintentional user errors and omissions were also found to be significant risks to system data and operations.

ABC System management has fully implemented 45 of 80 of the required information technology security controls (55%). Another two (2) controls (3%) have been partially implemented or are in the process of being implemented. Twenty-four (24) controls (30%) are not applicable to the system. Residual risk is being accepted for two (2) of the controls (3%). Seven controls (9%) have not been implemented at this time.

Statement of Compliance

Based on the state of security controls tested and evaluated during the ST&E, it is the judgment of the certifying agent that, with the exception of corrective actions specified in the attached plan of action and milestones (POA&M), the ABC System complies with the general requirements of OMB Circular A-130, Appendix III, and with minimum security requirements defined by the XYZ Company in accordance with National Institute of Standards and Technology (NIST) guidance. The most significant areas of noncompliance identified are

- Failure to review security controls on a quarterly basis
- Failure to update the risk assessment following significant changes to the system
- Failure to dispose of magnetic and optical media properly
- Failure to record successful user log-ons
- Failure to implement auditing

Recommendations

The security controls listed in the ABC System security plan have been tested and evaluated by an independent certification team using the verification techniques and the procedures described in the attached ST&E results report to determine if those controls meet minimum security requirements and are effective in their applications. Testing has reasonably demonstrated that the ABC System provides necessary assurance for secure processing. Based on the results of ST&E activities, the undersigned certifying agent recommends that the system owner take action to correct identified vulnerabilities according to the schedule documented in the POA&M, which describes the necessary corrective measures to reduce or eliminate the stated vulnerabilities in system controls. I further recommend that the system be authorized for operation by the DAA and that identified residual risks be accepted.

_____   _____
Joe Doaks   Date
Certifying Agent
Acme Consulting, Inc.

Appendix R

Certification Statement

Based on my review of documentation contained in the accompanying certification package, I concur with the findings and recommendations of the certifying agent. I certify that ABC System security controls have been tested at the appropriate certification level, and as of this date the ABC System meets applicable federal security requirements as it operates in its current environment with the exception of vulnerabilities identified in the attached POA&M. I recommend that the DAA accept identified residual risk and authorize ABC System processing in its current operational environment by accrediting the system under the provision that all risks be mitigated in accordance with the ABC System POA&M. A review of security controls protecting the system will be conducted on any major changes to the current operating environment.

_____   _____

Jane Doe, Chief Information Security Officer   Date

Certifying Official

XYZ Company

Appendix S

Sample Accreditation Letter

In accordance with the provisions of the Acme Corporation Certification and Accreditation Program, after reviewing the security controls that have been implemented and planned and weighing the remaining residual risks against operational requirements, I authorize continued operation of the Apollo System under the provision that necessary corrective action is taken to address the following weaknesses

- Lack of a documented agreement regarding the interconnection with the Ajax System
- Failure to conduct contingency plan testing
- Lack of separation of duties between those administering the system and personnel charged with managing security controls
- Failure to identify a backup storage site that is more than 10 miles from the primary processing location

This authorization is my formal declaration that security controls for the Apollo System have generally been implemented and are functioning correctly; however, additional security controls are needed to ensure that a heightened level of security has been achieved. The Apollo System may be operated in a restricted mode until all high and medium risks identified in the plan of action and milestones (POA&M) for the system can be implemented. This authorization is for the existing operating environment of the Apollo System, is contingent on continued operation and maintenance of the security controls in place, and is valid for a period of three (3) years from the date of this statement unless a significant change to the information technology system requires earlier reaccreditation. I authorize the Apollo System to operate with residual risks related to the following NIST SP 800-26 requirements:

- Lack of separation of duties between those administering the system and personnel charged with managing security controls

■ Failure to identify a backup storage site that is more than 10 miles from the primary processing location

I will ensure that the owner of the Apollo System analyzes any significant change in the system's configuration (i.e., hardware, software, and firmware) or in the system's operating environment to determine its impact on system security, and that the system owner takes appropriate action to maintain a level of security consistent with the requirements for this action.

The Acme Corporation information system security officer (ISSO) will retain a copy of this accreditation letter with all supporting documentation as a permanent record.

Theodore Postlewaithe   Date

Approving Authority

Office of the Chief Financial Officer

cc: Helen Bridgewater, Chief Information Officer
Attachments:

1. System security plan
2. Risk assessment
3. Security test and evaluation plan and results
4. Plan of action and milestones
5. Minimum security baseline assessment

Appendix T

Sample Interim Accreditation Letter

From: Accrediting Official

To: System Owner

Subject: Interim Authority to Operate for the ABC System

I have reviewed the results of the security certification of the ABC System and all supporting documentation provided in the ABC System accreditation package. Based on this review, I have determined that the risk resulting from the operation of the system to XYZ Company operations, assets, and personnel is not presently acceptable. However, I recognize that there is a continuing need to allow the system to continue its operation due to existing business needs. Therefore, this interim authorization to operate the ABC System in its existing operating environment is being granted. This interim authorization constitutes a limited authorization to operate the system under specific conditions and acknowledges increased risk to company operations for a specified period of time until specified operating conditions are met. The terms and conditions of this interim authority to operate are described in the enclosure.

This interim authorization is valid for 90 days. During this period, the system owner will submit weekly security status reports for the system. The system owner will take action to reduce or eliminate vulnerabilities in ABC System controls identified in the plan of action and milestones.

The system owner will immediately establish a process to monitor the effectiveness of the security controls in the information system during this period of limited authorization. Specific areas of concern identified during the security certification will be given priority for monitoring. The system owner will immediately report any significant changes in the security posture of the ABC System during the period of limited authorization. I will monitor the plan of action and milestones submitted with the accreditation package during the period of limited authorization.

At the end of the period of limited authorization, I will again review the risks to the ABC System and will either authorize it to operate or deny continued operation. I will not grant further renewals or extensions to this interim authorization to operate. The system owner will retain a copy of this authorization with all supporting security certification and accreditation documentation in accordance with the company's record retention schedule.

John Doe, Vice President for Operations
Enclosure

Appendix U

Certification and Accreditation Professional (CAP®) Common Body of Knowledge (CBK®)

The International Information Systems Security Certification Consortium or (ISC)²® offers the Certified Authorization Professional (CAP®) credential as an objective measure of the knowledge, skills, and abilities that personnel engaged in information system security authorization process. The CAP® credential offers hiring authorities assurance that personnel holding this credential are capable of ensuring information systems are secured to counter potential risks.

(ISC)²® developed the credential for application to a broad spectrum of organizations to include commercial firms, state and local governments, and all components of the U.S. government, including the defense, intelligence community, and civilian government organizations. The Department of Defense (DOD), as shown in the following matrix, has accepted the CAP® certification to satisfy its competency requirements. Personnel performing system security authorization roles, including security control assessors, system owners, information system security officers, and authorizing officials, can benefit through attainment of the CAP® credential.

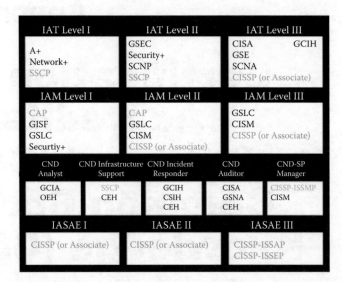

Award of the CAP® certification is based on a rigorous examination that tests the breadth and depth of a candidate's knowledge of authorization practices and principles as reflected in its CAP® Common Body of Knowledge (CBK®). While numerous National Institute of Standards and Technology (NIST) and Office of Management and Budget (OMB) publications constitute the CAP® exam, the seven domains for this exam conceptually mirror the NIST system authorization process that is described in NIST Special Publication (SP) 800-53, Revision 3, and NIST SP 800-37, Revision 1. These two documents are the foundation for the emerging harmonized control taxonomy and security authorization processes, respectively, that now govern across all federal government agencies. A candidate must understand and be able to apply knowledge in each domain to be successful. This requires a candidate to synthesize material from many sources to be successful. The CAP® CBK® is comprised of the seven security domains and related key areas of knowledge and are discussed next.

Domain 1: Understanding the Security Authorization of Information Systems

Security authorization includes a tiered risk management approach to evaluate both strategic and tactical risk across the enterprise. The authorization process incorporates the application of a Risk Management Framework (RMF), a review of the organizational structure, and the business process/mission as the foundation for the implementation and assessment of specified security controls. This authorization management process identifies vulnerabilities and countermeasures and determines residual risks. The residual risks are evaluated and deemed either acceptable or unacceptable. More controls must be implemented to reduce unacceptable risk. The system may be deployed only when the residual risks are acceptable to the enterprise.

Key Areas of Knowledge

- Understand the risk management approach to security authorization
  - Distinguish between applying risk management principles and satisfying compliance requirements
  - Identify and maintain information systems inventory
  - Understand the criticality of securing information
  - Understand organizational operations
- Understand and distinguish among the RMF steps
  - Categorize information system
  - Select security controls
  - Implement security controls
  - Assess security controls
  - Authorize information system
  - Monitor security controls
- Define and understand roles and responsibilities
  - Head of agency (chief executive officer)
  - Risk executive (function)
  - Chief information officer
  - Information system security officer
  - Security control assessor
  - Other defined roles
- Understand how the security authorization process relates to
  - Organization-wide risk management
  - System development life cycle (SDLC)
  - Information system boundaries
  - Authorization decisions
- Understand the relationship between the RMF and SDLC

- ■ Understand legal, regulatory, and other requirements for security authorization, including

  - – Federal information security and privacy legislation

  - – Office of Management and Budget

  - – Committee on National Security Systems (CNSS)

  - – Federal Information Processing Standards (FIPSs)

  - – NIST special publications

- ■ Understand common controls and security control inheritance

- ■ Understand ongoing monitoring strategies

Domain 2: Categorize Information Systems

Categorization of the information system is based on an impact analysis. It is performed to determine the types of information included within the security authorization boundary, the security requirements for the information types, and the potential impact on the organization resulting from a security compromise. The result of the categorization is used as the basis for developing the security plan, selecting security controls, and determining the risk inherent in operating the system.

Key Areas of Knowledge

- ■ Categorize the system

- ■ Register the system

- ■ Security plan analysis, update, and acceptance

Domain 3: Establish the Security Control Baseline

The security control baseline is established by determining specific controls required to protect the system based on the security categorization of the system. The baseline is tailored and supplemented in accordance with an organizational assessment of risk and local parameters. The security control baseline, as well as the plan for monitoring it, is documented in the security plan.

Key Areas of Knowledge

- Identify and document common (inheritable) controls
- Select and document security controls
- Develop security control monitoring strategy
- Review and approve security plan

Domain 4: Apply Security Controls

The security controls specified in the security plan are implemented by taking into account the minimum organizational assurance requirements. The security plan describes how the controls are employed within the information system and its operational environment. The security assessment plan documents the methods for testing these controls and the expected results throughout the system's life cycle.

Key Areas of Knowledge

- Implement selected security controls
- Document security control implementation

Domain 5: Assess Security Controls

The security control assessment follows the approved plan, including defined procedures, to determine the effectiveness of the controls in meeting security requirements of the information system. The results are documented in the security assessment report.

Key Areas of Knowledge

- Prepare for security control assessment
- Establish security control assessment plan
- Determine security control effectiveness
- Develop initial security assessment report
- Perform initial remediation actions
- Develop final security assessment report and addendum

Appendix U

Domain 6: Authorize Information System

The residual risks identified during the security control assessment are evaluated, and the decision is made to authorize the system to operate, deny its operation, or remediate the deficiencies. Associated documentation is prepared or updated depending on the authorization decision.

Key Areas of Knowledge

- Develop plan of action and milestones (POA&M)
- Assemble security authorization package
- Determine risk
- Determine the acceptability of risk
- Obtain security authorization decision

Domain 7: Monitor Security Controls

After an authorization to operate (ATO) is granted, ongoing continuous monitoring is performed on all identified security controls as well as the political, legal, and physical environment in which the system operates. Changes to the system or its operational environment are documented and analyzed. The security state of the system is reported to designated officials. Significant changes will cause the system to reenter the security authorization process. Otherwise, the system will continue to be monitored on an ongoing basis in accordance with the organization's monitoring strategy.

Key Areas of Knowledge

- Determine security impact of changes to system and environment
- Perform ongoing security control assessments
- Conduct ongoing remediation actions
- Update key documentation
- Perform periodic security status reporting
- Perform ongoing risk determination and acceptance
- Decommission and remove system

Answers to Review Questions

Domain 1

1. During which Risk Management Framework (RMF) step is the system security plan initially approved?

   A. RMF Step 1 Categorize Information System
   B. RMF Step 2 Select Security Controls
   C. RMF Step 3 Implement Security Controls
   D. RMF Step 5 Authorize Information System

   Answer is **B**.
   The system security plan is first approved by the authorizing official or AO designated representative during execution of RMF Step 2, Task 2-4.
   Security Plan Approval. See: CAP® CBK® Chapter 2, Task 2-4: Approval Security Plan; NIST SP 800-37, Revision 1, RMF Step 2, Task 2-4: Security Plan Approval.

2. Which organizational official is responsible for the procurement, development, integration, modification, operation, maintenance, and disposal of an information system?

   A. Information system security engineer (ISSE)
   B. Chief information officer (CIO)
   C. Information system owner (ISO)
   D. Information security architect

   Answer is **C**.

According to National Institute of Standards and Technology Special Publication (NIST SP) 800-37, Revision 1, Appendix D.9 Information System Owner, the information system owner is an organizational official responsible for the procurement, development, integration, modification, operation, maintenance, and disposal of an information system. The information system owner serves as the focal point for the information system. In that capacity, the information system owner (ISO) serves both as an owner and as the central point of contact between the authorization process and the owners of components of the system. See also CAP® CBK® Chapter 1, System Authorization Roles and Responsibilities, Primary Roles and Responsibilities.

3. Which authorization approach considers time elapsed since the authorization results were produced, the environment of operation, the criticality/sensitivity of the information, and the risk tolerance of the other organization?

A. Leveraged
B. Single
C. Joint
D. Site specific

Answer is **A**.

With this approach, the leveraging organization considers risk factors such as the time elapsed since the authorization results were originally produced; the current environment of operation (if different from the environment of operation reflected in the authorization package); the criticality/sensitivity of the information to be processed, stored, or transmitted (if different from the state of the original authorization); as well as the overall risk tolerance of the leveraging organization (in the event that the risk tolerance posture has changed over time). See NIST SP 800-37, Revision 1, Appendix F.6 Authorization Approaches.

4. System authorization programs are marked by frequent failure due to, among other things, poor planning, poor systems inventory, failure to fix responsibility at the system level, and

A. inability to work with remote teams.
B. lack of a program management office.
C. insufficient system rights.
D. lack of management support.

Answer is **D**.

Lack of management support results from failure to connect system authorization to budgeting for resources, as well as excessive paperwork, lack of enforcement, and poor timing and, among others. See CAP® CBK® Chapter 1, Why System Authorization Programs Fail.

5. In what phases of the Risk Management Framework (RMF) and system development life cycle (SDLC), respectively, does documentation of control implementation start?

A. Categorization and initiation
B. Implement security controls and development/acquisition
C. Authorization and operations/maintenance
D. Monitor and sunset

Answer is **B**.

Security control documentation that describes how system-specific, hybrid, and common controls are implemented are part of the RMF Step 3—implement security controls and the SDLC development/acquisition; implementation phases. The documentation formalizes plans and expectations regarding the overall functionality of the information system. The functional description of the security control implementation includes planned inputs, expected behavior, and expected outputs where appropriate, typically for those technical controls that are employed in the hardware, software, or firmware components of the information system. See CAP® CBK® Chapter 4, Application of Security Controls, Task 3-1: Implement Security Controls; NIST SP 800-37, Revision 1, Step 3, Task 3-1: Security Control Implementation.

6. The tiers of the National Institute of Standards and Technology (NIST) risk management framework are

A. operational, management, system.
B. confidentiality, integrity, availability.
C. organization, mission/business process, information system.
D. prevention, detection, recovery.

Answer is **C**.

According to NIST SP 800-39, 2.2 Multitiered Risk Management, the three tiers of the RMF are organization, mission/business process, and information systems. Answer A ("operational, management, system") is a distracter. Answer B ("confidentiality, integrity, availability") refers to security impacts of information and systems determined during categorization. Answer D relates to a common typology for security controls. See also CAP® CBK® Chapter 1, Fundamentals of Information Systems Risk Management, Guidance on Organization-Wide Risk Management.

7. National Institute of Standards and Technology (NIST) guidance classifies security controls as

   A. production, development. and test.
   B. people, process, and technology.
   C. system-specific, common and hybrid.
   D. technical, administrative, and program.

   Answer is **C**.
   According to NIST SP 800-37, Revision 1, Chapter Two—The Fundamentals, 2.4 Security Control Allocation, security control allocation classifies controls as either system specific, common controls, or a hybrid with qualities of each. Answer A relates to operating environments. Answer B is a common taxonomy for security components. Answer D is a common taxonomy for types of security controls but is not used in NIST guidance. See also CAP® CBK® Chapter 1, Fundamentals of Information Systems Risk Management.

8. Which of the following specifies security requirements for federal information and information systems in 17 security-related areas that represent a broad-based, balanced information security program?

   A. Federal Information Processing Standard (FIPS) 199, Standards for Security Categorization of Federal Information and Information Systems
   B. FIPS 200, Minimum Security Requirements for Federal Information and Information Systems
   C. Committee on National Security Systems (CNSS) Instruction No. 1253, Security Categorization and Control Selection for National Security Systems
   D. Section 3541 Title 44 U.S.C. Federal Information Security Management Act of 2002

   Answer is **B**.

FIPS 200 Minimum Security Requirements for Federal Information and Information Systems specifies minimum security requirements for federal information and information systems in 17 security-related areas that represent a broad-based, balanced information security program. The other selections do not reference those 17 security-related areas. See also CAP® CBK® Chapter 3, Minimum Security Baselines, Selecting Baseline Controls.

9. After a monthly change control board meeting at which the team determined the security impact of proposed changes to an application, what would be the team's next action?

   A. Prepare the plan of action and milestones based on the findings and recommendations of the security assessment report excluding any remediation actions taken.
   B. Prepare the security assessment report documenting the issues, findings, and recommendations from the security control assessment.
   C. Update the security plan, security assessment report, and plan of action and milestones based on the results of the change control board's security impact analysis.
   D. Assess a selected subset of the security controls employed within and inherited by the application in accordance with the organization-defined monitoring strategy.

   Answer is **C**.
   This question refers to NIST SP 800-37, Revision 1, RMF Task 6-1: Information System and Environment Changes, so the correct answer is C. Answer D refers to RMF Task 6-2. Answer A refers to RMF Task 5-1. Answer B refers to RMF Task 4-3. See CAP® CBK® Chapter 7, Task 6-1: Analyze Impact of Information System and Environment Changes.

10. When an authorization to operate (ATO) is issued, which of the following roles authoritatively accepts residual risk on behalf of the organization?

    A. Information owner
    B. Chief information security officer (CISO)
    C. Authorizing official (AO)
    D. AO or the AO's designated representative (DR)

    Answer is **C**.

The explicit acceptance of risk is the responsibility of the authorizing official and cannot be delegated to other officials within the organization. The authorizing official considers many factors when deciding if the risk to organizational operations (including mission, function, image, or reputation), organizational assets, individuals, other organizations, and the nation, is acceptable. Balancing security considerations with mission and operational needs is paramount to achieving an acceptable authorization decision. The authorizing official issues an authorization decision for the information system and the common controls inherited by the system after reviewing all of the relevant information and, if appropriate, consulting with other organizational officials, including the organization's risk executive (function). Also see the CAP® CBK® Chapter 6, Authorizing Decisions.

Domain 2

1. When attempting to categorize a system, which two Risk Management Framework (RMF) starting point inputs should be accounted for?

   A. Federal laws and organizational policies
   B. Federal laws and Office of Management and Budget (OMB) policies
   C. Federal Information Security Management Act (FISMA) and the Privacy Act
   D. Architectural descriptions and organizational inputs

   Answer is **D**.
   Architectural descriptions and organizational inputs are critical input to the system categorization process, as depicted in the NIST SP 800-37, Revision 1, RMF Figure 2-2, and in NIST SP 800-53, Revision 3, Section 3.1, Figure 3.1. See also CAP® CBK® Chapter 1, Task 1-2: Describe the Information System.

2. Documenting the description of the system in the system security plan is the primary responsibility of which Risk Management Framework (RMF) role?

   A. Authorizing official (AO)
   B. Information owner
   C. Information system security officer (ISSO)
   D. Information system owner

Answer is **D**.

NIST SP 800-37, Revision 1, Appendix D.9 Information System Owner, and CAP® CBK® Chapter 1, Primary Roles and Responsibilities, both describe the information system owner as the role with the primary responsibility of documenting the description of the system in the system security plan.

3. The registration of the system directly follows which Risk Management Framework (RMF) task?

A. Categorize the system
B. Describe the system
C. Review and approve the system security plan
D. Select security controls

Answer is **B**.

Refer to NIST 800-37, Revision 1, Step 1 (Categorize the Information System), Task 1-3 (Information System Registration), which describes the system registration process. See also CAP® CBK® Chapter 1, Task 3-1: Register the Information System.

4. When should the information system owner document the information system and authorization boundary description in the security plan?

A. After security controls are implemented
B. While assembling the authorization package
C. After security categorization
D. When reviewing the security control assessment plan

Answer is **C**.

During RMF Step 1, Task 1-2 (Information System Description) and CAP® CBK® Chapter 2, Task 1-2, the information system owner should describe the information system (including system boundary) and document the description in the security plan, including attachments to the plan, or references to other standard sources for information generated as part of the system development life cycle. The information system description and authorization boundary are prerequisites to security control implementation (answer A), to review of the security control assessment plan (answer D), and to the start of system authorization tasks (answer B).

5. Information developed from Federal Information Processing Standard (FIPS) 199 may be used as an input to which authorization package document?

    A. Security assessment report (SAR)
    B. System security plan (SSP)
    C. Plan of actions and milestones (POA&M)
    D. Authorization decision document

Answer is **B**.

NIST 800-37, Revision 1, RMF Step 1, Task 1-1 (Categorize Information System) uses the results of an FIPS 199 (Standards for Security Categorization of Federal Information and Information Systems) analysis as input to the system security plan. The POA&M (answer C) includes the corrective actions planned for remediation of a weakness discovered during assessment, and the SAR (answer A) includes the assessment results and recommendations for correcting weaknesses discovered during assessment, while the authorization decision document (answer D) is the decision made by the authorizing official to the information system owner to allow or disallow the information system to operate. See also CAP® CBK® Chapter 2, Task 1-1: Categorize and Document the Information System.

Domain 3

1. An organization's information systems are a mix of Windows and UNIX systems located in a single computer room. Access to the computer room is restricted by the use of door locks that require proximity cards and personal identification numbers (PINs). Only a small percentage of the organizations employees have access to the computer room. The computer room access restriction is an example of what type of security control relative to the hardware in the computer room?

    A. Managerial
    B. System specific
    C. Technical
    D. Inherited

Answer is **D**.

The computer room access restriction is a physical security control by itself, but it is a control inherited by all information systems located in the computer room that are protected by it. See: NIST SP 800-53, Revision 3, 2.3 Common Controls, Appendix G, PM-1 Supplemental Guidance; CAP® CBK® Chapter 1, Guidance on Security Control Allocation.

2. Why is security control volatility an important consideration in the development of a security control monitoring strategy?

   A. It identifies needed security control monitoring exceptions.
   B. It indicates a need for compensating controls.
   C. It establishes priority for security control monitoring.
   D. It provides justification for revisions to the configuration management and control plan.

   Answer is **C**.

   According to NIST SP 800-37, Revision 1, Appendix G.2 Selection of Security Controls for Monitoring: "Priority for security control monitoring is given to the controls that have the greatest volatility and the controls that have been identified in the organization's plan of action and milestones." Also see the CAP® CBK® Chapter 3 Establishment of the Security Control Baseline/NIST Guidance on Security Controls Selection, Task 2-3: Develop Monitoring Strategy.

3. An information system is currently in the initiation phase of the system development life cycle (SDLC) and has been categorized high impact. The information system owner wants to inherit common controls provided by another organizational information system that is categorized moderate impact. How does the information system owner ensure that the common controls will provide adequate protection for the information system?

   A. Supplement the common controls with system-specific or hybrid controls to achieve the required protection for the system.
   B. Ask the common control provider for the system security plan for the common controls.
   C. Consult with the information system security engineer and the information security architect.
   D. Perform rigorous testing of the common controls to determine if they provide adequate protection.

Answer is **A**.

NIST SP 800-37, Revision 1, RMF Step 2—Select Security Controls, Task 2-1 Common Control Identification, explicitly states each of the three activities associated with inheriting common controls, including "Supplement the common controls with system-specific or hybrid controls to achieve the required protection for the system." The other answers do not ensure that the common controls will provide appropriate protection for a high-impact information system. See also CAP® CBK® Chapter 3, Task 2-1: Identify Common Controls.

4. An effective security control monitoring strategy for an information system includes

   A. monitoring the security controls of interconnecting information systems outside the authorization boundary.
   B. active involvement by authorizing officials in the ongoing management of information system-related security risks.
   C. the annual assessment of all security controls in the information system.
   D. all controls listed in NIST SP 800-53, Revision 3.

   Answer is **B**.

   NIST SP 800-37, Revision 1, explicitly states (Appendix G, Monitoring Strategy): "An effective organization-wide continuous monitoring program includes:

   • Configuration management and control processes for organizational information systems;

   • Security impact analyses on proposed or actual changes to organizational information systems and environments of operation;

   • Assessment of selected security controls (including system-specific, hybrid, and common controls) based on the organization-defined continuous monitoring strategy;

   • Security status reporting to appropriate organizational officials; and

   • Active involvement by authorizing officials in the ongoing management of information system-related security risks."

5. A large organization has a documented information security policy that has been reviewed and approved by senior officials and is readily available to all organizational staff. This information security policy explicitly addresses

each of the 17 control families in NIST SP 800-53, Revision 3. Some system owners also established procedures for the technical class of security controls on certain of their systems. In their respective system security plans, control AC-1 Access Control Policy and Procedures (a technical class security control) must be identified as what type of control?

A. Fully inheritable
B. Hybrid
C. System specific
D. Inherited

Answer is **B**.
NIST SP 800-53, Revision 3, 2.3 Common Controls, states: "Organizations assign a hybrid status to a security control when one part of the control is deemed to be common and another part of the control is deemed to be system-specific. For example, an organization may implement the Incident Response Policy and Procedures security control (IR-1) as a hybrid control with the policy portion of the control deemed to be common and the procedures portion of the control deemed to be system-specific." Note that all NIST SP 800-53 XX-1 controls specify the requirements for a formal policy as well as formal procedures.

Domain 4

1. When determining the applicability of a specific security control, the security professional should utilize which type of guidance?

A. Categorization guidance
B. Selection guidance
C. Scoping guidance
D. Remediation guidance

Answer is **C**.
References: NIST SP 800-18, Section 2.5.1 "Scoping guidance provides an agency with specific terms and conditions on the applicability and implementation of individual security controls in the security control baselines defined in NIST SP 800-53"; NIST SP 800-37, Revision 1, RMF

Step 2—Select Security Controls, Task 2-2 Security Control Selection, Supplemental Guidance; NIST SP 800-53, Revision 3, 3.3 Selecting Security Controls, "Tailoring the Baseline Security Controls"; CAP® CBK® Chapter 3 Establishment of the Security Control Baseline/NIST Guidance on Security Controls Selection, Task 2-2: Select Security Controls.

2. When making a determination regarding the adequacy of the implementation of inherited controls for their respective systems, an information system owner (ISO) can refer to the authorization package prepared by which of the following?

   A. Information owner/steward (IO)
   B. Information system security engineer (ISSE)
   C. Information systems security officer (ISSO)
   D. Common control provider (CCP)

   Answer is **D**.
   The common control provider is responsible for the planning, development, implementation, assessment, authorization, and maintenance of common security controls inherited by other information systems. The common control provider is responsible for documenting those common controls in a system security plan. Information owners, ISSEs, ISSOs, and other security roles are not responsible for preparing authorization packages. Refer to CAP® CBK® Chapter 4, Task 3-1: Implement Security Controls; NIST SP 800-37, Revision 1, Step 3, Task 3-1: Security Control Implementation.

3. The initial security plan for a new application has been approved. What is the next activity in the Risk Management Framework (RMF)?

   A. Develop a strategy for the continuous monitoring of security control effectiveness.
   B. Assemble the security authorization package.
   C. Implement the security controls specified in the security plan.
   D. Assess a selected subset of the security controls inherited by the information system.

   Answer is **C**.
   Reviewing and approving the security plan is Task 2-4 in Step 2 of the Risk Management Framework. The next task is RMF Step 3, Task 3-1: Implement the security controls specified in the security plan.

4. Which role has the supporting responsibility to coordinate changes to the system, assess the security impact and update the system security plan?

   A. Information system security officer (ISSO)
   B. Information system owner (ISO)
   C. Common control provider
   D. Senior agency information security officer

   Answer is **A**.

   Per NIST SP 800-37, Revision 1, Appendix D Roles and Responsibilities, D.10, the Information System Security Officer is the only role listed that has a supporting responsibility in each of the activities in question, and NIST Chapter 3—The Process—elaborates on the RMF tasks, primary responsibility, and supporting roles.

   Coordination of changes to the system is an activity in RMF Task 6-1: Information System and Environment Changes. Assessment of security impact is an activity in RMF Task 6-2: Ongoing Security Control Changes. Updates to the security plan are an activity in RMF Task 6-4: Key Updates.

5. Who is primarily responsible for the development of system-specific procedures?

   A. The system owner
   B. The information systems security officer (ISSO)
   C. The system architect
   D. The system administrator

   Answer is **A**.

   The system owner is normally the official responsible for developing and approving system-specific procedures. This is because system owners have the most knowledge of the system and know what procedures are needed and what they need to address. See CAP® CBK® Chapter 4, The Problem with Procedures.

Domain 5

1. An initial remediation action was taken by the information system owner (ISO) based on findings from the security assessment report (SAR). What is the next appropriate step based on the Risk Management Framework (RMF)?

A. ISO documents the remedial action in the security plan.

B. Include the remediation action taken by information system owner as an addendum to the SAR.

C. Information system security officer (ISSO) documents the remediation action and informs the ISO.

D. Remedial action taken is sent for review to the ISSO.

Answer is **B**.

According to Supplemental Guidance to Risk Management Framework Step 4—Assess Security Controls, Task 4-4 Remedial Actions, "Organizations can prepare an optional addendum to the SAR that is transmitted to the authorizing official. The optional addendum provides ISO and common control providers an opportunity to respond to the initial findings of assessors. The addendum may include, for example, information regarding initial remediation actions taken by the ISO or common control providers in response to assessor findings, or provide an owner's perspective on the findings (e.g., including additional explanatory material, rebutting certain findings, and correcting the record). The addendum to the SAR does not change or influence, in any manner, the initial assessor findings provided in the original report. Information provided in the addendum is considered by authorizing officials in their risk-based authorization decisions." Also see CAP® CBK® Chapter 5, Task 4-4: Conduct Remediation Action.

2. Which of the following control families belongs to the management class of security controls?

A. Media protection

B. Configuration management

C. Access control

D. Risk assessment

Answer is **D**.

The RA Risk Assessment family of controls is of the management class. Media protection and configuration management are operational controls. Access control is a technical control. Refer to NIST SP 800-53, Revision 3, Appendix F Security Control Catalog for listings of security controls with family and class categories.

3. Prior to completion of the security assessment report (SAR), what type of analysis is performed when agile, iterative development is used?

A. Regression analysis
B. Interim assessment
C. Incremental assessment
D. Executive assessment

Answer is **C**.

An incremental assessment is appropriate when iterative development processes such as agile development are employed. This typically results in an iterative assessment as each cycle is conducted. Even when iterative development is not employed, organizations may choose to begin assessing security controls prior to the complete implementation of all security controls listed in the security plan. This type of incremental assessment is appropriate if it is more efficient or cost effective to do so. See CAP® CBK® Task 4-2: Assess Security Controls; see also Supplemental Guidance to NIST SP 800-37, Revision 1, Step 4 Assess Security Controls, Task 4-2: Security Control Assessment.

4. In the case of a complex information system, where a "leveraged authorization" that involves two agencies will be conducted, what is the minimum number of system boundaries/accreditation boundaries that can exist?

A. Only one.
B. Only two, because there are two agencies.
C. At least two.
D. A leveraged authorization cannot be conducted with more than one agency involved.

Answer is **A**.

Security authorizations are issued for single information systems; however, an existing information system may be leveraged by another agency provided that a review of the system security plan of the owing agency by the leveraging agency determines that adequate security and an interagency agreement are in place. See CAP® CBK® Chapter 1 Security Authorization of Information Systems, NIST SP 800-37, Revision 1, Guidance on System Boundary Definition; NIST SP 800-37, Revision 1, paragraphs 2.3.2 Boundaries for

Complex Information Systems, 2.3.3 Changing Technologies and the Effect of Information System Boundaries, External Subsystems, and Appendix I Security Controls in External Environments.

5. Who determines the required level of independence for security control assessors?

A. Information system owner (ISO)
B. Information system security manager (ISSM)
C. Authorizing official (AO)
D. Information system security officer (ISSO)

Answer is **C**.

The authorizing official, or designated representative, determines the required level of independence for security control assessors based on the results of the security categorization process for the information system and the ultimate risk to organizational operations and assets, individuals, other organizations, and the nation. The authorizing official determines if the level of assessor independence is sufficient to provide confidence that the assessment results produced are sound and can be used to make a risk-based decision on whether to place the information system into operation or continue its operation. See CAP® CBK® Chapter 5 Assessment of Security Controls, NIST Guidance on Assessment of Security Control Effectiveness, Task 4-1: Prepare for Controls Assessment, and Task 4-2: Assess Security Controls; NIST SP 800-37, Revision 1, Supplemental Guidance to Step 4 Assess Security Controls, Task 4-1 Assessment Preparation.

Domain 6

1. System authorization is now used to refer to which of the following terms?

A. System security declaration
B. Certification and accreditation
C. Security test and evaluation
D. Continuous monitoring

Answer is **B**.

NIST SP 800-37, Revision 1, substitutes use of the term *certification and accreditation* with *security authorization*. Answer A is a distracter. Answer C relates to another term changed by NIST SP 800-37, Revision 1 (this term was replaced by *security controls assessment*). Answer D is a distracter as it relates to Step 6 of the Risk Management Framework. See CAP® CBK® Chapter 1 Security Authorization of Information Systems, Introduction, Defining System Authorization, and Chapter 9 The Future of Information System Authorization.

2. What key information is used by the authorizing official (AO) to assist with the risk determination of an information system (IS)?

   A. Security authorization package (SAP)
   B. Plan of action and milestones (POA&M)
   C. Security plan (SP)
   D. Interconnection security agreement (ISA)

Answer is **A**.

A security authorization package contains the security plan, security assessment report, and the plan of action and milestones. The information in these key documents is used by authorizing officials to make risk-based authorization decisions. See CAP® CBK® Chapter 5 Assessment of Security Controls, NIST Guidance on Assessment of Security Control Effectiveness, Task 4-3: Prepare Security Assessment Report; NIST SP 800-37, Revision 1, Step 5—Authorize Information System, Task 5-3: Risk Determination.

3. When an authorizing official (AO) submits the security authorization decision, what responses should the information system owner (ISO) expect to receive?

   A. Authorized to operate (ATO) or denial authorization to operate (DATO), the conditions for the authorization placed on the information system and owner, and the authorization termination date
   B. Authorized to Operate (ATO) or Denial Authorization to Operate (DATO), the list of security controls accessed, and an system contingency plan
   C. Authorized to operate (ATO) or denial authorization to operate (DATO), and the conditions for the authorization placed on the information system and owner
   D. A plan of action and milestones (POA&M), the conditions for the authorization placed on the information system and owner, and the authorization termination date

Answer is **A**.

The original security authorization package that contains supporting documentation has been presented to the authorizing official (AO). The AO will make a decision based on the system security posture, operational need, and its functionality. See CAP® CBK® Chapter 6 Information System Authorization, NIST Guidance on Authorization of Information Systems, Task 5-4: Perform Risk Assessment; NIST SP 800-37, Revision 1, Step 5—Authorize Information System, Task 5-4: Risk Acceptance.

4. What should the system owner use to prioritize mitigation actions when developing the plan of action and milestones (POA&M)?

  A. Budget constraints
  B. Risk assessment results
  C. Continuous monitoring strategy
  D. Recommendations of the information owners

Answer is **B**.

The prioritization of POA&M items is guided by the risk assessment results. While budget constraints (answer A) may factor into overall decisions, they should not be the primary prioritization as no consideration of impact is given. A continuous monitoring strategy (answer C) is important but is not the correct method to prioritize POA&M items as it focuses only on operations and maintenance. Information owners may be biased in which areas of a system or weaknesses may relate to their information (answer D) and therefore should not be involved in POA&M prioritization.

5. According to NIST SP 800-39, when an organization responds to risk by eliminating the activities or technologies that are the basis for the risk, that organization is

  A. accepting the risk.
  B. avoiding the risk.
  C. transferring the risk.
  D. mitigating the risk.

Answer is **B**.

See NIST SP 800-39, Managing Information Security Risk, Chapter 3—The Process, Step 3 Risk Response, Task 3-1: Risk Response Identification, Responding to Risk; CAP® CBK® Chapter 4 Application of Security Controls, Remediation Planning, Managing Risk.

Domain 7

1. An effective continuous monitoring program can be used to

    A. meet the Federal Information Processing Standard (FIPS) Publication 200 requirement for monthly risk assessments.
    B. meet an organization's requirement for periodic information assurance training of all computer users.
    C. replace information system security audit logs.
    D. support the Federal Information Security Management Act (FISMA) requirement for annual assessment of the security controls in information systems.

    Answer is **D**.
    FISMA has a requirement for annual assessment of information systems. FIPS Publication 200 Minimum Security Requirements for Federal Information and Information Systems (answer A) does not have a requirement for monthly risk assessments. Continuous monitoring of systems is not a task performed by all of an organization's computer users and is not an information assurance training activity (answer B). Continuous monitoring does not collect the same data as audit logs and therefore does not replace the requirement for audit logs (answer C). See CAP® CBK® Chapter 7 Security Controls Monitoring, NIST Guidance on Ongoing Monitoring of Security Controls, Task 6-2: Conduct Ongoing Security Control Assessments; NIST SP 800-37, Revision 1, Step 6 Monitor Security Controls, Task 6-2: Ongoing Security Control Assessments.

2. According to the Risk Management Framework (RMF), which role has a primary responsibility to report the security status of the information system to the authorizing official (AO) and other appropriate organizational officials on an ongoing basis in accordance with the monitoring strategy?

    A. Information system security officer (ISSO)
    B. Common control provider
    C. Independent assessor
    D. Senior information assurance officer (SIAO)

    Answer is **B**.

NIST SP 800-37, Revision 1, Risk Management Framework (RMF) Task 6-5 states that the information system owner and the common control provider have the primary responsibility to report the security status of an information system to the authorizing official (AO). See also CAP® CBK® Chapter 7 Security Controls Monitoring, NIST Guidance on Ongoing Monitoring of Security Controls, Task 6-5: Report Security Status.

3. During an annual assessment, numerous high-risk findings are discovered on a critical organizational system. The system's Federal Information Processing Standard (FIPS) 199 rating is "high" integrity, "high" confidentiality, and "low" availability. The organization has a very low risk tolerance. What is the *best* decision that should be made in this situation?

A. The authorizing official should deny operation of the system until risk is reduced to an acceptable level.

B. The information system owner should resolve issues as quickly as possible while keeping the system up.

C. The security control assessor should implement immediate compensating controls.

D. The chief information security officer should scope and tailor the weak controls to ensure proper function.

Answer is **A**.

Given the FIPS 199 categorization, the best approach is to shut down the system and resolve the weaknesses. Informed risk-based decisions during continuous monitoring must be made by the authorizing official in coordination with the risk executive function. Given the high impact, the system should not be kept in operation by the information system owner (answer B) as this forces the organization to continue to accept risk. The security control assessor should not implement any changes to the system (answer C) as this will question their independence. The chief information security officer (CISO) is not responsible for resolving control issues (answer D) since that is the responsibility of the system owner. See NIST SP 800-37, Revision 1, Appendix D Roles and Responsibilities, D.6 Authorizing Official; CAP® CBK® Chapter 6 Information System Authorization, System Authorization Decision Making, the Authorization Letter.

A special case of a denial of authorization to operate is an authorization rescission. Authorizing officials can rescind a previous authorization decision at any time if there is a specific violation of (1) federal/organizational security policies, directives, regulations, standards, guidance, or practices; or (2) the terms and conditions of the original authorization. For example, failure to maintain an effective continuous monitoring program may be grounds for rescinding an authorization decision. Authorizing officials consult with the risk executive (function) and the senior information security officer before rescinding security authorizations.

4. Which National Institute of Standards and Technology Special Publication (NIST SP) 800 series document is concerned with continuous monitoring for federal information systems and organizations?

   A. SP 800-26
   B. SP 800-64
   C. SP 800-137
   D. SP 800-144

   Answer is **C**.
   NIST SP 800-137, published September 2011, is titled, "Continuous Monitoring for Federal Information Systems and Organizations." See also CAP® CBK® Chapter 7 Security Controls Monitoring, NIST Guidance on Ongoing Monitoring of Security Controls, Task 6-7 Information System Removal and Decommissioning.

5. Which of the following are phases of the National Institute of Standards and Technology (NIST) Risk Management Framework?

   A. Categorize, select, implement, authorize
   B. Assess, certify, accredit, manage
   C. Prepare, execute, authorize, monitor
   D. Assess, mitigate, authorize, monitor

   Answer is **A**.
   The six steps of the RMF are categorize, select, implement, assess, authorize, and monitor. See CAP® CBK® Chapter 1 Authorization of Information Systems. NIST SP 800-37, Revision 1, NIST's Risk Management Framework (RMF); NIST SP-800-37, Revision 1, Chapter 2—The Fundamentals, 2.1 Integrated Organization-Wide Risk Assessment.

Index